RETRACING THE PAST

RETRACING THE PAST

Readings in the History of the American People

Volume I

To 1877

Sixth Edition

Gary B. Nash
University of California, Los Angeles

Ronald Schultz
University of Wyoming

New York San Francisco Boston
London Toronto Sydney Tokyo Singapore Madrid
Mexico City Munich Paris Cape Town Hong Kong Montreal

Executive Editor: Michael Boezi
Executive Marketing Manager: Sue Westmoreland
Production Manager: Denise Phillip
Project Coordination, Text Design, and Electronic Page Makeup: WestWords, Inc.
Cover Designer/Manager: Wendy Ann Fredericks
Cover Art: *Sansome Street Market,* San Francisco by Wilhelm Hahn, c.1850 The Art Archive/EB
   Crocker Art Gallery Sacramento/Laurie Platt Winfrey © Picture Desk, Inc./Kobal Collection
Manufacturing Buyer: Roy Pickering
Cover Printer: Courier Corporation

Library of Congress Cataloging-in-Publication Data

Retracing the past : readings in the history of the American people / [edited by] Gary B.
   Nash, Ronald Schultz.—6th ed.
     p. cm.
   Contents: v. 1. To 1877—v. 2. Since 1865.
   ISBN 0-321-33379-9 (v. 1)—ISBN 0-321-33380-2 (v. 2)
   1. United States—History. I. Nash, Gary B. II. Schultz, Ronald

E178.6.R45 2005
973—dc22
                                                                    2005048910

Please visit out website at http://www.ablongman.com

ISBN 0-321-33379-9

  2 3 4 5 6 7 8 9 10—CRS—08 07 06

For Sara, Tristan and Hanna

CONTENTS

PART TWO   A Revolutionary People   100

PART THREE   An Expanding People   194

PREFACE

This two-volume reader has been constructed as a supplement to the many American history survey textbooks currently in use in the United States and beyond. The essays have been selected with three goals in mind: first, to blend political and social history; second, to lead students to a consideration of the roles of women, ethnic groups, and laboring Americans in the weaving of the nation's social fabric; and third, to explore life at the individual and community levels. The book is also intended to introduce students to the individuals and groups that made a critical difference in the shaping of American history or whose experience reflected key changes in society.

Some of the individuals highlighted are famous, such as James Madison and Lyndon Johnson. A number of others, George Whitefield and John Muir for example, are historically visible but are not quite household names. Many will be totally unknown to students, such as George Robert Twelves Hewes, a Boston shoemaker who participated in some of the most important events of the American Revolution; Thomas Peters, who escaped slavery by fleeing to the British during the Revolutionary War and later led several thousand escaped slaves to a new homeland in Sierra Leone; and Lozen, an Apache woman who functioned as an important war leader in the last decades of the nineteenth century. Often the focus is on groups whose role in history has not been adequately treated—the Chinese in the building of the transcontinental railroad, the grassroots black leaders during Reconstruction, and the rising African American middle and underclasses of the post–Civil Rights era.

Some of these essays take us inside American homes, farms, and factories, such as the essays on working women and their families in New York City before the Civil War and the people of Butte, Montana, who welcomed newly available radios into their homes during the 1920s and 1930s. Such essays, it is hoped, convey an understanding of the daily lives of ordinary Americans, who collectively helped shape their society. Other essays deal with the vital social and political movements that transformed American society: the debate over the Constitution in the 1780s; reform in the antebellum period; populism and progressivism in the late nineteenth and early twentieth centuries; and the rise of economic uncertainty and political conservatism in our own time.

Accessibility has been a guiding concern in preparing this edition of *Retracing the Past*. Consequently, we have continued with the significant changes made in the previous edition that were designed to make the readings more accessible and useful to student readers and more effective in the classroom. At the same time, we have replaced a third of the previous readings with new essays that better reflect current scholarship and current student interests. Especially important here is a new emphasis on the diversity of American society. For example, the first volume opens with James Axtell's depiction of the first encounters between Europeans and Native Americans in the sixteenth and seventeenth centuries, while the second volume brings the study of diversity into the present with Robin D.G. Kelley's portrayal of the simultaneous growth of poverty and middle-class prosperity in African American communities during the late twentieth century. We have edited each of the readings to make them more straightforward and understandable to students and, in addition, have included glossaries at the end of each reading to help students better identify the people and terms discussed in the essays.

One of the most important changes to the previous edition was the inclusion of thought-provoking questions at the end of each essay. These questions—**Implications**—ask students to move from the local and personal focus of the essays to consider the broader implications of what they have read, placing the essays in the wider perspective of the American past. We have continued these very successful questions in this edition. Another important change in the previous edition was the inclusion of primary documents to introduce each reading. These documents, often taken from sources used in the essays themselves, enliven the past, make the experiences of the American people more concrete, and set the stage for the readings that follow. These documents, too, have been continued in this edition. Finally, like its predecessors, this edition includes a brief introductory essay—**Sources and Interpretations**—that provides students with a strategy for reading these documents and the essays that follow in a way that is both efficient and effective. This strategy has been used at the University of Wyoming for a decade with excellent results, and we think this strategy will work equally well in any college or highschool classroom. In sum, we think these changes in the sixth edition of *Retracing the Past* will make this a more approachable and therefore more useful reader and will make the American past an engaging and rewarding subject for a new generation of students.

Gary B. Nash
Ronald Schultz

ACKNOWLEDGMENTS

In developing this volume of readings, the editors have been well-advised by the following academic colleagues, who reviewed the previous edition and read preliminary tables of contents: Ginette Aley, Virginia Tech; James A. Zimmerman, Tri-State University; Anthony Gulig, University of Wisconsin-Whitewater; Catherine Candy, Raritan Valley Community College; Peter Murray, Methodist College; Robert Sawrey, Marshall University; and Jeff Pasley, University of Missouri-Columbia.

INTRODUCTION

Sources and Interpretations

People often think that history is mostly about facts: Who invented the cotton gin? Where was the nation's first capital? When did women secure the vote? But, while no historian would dispute the importance of facts, historical writers are much more concerned with interpretation, that is, with giving facts historical meaning. In practice, historians normally spend very little time debating the facts of a particular historical process or event; instead they typically differ about what those established facts mean. Take, for example, a letter written by an early nineteenth-century New England farmer outlining his plan to purchase land on the western New York frontier. One historian might recall what she has read about the family-centeredness of New Englanders and find in the letter a father's concern to place each of his sons on freehold land, thus allowing them to re-create his own life as an independent family farmer. On the other hand, the contents of the same letter might lead another historian to remember the economic position of early American farmers and conclude that the father was purchasing land for speculation, hoping to sell the land at a higher price once settlers entered the region. Or a third historian might integrate both of these views and infer from the letter that the farmer's main aim was family continuance but that he was not above a little speculation along the way. In all of these cases, the historians have no dispute with the source (the letter) itself but draw very different and potentially conflicting conclusions from it.

This example points to one of the fundamental features of historical interpretation: the essential ambiguity of sources. Like the farmer's letter, no document or physical artifact is ever perfectly clear to the reader or observer. Instead, it requires the exercise of historical judgment—re-creating the context in which the source was produced and making collateral connections between it and other sources from the same time and place—to give it meaning. It is the historian's job to interrogate a source by asking a series of questions, most importantly, Who produced the source?; What was their purpose in doing so?; For whom was the source intended?; and How was the source received and how was it used? Historians employ this basic arsenal of questions when analyzing a source, and only when the source has been internally scrutinized and these questions answered satisfactorily can the source be used to build an interpretation.

Facts and interpretations are thus closely linked and historians acknowledge this linkage by dividing their materials into two groups: primary sources and secondary interpretations. Primary sources are items produced during the time period being investigated. These items might be written documents—such as letters, diaries, travel accounts, or contemporary books—or they might be statistical compilations—such as census tabulations, business records, or tax lists. They might even be material artifacts—such as houses, home furnishings, or clothing—that have survived from the period in question. It is from the broad array of such primary sources that historians draw the facts they will use in constructing interpretations of past events and processes.

History is a discipline that builds on the work of others, and historians continually measure the primary source data they gather against existing interpretations of their subject. These interpretations (sometimes called secondary sources) most commonly appear as articles in professional journals and as monographs that deal with a specific aspect of the period in question, say an essay about agricultural change in the early republic or a book about the origin of Jim Crow laws in the post–Reconstruction South. Historians use secondary sources to help them place their primary materials in context and to give those materials a wider meaning. In turn, they use primary sources to question the conclusions drawn by other writers. By utilizing primary sources and secondary interpretations in this way, historians advance historical understanding through a process of successive interrogation and refinement. Written history is thus a continuous dialogue between the past and the present, a dialogue that is always ongoing and provisional and one that is never final or complete.

As you read each of the essays in *Retracing the Past*, you will first encounter "Past Traces," a brief selection of primary documents drawn from the time period of the essay. The purpose of these documents is twofold: first, to give you a sense of the lives and concerns of ordinary people in a particular time period and, second, to involve you in the process of historical evaluation and interpretation. For example, in the opening essay of this volume you will find documents from some of the first encounters between Europeans and Native Americans in North America; one from the Indian perspective and one from that of the colonists. Read with care and imagination, the documents tell us much about Native American and European life and culture as well as the nature of their mutual encounters. We learn, for example, that both groups drew upon their own cultural assumptions in interpreting the appearance and actions of the other, the Montagnais villagers by describing the incoming French ships as "floating islands" and the Jesuit missionaries by bristling at what they saw as the native exploitation of women. If we look a little further, we also learn that both groups came from agrarian societies, although both practiced agriculture in different ways. These are just a few of the things that can be learned from the primary documents that follow; there are many others, as you will discover. As you read the documents, you will begin to ask your own questions and form your own interpretations. Most importantly, in learning to read the documents for their diverse meanings, you will already be thinking like a historian.

Following the documents, you will find six essays of historical interpretation. In each, a historian has consulted primary and secondary sources and constructed an interpretation that explains what he or she thinks the sources reveal about an individual or group of people in the chronological period in question. Thus, in "The Small Circle of Domestic Concerns," Mary Beth Norton uses contemporary women's letters and diaries to reconstruct the lives of eighteenth-century women and finds that household labor lay at the heart of women's roles, no matter what their class or status in life. At the same time, Norton uses these primary sources to challenge historians who have viewed the colonial era as a "golden age" for

American women, an age in which gender relations were more equal than they became in later times. This, then, is the procedure of the working historian, a procedure that depends on the mutual interrogation of primary sources and secondary interpretations in the process of reaching historical conclusions.

Reading with Purpose

One of the unusual aspects of written history is that, like literature, it is often read by nonhistorians for no other purpose than simple relaxation and pleasure. Thus, while few people will spend their leisure hours reading a new book on the biochemistry of enzymes, many nonspecialists will read the latest book about the American Civil War. This difference between a work of chemistry and a work of history lays a trap that often snares student readers. The chemistry book will most likely be read pragmatically, that is, it will be read in order to gain specific information about enzymes that can be used later in an experimental or classroom application. The history book, on the other hand, will more likely be read without any expectation of future use or application.

Each of the historical essays that follow can be read as an interesting story in its own right, whether about southern slave resistance, the Populist critique of big business, or the youth culture of the 1960s. As such, each essay invites a casual rather than a pragmatic reading. Yet, most history courses will ask for exactly that: a purposeful, pragmatic, and analytical reading that goes beyond the story line and focuses instead on what the essay and its evidence tell us about a person (or group of people) and their times. In his essay about slave resistance, for example, Peter Wood uses newspapers and contemporary journals to reveal ways in which southern slaves contested the terms of their enslavement and put the lie to slaveholder attempts to dehumanize their bondsmen and women. It is a compelling story in its own right, but in a college classroom or discussion section you would be expected to gain more from Wood's essay than a casual reading would allow. At a minimum, you would be expected to recount the main and subsidiary points of his essay and be able to say something about how the essay adds to our understanding of southern society in the colonial period.

How, then, does one avoid the pitfalls of a casual reading of an essay and grasp its most salient points? One of the most effective ways to accomplish this is to read each essay with a structured set of questions in mind, that is, to read with a purpose. There are five basic questions you should ask yourself as you read the essays in *Retracing the Past*.

First, you should be able to identify the main subject of the essay and place that person or group in the context of their times. Some questions you might wish to ask include: Who are the most important people in the essay? Is the essay about an individual or a group? What are the most important characteristics of this person or group for an understanding of the essay? What is their class? Their race? Their gender? Their occupation? Where did the events discussed in the essay take place? When?

Second, since history deals with human predicaments, you should be able to identify the major problem or problems faced by the subject of the essay. What did the subject hope to accomplish? What was the most important obstacle(s) or impediment(s) standing in the way of the fulfillment of the subject's desires? What was the source of this impediment(s)? Was it individual and personal or structural and impersonal?

Third, because people respond to their predicaments in many different ways, you should be able to locate major actions undertaken by the subject to solve the problem(s). How did the subject go about trying to solve the problem(s)? Does the person or group solve the problem alone? Who provides help? What help was given? Why was it given?

Fourth, since some actions lead to successful conclusions and others do not, make a judgment about the ultimate resolution of the actions taken by the people in the essay. Did they achieve what they set out to accomplish? Or did they realize only some of their goals? If they solved their problem(s), what allowed them to do this? If the problem remained unsolved, why wasn't it solved? What obstacles prevented a solution? What was the person's or group's response to the lack of a solution?

Lastly, since each essay in *Retracing the Past* is a case study of a larger historical process, you should be able to place the subject's problem(s) and resolution(s) into the larger context of the historical period in question. What ideas do you think the author wanted to convey in his or her article? How does the essay relate to other course materials, such as lectures, multimedia presentations, or points made in your textbook and other readings? Do the points made in the essay agree or disagree with other interpretations you've heard or read about in the course? How do they agree or disagree? If they disagree, which interpretation do you accept? Why?

By asking these questions as you read the essays in *Retracing the Past*, you will be engaged in reading pragmatically. This purposeful way of reading will help you to understand and enjoy the essays more fully and, at the same time, will actively engage you in the process of historical interpretation, thus helping you draw your own conclusions and form your own arguments about the historical period in question.

RETRACING THE PAST

PART ONE

A Colonizing People

The expansion of Europe westward across the Atlantic during the sixteenth and seventeenth centuries brought together peoples from Africa, Western Europe, and the Americas to create a new form of multiracial and multiethnic society. The local societies created by this unprecedented mixing of peoples were among the most complex in recorded human history. Reflecting this complexity, the history of colonization in North and South America was largely a story of conflict and accommodation in which people with different cultures and divergent ways of life struggled to create stable patterns of everyday life in a world of constant change.

The early experiences of people in the colonial era were decisively shaped by cultural interactions between the Old World and the New. James Axtell captures these early interactions in "Imagining the Other: First Encounters." Curiosity dominated these early interchanges, as both Europeans and Native Americans took the measure of each other and struggled to understand how to remake their lives now that they lived among strangers. In this essay, Axtell reminds us that Native Americans were not passive victims of European conquest, but sought to maintain the integrity of their social world in ways that paralleled those of the English settlers.

The realization of a stable social life was also an important goal of free Africans in the early Chesapeake. As T.H. Breen and Stephen Innes reveal in "The Patriarch of Pungoteague Creek," not only did a small number of free Africans live in the eastern shore of the Virginia colony, but they owned property and were comparatively integrated into white society. The story of Anthony Johnson and his family suggests that the future of Virginia society might have been very different from what developed in the Chesapeake colonies by the mid-seventeenth century.

Individualism posed less of a problem in New England than in Virginia. Settled mostly by established family groups and lacking a lucrative export crop that would

2

attract young, unattached men—as was the case in the tobacco colonies—, Massachusetts Bay established social stability from the very beginning. In her study of the original migrants to Massachusetts Bay, Virginia DeJohn Anderson tackles the recurring question of the relative importance of economics and religion in bringing about the settlement of the Bay Colony. She finds that in the early years of the colony, the corporate and religious ethos of Puritanism held sway over the search for individual economic gain.

By 1700, English settlers had achieved a substantial measure of social and political stability. Yet the new century would bring new challenges to colonists living in a changing world. Slavery was one of the most important legacies of the colonial era, creating divisions in American society that would lead to a civil war in 1861 and to distorted social relations for much of our nation's history. In "Patterns of Black Resistance," Peter H. Wood takes us into the private world of South Carolina slaves, showing us the many, often subtle, ways in which African bondspeople resisted the control of their masters and in the process reaffirmed their basic humanity and their own countervailing power.

Labor was the heart of slave life, just as it was for colonial women. In tracing "The Small Circle of Domestic Concerns," Mary Beth Norton provides us with an intimate look at the everyday lives of American women, whose experiences ranged from the drudgery faced by frontier wives to the more genteel—but no less demanding—duties of the plantation mistress.

Beginning in the early eighteenth century, the combined effects of imperial warfare and economic change began to transform America into a recognizably "modern" society. Looking beyond religion itself, Harry S. Stout examines the ways in which George Whitefield, the most famous evangelist of his day, employed the latest British publicity and marketing techniques to create a "Great Awakening" from a series of local revivals. Focusing on Whitefield's Philadelphia revivals, Stout suggests that the Great Awakening was as much the result of a rising cultural modernity as it was the result of a revival of religion. While much of American society remained traditional during the Great Awakening, there were unmistakable signs of change as well.

Past Traces

The New World encounters of Native American and European peoples during the sixteenth and seventeenth centuries inaugurated a complex period of social, cultural, and psychological adjustment. As both groups of people experienced the unsettling effects of confronting unfamiliar people with very different ways of life, they sought to make sense of what they saw by turning to established and familiar patterns of interpreting the world. In this way, Europeans and Native Americans attempted to explain each other in reference to the world in which they lived.

The following two documents provide telling glimpses into the world of early Euro–Indian interchange. The first document is an account of a Native American village's first encounter with French explorers in the sixteenth century. In it, Montagnais villagers attempt to explain the strangeness of the explorers' ship and the explorers themselves in terms of their own culture, comparing the French ship to the many islands that dotted the bays surrounding them. In the second, two Jesuit missionaries seek to explain the lives of Native American women in light of European gender roles. In most parts of Atlantic Europe, men, not women, were the primary agriculturists, and it was rare to find a woman performing heavy work in the fields. Thus, when Europeans, such as the Jesuit priests, encountered Indian women digging, planting, and harvesting village fields, they could only imagine them to be slaves of their husbands. Only gradually, and often imperfectly, did Europeans come to understand the division of gender roles in Native American society as simply different from their own.

Fr. Paul le Jeune, *Brief Relation of the Journey to New France (1633)*

Pierre Pastedechouan has told us that his grandmother used to take pleasure in relating to him the astonishment of the Natives, when they saw for the first time a French ship arrive upon their shores. They thought it was a moving Island; they did not know what to say of the great sails which made it go; their astonishment was redoubled in seeing a number of men on deck. The women [41] at once began to prepare houses for them, as is their custom when new guests arrive, and four canoes of Savages ventured to board these vessels. They invited the Frenchmen to come into the houses which had been made ready for them, but neither side understood the other. They were given a barrel of bread or biscuit. Having brought it on shore they examined it; and, finding no taste in it, threw it into the water. In a word, they were as much astonished as was the King of Calecut, in olden times, when he saw the first European ship nearing his shores; for, having sent some one to investigate the character and appearance of the men brought by that great house of wood, the messengers reported to their master that these men were prodigious and horrible; that they were dressed in [42] iron, ate bones, and drank blood. They had seen them covered with their cuirasses, eating biscuits, and drinking wine. Our Savages said the Frenchmen drank blood and ate wood, thus naming the wine and the biscuits.

Now as they were unable to understand to what nation our people belonged, they gave them the name which has since always clung to the French, *ouemichtigouchiou*; that is to say, a man who works in wood, or who is in a canoe or vessel of wood. They saw our ships, which were made of wood, their little canoes being made only of bark.

Jesuit Observations on the "Enslavement" of Native American Women (1633, 1710)

[1633]
To obtain the necessaries of life they [the Indians of Acadia] endure cold and hunger in an extraordinary manner. During eight or ten days, if the necessity is imposed on them, they will follow the chase in fasting, and they hunt with the greatest ardor when the snow is deepest and the cold most severe. And yet these same Savages, the offspring, so to speak, of Boreas [The North Wind] and the ice, when once they have returned with their booty and installed themselves in their tents, become indolent and unwilling to perform any labor whatever, imposing this entirely upon the women. The latter, besides the onerous role of bearing and rearing the children, also transport the game from the place where it has fallen; they are the hewers of wood and drawers of water; they make and repair the household utensils; they prepare food; they skin the game and prepare the hides like fullers; they sew garments; they catch fish and gather shellfish for food; often they even hunt; they make the canoes, that is, skiffs of marvelous rapidity, out of bark; they set up the tents wherever and whenever they stop for the night—in short, the men concern themselves with nothing but the more laborious hunting and the waging of war. For this reason almost every one has several wives, and especially the Sagamores, since they cannot maintain their power and keep up the number of their dependents unless they have not only many children to inspire fear or conciliate favor, but also many slaves to perform patiently the menial tasks of every sort that are necessary. For their wives are regarded and treated as slaves.

[1710]
. . . Now, if you inquire concerning the customs and character of this people [Canadian Indians in general], I will reply that a part of them are nomads, wandering during the winter in the woods, whither the hope of better hunting calls them—in the summer, on the shores of the rivers, where they easily

obtain their food by fishing; while others inhabit villages. They construct their huts by fixing poles in the ground; they cover the sides with bark, the roofs with hides, moss and branches. In the middle of the hut is the hearth, from which the smoke escapes through an opening at the peak of the roof. As the smoke passes out with difficulty, it usually fills the whole hut, so that strangers compelled to live in these cabins suffer injury and weakening of the eyes; the savages, a coarse race, and accustomed to these discomforts, ridicule this. The care of household affairs, and whatever work there may be in the family, are placed upon the women. They build and repair the wigwams, carry water and wood, and prepare the food; their duties and position are those of slaves, laborers and beasts of burden. The pursuits of hunting and war belong to the men. Thence arise the isolation and numerical weakness of the race. For the women, although naturally prolific, cannot, on account of their occupation in these labors, either bring forth fully-developed offspring, or properly nourish them after they have been brought forth; therefore they either suffer abortion, or forsake their newborn children, while engaged in carrying water, procuring wood and other tasks, so that scarcely one infant in thirty survives until youth. To this there is added their ignorance of medicine, because of which they seldom recover from illnesses which are at all severe.

1

Imagining the Other: First Encounters

James Axtell

News of Columbus's Caribbean landfall in October, 1492, set in motion a series of European trans-Atlantic expeditions that lasted throughout the sixteenth and early parts of the seventeenth centuries. Seeking land, wealth, trade, and a water passage to the lucrative markets of Asia, Spanish, Portuguese, French, Dutch, and English explorers encountered new lands and, most importantly, new peoples—the indigenous peoples of the New World. Confronted with these new people and novel situations, European explorers and North American Indians alike turned to familiar cultural understandings to help them explain themselves, their land, and the ways of "others." All along coastal North America, these cultural understandings became the first tools used by both Native American inhabitants and European explorers and traders to interpret, understand, and interact with each other.

In this essay, James Axtell investigates the early stages of European contact with the Eastern Woodland peoples whom explorers met in the sixteenth and seventeenth centuries. As he shows, Europeans—whether Spanish, French, Dutch, or English—brought with them to the New World a complex mixture of Old World ideas and trans-Atlantic anticipations. The early European explorers combined in their minds ancient fantasies about strange, semihuman inhabitants and hard-headed concerns about establishing trade and settlements in the new-found land. In these earliest encounters, however, simple curiosity and self-interest more often than not prevailed. Who were these people? How did they live? Would they make profitable trading partners? Would they allow, or could they prevent, settlement?

For their part, Native Americans drew on their own cultures to explain the strange people whom they confronted and the alien technologies the strangers brought with them. Viewed from an Eastern Woodland perspective, these newcomers were exceptional because they were so unusual, so unlike themselves. Their religious world-view had taught them that "unusual" beings such as these were either spirits or bearers of spiritual powers and, because of this, required both hospitality and, they hoped, incorporation. In this way, the native inhabitants of North America hoped to add the spiritual and technological power of these strangers to their own cultural repertory.

But, as Axtell reveals, the uneasy balance of power that characterized the initial contact period quickly gave way to conflict, domination, disruption, and defense. The "gentle and promising" interactions of the first Euro–Indian encounters were soon buried beneath accumulating layers of mistrust, aggression, and misunderstanding.

....

Before the "Barbarians" of Europe and America actually met, they each had some notion of what the "other" would probably be like. Thanics to their own recent experience of peoples and places and to the rediscovered libraries of the ancient world, Europeans had a rich "cabinet of curiosities," accumulated over many centuries on three continents, from which to draw. From Marco Polo's thirteenth-century travels in particular, they continued to learn of immense empires and fabulous riches in the Far East. Africa gradually revealed its cultural secrets to resourceful fleets of Portuguese seamen. Christian crusaders heading for the Holy City and pilgrims of every stripe left their footprints all around the sun-drenched rim of the Mediterranean. Hot on the heels of all these adventurers were eager avatars of trade, fanning out from the commercial capitals of Europe in search of useful knowledge as well as luxury goods and mineral wealth.

Beneath this growing knowledge of cultures and geographies lay a bedrock of ancient precedent—the Old and New Testaments and the classical heritage of Greece and Rome recently regained by the scholars of the Renaissance—and an even denser stratum of medieval legend. While the second-century Egyptian astronomer Claudius Ptolemy gave sixteenth-century Europeans a workable heaven by which to navigate and the fifth-century B.C. traveler-historian Herodotus provided a way to write

the history of "others," credulous tale-tellers of the Middle Ages topped their imaginations with a bestiary of human monsters, monstrosities, and wild, hairy men.

Accordingly, peoples of black, brown, yellow, and white skin; religions as diverse as Buddhism, pantheism, and atheism; and a spectrum of polities from divine monarchy to natural anarchy could be found in the collective wisdom of Europe. But also present, for learned and credulous alike, were strange people who ate human flesh, peered at the world from one large eye in the middle of their chests, and barked rather than spoke from canine snouts. To Europeans, "others" might appear in an infinite variety of shapes, hues, and habits, but they were always and distinctly unlike Europeans and, for the most part, therefore regarded as inferior. Before and after 1492, the occidental wall between "them" and "us" was high, and only a few thinkers like Michel de Montaigne in the sixteenth century were available to give their fellow Europeans a leg up.

The relatively isolated natives of the American, by contrast, were prepared by experience to see in "others" largely faithful reflections of themselves or of the anthropomorphic deities who populated their pantheons. While Europeans found "others" to be different and usually inferior, the "others" the Indians knew tended to be similar or superior. This is not to say that Indian cultures were blessedly lacking in ethnocentrism; they were as hidebound as the next group. But their human experience was limited solely to other Indian peoples, so their ethnographic categories appear to have been relatively few, perhaps some variation on three.

The Indians' first category consisted of their own immediate social group, whether band, tribe, chiefdom, or confederacy. As if to celebrate their ethnocentrism, tile names many, perhaps most, groups (Iroquois, Navajo, Penobscot) gave themselves meant "the original people" or "the true men"—in other words, the only folks who mattered. Their enemies and neighbors, on the other hand, were called names (Eskimo, Sioux, Nottoway) that meant "raw meat-eaters," "bark-eaters," or "rattlesnakes." In cultural retrospect, most of these perceived differences were minor or nonexistent and were simply inflated or invented by politics and inherited hatreds. Beneath the reciprocal epithets were brown-skinned Americans whose lives were strikingly similar, all things considered.

Even the third category of "others"—the spiritual beings with whom the Indian people closely shared the world—did not vary greatly from group to group. While these "supernatural" persons (a distinction they did not make) could easily change appearance and voice, particularly when encountered in dreams or induced trances, the Indians of North America shared a belief that all living things possessed "souls" or "spirits" capable of unrestricted movement in time and space and of banning or helping other "persons." Because the magnitude of their power was largely unknown and because they might appear in a strange guise, each "person" had to be treated with respect and circumspection, often in formal ceremonies of supplication and thanksgiving. Thus, when Europeans first appeared at the edge of the water, woods, plains, or desert, the Indians were prepared to treat with extraordinary "persons" whose physical manifestations might be very different from, but certainly not inferior to, their own.

NATIVE PROPHECIES AND MEMORIES

Even before the first white men materialized, they may have impressed themselves upon the Indian imagination. Shamans, who were thought capable of seeing into the future, and other prescient people may have prophesied the coming of the Europeans. I say "may have" because these prophecies were recorded only after contact with literate newcomers. In 1540 Francisco Vázquez de Coronado was glad to hear from Zuni elders in the desert Southwest that "it was foretold them more than fifty years ago that a people such as we are would come, and from the direction we have come, and that the whole country would be conquered." It is not unlikely that the natives' memories were jogged by the seventeen hundred men in the Spanish entrada, including 250 heavily armed horsesoldiers. A year later, under similar conditions, six leaders from an Indian town near the Mississippi River visited Hernando de Solo's camp, saying "they were come to see what people [the Spanish] were and that they had learned from their ancestors that a white race would inevitably subdue them."

A *wiochist* or shaman had a similar message for the Powhatans as they confronted English bellicosity in Virginia after 1607: he predicted that "bearded men should come & take away their Country & that there should none of the original Indians be left, within . . . a hundred & fifty" years. Another shaman was somewhat more ambiguous when he informed the "emperor" that "from the *Chesapeack* Bay a Nation should arise, which should dissolve and give end to his Empier." While the apparently feckless Jamestown colonists looked on, Powhatan exterminated the whole tribe of "*Chessiopeians*" to hedge his bets.

Confronting a different English challenge, natives in New England were given a prophecy appropriate to their circumstances. During the lethal plague that preceded the arrival of the Plymouth pilgrims in 1620, a Nauset man on Cape Cod dreamed of the advent of "a great many men" dressed in what proved to be English-style clothes. One of them, dressed all in black, stood on an eminence with a book in his hand and told the assembled Indians that "God was *moosquantum* or angry with them, and that he would kill them for their sinnes. . . ."

More prevalent than prophesies were oral traditions regarding the Europeans' arrival, a few collected shortly after contact, most of them several centuries later. When the natives recalled their first encounters with European "others," it was novel "persons" like their own deities whom they remembered.

In 1633 a young Montagnais on the north shore of the St. Lawrence related the story his grandmother had told him of the Indians' astonishment at seeing a French ship for the first time. Like many natives before and after, they thought it was a "moving Island." Having seen the men aboard, however, the Montagnais women began to prepare wigwams for them, "as is their custom when new guests arrive," and four canoes bade the strangers welcome. The French gave them a barrel of ship's biscuits and probably offered them some wine. But the natives were appalled that these people "drank blood and ate wood" and promptly threw the tasteless biscuits into the river. Obviously more impressed by French technology than cuisine, the Montagnais henceforth called the French *ouemichtigouchiou*, "men in a wooden canoe or boat."

The Micmacs were equally unimpressed by French fare, as tribal successors recalled in the nineteenth century. When the first Frenchmen arrived in the Gaspé, presumably in the early sixteenth century, the Micmacs "mistook the bread which was given them for a piece of birch tinder." When wine was proffered, perhaps a nice Bordeaux red, the natives became convinced that the strangers were "cruel and inhuman, since in their amusements . . . they drank blood without repugnance. . . . Therefore they remained some time not only without tasting it, but even without wishing to become in any manner intimate, or to hold

intercourse, with a nation which they believed to be accustomed to blood and carnage."

Farther west, perhaps around Lake Superior, an Ojibwa prophet dreamed that

> men of strange appearance have come across the great water. They have landed on our island [North America]. Their skins are white like snow, and on their faces long hair grows. These people have come across the great water in wonderfully large canoes which have great white wings like those of a giant bird. The men have long and sharp knives, and they have long black tubes which they point at birds and animals. The tubes make a smoke that rises into the air just like the smoke from our pipes. From them come fire and such terrific noise that I was frightened, even in my dream.

At once a flotilla of trusted men was sent through the Great Lakes and down the St. Lawrence to investigate. On the lower river they found a clearing in which all the trees had been cut down, which led them to conjecture that "giant beavers with huge, sharp teeth had done the cutting." The prophet disagreed, reminding them of the long knives in his dream. Knowing that their stoneheaded axes could not cut such large trees so smoothly, they were "filled with awe, and with terror also." Still more puzzling were "long, rolled-up shavings" of wood and scraps of "bright-colored cloth," which they stuck in their hair and wound around their heads. Farther downriver they finally came upon the white-faced, bearded strangers with their astonishing long knives, thunder tubes, and giant winged canoes, just as the prophet had foretold.

Having satisfied their curiosity and fulfilled the prophet's dream, the Indians returned home with their trophies; each villager was given a small piece of cloth as a memento. To impress their neighbors, the Ojibwas followed an old custom. Just as they tied the scalps of their enemies on long poles, "now they fastened the splinters of wood and strips of calico to poles and sent them with special messengers" from one tribe to another. Thus were these strange articles passed from hand to hand around the whole lake, giving the natives of the interior their first knowledge of the white men from Europe.

WHITE DEITIES

The Indians regarded the Europeans' ability to fashion incredible objects and make them work less as mechanical aptitude than as spiritual power. When the Delawares, who once lived along the New Jersey–New York coast, met their first Dutch ship in the early seventeenth century, they concluded that it was a "remarkably large house in which the Mannitto (the Great or Supreme Being) himself was present," Thinking he was coming to pay them a visit, they prepared meat for a sacrifice, put all their religious effigies in order, and staged a grand dance to please or appease him. Meanwhile, the tribal conjurers tried to fathom his purpose in coming because their people were all "distracted between hope and fear." While preparation went forward, runners brought the welcome news that the visitors were human, like themselves, only strangely colored and oddly dressed. But when the Dutchmen made their appearance, graced the assembly with a round of liquor, and distributed iron and cloth gifts, the natives were confirmed in their original belief that every white man was an "inferior Mannitto attendant upon the Supreme Deity"—the ship's captain—who "shone superior" in his red velvet suit glittering with gold lace.

The earliest European objects of native awe corroborated native testimony about their godlike reception. The gentle inhabitants of the West Indies, Columbus assured his sovereign sponsors, were "very firmly convinced that I, with these ships and men, came from the heavens, and in this belief they everywhere received me after they had mastered their fear." Even the Taínos he kidnapped as guides and interpreters and brought to Spain to support his discoveries were "still of the opinion that I come from Heaven, for all the intercourse which they

have had with me. They were the first to announce this wherever I went . . . 'Come! Come! See the men from Heaven!'"

Four survivors of the ill-fated Florida expedition of Pánfilo de Narváez (1528) also traded on their reputation for divinity, as they walked from eastern Texas to Mexico. After some success in curing Indians with Christian prayers, elementary surgery, and the power of positive thinking, Alvar Nuñez Cabeza de Vaca and his three cohorts were regarded wherever they went as "children of the sun." The crowds of native acolytes who accompanied them swore at each new village that the Spaniards "had power to heal the sick and to destroy," just like their own shamans. In order to preserve their tremendous influence over the natives, the Spanish "gods" cultivated an inscrutable public silence, letting their black servant, Estevánico, make their mundane arrangements. The strange caravan of white and black beings, apparently endowed with extraordinary spiritual power and attended by an adoring cast of hundreds, sometimes thousands, gave them "control throughout the country in all that the inhabitants had power, or deemed of any value, or cherished."

Having read the accounts of his Spanish predecessors before launching his own gold-seeking entrada into the Southeast in 1539, Hernando de Soto burnished his divine attributes to a high luster. Whenever he came to a new province and needed bearers, food, and guides, he announced through his interpreter that "he was a son of the sun and came from where it dwelt," that he and his men were immortal, and that the natives could hide nothing because the face that appeared in the mirror he held before them "told him whatever they were planning or thinking about." Only when Soto visibly weakened and took to his bed did a chief near the Mississippi call his bluff, "saying that with respect to what he said about being a son of the sun, let him dry up the great river and he would believe him." Nor, when Soto died three days later, did the natives swallow the Spanish story that he was not dead but had only "gone to the sky as he had often done before."

In the seventeenth century, Indians who first encountered French and English explorers also regarded them as deities from a familiar cosmos. When the English at Roanoke failed to sicken during Indian epidemics and seemed to show no sexual interest in native women—and had no women of their own—several of the local Indians "could not tel whether to thinke [them] gods or men." Believing in general that "all the gods are of human shape," others thought the English immortal because they "were not born of women." Likewise, when French traders and missionaries canoed into the upper Great Lakes in the 1660s, the Indians "often took them for spirits and gods." Having heard that the French were "a different species from other men," the Potawatomis near Green Bay were astonished to see in Nicolas Perrot, a French emissary, that the strangers possessed human form and "regarded it as a present that the sky and spirits had made them in permitting one of the celestial beings to enter their land." Forty years later, wrote a missionary in 1700, the French in Louisiana had some difficulty in disabusing the Bayogoulas of the notion that "we are spirits descended from heaven, and that the fire of our cannon is the same sort as celestial fire."

Welcoming the Strangers

The welcome and treatment the natives lavished on them convinced the Europeans even farther that they were regarded as the bearers of divine tidings or at least of special human talents that were nonexistent or in very short supply in native society. It is difficult to tell from credulous European sources when the natives first realized that the intruders in their midst were not gods from another realm but were humans nonetheless possessed of extraordinary "spirits" or "souls," on a par with their own shamans and witches who practiced the black and white arts. In large part, the Europeans were treated as any native dignitaries would have been, but some aspects of their reception were clearly intended to honor celestial rather than earthly visitors.

Europeans first realized that Indians had placed them in a category by themselves when they caused a sensation by walking into native villages. When Columbus sent two of his men to explore a large island town, the inhabitants "touched them and kissed their hands and feet, marveling and attempting to see if they were, like themselves, of flesh and bone." After a five-day stay, the men returned to the ship but had some difficulty persuading five hundred natives not to accompany them in hopes of seeing them "return to the heavens." The southwestern Indians who wanted to touch Cabeza de Vaca's band of wandering medicine men "pressed us so closely," he half-boasted, "that they lacked little of killing us; and without letting us put our feet to the ground, carried us to their dwellings. We were so crowded upon by numbers, that we escaped into the houses they had made for us."

The natives of the Great Lakes and upper Mississippi Valley also "devoured [the first Europeans] with their eyes." In the 1660s, Green Bay Potawatomis did not "dare look [Nicolas Perrot] in his face; and the women and children watched him from a distance." About the same time, Father Claude Allouez felt slightly more discommoded by the villagers at Chequamegon on Lake Superior. "We were so frequently visited by these people," he recalled, "most of whom had never seen any Europeans, that we were overwhelmed" and religious instruction went slowly. He was happier with the visits of the teachable children, who came to him "in troops to satisfy their curiosity by looking at a stranger." Eight years later, Father Jacques Marquette was likewise showered with attention by the Illinois, not far from the Mississippi River. "All these people, who had never seen any Frenchmen among them," he wrote, "could not cease looking at us. They lay on the grass along the road; they preceded us, and then retraced their steps to come and see us again. All this was done noiselessly, and with marks of great respect for us." When the Frenchmen were walked through the three-hundred house village after a feast, "an orator continually harangued to oblige all the people to come to see us without annoying us."

Even relative latecomers among the English sometimes had to endure the astonished stares of native hosts. In 1674 three English-men in two different parts of the Southeast met Indians who had apparently not laid eyes on their like. At the Westo village on the Savannah River, the chief's house could not hold the crowd that wanted to admire Henry Woodward, a surgeon and early planter of South Carolina. The smaller fry solved the problem by climbing up on the roof and peeling it back to get a clear view. Meanwhile, beyond the Great Smoky Mountains, a town of western Cherokees welcomed two servants of a Virginia gentleman-trader "even to addoration in their cerrimonies of courtesies." The visitors' equally unusual packhorse was tethered to a stake in the middle of town and given a royal diet of corn, fish, and bear oil. Similarly, the white guests were invited to squat on a specially-built scaffold so that the natives "might stand and gaze at them and not offend them by theire throng." None of these celebrated Europeans ever talked about his embarrassment or self-consciousness under such

exposure, but we can well imagine that even the most self-possessed and arrogant men must occasionally have developed a healthy blush.

An even surer sign that the first Europeans were exalted in Indian eyes was the official welcome they received. Those who arrived by water were first guided to the best anchorages and landings. If smaller boats then could not reach dry land, the natives often plowed into the surf or stream to carry the sailors piggyback. On Hispaniola in 1492, villagers "insisted on carrying [Columbus and his men] on their backs . . . through some rivers and muddy places." French officers in sixteen-century Florida traveled to an important chief's village perched on the shoulders, not merely the backs, of several Indians who sought to keep them out of the marshy mire surrounding it. In 1535, en route to Hochelaga on the upper St. Lawrence, wiry Jacques Cartier had been lifted from his longboat by a husky Indian and carried to shore in the man's arms "as easily as if he had been a six-year-old child." Having been carted around in a red blanket on other occasions, Nicolas Perrot and a French companion drew the line at being piggybacked. They politely told their Mascouten hosts that "as they could shape . . . iron, they had strength to walk." Few other Europeans let pride get in the way of a free ride.

If getting there was half the fun, the arrival must have been somewhat discomfiting to those who had no idea what to expect. As soon as the newcomers were deposited in the village square or the chief's house, a startling round of touching and rubbing began, the import of which was not immediately clear. On their eight-year trek trough the Southwest after 1528, Cabeza de Vaca and his comrades received at least two different greetings. One village, after quelling their fear of the strangers, "reached their hands to our faces and bodies, and passed them in like manner over their own." Another group somewhat farther west greeted the Spaniards "with such yells as were terrific, striking the palms of their hands violently against their thighs," a response that might have scared the wits out of Europeans less accustomed to native ways.

Fortunately for most landed immigrants, the former gentle greeting was much more typical in eastern America. On the Gaspé Peninsula, both the Micmacs and the visiting Stadaconans who met Cartier "rubbed his arms and his breast with their hands" in welcome. Fifty years later, in 1584, Arthur Barlowe was greeted at Roanoke by Granganimeo, the local chief's brother, who struck his head and chest and then Barlowe's "to shewe [they] were all one." Several hundred miles away, on the icy coasts of Baffin Island, Eskimo traders were initiating relations with John Davis and his crew by pointing to the sun, striking their chests "so hard that [the sailors] might heare the blow," and crying "*Iliauote*", in a loud voice. When Davis stuck out his hand to greet one of them English-style, the man kissed it instead.

The customary greeting in South Carolina, as the English noted in the late 1660s, was the "stroaking of our shoulders with their palmes and sucking in theire breath the whilst." In Louisiana the French experienced a variation on the same theme. At their first camp near Biloxi in 1699, Pierre LeMoyne d'Iberville and his officers had their faces rubbed with white clay before being saluted in friendly fashion, which was, he wrote, "to pass their hands over their faces and breasts, and then pass their hands over yours, after which they raise them toward the sky, rubbing them together again and embracing again." Antoine de Sauvole, the fort commander, obviously found one party of Pascagoulas almost too much for his Gallic sensibilities. "I have never seen natives [*sauvages*] less inhibited," he confided to his journal. "They have embraced us, something that I have never seen the others do." The most sensual treatment, however, was reserved for Europeans who had hiked into Indian country: their hosts massaged their feet, legs, joints, and even eyelids with soothing bear oil.

But the cossetting had only begun. The visitors were next sealed on fresh skins or reed mats, "harangued" (as they put it) with unintelligible speeches, entertained with dancing, singing, and games, and feasted to surfeit on such delicacies as *sagamité* (cornmeal mush seasoned with fat) and roasted dog. An Illinois master of ceremonies, recalled Father Marquette, "filled a spoon with sagamité three or four times, and put it to my mouth as if I was a little child." After removing the bones, from the second—fish—course and blowing on some pieces to cool them, the genial host put them in the Frenchmen's mouths "as one would give food to a bird." They passed on the dog course, as "gods" had some leave to do, but happily chewed the fat buffalo morsels again placed in their mouths. Most European guests, however, were allowed to feed themselves and so could take more time to appreciate native foods, upon which most of them would be dependent far longer than they could imagine.

BECOMING AMERICANIZED

The next step after greeting and feting the Europeans was the serious business of assimilating the strangers into native society, of making the "others" even more like themselves, and securing peace until the newcomers displayed behavior that was less than "divine" or even, in native terms, "human." Throughout much of eastern America in the seventeenth and eighteenth centuries, the major vehicle of peaceful alliance was the calumet, a four-foot-long wood and stone pipe richly decorated with paint and a fan of long feathers. (After his Canadian experience, Iberville brought his own to Louisiana, an iron one "made in the shape of a ship with the white flag adorned with fleur-de-lis and ornamented with glass beads.") The Europeans soon learned that possession of a calumet was a passport through even hostile Indian country and that sharing its consecrated smoke was the major ticket to diplomatic success. To refuse a calumet ceremony—which in the lower Mississippi Valley invariably lasted three days—was to declare war upon, or at least to risk affronting, the offering party. In 1701 Iberville took such a risk in passing a village of Mobilians because he did not have three days to spare. But he managed to unfurrow their brows by distributing several presents and taking a chief with him to receive the hospitality of Fort Biloxi.

As early as the sixteenth century, smoke played another key role in welcoming the god-like Europeans. In native America, tobacco was sacred, and on its smoke prayers were lifted to heaven. The best way to honor any great-spirited being, therefore, was to offer it tobacco or smoke. When Father Allouez advised a Fox man to have his dangerously ill parents bled, the man poured powdered tobacco all over the priest's gown and said, "Thou art a spirit; come now, restore these sick people to health; I offer thee this tobacco in sacrifice." A dusty gown was small enough price to pay for such status, but other Frenchmen paid more dearly. In another part of the Great Lakes, Nicolas Perrot had smoke blown directly into his face "as the greatest honor they could render him; he saw himself smoked like meat," but gamely "said not a word." With Iberville on the Mississippi, Father Paul du Ru reported that, after puffing two or three times on a calumet, one of the Indians "came and blew smoke from his pipe into my nose as though to cense me." Du Ru may have come off better than the first French captain who sailed to the Menominees on Lake Michigan: he had tobacco ground into his forehead. One of the earliest Europeans to be honored with smoke was too ethnocentric to recognize his good fortune. When some Baffin Island Eskimos tried to place John Davis in the consecrating smoke of their fire, he pushed one of them into the smoke instead and testily had the fire stomped out and kicked into the sea.

If being smoked connoted some kind of religious affirmation, other ceremonies spelled political and social acceptance of the newcomers. At least two European leaders had the honor of being "crowned" by their native counterparts, but the exact meaning of their coronation is still unclear. At the future site of La Navidad on Hispaniola, Columbus was feted by the paramount chief Guacanagarí and five subordinate "kings," as the Admiral called them, "all with their crowns displaying their high rank." Guacanagarí led Columbus to a chair on a raised platform and "took off the crown from his own head and put it on the Admiral's." In return the grateful don dressed the chief in a collar of beautiful beads and agates, his own scarlet cloak, colored buskins, and a large silver ring. Probably the Indian got the better deal, as did the *Agouhanna* or head chief of Hochelaga in 1535. When Jacques Cartier rubbed the chief's paralyzed arms and legs at his request, the grateful man took off the red hedgehog-skin band he wore as a crown and presented it to the Frenchman. Before he left, Cartier distributed an array of metal tools and jewelry to repay the Hochelagans for their generous hospitality and political friendship.

Cartier's education in native politics had begun even before he left his base near the future Quebec City. In an effort to dissuade Cartier from going upriver to visit the Hochelagans on Montreal Island, Donnacona, the chief of the rival Stadaconans, made him a present of three children, including the ten-year-old daughter of his own sister and the younger brother of Cartier's native interpreter. These human gifts, Cartier quickly learned, were meant as seals on a firm political alliance to prevent any trafficking with enemies. When the French persisted in their travel plans and threatened to give the children back, the Stadaconans relented and put the best face they could on the necessity of dealing with ignorant intruders who refused to play by the established rules of the diplomatic game. But Cartier had already learned enough to accept the eight-year-old daughter of the chief of Achelacy, some twenty-five leagues upriver, an alliance that paid dividends during French difficulties with Donnacona later that winter.

More than a century and a half later, another French captain was given an Indian child to seal an alliance. In 1699 the chief of the Bayogoulas gave an adopted twelve-year-old slave boy to Jean Baptiste LeMoyne de Bienville, Iberville's younger brother and lieutenant in Louisiana. Perhaps realizing that he was slated to be shipped to France for training as an interpreter, the "poor boy regretted leaving the Indians so much that he cried incessantly without being able to stop." Sadly, he died of a throat ailment just after returning to his homeland "without getting to talk to any of his people."

In native eyes, the integration of the European "others" was nearly complete. Yet one thing was missing. Although the strangers were religiously honored and politically allied, they were not bound by the gossamer ties of marriage or adoption as kinsmen. In the earliest sources, foreign observers seldom distinguished clearly between marriage *à la façon du pays* (according to native custom) and hospitable short-term companionship—and even less seldom recognized adoption ceremonies when they occurred. So we have to rely on later evidence to interpret the faint signals left by the first Europeans, who seldom understood their hosts' language.

We know generally that in native society, an unattached person was *persona non grata*. To be accepted as a full member of a tribe or band was to be related—biologically or fictively—to other members. So a European trader, diplomat, missionary, or officer who wanted to exercise any sway over native life had to become part of an Indian family, either by adoption or marriage. More specifically, we know that throughout the sixteenth century the Indians of Florida readily adopted Spanish shipwreck victims, including several women who took native husbands and had *mestizo* children by them. We also know that all over eastern America in subsequent centuries, European war captives and runaways were adopted, married, and treated as if they had been born of Indian mothers. It is therefore likely that many of the chiefly "harangues," elaborate gift-givings, exchanges of official insignia, and bestowal of Indian names reported by European leaders marked the newcomers' adoption as fictive kin.

By the same token, the bestowal of native women upon the strangers was probably meant not only to betoken temporary hospitality but often to pledge long-term fidelity in marriage, which in Indian society did not require banns, dowries, rings, or church weddings. On the Mississippi River in 1541, the caciques of Casqui and Pacaha offered Soto three of their close relatives as "testimonial[s] of love." Begging the Spaniard to take his daughter as his wife, one chief said that "his greatest desire was to unite his blood with that of so great a lord as he was." The other was willing to give up two of his sisters, Macanoche and Mochila, to cement relations with the dangerous "children of the sun."

William Hilton was similarly if somewhat more ambiguously propositioned on the Cape Fear River in 1663. After repulsing several minor attacks upriver, Hilton and his crew were called to shore by forty warriors crying, "Bonny, Bonny." When the English landed, the natives threw beads into their boat, made a long, indecipherable speech, and presented the nonplussed crew with "two very handsom proper young Indian women, the tallest," Hilton wrote, "that we have seen in the Countrey; which we supposed to be the Kings Daughters, or persons of some great account amongst them. These young women were ready to come into our Boat." Indeed, he hurried to assure his sensitive English readers, "one of them crouding in, was hardly perswaded to go out again." Three years later, Henry Woodward discovered what such a gift entailed. Having been left with the Port Royal Indians to learn their language and to serve as hostage for the return of the chief's nephew, who was taken to Barbados for a similar purpose, Woodward was given by the chief a large cornfield and his Indian counterpart's sister, "telling him that she should tend him and dresse his victuals and be careful of him that soe her Brother might be the better used amongst [the English]."

The sixty men who stopped with Iberville at the Bayogoula village in 1700 undoubtedly would have sold their honor cheap to share Woodward's fate. As the French arrived for the requisite three days of the calumet, the chiefs asked Iberville whether they "would require as many women as there were men in [their] party." Just as he, a non-smoker, was not eager to smoke the calumet, so Iberville "spoiled" what he perceived as his men's sport by show-ing his hand to his hosts and making them understand that "their skin—red and tanned—should not come close to that of the French, which was white."

The attention and welcome generated among the Indians by the advent of the first Europeans was clearly exceptional; whether gods in human shape or rare mortals, these beings were quite unlike any of the "original peoples" of America. As such they deserved the most respectful treatment possible and required full incorporation into native society in order to harness their assets and to forestall any harm they might do. But what exactly was the source of the Europeans' fascination and power?

White Power

What did the Indians see in the Europeans that was not, or only dimly, seen in their own kind? One difference was the whiteness of European skin. On Arthur Barlowe's recon-naissance of Roanoke Island in 1584, the natives "wondred mervelously when we were amongst them, at the whiteness of our skinnes, ever coveting to touch our breastes, and to view the same." Sixty years earlier, the natives of the Outer Banks had been equally aston-ished by the newcomers' whiteness. When one of Giovanni da Verrazzano's sailors was nearly drowned trying to swim with some small gifts to a group of Indians, they rescued him, took off his shoes, stockings, and shirt, built a large warming fire, "placed him on the ground in the sun . . . and made gestures of great admiration, looking at the whiteness of his flesh and exam-ining him from head to foot." The Biloxi Indians who first laid eyes on the French in 1699 also gaped at the "white-skinned people" in their midst. "Thus," noted André Pénicaut,

the literate ship's carpenter, "we appeared to be quite different from them, who have very tawny skin. . . ."

But the close examination that the Indians gave the explorers' chests, faces, and arms may have been focused on the skin's hairiness as well as its pallor. For Pénicaut went on to say that the Biloxis were also astonished by the heavy beards and bald heads among the French, for the Biloxis had "heavy black hair which they groom very carefully" and, like the other Mississippi tribes, "remove the hair from their faces as well as from other parts of the body . . . with shell ash and hot water as one would remove the hair from a suckling pig." Undiluted Indian genes still carry no chromo-somes for baldness. Understandably, European beards and tufted chests held an ugly fas-cination for the smooth-skinned Americans. Before they actually saw a white man, the Potawatomis and Menominees around Green Bay believed the French to be a different species from other men, not because their skin was a shade or two lighter, but because they were "covered" with hair.

The first Europeans were celebrated less because they were pale or hairy than because they were spiritually powerful men, "gods" (as the Europeans put it) or *manitous* (in Algonquian parlance), like Indian shamans and conjurers. There were two chief sources of their power. The first was their reputation among the Indians as purveyors or preventers of disease, exactly comparable to native shamans, who were also thought to wield powers of life and death. Jacques Cartier was asked to lay hands on all the sick and handicapped at Hochelaga as if, he said, "Christ had come down to earth to heal them." The three Spanish doctors in Cabeza de Vaca's traveling medicine show were thought to raise men from the dead as well as to cure a variety of ailments. They got into this profitable business— satisfied customers paid them fees of food and goods beyond their ability to consume—when their Texas captors forced them to practice traditional shamanic blowing and rubbing techniques for their keep, convinced that "we who were extraordinary men must possess power and efficacy over all other things." Not surprisingly, the cacique thought it only sensible to ask the "son of the sun"—Soto—to restore sight to a number of his blind villagers.

At the same time, the Indians believed that all spiritual power was double-edged: those who could cure could also kill. Only powerful "spirits" possessed the ability to bewitch or to counteract another's witchcraft. When the Roanoke colonists inadvertently carried deadly European diseases into the North Carolina coastal region, they were deified by their hosts for their ability to kill Indians at a distance and to remain unscathed themselves. "There could at no time happen any strange sicknesses, losses, hurtes, or any other crosse unto [the natives]," wrote Thomas Harriot, the expedition's Indian expert, "but that they would impute to us the cause or means thereof for offending or not pleasing us." The Indians had

extra cause to worry when four or five towns that had practiced some "subtle devise" against the English were ravaged by an unknown disease shortly after the colonists' departure. The English rivals under chief Wingina deduced that the havoc was wrought by "our God through our meanes, and that wee by him might kil and slaie whom wee would without weapons and not come neere them."

The second and more important source of the white man's power in native America was his technological superiority. As native oral traditions suggest, European ships initially impressed the Americans who piloted nothing larger than dug-out canoes. Columbus attributed his divine reception largely to his clothes and his ships. Arthur Barlowe told Sir Walter Ralegh that the natives of Roanoke "had our ships in marvelous admiration, and all things els was so strange unto them, as it appeared that none of them had even seene the like." As late as 1700 many Mississippi Valley tribes had never seen a European sailing ship. So when Iberville returned to Louisiana with the French fleet, Sauvole took four native dignitaries to view the frigates. As predicted, they were "ecstatic to see such big contraptions." When they returned to Fort Biloxi, they told waiting tribesmen that "they had been on the ships that went up to the clouds, that there were more than fifty villages on each one and crowds that one cannot pass through, and one made them climb down to a place where they did not see sun or moon." Then they all left for Choctaw country upriver "to teach them these wonders."

Another cause of wonderment was firearms, which Verrazzano noted as early as 1524. On an "Arcadian" coast somewhere south of New York harbor, a handsome, naked Indian man approached a group of French sailors and showed them a burning stick, "as if to offer [them] fire." But when the Europeans trumped his hospitality by firing a matchlock, "he trembled all over with fear" and "remained as if thunderstruck, and prayed, worshiping like a monk, pointing his finger to the sky; and indicating the sea and the ship, he appeared to bless us."

Not without reason, European metal weapons continued to impress the natives who saw them in action for the first time. When chief Donnacona asked Cartier in 1535 to demonstrate his artillery, of which two of the chief's men had given "great account," the Frenchman obliged by firing a dozen cannon into the nearby woods. The Stadaconans were "so much astonished as if the heavens had fallen upon them, and began to howl and to shriek in such a very loud manner that one would have thought hell had emptied itself there." When Pierre Radisson and Nicolas Perrot traveled among the Indians of Wisconsin in the 1650s and 1660s, the natives literally worshipped their guns, knives, and hatchets by blowing sacred smoke over them "as if it were incense." Likewise, the woodland Sioux who captured the Recollect missionary Louis Hennepin in 1680 called a gun *Manza Ouckange*, "iron which has a spirit." Understandably, the gun's noise and smoke initially did as much to terrify the natives as did its lead balls, which everyone conceded did more crippling damage to internal organs than did flinttipped arrows.

Weapons were of paramount importance to the feuding polities of North America, but metal objects of any kind, cloth goods, and cleverly designed or sizable wooden objects also drew their admiration. Thomas Harriot put his finger on the primary cause of the Indians' initially exalted opinion of the white strangers when he noted that

> most things they sawe with us, as Mathematicall instruments, sea compasses, the vertue of the loadstone in drawing iron, a perspective glasse whereby was shewed manie strange sightes, burning glasses, wildfire woorkes, gunnes, bookes, writing and reading, spring clocks that seeme to goe of themselves, and manie other things that wee had, were so straunge unto them, and so farre exceeded their capacities to comprehend the reason and meanes how should be made and

done, that they thought they were rather the works of gods than of men, or at the leastwise they had bin given and taught us of the gods.

The Sioux, Illinois, and Seneca Indians among whom Father Hennepin journeyed frequently clapped their hands over their mouths in astonishment at such things as printed books, silver chalices, embroidered chasubles, and iron pots, all of which they designated as "spirits." In the 1630s the natives of southern New England considered a windmill "little less than the world's wonder" for the whisking motion of its long arms and its "sharp teeth biting the corn," and the first plowman little less than a "juggler" or shaman. Being shown the iron coulter and share of the plow, which could "tear up more ground in a day than their clamshells [hoes] could scrape up in a month," they told the plowman "he was almost Abamacho, almost as cunning as the Devil."

In a very short time, the enterprising newcomers discovered how to turn the natives' awe of European technology to private advantage. Columbus's crewmen found that they could make a killing in a trade with the Taínos—over the Admiral's objections—for pieces of broken wine-barrel hoops, earthenware shards, scraps of broken glass, and lace tips. In the next century, European colonists on the coasts of Florida and Georgia took advantage of the Indians' eagerness to swap decorative but otherwise useless gold and silver from Spanish shipwrecks for pieces of paper and playing cards. A Calusa man once gave a Spanish soldier seventy ducats of gold for an ace of diamonds. But Captain George Waymouth may have been the most calculating of all. In 1605 he used a magnetized sword to pick up a knife and a needle before a Maine band of potential fur-trading partners. "This we did," he confessed, "to cause them to imagine some great power in us: and for that to love and feare us."

The white man's varied powers were celebrated in the generic names given to him by different native groups. The Narragansetts of

Rhode Island called all Europeans "Coatmen" or "swordmen." The Mohawks of New York referred to the Dutch as "Iron-workers" or "Cloth makers," while the Hurons of southern Ontario called the French *Agnonha*, "Iron People." In northern New England the Pocumtucks knew the French as "Knife men," just as the Virginians, and later all white Americans, were known as "Longknives." The strong identification of the European "others" with their metal instruments of death seems sadly appropriate. After all, on the very first day the Taínos met Columbus on the sands of Guanahaní in 1492, the Admiral "showed them swords and they took them by the edge and through ignorance cut themselves."

THE DOMESTICATION OF DIFFERENCE

The Taíno experience notwithstanding, European encounters with the North American Indians were, at the very beginning, predominantly peaceful, and the natives generally welcomed the newcomers. The white explorers had too much curiosity about, and especially too much need for, the new peoples they had "discovered" to pick gratuitous fights; enough skirmishes would eventually break out through mutual misunderstanding and ham-handed tactics. The Europeans' immediate need was to learn enough about the natives and the land to be able to classify, utilize, and, ultimately, dominate both. In all these efforts, they assumed that the American "others" were inferior—culturally and religiously rather than racially—to themselves. So they began by trying to remake America in the images of the various Europes they had left behind and to remake America's inhabitants less in their own European likenesses than according to a venerable set of normative stereotypes of aliens and "others."

Despite determined efforts, the Europeans foundered on the palpable reality of America. Although the various imperial competitors shared many goals and pursued them over several centuries, they were often stymied in the colonial period by the great number, variety, and determination of native societies living within equally stubborn and varied geographies. But the pattern of thought and activity initially laid down by these argonauts of empire allows us to glimpse the other side of America's post-Columbian encounters.

TAMING THE LAND

In some ways, the "otherness" of the land was easier to domesticate, at least intellectually, than were the people. Usually before meeting any natives, the Europeans assimilated the land by relating it to familiar scenes at home or abroad, renaming its major features, and claiming it for their sovereigns to forestall competing European claims. The well-traveled Columbus established precedent once again by comparing the green of Antillian trees to those of his adopted Andalusia "in the month of May," and the cultivated fields of Tortuga to "the plain of Cordova." He also thought he recognized mastic like that grown on the Aegean island of Chios, noticed the difference between island palms and those of African Guinea, and believed (wrongly) that the mountains of Hispaniola were loftier than "Tenerife in the Canaries." By contrast, the best way a more sedentary Englishman could describe a large yellow-flowered meadow in South Carolina was "a pasture not inferior to any I have seen in England."

Although the Indians had already endowed many prominent geographical features with names, the first Europeans signaled their imperial intentions by naming or renaming everything in sight. In choosing names they paid homage to their religions, homelands, social superiors, and, not least, their own egos. Catholic explorers were the most eager donors of religious names, such as "San Salvador," given "in remembrance of the Divine Majesty, Who had marvellously bestowed all this," said

Columbus; "the Indians call it 'Guanahaní.'" Other Spaniards dubbed two of their earliest towns "St. Augustine" and "Santa Fe." Cartier baptized the majestic Canadian river "St. Lawrence," and wherever Christians came upon bone-covered sites of former epidemics or massacres they dubbed them "Golgotha." The hearth-hugging English, of course, were famous for transferring English place-names to the localities of "*New* England," but the French in sixteenth-century Florida also renamed eight rivers after well-known French ones. Flattery, too, had its place in the nominating process, as is proved by the existence of "Virginia" (after Elizabeth I, the Virgin Queen), "Montreal" (*mont Royal*, for King Francis I), "Monterey" (for the viceroy of New Spain), and "Lake Pontchartrain" (after the French minister of marine in 1699). And self-flattery was never far behind, as "Lake Champlain," "Frobisher Bay," and "Pennsylvania" attest.

Claiming the land was hardly more taxing than naming it: The "discoverers" simply stepped off the boat and performed a small number of symbolic acts, thereby accessioning whole islands, regions, and continents for their nation-states. On October 12, 1492, Columbus rowed to the beach at Guanahaní, unfurled the royal standard and two banners of the Green Cross (one for each sovereign), made legal proclamations of possession which his fleet secretary duly recorded and his captains witnessed, and transferred the island to Ferdinand and Isabella. As he continued through the Antilles, he wrote, "my intention was not to pass by any island of which I did not take possession, although if it is taken of one," he assumed, "it may be said that it is taken of all."

Even more popular as symbols of possession were large wooden crosses, which also marked convenient harbors and landmarks for countrymen who followed. Simple crosses heralded the claims of Christians but did not specify their nationality unless coats of arms or other telltale insignia were attached. Thus when the Virginia colonists claimed Powhatan's empire for England, they insured against ambiguity by leaving a cross at the head of the newly-renamed James River with the inscription "Jacobus Rex. 1607."

More than one native leader, besides Powhatan, was suspicious of the meaning of these arrogant constructions. When Cartier erected at the entrance of Gaspé harbor a thirty-foot cross, complete with shield and plaque reading "VIVE LE ROY DE FRANCE" in bold Gothic letters, he got an argument from a Micmac chief. "Pointing to the cross," Cartier recalled, "he made us a long harangue, making the sign of the cross with two of his fingers; and then he pointed to the land all around about, as if he wished to say that all this region belonged to him, and that we ought not to have set up this cross without his permission."

The French Huguenots who tried to preempt the Spanish in Florida may have gotten a similar message when they planted a white stone pillar on a riverbank. This was one of five man-sized columns they had brought to assert their claims, each inscribed with a royal shield, three fleurs-de-lis, the Queen Mother's initial, and the date "1561." One of the local chiefs, however, was not amused by their audacity. When Jean Ribault, the French captain, went to visit him with gifts, the chief put on a grave face and only shook his head a little to show that "he was not well pleased" either with the column or the fact that the French had first planted one across the river in the domain of a rival. Before long, the disgruntled chief was vindicated. When the French returned three years later to establish a military presence, they were gleefully taken to see the first pillar, which had been protected by the Indians and decorated with "crownes of Bay" and "little baskets of Mill [grain]." Within a year, however, the Spanish demolished the French fort, murdered the garrison, and carried off the offensive column to Havana.

Situational Ethics

Claiming allegedly "virgin" land was one thing, mastering it and turning it to profit was quite another. The Europeans quickly found that the latter was impossible without the active aid of the natives, whom even the most contemptuous invaders realized had strong attachments, if not "legitimate" claims or "natural rights," to the land. The Indians also had unique knowledge of the land and its environmental limits, something European dreamers and schemers often sorely lacked. Before newcomers could proceed to their larger goals of profiteering and domination, they had to learn enough about the American "others" to win their confidence and friendship, get them to supplement always-inadequate supplies, and induce them to reveal the sources of America's presumed wealth. Beginning with Columbus, European leaders initially instructed their men to avoid any behavior that would offend the numerically superior natives. "For if any rude and rigorous meanes shuldbe used towardes this people," Ribault predicted, "they would flye hither and thither through the woodes and forestes and abandon there habitations and cuntrye" or else, he did not have to say, they would turn and attack the offending parties.

EUROPEAN HOSPITALITY

So, on the ancient principle of "When in Rome," the Europeans tamed their haste for results and bent their initial efforts to reciprocating native hospitality as fully as possible. As they sought to earn reputations for generosity, perhaps the supreme virtue in communal Indian society, they also hoped to impress the natives with their superior technology, intelligence, and spiritual power, all of which they assumed gave them just claim to rule the new land and its people. European hospitality was not much different from Indian, except that its spirit was more calculating, and the newcomers had no desire to reduce native difference and "inferiority" by incorporating them into their families, which were largely absent in any event. The staples of both welcomes were feasting, entertainment, and gift-giving, the essential lubricant of Indian social relations. For Indians, spending the night in a tarry, creaking ship was apparently considered a treat, perhaps more for the novel food and drink offered than for comfort or company. European-prepared meat, pease, beans, bread, and even ship's biscuits were eaten with gusto. A band of southern New England Indians liked everything Captain Bartholomew Gosnold served them but the mustard, "whereat they made many a sowre face." Alcoholic beverages got a mixed reception. A Timucua chief grew so fond of French wine—or company—that he broke a ban on daytime eating to request a cup in order to drink with Jean Ribault. Yet the Bayogoulas took "very little" of the wine and brandy Iberville offered them, being more stunned by the brandy he set on fire. In 1605 the Abenakis on St. George's River in Maine tasted English aqua vitae "but would by no meanes drinke." Sugar candy and raisins were more to their taste.

What caught the attention of the European hosts was not the natives' palate but their unselfish sharing of everything they received. Columbus was the first to notice that when a Haitian cacique left his retinue on deck to go below to join the Admiral at dinner, he took only a small sample of each dish for tasting and "afterward sent the rest to his people, and all ate of it." A century later, Captain Waymouth similarly entertained two Abenakis, who, after eating a modest amount, characteristically "desired pease to carry a shore to their women, which we gave them, with fish and bread," wrote the ship's scribe, "and lent them pewter dishes, which they carefully brought [back] againe."

Once the Indians had been wined and dined, they were serenaded by the European equivalents of native drums, flutes, and rattles. Most expeditions on land and sea carried a complement of martial drummers and trumpeters, who were often pressed into social service to entertain visiting natives. But some ships' crews included bona fide musicians: Sir Humphrey Gilbert had six, John Davis, four. Davis lured several Eskimo groups to trade by playing music and having his crew dance to it on shore. In 1603 some Massachusetts Algonquians were diverted by the "homely Music" of a young guitarist in Martin Pring's crew. After showering the musician with gifts, they danced around him "twentie in a Ring . . . using many Savage gestures [and] singing Io, Ia, Io, Ia, Ia, Io." In Louisiana a century later, the Colapissa villagers who hosted a dozen Frenchmen during one of their periodic supply shortages learned to dance the minuet and *la bourrée* to the fine fiddling of a violinist named Picard. His companions "nearly d[ied] of laughter" over their hosts' capers, but the natives obviously enjoyed themselves and even had the last laugh when Picard could not keep time with the intricate drumming at their traditional dances.

European rituals of hospitality were brought to a close by the giving of gifts to the visiting natives. Fresh from the corrupt courts and countinghouses of Europe, the newcomers tended to see gifts as bribes, necessary palm-crossings to get a job done. In native America, by contrast, gifts were at once "words" in the rich metaphorical language of political councils and sureties for one's word. The potential conflict between these two meanings was largely avoided by the necessity of employing gifts in a native context. Since nothing could be done without them, the Europeans quickly learned that in using them they were bound by the promises made on each occasion. In such a setting, words could not be taken lightly and

stark honesty was a necessity, particularly on formal or ceremonial occasions. If the Europeans wanted peace with the natives, reciprocal gift-giving was the only reliable way to secure it.

As in Europe, gifts to leaders usually led to the best results. So it was chiefs and caciques who received an eye-catching drapery from Columbus's bed, red wool caps from Cartier, and "gownes of blewe clothe garnished with yellowe flowers de luce" from Ribault. Since Europe and America were alike in generally adhering to social hierarchy, appropriate gifts were best given to the several ranks. When Cartier was ready to distribute gifts to the Hochelagans, he made the men, women, and children line up separately. "To the headmen he gave hatchets, to the others knives, and to the women, beads and other small trinkets. He then made the children scramble for little rings and tin *agnus Dei*, which afforded them great amusement."

TAKING THE AMERICANS' MEASURE

Having earned provisional reputation as "generous men," the explorers could then proceed to two final acts of preparation before attempting to impose their will on the land and the people. The first was to take the measure of the natives, for both intellectual and practical purposes. Attempting to make sense of the natives' novelty was natural to literate people whose culture relied heavily on encyclopedias and other compendia of knowledge to assimilate all that was known about their burgeoning world. And knowing the American "others" was the only way to beat them in the competition for their continent.

Like most people, Europeans tended to conceive of the new in terms of the old, to classify novelties according to conventional wisdom. Most explorers, therefore, began to cope with the shiny newness of the natives by putting them in mental pigeonholes constructed from ancient precedent and proximate experience. This had the added advantage of helping the homebound readers of their New World narratives learn by comparison with the known and the familiar.

When Europeans first sought to describe Indians and Indian culture, they slipped their often keen-eyed observations into interpretive slots marked "Ancients," "Africans," "Wild Irish," or, the most capacious and indefinite of all, "Savages." The people Verrazzano met in Narragansett Bay exhibited the "sweet and gentle . . . manner of the ancients." Arthur Barlowe found the natives of Roanoke "such as lived after the manner of the golden age." But other "ancient" analogies were less flattering to the Indians. When Theodor de Bry republished Harriot's account of Roanoke in 1590, he included many engravings of John White's paintings of "Virginia" Indians and life. After the index, he tucked in a section of five pictures of Picts and Ancient Britons "to showe how . . . the Inhabitants of the great Bretannie have bin in times past as sauvage as those of Virginia." Long-haired, naked, and tattooed from head to toe, a fierce Pict warrior is depicted wearing a deadly curved sword at his belt and holding a shield in one hand and the bloody head of a victim in the other.

Since few other European colonizers had as much experience in Africa as the Portuguese had, the earliest comparisons of American Indians and Africans were limited largely to physical appearance, such as skin color, hair texture, and lip size. These comparisons tended to emphasize contrasts rather than similarities and to favor the Americans, who came closer to European norms of appearance and beauty. The "wild Irish" and their culture, on the other hand, were quite familiar to many English adventurers in North America because the latter had served in Ireland, trying to bring it under Queen Elizabeth's royal wing. It was understandable that Captain John Smith likened the Virginians' deerskin robes to "Irish mantels," and Harriot compared their spear-fishing to "the maner as Irish men cast darts [short spears]."

Any other native behavior or social custom that could not be easily classified was assigned to the "Savage" category, an *omniumgatherum* for temporarily isolating the unfamiliar until it could be defused by myopic familiarity or accepted on its own terms as the stubborn reality of Indian life. In many ways, the first Europeans to meet America's natives were the most open to that reality, before the frustration of their dominating designs permanently warped their vision and judgment.

TAMING TONGUES

The Europeans' final preparation for New World domination was to learn how to communicate with the Indians. For without the ability to plumb the nuances of their languages, their thoughts and feelings would remain dangerously hidden. The Indians faced the same task: the "other" must become intelligible in order to become predictable and, thereby, controllable. In the beginning, the natives enjoyed numerical superiority and could dictate the terms of engagement. A Frenchman who made a grand tour of the Great Lakes in 1669 spoke for all European explorers when he realized early in his journey "how important it was not to engage one's self amongst the tribes of these countries without knowing their language or being sure of one's interpreter. The lack of an interpreter under our own control prevented the entire success of our expedition," he lamented.

Since the crude pantomimes of sign language were clearly not sufficient for reliable discourse, interpreters on both sides had to be trained. This generally entailed a voluntary program of student exchanges, at which the French both in Canada and later in Louisiana proved to be the most adept. Quick-witted children were sent to live with the "others" in order to learn not only their words but the social and cultural realities that lay behind them. It did not tarnish the exchange that the foreign students also served as hostages for the peaceful conduct of their people.

Some interpreters, however, were not volunteers. A few European expeditions that arrived after the initial waves of invasion were fortunate to find countrymen who had been taken captive or saved from shipwrecks and adopted by the Indians and who were already fluent in the regional tongues. Soto's entrada would never have left the coast of Florida had he not redeemed Juan Ortiz, a survivor of the Narváez debacle in 1528 who had lived with the natives for twelve years. Fortunately, although he closely resembled the Indians, down to his arm tattoos and breechclout, Ortiz had not forgotten the Spanish he had learned in Seville. When he died somewhere west of the Mississippi in March 1542, the expedition began to unravel, for the only interpreter left was a young Indian slave acquired in northeastern Georgia, where different languages were spoken. "So great a misfortune was the death of . . . Ortiz . . . that to learn from the Indians what he stated in four words, with the youth the whole day was needed; and most of the time he understood just the opposite of what was asked."

The need for interpreters among the early Europeans was so urgent that many ship captains endangered future relations with the natives by kidnapping tribesmen (never women) to take back to Europe for language instruc-tion. Since it was nearly impossible for the Indians to distinguish the temporary "borrow-ing" of interpreters from the permanent kid-napping of slaves, which Europeans also snatched in alarming numbers, they could be forgiven a certain amount of violence toward the next ships to appear. Columbus inaugu-rated the sordid practice on his first voyage, but the pairs of interpreters taken by Jacques Cartier and Arthur Barlowe are the more famous because they were safely returned after a year abroad to play key roles in the colonial ventures of Canada and Roanoke respectively. Chief Donnacona's two sons, Domagaya and especially Taignoagny, did their best to foil French incursions into the St. Lawrence before they were shanghaied a second time, but Manteo and Wanchese from the Outer Banks left a mixed legacy. Wanchese, one of chief Wingina's warriors, was also hostile to European pretensions, but Manteo, a rival Croatoan, was instrumental in securing an English foothold, however briefly, in North Carolina. In 1587 he became the first native convert to the Church of England and was appointed chief of Roanoke Island by the last English governor.

GLOSSARY

Francisco Vásquez de Coronado (1510–1554): Spanish explorer who in his quest for the fabled Seven Cities of Cibola was the first to explore Arizona and New Mexico.

Hernando de Soto (c.1500–1542): Spanish explorer. In 1539 he set out to conquer Florida. In search of treasure, his group explored much of present-day Georgia, the Carolinas, Tennessee, Alabama, and Oklahoma. De Soto died on the expedition and was buried in the Mississippi.

Zuni: A pueblo people located in western New Mexico.

Green Bay Potawatomis: A Native American people variously located in Michigan, Wisconsin, northern Illinois, and northern Indiana in the seventeenth to the nineteenth centuries. Green Bay, in present-day Wisconsin, was the Potawatomi trading center.

Jacques Cartier (1491–1557): French explorer who navigated the St. Lawrence River (1535) and laid claim to the region for France.

Samuel de Champlain (1567?–1635): French explorer who explored present-day Canada and in 1608 established the settlement of Quebec.

Giovanni da Verrazzano (1485?–1528?): Italian explorer of the Atlantic coast of North America during the mid-sixteenth century.

IMPLICATIONS

In this essay, Axtell depicts a process of mutual assessment on the part of natives and newcomers alike. From what you've read in this essay, how do you think Native Americans and European evaluated each other? What were the positive and the negative aspects of Native American culture for the Europeans? Of European culture for the Native Americans?

Past Traces

Life in early Virginia was dominated by disease and hard labor. This reading begins with a letter home from Richard Frethorne, a typical indentured servant in early seventeenth-century Virginia. Like many others before and after him, Frethorne was shocked and dismayed by the daily routine of unremitting work and poor provisions that was the lot of indentured servants in the Chesapeake colony. The harshness of early Virginia life often brought immigrants, like Frethorne, to question their decision to leave England for the promise of the New World.

Richard Frethorne's Letter Home (1623)

Loveing and kind father and mother my most humble duty remembered to you hopeing in God of your good health, as I my selfe am at the makeing hereof, this is to let you understand that I your Child am in a most heavie Case by reason of the nature of the Country is such that it Causeth much sicknes [including scurvy and "the bloody flux"] . . . and when wee are sicke there is nothing to comfort us; for since I came out of the ship, I never at anie thing but pease, and loblollie (that is water gruell)[.] as for deare or venison I never saw anie since I came into this land there is indeed some foule, but Wee are not allowed to goe, and get yt, but must Worke hard both earelie, and late for a messe of water gruell, and a mouthfull of bread, and beife[.] a mouthfull of bread for a pennie loafe must serve for 4 men which is most pitifull if you did knowe as much as I, when people crie out day, and night, Oh that they were in England without their lymbes and would not care to loose anie lymbe to bee in England againe, yea though they beg from doore to doore. . . . I have nothing at all, no not a shirt to my backe, but two Ragges nor no Clothes, but one poore suite, nor but one paire of shooes, but one paire of stockins, but one Capp, but two bands, my Cloke is stollen by one of my owne fellowes, and to his dying hower would not tell mee what he did with it [although some friends saw the "fellowe" buy butter and beef from a ship, probably purchased with Frethorne's cloak]. . . . but I am not halfe a quarter so strong as I was in England, and all is for want of victualls, for I doe protest unto you, that I have eaten more in a day at home than I have allowed me here for a Weeke. . . .

O that you did see may daylie and hourelie sighes, grones, and teares, and thumpes that I afford mine owne brest, and rue and Curse the time of my birth with holy Job. I thought no head had beene able to hold so much water as hath and doth dailie flow from mine eyes.

2
....

Anthony Johnson:
Patriarch on Pungoteague Creek
T.H. Breen and Stephen Innes

The seventeenth-century Chesapeake offered high risks and potential advancement to any who would come to the first sustained English colony in North America. More than 90 percent of white English men and women who came to the Chesapeake arrived as indentured servants, living a life of constricted freedom and hard labor in exchange for the prospect of land and relative prosperity that might come in the near future. But non-whites came to the early Chesapeake as well, although they seldom did so voluntarily. Africans arrived in Virginia sometime shortly before 1619 as captives of a burgeoning Atlantic slave system that transported captured Africans to the labor-starved plantations of the New World.

In the early years of Virginia, many of these Africans were creoles: mostly men, but some women, who had created biracial lives in the settlements and trading posts of the Atlantic basin. Combining knowledge of European languages and customs with that of their native African traditions, these African creoles inhabited a fluid world in which the rigid racial caste system of the eighteenth and nineteenth centuries did not yet exist. Living in a world that was neither completely black nor white, many creoles found a measure of freedom and financial success that provided them the space to pursue the same goals of family and personal independence that dominated the white settler ethic in the Chesapeake.

Anthony Johnson was one of these Atlantic creoles. As T.H. Breen and Stephen Innes recount Johnson's story, they reveal the ways in which one African man and his wife created a place for themselves and their growing family in the fluid world of early Virginia. Settling on the remote eastern shore of the Virginia colony, Anthony Johnson used his well-honed interracial social skills to claim a position as family head and independent property-holder that was identical to that of his white counterparts.

....

Anthony Johnson would have been a success no matter where he lived. He possessed immense energy and ingenuity. His parents doubtless never imagined that their son would find himself a slave in a struggling, frontier settlement called Virginia. Over his original bondage, of course, Johnson had no control. He did not allow his low status in the New World to discourage him, however, and in his lifetime he managed to achieve that goal so illusive to immigrants of all races, the American dream. By the time Johnson died he had become a freeman, formed a large and secure family, built up a sizable estate, and in the words of one admiring historian, established himself as the "black patriarch" of Pungoteague Creek, a small inlet on the western side of Northampton County.

Johnson arrived in Virginia sometime in 1621 aboard the *James*. People referred to him at this time simply as "Antonio a Negro," and the overseers of the Bennett or Warresquioake (Wariscoyack) plantation located on the south side of the James River purchased him to work in their tobacco fields. In a general muster of the inhabitants of Virginia made in 1625, Anthony appeared as a "servant," and while some historians argue that many early blacks were indentured servants rather than slaves, Anthony seems to have been a slave. Like other unfree blacks in seventeenth-century Virginia, he possessed no surname. Had he been able to document his conversion to Christianity—preferably by providing evidence of baptism—he might have sued for freedom, but there is no record that he attempted to do so. He settled on Bennett's plantation, no doubt more concerned about surviving from day to day than about his legal status.

The 1620s in Virginia were a time of great expectations and even greater despair. The colony has been described as "the first American boom country," and so it was for a very few men with money and power enough to purchase gangs of dependent laborers. For the servants and slaves, however, the colony was a hell. Young men, most of them in their teens, placed on isolated tobacco plantations, exposed constantly to early, possibly violent, death, and denied the comforts and security of family life because of the scarcity of women, seemed more like soldiers pressed into dangerous military service than agricultural workers. They would certainly have understood Lytton Strachey's poignant phrase, "the abridgment of hope."

Immediately before Johnson arrived at Warresquioake, the Virginia Company of London launched an aggressive, albeit belated, program to turn a profit on its American holdings. Sir Edwin Sandys, the man who shaped company policy, dreamed of producing an impressive array of new commodities, silk and potash, iron and glass, and he persuaded wealthy Englishmen to finance his vision. One such person was Edward Bennett, possibly a man of Puritan leanings, who won Sandys's affection by writing a timely treatise "touching the inconvenience that the importacon of Tobacco out of Spaine had brought into this land [England]." Sandys dispatched thousands of settlers to the Chesapeake to work for the company, but favored individuals like Bennett received special patents to establish "particular plantations," semi-autonomous economic enterprises in which the adventurers risked their own capital for laborers and equipment and, in exchange, obtained a chance to collect immense returns. Bennett evidently sent his brother Robert and his nephew Richard to Virginia to oversee the family plantation. At one time, the Bennetts owned or employed over sixty persons.

On Good Friday, March 22, 1622, the Indians of Tidewater Virginia put an end to Sandys's dream. In a carefully coordinated attack, they killed over three hundred and fifty colonists in a single morning. Fifty-two of these people fell at the Bennett plantation, and in the muster of 1625 only twelve servants were reported living at Warresquioake, which perhaps to erase the memory of the attack was now renamed Bennett's Welcome. One of the survivors was Anthony. Somehow he and four other men had managed to live through the Indian assault; the other seven individuals listed in 1625 had settled in Virginia after the Indian uprising. Johnson revealed even at this early date one essential ingredient for success in Virginia: good luck. In 1622 the *Margrett and John* brought "Mary a Negro Woman" to Warresquioake. She was the only woman living at Bennett's plantation in 1625, and at some point—we do not know when—she became Anthony's wife. He was a very fortunate man. Because of an exceedingly unequal sex ratio in early Virginia, few males, black or white, had the opportunity to form a family. Mary bore Anthony at least four children, and still managed to outlive her husband by several years. In a society in which marriages were routinely broken by early death, Mary and Anthony lived together for over forty years. The documents reveal little about the quality of their relationship, but one infers that they helped each other in myriad ways that we can never recapture. In 1653 Anthony Johnson and Mary "his wife" asked for tax relief from the Northampton County court. The local justices observed that the two blacks "have lived Inhabitants in Virginia (above thirty yeares)" and had achieved widespread respect for their "hard labor and known service." The interesting point is that both Mary and Anthony received recognition; both contributed to the life of their community.

Johnson's movements between 1625 and 1650 remain a mystery. Court records from a later period provide tantalizing clues about his life during these years, but they are silent on how "Antonio a Negro" became Anthony Johnson. Presumably someone named Johnson helped Anthony and Mary to gain freedom, but the details of that agreement have been lost.

During the 1640s the Johnsons acquired a modest estate. Raising livestock provided a reliable source of income, and at mid-century, especially on the Eastern Shore, breeding cattle and hogs was as important to the local economy as growing tobacco. To judge by the extent of Johnson's livestock operations in the 1650s, he probably began to build up his herds during the 1640s. In any case, in July 1651 Johnson claimed that 250 acres of land were due him for five headrights. The names listed in his petition were Thomas Bembrose, Peter Bughby, Anthony Cripps, John Gesororo, and Richard Johnson. Whether Anthony Johnson actually imported these five persons into the colony is impossible to ascertain. None of them, with the exception of Richard Johnson, his son, appeared in later Northampton tax lists. Like John Upton, Anthony may have purchased headright certificates from other planters. Two hundred and fifty acres was a considerable piece of land by Eastern Shore standards, and though the great planters controlled far more acreage, many people owned smaller tracts or no land at all. Johnson's 250 acres were located on Pungoteague Creek.

In Feburary 1653 Johnson's luck appeared to have run out. A fire destroyed much of his plantation. This event—the Northampton Court called it "an unfortunate fire"—set off in turn a complicated series of legal actions that sorely tested Anthony's standing within the Pungoteague community, and at one point even jeopardized much of his remaining property. The blaze itself had been devastating. After the county justices viewed the damage, they concluded that without some assistance the Johnsons would have difficulty in the "obtayneing of their Livelyhood," and when Anthony and Mary formally petitioned for relief, the court excused Mary and the Johnsons' two daughters from paying "Taxes and Charges in Northampton County for public use" for "their naturall lives." The court's decision represented an extraordinary concession. The reduction of annual taxes obviously helped Johnson to reestablish himself, and the fact that he was a "Negro" and so described during the proceedings seems to have played no discernible part in the deliberations of the local justices. Moreover, the court did more than simply lighten the Johnsons' taxes. By specifically excusing the three black women from public levies, the justices made it clear that, for tax purposes at least, Mary and her daughters were the equals of any white woman in Northampton County. Taxes in seventeenth-century Virginia were assessed on people, not on land or livestock. The definition of a tithable—someone obliged to pay taxes—changed from time to time. In the 1620, the Burgesses had included "all those that worke in the grounde." The Virginia legislators apparently intended to exempt the wives of white planters. Such women, it was assumed, busied themselves with domestic chores and therefore, did not participate directly in income producing activities. Indeed, it was commonly believed that only "wenches that are nasty, and beastly" would actually cultivate tobacco. Black women, alone, in other words, demeaned themselves by engaging in hard physical labor. In a 1645 act concerning tithables the colonial legislators declared: "And because there shall be no scruple or evasion who are and who are not tithable, It is resolved by this Grand Assembly, That *all negro men and women,* and all other men from the age of 16 to 60 shall be adjudged tithable." Why the Northampton Court made a gratuitous exception to statute law is not clear. Perhaps the Johnsons' economic success coupled with their "hard labor and known service" pointed up the need for local discretion in enforcing racial boundaries.

Anthony Johnson's next court appearance came on October 8, 1653. This time his testimony "concerned a cowe" over which he and Lieutenant John Neale had had a difference of opinion. The court records unfortunately provide no information about the nature of the conflict. The Northampton justices ordered two men familiar with the affairs of Pungoteague Creek, Captain Samuel Gouldsmith and Robert Parker, to make an "examination and finall determination" of the case. Since the Neales were a powerful family on the Eastern Shore, the decision of the justices reveals the high regard in which Johnson was held. Had he been a less important person in that society, they might have immediately found for Neale. Of greater significance, however, was the involvement of Gouldsmith and Parker in Johnson's personal business. Neither of them was a great planter; but both were ambitious men, who apparently concluded after their investigation that Johnson's fire losses had left him vulnerable to outside harassment.

A year after this litigation had been resolved, Captain Gouldsmith visited the Johnson plantation to pick up a hogshead of tobacco. Gouldsmith presumably expected nothing unusual to happen on this particular day. Like other white planters on the Eastern Shore, he carried on regular business transactions with Anthony Johnson. Gouldsmith was surprised, however, for soon after he arrived, "a Negro called John Casor" threw himself upon the merchant's mercy. He declared with seemingly no prompting that he was not a slave as Johnson claimed in public. He asserted that the Johnsons held him illegally and had done so for at least seven years. Casor insisted that he entered Virginia as an indentured servant, and that moreover he could verify his story. An astonished Johnson assured Gouldsmith that he had never seen the indenture. Whether Casor liked it or not, he was Johnson's "Negro for life."

Robert Parker and his brother George took Casor's side in the dispute. They informed the now somewhat confused Gouldsmith that the black laborer had signed an indenture with a certain Mr. Sandys, who lived "on the other side of the Baye." Nothing further was said about Sandys, and he may have been invented conveniently to lend credibility to Casor's allegations. Whatever the truth was, Robert Parker led Casor off to his own farm, "under pretense that the said John Casor is a free-man," noting as he went that if Johnson resisted, Casor "would recover most of his Cows from him the said Johnson."

The transfer involved a carefully calculated gamble. Parker was tampering with another man's laborer, a serious but not uncommon practice in mid-century Virginia. Like other enterprising tobacco planters, Parker needed fieldhands and he was not overly scrupulous about the means he used to obtain them. The House of Burgesses regularly passed statutes outlawing the harboring of runaway servants, explaining, no doubt with people like Parker in mind, that "complaints are at every quarter court exhibitted against divers persons who entertain and enter into covenants with run-away servants . . . to the great prejudice if not the utter undoeing of divers poor men." Regardless of the letter of the law, Gouldsmith reported that Johnson "was in a great feare." In this crisis Anthony called a family conference and, after considerable discussion about the Parkers' threats, "Anthony Johnson's sonne-in-law, his wife and his owne twoe sonnes persuaded the old Negro Anthony Johnson to set the said John Casor free now." The word "old" stands out in this passage. In seventeenth-century Virginia, few men lived long enough to be called old. When they did so, they enjoyed special status as "old planters" or "Antient Livers," people who were respected if for no other reason than they had managed to survive.

This dramatic conference revealed the strong kinship ties that bound the Johnsons together. The group functioned as a modified extended family. The members of each generation lived in separate homes, but in certain economic matters they worked as a unit. Indeed, they thought of themselves as a clan. The bonds between Anthony and his sons were especially important. In 1652 John Johnson patented 450 acres next to his father's lands. Two years later, Richard Johnson laid out a 100-acre tract adjacent to the holdings of his father and brother. Both sons were married and had children of their own. In family gov-ernment, Mary had a voice, as did the son-in-law, but as all the Johnsons understood, Anthony was the patriarch. The arguments advanced at the family meeting, however, impressed Anthony. Perhaps he was just an "old" man who had allowed anger to cloud his better judgment. In any case, he yielded as gracefully as possible to the wishes of the clan. In a formal statement he discharged "John Casor Negro from all service, claims and demands . . . And doe promise accordinge to the custome of servants to paye unto the Said John Casor corne and leather." The inclusion of freedom dues gives us some sense of the extent of Johnson's fear. Colony law obliged a master to provide his indentured servants with certain items, usually food and clothes, at the end of their contracts, but it was a rare planter who paid the "custom of the country" without wringing some extra concession out of the servant. Johnson, however, was in no position to haggle.

But the decision did not sit well with Johnson. After brooding over his misfortune for three and one-half months, Johnson asked the Northampton County court to punish Robert Parker for meddling with his slave and to reverse what now appeared a precipitant decision to free Casor. The strategy worked. On March 8, 1655, "complaint was this daye made to the Court by the humble petition of Anthony Johnson Negro; agt Mr. Robert Parker that he detayneth one Jno Casor a Negro the plaintiffs servant under pretense that the said Jno Casor is a free man." After "seri-ously consideringe and maturely weighinge" the evidence, including a deposition from Gouldsmith, the members of the court ruled that "the said Mr. Robert Parker most unjustly kept the said . . . Negro (Jno Casor) from his master Anthony Johnson . . . [and] the said Jno Casor Negro shall forthwith bee returned unto the service of his master Anthony Johnson." As a final vindication of Johnson's position, the justices ordered Parker to "make payment of all charges in the suite." Johnson was elated. Casor was reenslaved and remained the prop-erty of the Johnson family. In the 1660s he accompanied the clan when it moved to Maryland. George Parker, who had taken an early interest in the controversy, managed to divorce himself from the last round of legal proceedings. His brother, Robert, of course, lost face. A few years later Robert returned to England, wiser perhaps but not richer for his experiences on the Eastern Shore.

It is important to recognize the cultural significance of this case. Throughout the entire affair the various participants made assumptions not only about the social organization of Northampton County and their place within that organization but also about the value orientations of the other actors. This sort of gambling can be dangerous, as Casor discovered. He wagered that he could forge patronage links stronger than those which his master had built up over the years. In other words, he viewed the controversy largely in terms of patron-client relations. Johnson, however, was much more alert to the dynamics of the situation than was his slave. Anthony realized that he and the local justices shared certain basic beliefs about the sanctity of property before the law. None of the parties involved, not even Casor, questioned the legitimacy of slavery nor the propriety of a black man owning a black slave. Tensions were generated because of conflicting personal ambitions, because tough-minded individuals were testing their standing within the community. In this particular formal, limited sphere of interaction, the values of a free black slaveowner coincided with those of the white gentry. In other spheres of action—as we shall discover—this value congruence did not exist. Johnson owed his victory to an accurate assessment of the appropriate actions within this particular institutional forum.

In the mid-1660s the Johnson clan moved north to Somerset County, Maryland. The Johnsons, like many other people who left Virginia's Eastern Shore during this period, were in search of fresh, more productive land. As in the Casor affair, everyone in the family participated in the decision to relocate. None of the Johnsons remained at Pungoteague. In 1665 Anthony and Mary sold 200 acres to two

planters, Morris Matthews and John Rowles. The remaining fifty acres were transferred to Richard, a gift that may have been intended to help their youngest son and his growing family establish themselves in Maryland. Whatever the motive, Richard soon sold the land, his buyer being none other than George Parker. John Johnson, the eldest son, also went to Somerset. He had already acquired 450 acres in Northampton and thus, apparently did not require his parents' financial assistance. A paternity suit, however, clouded John's departure from Virginia. He fathered an illegitimate child, and the local authorities, fearful of having to maintain the young mother and child at public expense, placed John in custody, where he stayed until his wife, Susanna, petitioned for his release. John pledged good behavior and child support and hurried off to Maryland, where he resumed his successful career.

For reasons that are unclear, the Johnsons closely coordinated their plans with those of Ann Toft and Randall Revell, two wealthy planters from Virginia's Eastern Shore. When Toft and Revell arrived in Maryland, they claimed 2,350 acres and listed Anthony, Mary, and John Casor as headrights. Whatever the nature of this agreement may have been, the Johnsons remained free. Anthony leased a 300-acre plantation which he appropriately named "Tonies Vineyard." Within a short time, the family patriarch died, but Mary renegotiated the lease for ninety-nine years. For the use of the land she paid colony taxes and an annual rent of one ear of Indian corn.

Anthony's death did not alter the structure of the family. John assumed his father's place at the head of the clan. He and Susanna had two children, John, junior, and Anthony. Richard named his boys Francis and Richard. In both families we see a self-conscious naming pattern that reflected the passing of patriarchal authority from one generation to the next. Another hint of the tight bonds that united the Johnsons was Mary's will written in 1672. She ordered that at her death three cows with calves be given to three of her grandchildren, Anthony,

Francis, and Richard. She apparently assumed that John, junior, the patriarch's son, would do well enough without her livestock. The Johnsons' financial situation remained secure. John increased his holdings. In one document he was described as a "planter," a sign that his property had brought him some economic standing within the community. One of his neighbors, a white man named Richard Ackworth, asked John to give testimony in a suit which Ackworth had filed against a white Marylander. The Somerset justices balked at first. They were reluctant to allow a black man to testify in legal proceedings involving whites, but when they discovered that John had been baptized and understood the meaning of an oath, they accepted his statement. Even Casor prospered in Maryland. He raised a few animals of his own, and in 1672 recorded a livestock brand "With the Said Marys Consent." No doubt, Casor had learned an important lesson from his dealings with Anthony. Property, even a few cows or pigs, provided legal and social identity in this society; it confirmed individuality.

GLOSSARY

Cavaliers: Aristocratic supporters of Charles I during the English Civil War (1640–1660).

Lytton Strachey: (1880–1932) British historian and biographer noted for his urbane, witty, and critical biographical works, including *Eminent Victorians* (1918).

Headrights: A grant of land in return for bringing servants and laborers to the labor-starved early Chesapeake.

IMPLICATIONS

For Breen and Innes, the story of Anthony Johnson suggests that integration of Africans into British colonial society was a real possibility in early Virginia and by implication throughout British North America. From what you've learned about the tobacco colony, do you think that the incorporation of African and African American people into the mainstream of colonial life was a real possibility?

Unlike Virginia, which verged on anarchy during its early years, Massachusetts Bay was a stable venture from its inception. Beyond the painstaking planning of the colony's leaders and the family-centeredness of the early immigrants, much of this initial stability came from the common religious focus of the Puritan settlers. This reading is introduced by one of the most important statements of the Puritan ideal in New England, *A Model of Christian Charity*. Written by John Winthrop, one of the colony's founders and its first governor, *A Model of Christian Charity* was designed as a model compact for the pious and community-minded Massachusetts Bay colony. Although Winthrop would later complain that his Massachusetts colonists too often failed to live up to these ideals, *A Model of Christian Charity* nevertheless remains one of the most powerful statements of Puritan religious and community sentiment.

John Winthrop, *"A Model of Christian Charity"* (1630)

God almighty in His most holy and wise providence hath so disposed of the condition of mankind, as in all times some must be rich, some poor, some high and eminent in power and dignity, others mean and in subjection.

Reason: First, to hold conformity with the rest of His works, being delighted to show forth the glory of His wisdom in the variety and difference of the creatures and the glory of His power, in ordering all these differences for the preservation and good of the whole.

Reason: Secondly, that He might have the more occasion to manifest the work of His spirit. First, upon the wicked in moderating and restraining them, so that the rich and mighty should not eat up the poor, nor the poor and despised rise up against their superiors and shake off their yoke. Secondly, in the regenerate in exercising His graces in them, as in the great ones, their love, mercy, gentleness, temperance, etc., in the poor and inferior sort, their faith, patience, obedience, etc.

Reason: Thirdly, that every man might have need of other, and from hence they might all be knit more nearly together in the bond of brotherly affection. From hence it appears plainly that no man is made more honorable than another, or more wealthy, etc., out of any particular and singular respect to himself, but for the glory of his creator and the common good of the creature, man.

Thus stands the cause between God and us. We are entered into covenant with Him for this work, we have taken out a commission, the Lord hath given us leave to draw our own articles we have professed to enterprise these actions upon these and these ends, we have hereupon besought Him of favor and blessing. Now if the Lord shall please to hear us, and bring us in peace to the place we desire, then hath He ratified this covenant and sealed our commission, [and] will expect a strict performance of the articles contained in it, but if we shall neglect the observations of these articles which are the ends we have propounded, and dissembling with our God, shall fall to embrace this present world and prosecute our carnal intentions seeking great things for ourselves and our posterity, the Lord will surely break out in wrath against us, be revenged of such a perjured people, and make us know the price of the breach of such a covenant.

Now the only way to avoid this shipwreck and to provide for our posterity is to follow the counsel of Micah, to do justly, to love mercy, to walk humbly with our God. For this end we must be knit together in this work as one man, we must entertain each other in brotherly affection, we must be willing to abridge ourselves of our superfluities for the supply of others' necessities, we must uphold a familiar commerce together in all meekness, gentleness, patience, and liberality, we must delight in each other, make others' conditions our own, rejoice together, mourn together, labor and suffer together, always having before our eyes our commission and community in the work, our community as members of the same body So shall we keep the unity of the spirit in the bond of peace. The Lord will be our God and delight in all our ways, so that we shall see much more of His wisdom, power, goodness, and truth than formerly we have been acquainted with. We shall find that the God of Israel is among us, when ten of us shall be able to resist a thousand of our enemies, when He shall make us a praise and glory, that men shall say of succeeding plantations, the Lord make it like that of New England. For we must consider that we shall be as a city upon a hill, the eyes of all people are upon us. So that if we shall deal falsely with our God in this work we have undertaken and so cause Him to withdraw His present help from us, we shall be made a story and byword throughout the world, we shall open the mouths of enemies to speak evil of the ways of God and all professors for God's sake, we shall shame the faces of many of God's worthy servants, and cause their prayers to be turned into curses upon us till we be consumed out of the good land whither we are going. And to shut up this discourse with that exhortation of Moses, that faithful servant of the Lord in His last farewell to Israel, Deut. 30., Beloved there is now set before us life and good, death and evil, in that we are commanded this day to love the Lord our God, and to love one another, to walk in His ways and to keep His commandments and His ordinance, and His laws, and the articles of our covenant with Him that we may live and be multiplied, and that the Lord our God may bless us in the land whither we go to possess it. But if our hearts shall turn away so that we will not obey, but shall be seduced and worship other Gods, our pleasures, our profits, and serve them, it is propounded unto us this day we shall surely perish out of the good land whither we pass over this vast sea to possess it. Therefore let us choose life, that we, and our seed, may live, and by obeying His voice, and cleaving to Him, for He is our life and our prosperity.

3

Migrants and Motives: Religion and the Settlement of New England, 1630–1640

Virginia DeJohn Anderson

English men and women emigrated from their native land for many reasons. Some, such as the Chesapeake settlers, came to the New World seeking to better their lot in life. Others sought to add a measure of adventure to their lives. For many English dissenters, however, the New World offered the unique prospect of recreating what they saw as God's true church free from the interfering hand of the established Church of England. One of the most important of these dissenting groups was the English Puritans. The Puritans had been staunch critics of the established Church of England since the late sixteenth century, believing that the English church was insufficiently reformed in both structure and doctrine. Drawing on the ideas of the French Protestant reformer John Calvin, the Puritans criticized not only the doctrines of the established English church but its elaborate ceremonies and its close connections with the monarchy as well. For Puritans, who believed that God had predestined some souls to salvation and others to damnation, only the "saved" ought to form and control the congregations of God's "true" church. The Church of England, which admitted every English man and woman to membership and was controlled by an established church hierarchy, was for the Puritans as distant from their vision of the true church as was the church in Rome.

By the 1620s, the spread of Puritanism to a growing number of English communities became a threat to the established church as well as to Charles I's ambition to make England into an absolutist state. Under the policy of William Laud, Archbishop of Canterbury and titular head of the national church, Puritan ministers and their con-

From "Migrants and Motives: Religion and the Settlement of New England, 1630–1640." *New England Quarterly*, 58, pp. 339–383. Reprinted by Permission.

gregations were harshly persecuted both as heretics and as enemies of the state. In the minds of many Puritans, their only hope lay in migration to the wilderness of New England, where they hoped to create the kind of pure and religiously cohesive communities that English conditions prevented them from achieving at home. It was against this backdrop that over 16,000 Puritan men, women, and children uprooted themselves from their local communities between 1630 and 1641 and set sail for the unpredictable wilderness of New England.

Given the risks and uncertainties of moving to the New World, some historians have doubted that religion alone can explain the source of the Puritan migration. More prosaic motives—escaping the effects of economic decline in England or the hope of economic gain—they claim, were at least as important as religious commitment in explaining the Puritan exodus. In this study of the Puritan "Great Migration," Virginia Dejohn Anderson answers these historians with a close study of the original migrants to Massachusetts Bay. The early Massachusetts Puritans, she finds, were little different from typical English men and women. New England Puritans, Anderson concludes, were not religious ascetics who dismissed economic well-being in their pursuit of religious perfection. Rather they were pragmatic realists who kept a firm eye on God's ordinances while providing amply for themselves in the New World.

....

No man, perhaps, would seem to have been an unlikelier candidate for transatlantic migration than John Bent. He had never shown any particular interest in moving; indeed, in 1638, at the age of forty-one, Bent still lived in Weyhill, Hampshire, where both he and his father before him had been born. Having prospered in the village of his birth, John Bent held enough land to distinguish himself as one of Weyhill's wealthiest inhabitants. One might reasonably expect that Bent's substantial economic stake, combined with his growing familial responsibilities—which by 1638 included a wife and five children—would have provided him with ample incentive to stay put. By embarking on a transatlantic voyage—moving for the first time in his life and over a vast distance—Bent would exchange an economically secure present for a highly uncertain future and venture his family's lives and fortunes no less than his own. Yet in the spring of 1638, Bent returned his Weyhill land to the lord of the manor, gathered his family and possessions, and traveled twenty-five miles to the port of Southampton. There, he and his family boarded the *Confidence*, bound for Massachusetts Bay.

In doing so, the Bent family joined thousands of other men, women, and children who left for New England between 1630 and 1642. We know more about John Bent than about the vast majority of these other emigrants because certain information has fortuitously survived. Bent's name appears on one of the few extant ship passenger lists of the Great Migration, and genealogists and local historians have compiled enough additional data to sketch in the outlines of his life in Old and New England. Yet despite this rare abundance of information, John Bent's reasons for moving to Massachusetts remain obscure. In fact, the surviving biographical details render the question of motivation all the more tantalizing because they provide no identifiable economic reason for leaving but rather depict a man firmly rooted in his English homeland.

Most accounts of early New England include a general discussion of the emigrants' motivations, but none has dealt with the issue systematically. If we are ever to comprehend the nature and significance of the Great Migration, however, we must understand why men like John Bent left their homes. The Great Migration to New England, unlike the simultaneous outpouring of Englishmen to other New World colonies, was a voluntary exodus of families and included relatively few indentured servants. The movement, which began around 1630, effectively ceased a dozen years later with the outbreak of the English Civil War, further distinguishing it from the more extended period of emigration to other colonies.

These two factors—the emigrants' voluntary departure and the movement's short duration—suggest that the Great Migration resulted from a common, reasoned response to a highly specific set of circumstances. Such circumstances must have been compelling indeed to dislodge a man like John Bent from a comfortable niche in his community. And while Bent and his fellows could not have known it, their reasons for embarking for New England would not only change their own lives but also powerfully shape the society they would create in their new home.

The New England settlers more closely resembled the nonmigrating English population than they did other English colonists in the New World. The implications of this fact for the development of colonial societies can scarcely be overstated. While the composition of the emigrant populations in the Chesapeake and the Caribbean hindered the successful transfer of familiar patterns of social relationships, the character of the New England colonial population ensured it. The prospect of colonizing distant lands stirred the imaginations of young people all over England, but most of these young adults made their way to the tobacco and sugar plantations of the South. Nearly half of a sample of Virginia residents in 1625 were between the ages of twenty and twenty-nine, and groups of emigrants to the Chesapeake in the seventeenth century consistently included a majority of people in their twenties. In contrast, only a quarter of the New England settlers belonged to this age group.

The age structure of New England's emigrant population virtual mirrored that of the country they had left. Both infancy and old age were represented: the *Rose* of Great Yarmouth carried one-year-old Thomas Baker as well as Katherine Rabey, a widow of sixty-eight. The proportion of people over the age of sixty was, not surprisingly, somewhat higher in the general English population than among the emigrants. Although Thomas Welde reported in 1632 that he traveled with "very aged" passengers, "twelve persons being all able to make well nigh one thousand years," a transatlantic voyage of three months' duration was an ordeal not easily undertaken, and the hardships involved in settling the wilderness surely daunted prospective emigrants of advanced years. On the whole, however, New England attracted people of all ages and thus preserved a normal pattern of intergenerational contact.

Similarly, the sex ratio of the New England emigrant group resembled that of England's population. If women were as scarce in the Chesapeake as good English beer, they were comparatively abundant in the northern colonies. In the second decade of Virginia's settlement, there were four or five men for each woman; by the end of the century, there were still about three men for every two women. Among the emigrants studied here, however, nearly half were women and girls. Such a high proportion of females in the population assured the young men of New England greater success than their southern counterparts in finding spouses.

These demographic characteristics derive directly from the fact that the migration to New England was primarily a transplantation of families. Fully 87.8 percent (597 out of 680) of the emigrants traveled with relatives of one sort or another. Nearly three-quarters (498 out of 680) came in nuclear family units, with or without children. Occasionally, single spouses migrated with their children, either to meet a partner already in the New World or to wait for his or her arrival on a later ship. Grandparents comprised a relatively inconspicuous part of the migration, but a few hardy elders did make the trip. In 1637, Margaret Neave sailed to

Massachusetts with her granddaughter Rachel Dixson, who was probably an orphan. In the following year, Alice Stephens joined her sons William and John and their families for the voyage to New England. More frequently, emigrant family structure extended horizontally, within a generation, rather than vertically, across three generations. Several groups of brothers made the trip together, and when the three Goodenow brothers decided to leave the West Country, they convinced their unmarried sister Ursula to come with them as well.

Thus, for the majority of these New England settlers, transatlantic migration did not lead to permanent separation from close relatives. Some unscrupulous men and women apparently migrated in order to flee unhappy marriages, but most nuclear family units arrived intact. When close kin were left behind, they usually joined their families within a year or so. Samuel Lincoln, for instance, who traveled aboard the *Rose* in 1637, soon joined his brother Thomas, who had settled in Hingham in 1633. Another brother, Stephen, arrived in the following year with both his family and his mother. Edward Johnson, who had first crossed the ocean with the Winthrop fleet in 1630, returned to England in 1637 to fetch his wife and seven children. For Thomas Starr, who left Sandwich in 1637, migration meant a reunion with his older brother Comfort, a passenger on the *Hercules* two years earlier. Although some disruption of kin ties was unavoidable, it was by no means the rule.

Further exploration of demographic patterns reveals other subtle but significant differences between the migrating population and that of England. These differences illustrate the important fact that migration was a selective process; not all people were equally suited to or interested in the rigors of New World settlement. Since the movement to New England was a voluntary, self-selective affair, most of this winnowing-out process occurred before the hearths of English homes, as individuals and families discussed whether or not to leave.

Although family groups predominated within the emigrant population, many individuals came to New England on their own. The vast majority of these solitary travelers were male—men outnumbered women by a factor of ten to one—and together they constituted 38 percent of the emigrant households. This figure stands in sharp contrast to England's population, where only about 5 percent of all households were composed of one individual. About one in six emigrants aged twenty-one to thirty sailed independently, perhaps drawn to New England by hopes of employment or freeholdership. These men were hardly freewheeling adventurers; instead, they provided the new settlements with skilled labor. The unaccompanied travelers included shoemakers, a carpenter, butcher, tanner, hempdresser, weaver, cutler, physician, fuller, tailor, mercer, and skinner. Some were already married at the time of the voyage, and those who were single seldom remained so for more than a couple of years after their arrival. Through marriage, the men became members of family networks within their communities. Within a few years of his arrival in 1635, for instance, Henry Ewell, a young shoemaker from Sandwich in Kent, joined the church in Scituate and married the daughter of a prominent local family. William Paddy, a London skinner, managed to obtain land, find a wife, and get elected to Plymouth's first general court of deputies within four years of his voyage.

New England clearly attracted a special group of families. The average age of emigrant husbands was 37.4 years; for their wives the average was 33.8. The westward-bound ships carried couples who were mature, who had probably been married for nearly a decade, and who had established themselves firmly within their communities. The typical migrating family was complete—composed of husband, wife, and three or four children—but was not yet completed. They were families in process, with parents who were at most halfway through their reproductive cycle and who would continue to produce children in New England. They would be responsible for the rapid population growth that New England experienced in its first decades of settlement. Moreover, the numerous children who emigrated with their parents contributed their efforts to a primitive economy sorely lacking in labor.

The task of transforming wilderness into farmland, however, demanded more labor than parents and their children alone could supply, and more than half of the emigrating families responded to this challenge by bringing servants with them to the New World. Perhaps some had read William Wood's advice in *New England's Prospect* and learned that "men of good estates may do well there, always provided that they go well accommodated with servants." In any case, servants formed an integral part, just over 17 percent, of the colonizing population and in fact were at first somewhat more commonplace in New England than in England. Most were males (80 of 114) and labored alongside their masters, clearing land, planting corn, and building houses and barns. Their presence substantially increased the ratio of producers to consumers in the newly settled towns.

Household heads, however, knew that servants might easily become a drain on family resources in the critical early months of settlement. Their passages had to be paid and food and shelter provided at a time when those commodities were at a premium. Hence, when arranging for a suitable labor supply, masters heeded the advice of writers like William Wood, who emphasized that emigrants should not take too many servants and should choose men and women of good character. "It is not the multiplicity of many bad servants (which presently eats a man out of house and harbor, as lamentable experience hath made manifest)," he warned, "but the industry of the faithful and diligent laborer that enricheth the careful master; so that he that hath many dronish servants shall soon be poor and he that hath an industrious family shall as soon be

rich." Most families attempted to strike a balance between their need for labor and available resources by transporting only a few servants. Nearly half of the families brought just one and another quarter of them brought only two.

The diversity of the emigrants' English backgrounds—and their urban origins in particular—influenced the distribution of their occupations. Virtually the same number of men were engaged in farming and in artisanal trades not involved with cloth manufacture; slightly fewer earned their livings in the textile industry. Most of the cloth workers emigrated from cities well known for their textile manufacture; half of the fourteen weavers left Norwich, while five of the sixteen tailors had lived in Salisbury. The geographical distribution of the other artisans was more even, yet many also had congregated in urban areas. Ten of the eleven shoemakers came from Norwich, Great Yarmouth, Sandwich, and Marlborough, while the only two joiners had lived in Canterbury and Norwich. Nearly all of the men with highly specialized skills lived in large towns; the locksmith William Ludkin in Norwich, the cutler Edmund Hawes in London, the surgeon John Greene (who appears to have been a physician, not a barber-surgeon) in Salisbury. Artisans, both in the cloth trades and in other pursuits, formed a greater proportion of the emigrant population than tradesmen did in the English population as a whole. In 1696, Gregory King estimated that "freeholders" and "farmers" outnumbered "artizans and handicrafts" by a factor of more than seven to one; among the emigrants to New England, however, artisans predominated by a ratio of nearly two to one.

The occupational spectrum of future New Englanders placed them at the more prosperous end of English society. As farmers and artisans, prospective emigrants belonged to that part of the population that—according to Gregory King—"increased the wealth of the kingdom." Yet in striking contrast to Virginia, where, at least initially, the population included "about six times as large a proportion of gentlemen as England had," New England attracted very few members of the upper class. Sir Henry Vane and Sir Richard Saltonstall were unique among the leaders of the migration, and for the most part even they submitted to government by such gentle but untitled figures as John Winthrop and Thomas Dudley. On the whole, emigrants were neither very high nor very low in social and economic status. Husbandmen predominated among the farmers who came to Massachusetts; thirty of them emigrated compared to just five yeomen. By the seventeenth century, the legal distinctions between the status of yeoman and that of husbandman had largely eroded and evidence indicates that the labels generally denoted relative position on the economic and social ladder. Both groups primarily made their livings from the land, but yeomen were generally better off. New England, however, was peopled by less affluent—but not necessarily poor—husbandmen.

Emigrant clothworkers practiced trades that also placed them on the middle rungs of the economic ladder. Textile manufacturing in the early seventeenth century employed the skills of dozens of different craftsmen, from the shearmen, carders, and combers who prepared wool for spinning to the wealthy clothiers who sold the finished product. But the emigrant clothworkers did not represent the entire spectrum of skills; most were weavers and tailors who made a modest living at their trade. While it is true that, during his impeachment trial, the former bishop of Norwich was accused of harrying some of the city's most important and prosperous tradesmen—including the weavers Nicholas Busby, Francis Lawes, and Michael Metcalf—out of the land, these emigrants' economic status was probably exaggerated. Most urban weavers from Norfolk in this period had goods worth no more than £100, and one out of five did not even own his own loom. Among the non-clothworking artisans, shoemakers and carpenters predominated, and they too worked in trades that would bring comfort, if not riches. All in all, the New England-bound

ships transported a population characterized by a greater degree of social homogeneity than existed in the mother country. Despite Winthrop's reminder to his fellow passengers on the *Arbella* that "some must be rich some poor, some highe and eminent in power and dignitie; others meane and in subieccion," New Englanders would discover that the process of migration effectively reduced the distance between the top and the bottom of their social hierarchy.

In a letter to England written in 1632, Richard Saltonstall commented on the social origins of New England's inhabitants. "It is strange," he wrote, "the meaner sort of people should be so backward [in migrating], having assurance that they may live plentifully by their neighbors." At the same time, he expressed the hope that more "gentlemen of ability would transplant themselves," for they too might prosper both spiritually and materially in the new land. For young Richard, the twenty-one-year-old son of Sir Richard Saltonstall, New England promised much but as yet lacked the proper balance of social groups within its population that would ensure its success. The migration of the "meaner sort" would help lower the cost of labor, while richer emigrants would "supply the want we labor under of men fitted by their estates to bear common burdens." Such wealthy men would invest in the colony's future even as they enhanced their own spiritual welfare by becoming "worthy instruments of propagating the Gospel" to New England's natives.

Saltonstall wrote early in the migration decade, but the succeeding years did little to redress the social imbalance he perceived in Massachusetts. Two years later, William Wood could still write that "none of such great estate went over yet." Throughout the decade of the 1630s, New England continued to attract colonists who were overwhelmingly ordinary. Demographically they presented a mirror image of the society they had left behind, and socially and economically they fairly represented England's relatively prosperous middle class. The question is inescapable: why did so many average English men and women pass beyond the seas to Massachusetts' shores?

Whether or not they have assigned it primary importance, most historians of the period have noted that economic distress in England in the early seventeenth century must have been causally related to the Great Migration. These were years of agricultural and industrial depression, and farmers and weavers were conspicuous passengers on the transatlantic voyages. A closer examination of the connections between economic crisis and the movement to New England, however, indicates that the links were not as close as they have been assumed to be.

Agriculture—especially in the early modern period—was a notoriously risky business. Success depended heavily upon variables beyond human control. A dry summer or an unusually wet season rendered futile the labor of even the most diligent husbandman, and English farmers in the early seventeenth century had to endure more than their share of adversity. While the decade of the 1620s began propitiously, with excellent harvests in 1619 and 1620, the farmers' luck did not hold. The next three years brought one disastrous harvest after another; improvement in 1624 was followed by dearth in 1625. The beginning of the 1630s, especially in the eastern counties, was marked by further distress; in 1630, the mayor of Norwich complained that "scarcity and dearth of corn and other victuals have so increased the number and misery of the poor in this city" that civic taxes had to be boosted to unprecedented heights and the city's stock of grain dwindled dangerously. In 1637, a severe drought spawned further hardship.

Although this period of agricultural depression undoubtedly touched the lives of many English families, it did not necessarily compel them to emigrate. The worst sustained period of scarcity occurred in the early 1620s, a decade or so before the Great Migration began; if agrarian distress was a "push" factor, it produced a curiously delayed reaction.

Furthermore, annual fluctuations were endemic in early modern agriculture. Englishmen knew from experience that times would eventually improve, even if that day were unpleasantly distant; moreover, they had no reason to suppose that farmers in New England would somehow lead charmed lives, exempt from similar variations in the weather. In addition, dearth was not an unmitigated disaster for families engaged in husbandry: as supplies of grain and other products shrank, prices rose. In 1630, a year with one of the worst harvests in the first half of the seventeenth century, the price of grain was twice what it had been in the more plentiful years of 1619 and 1620. Thus for farmers involved in market agriculture, a bad year, with half the yield of a good one, could still bring the same income. As the Norwich mayor's lament amply demonstrates, the people really hurt in times of scarcity were city-dwellers dependent on the countryside for their food. That urban dwellers left for New England to assure themselves of a steady food supply, however, is highly unlikely. Emigrants would surely have anticipated the primitive state of the region's agriculture; reports of scarcity at Plymouth and the early Massachusetts Bay settlements had quickly filtered back to England. Moreover, emigrating urban artisans certainly understood that, in the New World, responsibility for feeding their families would lie in their own hands—hands more accustomed to the loom or the last than the plow.

The slump in England's textile industry has also been accounted an incentive for emigration. The industry was indeed mired in a severe depression in the early seventeenth century; it is true as well that a quarter of the adult male emigrants were employed in a trade related to cloth manufacture. The weavers Nicholas Busby, Francis Lawes, and Michael Metcalf of Norwich all completed their apprenticeships at a time when the textile trade "like the moon [was] on the want," and the future of Norfolk's preeminent industry was growing dimmer each year. Throughout the sixteenth century, the county's traditional worsted manufacture had steadily lost ground in its European markets to a developing continental industry. In southern England and the West Country, broadcloth producers suffered reverses as well. In 1631, the clothiers of Basingstoke, Hampshire—a town about fifteen miles southwest of the home of the emigrant weaver Thomas Smith of Romsey—informed the county's justices that the "poor do daily increase, for there are in the said town 60 householders, whose families do amount to 300 persons and upwards being weavers, spinners, and clothworkers, the most of them being heretofore rated towards the relief of the poor, do now many of them depend upon the alms of the parish" and begged for some kind of relief.

The decline in sales of the white, undressed fabric that had been the mainstay of English clothiers proved to be irreversible. At the same time, however, certain sectors in the textile industry recovered by switching over to the production of "new draperies." These fabrics, lighter in weight and brighter in color than the traditional English product, were made from a coarser—and therefore cheaper—type of wool. They were introduced in England largely by immigrant Dutch and Walloon artisans, who were frequently encouraged by local authorities to take up residence in England. East Anglia and Kent became centers of the revitalized industry; the cities of Norwich, Canterbury, and Sandwich counted scores of these north European "strangers" among their inhabitants. With the end of hostilities between England and Spain in 1604, trade expanded, and the new fabrics found ready markets in the Mediterranean and the Levant. By the mid-seventeenth century, the production of Norwich stuffs—new versions of worsted wool—had "probably raised the prosperity of the industry to an unprecedented level" and brought renewed prosperity to a number of beleaguered artisans as well.

We cannot know whether worsted weavers like Nicholas Busby, William Nickerson, or Francis Lawes adapted to prevailing trends in their trade, but they seem not to have been in serious economic straits at the time they decided to go to Massachusetts. The identification of Busby, Lawes, and Michael Metcalf among Norwich's most important tradesmen at Bishop Wren's impeachment trial, even if those claims were somewhat exaggerated, attested to their standing in the community. Busby's service as a *jurat* responsible for checking the quality of worsted wool produced in the city certainly indicated that he had achieved considerable status in his profession. Economic advancement attended professional prominence: before their departure for the New World, Busby and his wife owned a houselot in a prospering parish in the northern part of the city. In the countryside as well, some cloth workers managed to make a good living in hard times. Thomas Payne, a weaver from the village of Wrentham in Suffolk, emigrated to Salem in 1637 but died soon thereafter. His will, written in April 1638, not only listed property recently acquired in Salem, but also mentioned his share in the ship *Mary Anne*, on which he had sailed to Massachusetts. At the time of the departure from Suffolk, then, Payne could not only afford his family's transportation costs but also had funds to invest in the New England enterprise.

Even if evidence did suggest that emigrant weavers were compelled by economic adversity to leave their homeland, Massachusetts would not have been a wise choice of destination if they hoped to continue in their trade. Flight to the Netherlands, a place with a well-developed textile industry, would have been a more rational choice for artisans worried about the fate of their trade in England and anxious to persist in its practice. Massachusetts lacked both the wool supply and the intricate network of auxiliary tradesmen—such as combers, carders, calenderers, fullers, dyers, etc.—upon which England's weavers depended. Several of the emigrants packed up their looms along with their other belongings, but there is little evidence that they were able to earn their livings in Massachusetts solely by weaving.

Arguments linking the Great Migration to economic hardship in England all share an important weakness. Although historians have discovered that many *places* from which emigrants came suffered from agricultural or industrial depression, they have had little success in connecting those unfavorable economic circumstances to the fortunes of individual emigrants. On the contrary, it appears that the families that went to New England had largely avoided the serious setbacks that afflicted many of their countrymen during those years.

An alternative interpretation of the colonists' economic motivation has recently been proposed by Peter Clark, who discovered similarities between the New England settlers and "betterment migrants" traveling within the county of Kent during the decades preceding the English Civil War. Betterment migrants, like the New England colonists, were persons of solid means who, Clark argues, sought further to improve their economic positions. Most betterment migrants traveled only a short distance, usually to a nearby town; the New Englanders differed from them primarily through the immense length of their transatlantic journeys. On the whole, betterment migrants were not especially mobile; in their search for opportunity, they generally moved just once in their lives. New England emigrants like John Bent, while they lived in England, also tended to be geographically stable. In addition, betterment migrants shared with the Massachusetts settlers a tendency to rely on kin connections in their choice of destinations.

Clark's model of betterment migration fits the New England movement in certain particulars, but it makes little sense within the larger context of the transatlantic transplantation. If migration to New England was not a sensible economic decision for farmers or weavers hurt by hard times in England, it was even less sensible for people doing well. Most emigrants exchanged an economically viable present for a very uncertain future. As we have seen, nearly one in ten was over forty years old at the time of the migration and had little reason to expect to live long enough to enjoy whatever prosperity the New World might bring. The emigrant groups studied here all left England five or more years after the Great Migration had begun and a decade and a half after the landing at Plymouth; they surely heard from earlier arrivals that New England was no land of milk and honey. If any had a chance to read Edward Winslow's *Good Newes from New England*, published in 1624, he or she would have learned that the "vain expectation of present profit" was the "overthrow and bane" of plantations. People might prosper through "good labor and diligence," but in the absence of a cash crop, great wealth was not to be expected. The message of William Wood's *New England's Prospect*, published a decade later, was similar. Some colonists were lured westward by descriptions of plenty, Wood acknowledged, but they soon fell to criticizing the new society, "saying a man cannot live without labor." These disgruntled settlers "more discredit and disparage themselves in giving the world occasion to take notice of their dronish disposition that would live off the sweat of another man's brows. Surely they were much deceived, or else ill informed, that ventured thither in hope to live in plenty and idleness, both at a time." Letters as well as published reports informed would be settlers that New England was not a particularly fertile field for profit. In 1631, one young colonist wrote to his father in Suffolk, England, that "the cuntrey is not so as we ded expecte it." Far from bringing riches, New England could not even provide essentials; the disillusioned settler begged his father to send provisions, for "we do not know how longe we may subeseiste" without supplies from home.

If prospective emigrants were not hearing that New England offered ample opportunities for economic betterment, they *were* informed that life in Massachusetts could bring betterment of another sort. When Governor Thomas Dudley provided the countess of Lincoln with an account of his first nine months in New England, he announced that "if any come hether to plant for worldly ends that canne live well at home hee comits an errour of which he will soon repent him. But if for spirituall [ends] and that noe particular obstacle hinder his removeall, he may finde here what may well content him." Dudley worried that some might be drawn to Massachusetts by exaggerations of the land's bounty and wanted to make clear who would benefit most from emigration. "If any godly men out of religious ends will come over to helpe vs in the good worke wee are about," the governor wrote, "I think they cannot dispose of themselves nor of their estates more to God's glory and the furtherance of their owne reckoninge." New England promised its settlers *spiritual* advantages only; men merely in search of wealth could go elsewhere. Emmanuel Downing, in a letter to Sir John Coke, clarified the important difference between New England and other colonial ventures. "This plantation and that of Virginia went not forth upon the same reasons nor for the same end. Those of Virginia," he explained, "went forth for profit. . . . These went upon two other designs, some to satisfy their own curiosity in point of conscience, others . . . to transport the Gospel to those heathen that never heard thereof."

Both published tracts and private correspondence advertised New England's religious mission. In *The Planter's Plea*, Rev. John White proclaimed that "the most eminent and desirable end of planting Colonies, is the propagation of Religion." Prospective emigrants learned from the Rev. Francis Higginson's *New-England's Plantation*, published in 1630, that "that which is our greatest comfort . . . is, that we haue here the true Religion and holy Ordinances of Almightie God taught amongst us: Thankes be to God, we haue here plentie of Preaching, and diligent Catechizing, with strickt and carefull exercise, and good and commendable orders to bring our People into a Christian conuersation with whom we haue to doe withall." Indeed, New England's Puritan predilections were so well known that colonial leaders feared retribution from the Anglican establishment in England. *The Planter's Plea* specifically sought to dispel rumors that Massachusetts was overrun with Separatists, and, during the early 1630s, Edward Howes maintained a steady correspondence with John Winthrop, Jr. concerning similar allegations of New England radicalism. In 1631, Howes reported that "heare is a mutteringe of a too palpable seperation of your people from our church gouernment." The following year, he again informed Winthrop of claims that "you neuer vse the Lords prayer, that your ministers marrie none, that fellowes which keepe hogges all the weeke preach on the Saboth, that euery towne in your plantation is of a seuerall religion; that you count all men in England, yea all out of your church, and in the state of damnacion." Howes knew such rumors were false but feared that many other Englishmen believed them. The spread of such lies endangered not only the colony's reputation but perhaps its very survival as well.

Prospective emigrants, then, could hardly have been unaware of the peculiar religious character of New England society. Accounts of the region's commitment to Puritanism were too numerous to be overlooked; those who made the voyage had to know what they were getting into. Adherence to Puritan principles, therefore, became the common thread that stitched individual emigrants together into a larger movement. As John White declared, "Necessitie may presse some; Noveltie draw on others; hopes of gaine in time to come may prevaile with a third sort: but that the most and most sincere and godly part have the advancement of the *Gospel* for their maine scope I am co[n]fident."

White's confidence was by no means misplaced. The roster of passengers to New England contains the names of scores of otherwise ordinary English men and women whose lives were distinguished by their steadfast commitment to nonconformity, even in the face of official harassment. The *Hercules* left Sandwich in 1635 with William Witherell and Comfort Starr aboard; both men had been in trouble with local ecclesiastical authorities. Anthony Thacher, a nonconformist who had been living in Holland for two decades, returned to Southampton that same year to embark for New England on the *James*. Two years later, the *Rose* carried Michael Metcalf away from the clutches of Norwich diocesan officials. Metcalf had appeared before ecclesiastical courts in 1633 and again in 1636 for refusing to bow at the name of Jesus or to adhere to the "stinking tenets of Arminius" adopted by the established Church. Before his departure, Metcalf composed a letter "to all the true professors of Christs gospel within the city of Norwich" that chronicled his troubled encounters with church officials and explained his exclusively religious reasons for emigration. Thomas and Mary Oliver, Metcalf's fellow parishioners at St. Edmund's in Norwich, had also been cited before the archepiscopal court in 1633 and set sail for Massachusetts the same year as Metcalf. Other emigrants leaving in 1637 were John Pers and John Baker, two Norwich residents evidently also in trouble with church officials; Joan Ames, the widow of the revered Puritan divine William Ames, who had only recently returned from a lengthy stay in Rotterdam; and Margaret Neave and Adam Goodens, whose names appeared on Separatist lists in Great Yarmouth. Peter Noyes, who emigrated in 1638, came from a family long involved in nonconformist activities in England's southwest.

Although New England was not populated solely by unsuccessful defendants in ecclesiastical court proceedings, the nonconformist beliefs of other emigrants should not be underestimated merely because they avoided direct conflict with bishops and deacons. John Winthrop's religious motivation has never been in doubt even though he was never convicted of a Puritan offense. Winthrop's "General Observations for the Plantation of New England," like Metcalf's letter to the citizens of Norwich, emphasized the corrupt state of England's ecclesiastical affairs and concluded that emigration "wilbe a service to the church

of great consequens" redounding to the spiritual benefit of emigrants and Indians alike. Those few men who recorded their own reasons for removal likewise stressed the role of religion. Roger Clap, who sailed in 1630, recalled in his memoirs that "I never so much as heard of *New-England* until I heard of many godly Persons that were going there" and firmly believed that "God put it into my Heart to incline to Live abroad" in Massachusetts. John Dane, who seems to have spent most of his youth fighting off his evil inclinations, "bent myself to cum to nu ingland, thinking that I should be more fre here then thare from temptations." Arriving in Roxbury in the mid-1630s, Dane soon discovered that relocation would not end his struggle with sinfulness; the devil sought him out as readily in the New World as in the Old.

To declare that most emigrants were prompted by radical religious sentiment to sail to the New World, however, does not mean that these settlers resembled Hawthorne's memorable "stern and blackbrowed Puritans" in single-minded pursuit of salvation. The decision to cross the seas indelibly marked the lives of those who made it. Even the most pious wrestled with the implications of removal from family, friends, and familiar surroundings. Parents often objected to the departure of their children; a son following the dictates of his conscience might risk the estrangement of a disappointed father. Although religious motivation is the only factor with sufficient power to explain the departure of so many otherwise ordinary families, the New England Puritans should not be seen as utopians caught up in a movement whose purpose totally transcended the concerns of daily life.

Solitary ascetics can afford to reject the things of this world in order to contemplate the glories of the next; family men cannot. Even as prospective settlers discussed the spiritual benefits that might accompany a move to New England, they worried about what they would eat, where they would sleep, and how they would make a living. In the spring of 1631,

Emmanuel Downing wrote with considerable relief to John Winthrop that the governor's encouraging letters "haue much refreshed my hart and the myndes of manie others" for "yt was the Iudgement of most men here, that your Colonye would be dissolved partly by death through want of Food, howsing and rayment, and the rest to retorne or to flee for refuge to other plantacions." Other leaders and publicists of the migration continued both to recognize and to sympathize with the concerns of families struggling with the decision of whether or not to move, and they sought to reassure prospective settlers that a decision in favor of emigration would not doom their families to cold and starvation in the wilderness. At the same time, the way in which these writers composed their comforting messages to would-be emigrants underscored the settlers' understanding of the larger meaning of their mission.

Although several of the tracts and letters publicizing the migration contained favorable descriptions of the new land, they were never intended to be advertisements designed to capture the interest of profit seekers. When John White, Thomas Dudley, and others wrote about the blessings of New England's climate, topography, and flora and fauna, they simply hoped to assure godly English men and women that a move to the New World would not engender poverty as well as piety. In *The Planter's Plea*, John White succinctly answered objections that New England lacked "meanes if wealth." "An unanswerable argument," White replied, "to such as make the advancement of their estates, the scope of their undertaking." But, he added, New England's modest resources were in "no way a discouragement to such as aime at the propagation of the Gospell, which can never bee advanced but by the preservation of Piety in those that carry it to strangers." For, White concluded, "nothing sorts better with Piety than Compete[n]cy." He referred his readers to Proverbs 30:8— "Remove far from me vanity and lies: give me neither poverty nor riches; feed me with food convenient for me." Thomas Dudley in effect

explicated the meaning of "competency" in a New England context when he listed such goods as "may well content" a righteous colonist. In Massachusetts, Dudley noted, settlers could expect to have "materialls to build, fewell to burn, ground to plant, seas and rivers to fish in, a pure ayer to breath in, good water to drinke till wine or beare canne be made, which togeather with the cowes, hoggs, and goates brought hether allready may sufffice for food." Such were the amenities that emigrants not only could but should aspire to enjoy.

John White repeatedly assured his readers that "all Gods directions"—including the divine imperative to settle New England— "have a double scope, mans good and Gods honour." "That this commandement of God is directed unto mans good *temporall and spirituall*," he went on, "is as cleere as the light." The Lord, in other words, would take care of His own. To providentialists steeped in the conviction that God intervened directly in human lives, that divine pleasure or disapproval could be perceived in the progress of daily events, White's statement made eminent sense. If emigrant families embarked on their voyages with the purpose of abandoning England's corruption in order to worship God according to biblical precepts in their new homes, and if they adhered to this purpose, they might expect as a sign of divine favor to achieve a competency, if not riches. Thus John Winthrop could assert that "such thinges as we stand in neede of are vsually supplied by Gods blessing vpon the wisdome and industry of man." The governor's firm belief in the connection between divine favor and human well-being explains why in his "Particular Considerations" concerning his own removal out of England, he admitted that "my meanes heere [in England] are so shortned (now my 3 eldest sonnes are come to age) as I shall not be able to continue in this place and imployment where I now am." If he went to Massachusetts, Winthrop anticipated an improvement in his fortunes, noting that "I [can] live with 7. or 8: servants in that place and condition where for many years I have spent 3: or 400 *li.* per an[num]." Winthrop, despite these musings on his worldly estate, did not emigrate in order to better his economic condition. Rather, he removed in order to undertake the "publike service" that God had "bestowed" on him and hoped that God might reward him if his efforts were successful. In similar fashion, thousands of other emigrants could justify their decisions to move to New England. They believed that, by emigrating, they followed the will of God and that their obedience would not escape divine notice. In return for their submission to His will, the emigrants sincerely hoped that God might allow them—through their own labor—to enjoy a competency of this world's goods.

GLOSSARY

Nonconformity: Refusing to conform to the doctrines and practices of the Church of England; also dissent; the people known as dissenters.

Covenant: Literally, a contract with God struck by the first settlers of New England villages, who agreed to live in harmony with one another while following God's ordinances.

IMPLICATIONS

In this essay, Anderson explores the motivations for the Great Migration of the 1630s and concludes that Puritans migrated to New England largely for religious reasons, although most also expected to attain modest well-being in the process. How does this portrayal of the early Puritans compare with Breen's depiction of the motives of those who traveled to early Virginia? Although apparently so dissimilar, do you find any common themes or motives among the Virginia and New England colonists? Were the differences between the two groups of colonists due to their motives or to the different situations they encountered in the New World?

Slavery was never a static institution and always involved an intricate process of negotiation between slave owners and slaves. This reading begins with an account of one aspect of this process, an observer's depiction of the ways in which South Carolina slaves created their own recreations away from their masters' gaze. In scenes such as these ranging from the colonial era to the Civil War, African and African American slaves asserted their basic humanity as well as their determination to shape the contours of their own lives.

The Stranger on Slave Recreation (1772)

The *Stranger* had once an opportunity of seeing a Country-Dance, Rout, or Cabal of *Negroes*, within 5 miles distance of this town, on a Saturday night; and it may not be improper here to give a description of that assembly. It consisted of about 60 people, 5–6th from Town, every one of whom carried something, in the manner just described; as, bottled liquors of all sorts, Rum, Tongues, Hams, Beef, Geese, Turkies and Fowls, both drest and raw, with many luxuries of the table, as sweetmeats, pickles &c. (which some did not scruple to acknowledge they obtained by means of false keys, procured from a Negro in Town, who could make any Key, whenever the impression of the true one was brought to him in wax) besides other articles, which, without doubt, were stolen, and brought thither, in order to be used on the present occasion, or to be concealed and disposed of by such of the gang as might have the best opportunities for this purpose: Moreover, they were provided with Music, Cards, Dice, &c. The entertainment was opened, by the men copying (or *taking off*) the manners of their masters, and the women those of their mistresses, and relating some highly curious anecdotes, to the inexpressible diversion of that company. Then they *danced*, *betted*, *gamed*, *swore*, *quarrelled*, *fought*, and did *everything* that the *most modern* accomplished gentlemen are *not ashamed of*; except *breaking of lamps*, *abusing the watch*, and what is commonly called *beating up of quarters*, which would have endangered their own safety. They had also their private committees; whose deliberations were carried on in too low a voice, and with so much caution, as not to be overheard by the others; much less by the *Stranger*, who was concealed in a deserted adjacent hut, where the humanity of a well-disposed grey headed Negro man had placed him, pitying his *seeming* indigence and distress. The members of this *secret council*, had much the appearance of Doctors, in deep and solemn consultation upon life or *death*; which indeed might have been the scope of their meditations at that time. Not less than 12 fugitive slaves joined this respectable company before midnight, 8 of whom were mounted on good horses; these, after delivering a good quantity of Mutton, Lamb, and Veal, which they brought with them, directly associated with one or other of the private consultators; and went off about an hour before day, being supplied with liquor, &c. and perhaps having also received some instructions.—The *Stranger* is informed, that such assemblies *have been* very common, and that the company has sometimes amounted to 200 persons, even within one mile's distance of this place: Nay, he has been told, that intriguing meetings of this sort *are* frequent even in Town, either at the houses of *free Negroes* apartments *hired to slaves*, or the *kitchens of* such Gentlemen as frequently retire, with their families, into the country, for a few days; and that, at these assemblies, there are seldom fewer than 20 or 30 people, who commit all kinds of excesses. Whenever or wherever such nocturnal rendezvouses are made, may it not be concluded, that their deliberations are never intended for the advantage of the white people?

4

Patterns of Slave Resistance

Peter H. Wood

As English colonists gained a foothold on the mainland of North America and began the process of establishing permanent communities, the need for labor became increasingly acute. The small farmers of New England and the Middle Atlantic colonies needed labor to clear land, harvest crops, and maintain livestock. In the South, large plantations required flocks of fieldhands to tend labor-intensive crops such as tobacco and rice. And in the growing seaport cities, labor was needed to handle a growing volume of goods, to build houses for a burgeoning population, and to augment the production of local artisans. During the colonial period, much of this labor was supplied by indentured servants, who exchanged four to seven years of their labor for passage to America.

But by the end of the seventeenth century, colonists began to turn to a new source of labor: African slaves. Slavery was not new to the Americas: Spain and Portugal had been conducting a profitable slave trade since the sixteenth century. English mainland colonists could also draw upon the experiences of their West Indian counterparts, whose sugar plantations depended on a constant supply of slaves for their operation. By the early eighteenth century, southern plantation owners as well as northern artisans and merchants had turned to large-scale importations of slaves in order to maintain their tobacco and rice plantations, their shops, and their homes.

While the importance of early American slavery has long been recognized, historians have only recently turned their attention to the lives of the slaves themselves. One of the most important outcomes of this research is our growing understanding of the African-American response to enslavement. In this essay, Peter H. Wood explores one aspect of this response, the subtle and varied ways in which slaves resisted their bondage. Slave resistance was continuous, he suggests, and took place along a continuum that ranged from collective violence at one extreme to individual acts of defiance and dissimulation on the other. While America witnessed no successful large-scale rebellions, African-American slaves nonetheless engaged in a continuous struggle with their owners and overseers throughout the colonial and antebellum periods.

....

It is by no means paradoxical that increasingly overt white controls met with increasingly forceful black resistance. The stakes for Negroes were simply rising higher and the choices becoming more hopelessly difficult. As the individual and collective tensions felt by black slaves mounted, they continued to confront the immediate daily questions of whether to accept or deny, submit or resist, remain or flee. Given their diversity of background and experience, it is not surprising that slaves responded to these pressures in a wide variety of ways. To separate their reactions into docility on the one hand and rebellion on the other, as has occasionally been done, is to underestimate the complex nature of the contradictions each Negro felt in the face of new provocations and new penalties. It is more realistic to think in terms of a spectrum of response, ranging from complete submission to total resistance, along which any given individual could be located at a given time.

At one end of the spectrum of individual resistance were the extreme incidents of physical violence. There are examples of slaves who, out of desperation, fury, or premeditation, lashed out against a white despite the consequences. Jemmy, a slave of Capt. Elias Ball, was sentenced to death in 1724 "for striking and wounding one Andrew Songster." The master salvaged the slave's life and his own investment by promising to deport Jemmy forever within two months. For others who vented individual aggression there was no such reprieve. In August 1733 the *Gazette* reported tersely: "a Negro Man belonging to Thomas Fleming of Charlestown, took an Opportunity, and kill'd the Overseer with an Axe. He was hang'd for the same yesterday." An issue during 1742 noted: "Thursday last a Negro Fellow belonging to Mr. Cheesman, was brought to Town, tried, condemn'd and hang'd, for attempting to murder a white lad."

Such explosions of rage were almost always suicidal, and the mass of the Negro population cultivated strict internal constraints as a means of preservation against external white controls. (The fact that whites accepted so thoroughly the image of a carefree and heedless black personality is in part a testimony to the degree to which black slaves learned the necessity of holding other emotional responses in outward check.) This essential lesson of control, passed on from one generation to the next, was learned by early immigrants through a painful process of trial and error. Those newcomers whose resistance was most overt were perceived to be the least likely to survive, so there ensued a process of conscious or unconscious experimentation (called "seasoning" or "breaking" by the whites) in which Africans calculated the forms and degrees of resistance which were most possible.

Under constant testing, patterns of slave resistance evolved rapidly, and many of the most effective means were found to fall at the low (or invisible) end of the spectrum. For example, for those who spoke English, in whatever dialect, verbal insolence became a consistent means of resistance. Cleverly handled, it allowed slaves a way to assert themselves and downgrade their masters without committing a crime. All parties were aware of the subversive potential of words (along with styles of dress and bearing), as the thrust of the traditional term "uppity" implies, and it may be that both the black use of this approach and the white perception of it increased as tensions grew. In 1737 the Assembly debated whether the patrols should have the right "to kill any resisting or saucy Slave," and in 1741 the Clerk of the Market proposed that "if any

Slave should in Time of Market behave him or herself in any insolent abusive Manner, he or she should be sent to the Work-house, and there suffer corporal Punishment."

At the same time traits of slowness, carelessness, and literal-mindedness were artfully cultivated, helping to disguise countless acts of willful subterfuge as inadvertent mistakes. To the benefit of the slave and the frustration of the historian, such subversion was always difficult to assess, yet considerable thought has now been given to these subtle forms of opposition. Three other patterns of resistance—poisoning, arson, and conspiracy—were less subtle and more damaging, and each tactic aroused white fears which sometimes far exceeded the actual threat. All three are recognized as having been methods of protest familiar in other slave colonies as well, and each is sufficiently apparent in the South Carolina sources to justify separate consideration.

African awareness of plants and their powers [was widespread], and it was plain to white colonists from an early date that certain blacks were particularly knowledgeable in this regard. In 1733 the *Gazette* published the details of a medicine for yaws, dropsy, and other distempers "for the Discovery whereof, a Negroe Man in Virginia was freed by the Government, and had a Pension of Thirty Pounds Sterling settled on him during his Life." Some of the Negroes listed by the name "Doctor" in colonial inventories had no doubt earned their titles. One South Carolina slave received his freedom and £100 per year for life from the Assembly for revealing his antidote to poison; "Caesar's Cure" was printed in the *Gazette* and appeared occasionally in local almanacs for more than thirty years.

In West Africa, the obeah-men and others with the herbal knowledge to combat poisoning could inflict poison as well, and use for this negative capability was not diminished by enslavement. In Jamaica, poisoning was a commonplace means of black resistance in the eighteenth century, and incidents were familiar on the mainland as well. At least twenty slaves

were executed for poisoning in Virginia between 1772 and 1810. In South Carolina, the Rev. Richard Ludlam mentioned "secret poisonings" as early as the 1720s. The administering of poison by a slave was made a felony (alongside arson) in the colony's sweeping Negro Act of 1740. No doubt in times of general unrest many poisoning incidents involved only exaggerated fear and paranoia on the part of whites, but what made the circle so vicious was the fact that the art of poisoning was undeniably used by certain Africans as one of the most logical and lethal methods of resistance.

The year 1751 was striking in this regard. The Rev. William Cotes of Dorchester expressed discouragement about the slaves in St. George's Parish, a "horrid practice of poisoning their Masters, or those set over them, having lately prevailed among them. For this practice, 5 or 6 in our Parish have been condemned to die, altho [*sic*] 40 or 50 more were privy to it." In the same year the assemblymen attempted to concoct a legal antidote of their own. They passed an addition to the existing Negro Act, noting that "the detestable crime of poisoning hath of late been frequently committed by many slaves in this Province, and notwithstanding the execution of several criminals for that offence, yet it has not been sufficient to deter others from being guilty of the same." The legislation declared that any Negroes convicted of procuring, conveying, or administering poison, and any other privy to such acts, would suffer death. A £4 reward was offered to any Negro informing on others who had poison in their possession, and a strict clause was included against false informers.

Three additional clauses in the measure of 1751 suggest the seriousness with which white legislators viewed the poisoning threat. They attempted belatedly to root out longstanding Negro knowledge about, access to, and administration of medicinal drugs. It was enacted "That in case any slave shall teach or instruct another slave in the knowledge of any poisonous root, plant, herb, or other poison whatever, he or she, so offending, shall, upon conviction thereof, suffer death as a felon." The student was to receive a lesser punishment. "And to prevent, as much as may be, all slaves from attaining the knowledge of any mineral or vegetable poison," the act went on, "it shall not be lawful for any physician, apothecary or druggist, at any time hereafter, to employ any slave or slaves in the shops or places where they keep their medicines or drugs." Finally, the act provided that "no negroes or other slaves (commonly called doctors,) shall hereafter be suffered or permitted to administer any medicine, or pretended medicine, to any other slave; but at the instance or by the direction of some white person," and any Negro disobeying this clause was subject to "corporal punishment, not exceeding fifty stripes." No other law in the settlement's history imposed such a severe whipping upon a Negro.

A letter written years later by Alexander Garden, the famous Charlestown physician, sheds further light on the subject of poisonings. The outspoken Garden was forthright in criticizing his own profession, observing to his former teacher in Edinburgh that among South Carolina's whites, "some have been actually poisoned by their slaves and hundreds [have] died by the unskilfulness of the practitioners in mismanaging acute disorders." He claimed that when local doctors confronted cases

proving both too obstinate and complicated for them, they immediately call them poisonous cases and so they screen their own ignorance, for the Friends never blame the doctors neglect or ignorance when they think that the case is poison, as they readily think that lies out of the powers of medicine. And thus the word *Poison* . . . has been as good a screen to ignorance here as ever that of *Malignancy* was in Britain.

But apparently neither strict legislation nor scientific observation could be effective in suppressing such resistance, for in 1761 the *Gazette* reported that "The negroes have again begun the hellish practice of poisoning." Eight years later several more instances were

detected, and although the apparent "instigator of these horrid crimes," a mulatto former slave named Dick, made good his escape, two other Negroes were publicly burned at the stake. According to the account in a special issue of the *Gazette*, Dolly, belonging to Mr. James Sands and a slave man named Liverpool were both burned alive on the workhouse green, "the former for poisoning an infant of Mr. Sands's which died some time since, and attempting to put her master out of the world the same way; and the latter (a Negro Doctor) for furnishing the means." The woman was reported to have "made a free confession, acknowledged the justice of her punishment, and died a penitent," but the man denied his guilt until the end.

The act of arson, highly destructive and difficult to detect, provided another peculiarly suitable means of subversion. Early in the century, with considerable forced labor being used to produce naval stores, the governor urged the Assembly "to make it ffelony without benefitt of Clergy, willfully to Sett ffire to any uncovered Tarrkiln or Pitch and Tarr in Barrells, as in like cases, ffiring Houses and Barnes." In later decades arsonists also fired stores of rice, and the Negro Act of 1740 was explicit in declaring death for "any slave, free negro, mulattoe, Indian or mustizoe, [who] shall wilfully and maliciously burn or destroy any stack of rice, corn, or other grain."

Indeed, as rice production intensified, the number of barns which burned between the months of October and January (when the majority of slaves were being pressed to clean and barrel the annual crop) increased suspiciously. A telling to the *Gazette* in October 1732 reads:

Sir,
I Have taken Notice for Several Years past, that there has not one winter elapsed, without one or more Barns being burnt, and two winters since, there was no less than five. Whether it is owing to Accident, Carelessness, or Severity, I will not pretend to determine; but am afraid, chiefly to

the two latter. I desire therefore, as a Friend to the Planters, that you'll insert the following Account from Pon Pon, which, I hope, will forewarn the Planters of their Danger, and make them for the future, more careful and human.

About 3 Weeks since, Mr. James Gray work'd his Negroes late in his Barn at Night and the next Morning before Day, hurried them out again, and when they came to it, found it burnt down to the Ground, and all that was in it.

Several years later, just after Christmas, "the Barn of Mr. John Fairchild at Wassamsaw, with all his Crop was burnt down to the Ground," and in November 1742, "a Barn, belonging to Mr. Hume, at Goose-Creek, was burnt in the Night, and near 70 Barrels of Rice consumed." Undoubtedly Negroes were occasionally made the scapegoats for fires which occurred by chance. The Rev. Le Jau relates vividly how a woman being burned alive on the charge of setting fire to her master's house in 1709 "protested her innocence . . . to the last." But as with accusations of poisoning, numerous Negroes charged with burning their masters' homes had actually resorted to such sabotage. Moreover, arson could occur in conjunction with other offenses, serving to cover evidence or divert attention. Runaways sometimes resorted to setting fires, and arson was occasionally linked to crimes of violence as well. The following news item from South Carolina appeared in Ireland's *Belfast News Letter*, May 10, 1763:

Charlestown, March 16. A most shocking murder was committed a few weeks ago, near Orangeburg by a Negro fellow belonging to one John Meyer, who happened to come to Charlestown; the cruel wretch murdered Mrs. Meyer, her daughter, about 16 years of age, and her sucking infant; he then dressed himself in his Master's best cloaths and set fire to the house, which was burnt to the ground; three other children of Mr. Meyers made their escape and alarmed the neighbors, some of whom did not live above half a mile distant. The murderer was taken up next day and by a Jury of Magistrates and Freeholders condemned to be burnt alive at

a stake which was accordingly executed. The unfortunate husband and father, we are told, is almost, if not entirely distracted by his misfortunes; it is said both he and his wife used the barbarous destroyer of their family and substance with remarkable tenderness and lenity.

It was fires within the town limits which aroused the greatest concern among white colonists, for not only were numerous lives and buildings endangered, but the prospect of subsequent disorder and vandalism by the city's enslaved residents was obvious. A fire engine was purchased by public subscription in the 1730s. But it proved of little use in 1740, when the Carolina colony, having experienced several epidemics and a series of slave conspiracies in rapid succession, added a severe fire to its "Continued Series of misfortunes." On the afternoon of Tuesday, November 18, flames broke out near the center of Charlestown, and whipped by a northwest wind, burned out of control for six hours, consuming some three hundred houses, destroying crucial new fortifications, and causing property losses estimated at £250,000 sterling.

Even though 2 P.M. seemed an unlikely hour for slave arson, there were strong suspicions about the origin of the holocaust. Not long before, in the strained atmosphere following the Stono Uprising, a slave had been accused of setting fire to the home of Mr. Snow and had been burned to death for the crime. Officials suspected the Spanish of instigating arson by Negroes as one form of resistance, for an act passed the previous April charged the Spaniards in St. Augustine with, "encouraging thither the desertion of our Slaves and . . . exciting them to rise here in Rebellion and to commit Massacres and Assassinations and the burning of Houses in divers parts of this Province of which practices there have of late been many proof[s]."

Word of the November fire reaching northern ports was accompanied by rumors of arson and insurrection. In January a Boston paper had to print a revised account of the fire, saying the story "that the Negroes rose upon the Whites at the same Time, and that therefore it was supposed to be done by them, turns out to be a Mistake, it happening by some Accident." The story finally reaching London was that the flames were "said to have begun among some Shavings in a Saddler's Shop."

Whatever the actual cause of the fire, the white minority feared Negro violence in the aftermath of the blaze. "It is inexpressible to relate to you the dismal Scheme [scene?] . . . ," Robert Pringle wrote to his brother in London, "the best part of this Town being laid in Ashes." He blamed his "Incorrect Confus'd Scrawl" on the fact that he had hardly slept in the three days since the fire. He cited as an explanation "the great Risque we Run from an Insurrection of our Negroes which we were very apprehensive of but all as yet Quiet by the strict Guards & watch we are oblig'd to keep Constantly night & Day." In a letter the next week he mentioned that much property had been stolen and concealed apparently by freemen and slaves alike. But large-scale disorder was prevented, and Negro labor was soon at work "pulling down the Ruin of Charles Town" and clearing away rubble for the arduous task of rebuilding.

Regardless of its true origins, the November fire could only have confirmed to slaves the effectiveness of arson. Moreover, there was word the following spring of Negro incendiaries at work in the northern colonies, supposedly with Spanish connections. On July 30, 1741, the *Gazette* contained a front-page story about a rash of barn-burnings in Hackensack, New Jersey. The next page was given over to details of an arson plot in New York City, for which nine Negroes had already been burned at the stake. The conspiracy, stated the report from New York,

> was calculated, not only to ruin and destroy this city, but the whole Province, and it appears that to effect this their Design was first to burn the Fort, and if Opportunity favoured to seize and carry away the Arms in store there, then to burn the whole Town, and kill and murder all the Male

> Inhabitants thereof (the Females they intended to reserve for their own use) and this to be effected by seizing their Master's Arms and a general Rising, it appears also as we are informed, that these Designs were not only carried on in this City, but had also spread into the country. . . . And so far had they gone that the particular Places to be burnt were laid out, their Captains and Other Officers appointed, and their places of general Rendezvous fixed, and the Number of Negroes concern'd is almost incredible, and their barbarous Designs still more so. . . .

It may not be coincidence that within five days after these lurid reports appeared in Charlestown several slaves attempted to kindle another fire in the city. After dark a mulatto slave woman named Kate and a man named Boatswain entered Mrs. Snowden's house in Unity Alley, climbed to the roof, and placed a small bundle of straw on the shingles so that it rested under the gables of the adjoining house, belonging to Moses Mitchell and fronting on Union Street. They lit the tinder with a brand's end, and the fire they started might have been capable "of burning down the remaining Part of the Town," had not Mrs. Mitchell, walking in her yard, spotted the blaze so promptly that it could be dowsed with several pails of drinking water.

An old Negro woman who heard one of the arsonists stumble descending the stairs testified against Kate, and within forty-eight hours she had been tried, convicted, and sentenced to die. At the eleventh hour, upon promise of pardon, Kate named Boatswain as a co-conspirator, and he in turn was sentenced to burn alive. According to the *Gazette's* account, "On his Tryal after much Preverication and accusing many Negroes, who upon a strict Examination were found to be innocent, he confessed that none but he and *Kate* were concerned." Since Boatswain "looked upon every white Man he should meet as his declared Enemy," his prosecutors concluded that the incident stemmed from "his own sottish wicked Heart," and that there was probably no larger plot. The same people may have been somewhat less sanguine several months later, when two slaves were found guilty of attempting to set fire to the city's powder magazine.

Arson, real and suspected, remained a recurring feature in eighteenth-century South Carolina. In 1754, for example, a slave named Sacharisa was sentenced to burn at the stake for setting fire to her owner's house in Charlestown. Two years later a suspicious fire started on a town wharf in the middle of the night. In 1797 two slaves were deported and several others were hanged for conspiring to burn down the city. In some ways the protracted Charleston Fire Scare of 1825 and 1826, which came four years after the Denmark Vesey Plot, was reminiscent of the concern for arson which followed in the wake of the Stono Uprising of 1739.

While poisoning and arson rarely involved more than one or two compatriots, organized forms of resistance, which involved greater numbers (and therefore higher risks), were not unknown in the royal colony. In fact uprisings appear to have been attempted or planned repeatedly by slaves. For obvious reasons, published sources are irregular on these matters—the *South Carolina Gazette* refrained from mentioning the Stono incident, which occurred within twenty miles of Charlestown—but a number of conspiracies were recorded. In these instances it is sometimes difficult to categorize the objectives of the insurgents, since often a will to overpower the Europeans and a desire to escape from the colony were intertwined in the same plot. The province's first major conspiracy, uncovered in 1720, provides a case in point. "I am now to acquaint you," wrote a Carolina correspondent to the colony's London agent in June, "that very lately we have had a very wicked and barbarous plott of the designe of the negroes rising with a designe to destroy all the white people in the country and then to take the town in full body." He continued that through God's will "it was discovered and many of them taken prisoners and some burnt some hang'd and some banish'd." At least some participants in the scheme "thought to

gett to Augustine" if they could convince a member of the Creek tribe to guide them, "but the Savanna garrison tooke the negroes up half starved and the Creeke Indians would not join them or be their pylott." A party of whites and Indians had been dispatched to "Savanna Towne," where fourteen captives were being held, and it was planned that these rebels would "be executed as soon as they came down."

Despite harsh reprisals, however, secret gatherings of slaves, sometimes exceeding one hundred people, were again reported within several years. In February 1733 the Assembly urged the slave patrols to special watchfulness and ordered a dozen slaves brought in for questioning, but there is no sign that any offense was uncovered. Late in 1736 a white citizen appears to have sought a reward for uncovering a Negro plot. Early in the following year the provost marshal took up three Negroes "suspected to be concerned in some Conspiracy against the Peace of this Government," and although the Assembly cleared and released the most prominent suspect, it did not deny the existence of a plot.

By September 1738 the government had completed "An Act for the further Security and better Defence of this Province" and given instructions that the two paragraphs relating to slaves were to be reprinted in the *Gazette*. The paper complied several days later by publishing the section which ordered that within a month every slaveowner in the colony was to turn in to the militia captain of his local precinct "a true and faithful List, in Writing, of all the Slaves of such Persons, or which are under their Care or Management, from the Age of 16 Years to the Age of Sixty Years." Each list was required to specify "the Names, Ages and Country of all such Slaves respectively, according to the best of the Knowledge and Belief of the Persons returning the same."

The statute imposed a heavy fine of £100 upon any master who neglected or refused to comply, so that the required local lists (if collected and sent to the governor annually as authorized) must have constituted a thorough census of the colony's adult slaves. The unlikely reappearance of even a portion of these lists would be a remarkable boon to historians, in light of the unique request for the original country of all slaves. This detail appears to bear witness to the fact that masters were generally interested and informed as to the origins of the Negroes they owned. It may also reflect the belief, commonly accepted in the Carolinas as elsewhere, that new slaves from Africa posed the greatest threat to the security of the white settlers. John Brickell explained at this time, "The Negroes that most commonly rebel, are those brought from Guinea, and who have been inured to War and Hardship all their lives; few born here, or in the other Provinces have been guilty of these vile Practices." When country-born slaves did contemplate rebellion, Brickell claimed, it was because they were urged to it by newcomers "whose Designs they have sometimes discovered to the Christians" in order to be "rewarded with their Freedom for their good Services."

The thought that newcomers from Africa were the slaves most likely to rebel does not appear to have been idle speculation, for the late 1730s, a time of conspicuous unrest, was also a time of massive importation. In fact, at no earlier or later date did recently arrived Africans (whom we might arbitrarily define as all those slave immigrants who had been in the colony less than a decade) comprise such a large proportion of South Carolina's Negro population. By 1740 the black inhabitants of the colony numbered roughly 39,000. During the preceding decade more than 20,000 slaves had been imported from Africa. Since there is little evidence that mortality was disproportionately high among newcomers, this means that by the end of the 1730s fully half of the colony's Negroes had lived in the New World less than ten years. This proportion had been growing steadily. In 1720 fewer than 5 per cent of black adults had been there less than a decade (and many of these had spent time in

the West Indies); by 1730 roughly 40 per cent were such recent arrivals. Heavy importation and low natural increase sent the figure over 50 per cent by 1740, but it dropped sharply during the nearly total embargo of the next decade, and after that point the established black population was large enough so that the percentage of newcomers never rose so high again.

Each of the lowland parishes must have reflected this shift in the same way. In St. Paul's, for example, where the Stono Uprising originated, there were only 1,634 slaves in 1720, the large majority of whom had been born in the province or brought there long before. By contrast, in 1742 the parish's new Anglican minister listed 3,829 "heathens and infidels" in his cure, well over 3,000 of whom must have been slaves. Of these, perhaps as many as 1,500 had been purchased in Charlestown since 1730. A predominant number of the Africans reaching the colony between 1735 and 1739 have been shown to have come from Angola, so it is likely that at the time of the Stono Uprising there were close to 1,000 residents of St. Paul's Parish who had lived in the Congo-Angola region of Africa less than ten years before. While this figure is only an estimate, it lends support to the assertion in one contemporary source that most of the conspirators in the 1739 incident were Angolans. The suggestion seems not only plausible, but even probable.

European settlers contemplating the prospects of rebellion, however, seem to have been more concerned with the contacts the slaves might establish in the future than with experience that came from their past. White colonists were already beginning to subscribe to the belief that most Negro unrest was necessarily traceable to outside agitators. Like most shibboleths of the slave culture, this idea contained a kernel of truth, and it is one of the difficult tasks in considering the records of the 1730s and 1740s to separate the unreasonable fears of white Carolinians from their very justifiable concerns.

Of the various sources of outside agitation none seemed so continually threatening after 1720 as St. Augustine, for the abduction and provocation of slaves by the Spanish were issues of constant concern. While London and Madrid were reaching a peace settlement in 1713, Charlestown and St. Augustine had renewed their agreement concerning the mutual return of runaways, but Spanish depredations continued long after the conclusion of the Yamasee War.

In June 1728 Acting Gov. Arthur Middleton sent a formal complaint to authorities in London that not only were the Spanish "receivieing and harbouring all our Runaway Negroes," but also, "They have found out a New way of sending our own slaves against us, to Rob and Plunder us;—They are continually fitting out Partys of Indians from St. Augustine to Murder our White People, Rob our Plantations and carry off our slaves," Middleton stated, "soe that We are not only at a vast expence in Guarding our Southern Frontiers, but the Inhabitants are continually Allarmed, and have noe leizure to looke after theire Crops." The irate leader added that "the Indians they send against us are sent out in small Partys . . . and sometimes joined wth Negroes, and all the Mischeife they doe, is on a sudden and by surprize."

These petty incursions soon subsided. Nevertheless, rumors reached South Carolina in 1737 from the West Indies of a full-scale Spanish invasion intended, in the words of Lt. Gov. Thomas Broughton, to "unsettle the colony of Georgia, and to excite an Insurrection of the Negroes of this Province." He reported to the Lords of Trade that the militia had been alerted, "and as our Negroes are very numerous An Act of the General Assembly is passed, to establish Patrols throughout the Country to keep the Negroes in order."

The threatened assault never materialized, but in the meantime a new element was added to the situation. Late in 1733 the Spanish king issued a royal *cédula* granting liberty to Negro fugitives reaching St. Augustine from the

English colonies. The edict was not immediately put into effect, and incoming slaves continued to be sold, but in March 1738 a group of these former runaways appealed successfully to the new governor for their freedom and obtained it. Seignior Don Manuel de Montiano established them on land two and a half miles north of St. Augustine at a site called the Pueblo de Gracia Real de Santa Terese de Mose, which soon became known as "Moosa." With the approval of the Council of the Indies, the governor undertook to provision this settlement of several dozen families until its first harvest and arranged for a Catholic priest to offer them instruction. He may also have urged other slaves to join them, for the captain of an English coasting schooner returning to Beaufort the following month testified that "he heard a Proclamation made at St. Augustine, that all Negroes, who did, or should hereafter, run away from the English, should be made free." As a result, according to the captain, "several Negroes who ran away thither, and were sold there, were thereupon made free, and the Purchasers lost their Money."

In November 1738 nineteen slaves belonging to Capt. Caleb Davis "and 50 other Slaves belonging to other Persons inhabiting about Port Royal ran away to the Castle of St. Augustine." Those who made it joined the Negro settlement at Moosa. It was apparently at this time that the Catholic king's edict of 1733 was published (in the words of a South Carolina report)

by Beat of Drum round the Town of St. Augustine (where many Negroes belonging to English Vessels that carried thither Supplies of Provisions &c. had the Opportunity of hearing it) promising Liberty and Protection to all Slaves that should desert thither from any of the English Colonies but more especially from this. And lest that should not prove sufficient of itself, secret Measures were taken to make it known to our Slaves in general. In consequence of which Numbers of Slaves did from Time to Time by Land and Water desert to St. Augustine, and the better to facilitate their Escape carried off their

Master's Horses, Boats &c. some of them first committing Murder; and were accordingly received and declared free.

When Capt. Davis went to St. Augustine to recover his slaves he was pointedly rebuffed, a sign for Carolina's legislature that this difficulty might grow worse in the coming year.

Any premonitions which colonial officials might have felt were to prove justifiable, for the year 1739 was a tumultuous and decisive one in the evolution of South Carolina. Only the merest twist of circumstances prevented it from being remembered as a fateful turning point in the social history of the early South.

GLOSSARY

Stono Uprising: British America's only "successful" slave revolt, taking place along the Stono River, South Carolina, in 1739; the slaves were all eventually killed or captured.

Denmark Vesey Plot: A failed slaved uprising in South Carolina in 1822.

St. Augustine, Florida: Spanish fortress and city that offered freedom to any slave fleeing their English master or mistress.

Yamasee War: War between British and native peoples of coastal South Carolina and Georgia. Allied with the Spanish, the Yamassees had raided English plantations and welcomed escaping slaves; they were defeated by British forces in 1715.

Cédula: A formal Spanish imperial decree or law.

IMPLICATIONS

In this essay, Wood asks us to view slave resistance as a conscious and measured response to enslavement, a response that was part of a larger relationship of negotiated power. If slave owners had the power to enslave Africans and African Americans and to coerce labor from them, what factors do you think made it possible for slaves to resist their masters' demands and to create their own lives under the heavy yoke of slavery?

Past Traces

In the following essay, Mary Beth Norton relies on surviving diaries and letters to capture the substance of women's lives in the eighteenth century. Her essay is introduced by selections from the poetry and prose of Anne Bradstreet, English America's most famous woman writer. At a time when few women put their thoughts on paper, Bradstreet's writings reveal the central place of religious and domestic concerns in the lives of colonial women.

Anne Bradstreet, *Thoughts on Her Husband and Children (1650)*

A Letter to Her Husband, Absent upon Public Employment

My head, my heart, mine eyes, my life, nay, more,
My joy, my magazine of earthly store,
If two be one, as surely thou and I,
How stayest thou there, whilst I at Ipswich lie?
So many steps, head from the heart to sever,
If but a neck, soon should we be together:
I, like the earth this season, mourn in black,

My sun is gone so far in's zodiac,
Whom whilst I 'joyed, nor storms, nor frost I felt,
His warmth such frigid colds did cause to melt.
My chillèd limbs now numbèd lie forlorn;
Return, return, sweet Sol, from Capricorn;
In this dead time, alas, what can I more
Than view those fruits which through thy heat I bore?

Which sweet contentment yield me for a space,
True living pictures of their father's face.
O strange effect! now thou art southward gone,
I weary grow, the tedious day so long;
But when thou northward to me shalt return,
I wish my sun may never set, but burn
Within the Cancer of my glowing breast,
The welcome house of him, my dearest guest.
Where ever, ever stay, and go not thence,
Till nature's sad decree shall call thee hence;
Flesh of thy flesh, bone of thy bone,
I here, thou there, yet both but one.

In Reference to Her Children, 23 June 1659

I had eight birds hatch in one nest,
Four cocks there were, and hens the rest.
I nursed them up with pain and care,
Nor cost, nor labor did I spare,
Till at the last they felt their wing,

Mounted the trees, and learned to sing.
Chief of the brood then took his flight
To regions far, and left me quite:
My mournful chirps I after send,
Till he return, or f do end:
Leave not thy nest, thy dam and sire,
Fly back and sing amidst this choir.
My second bird did take her flight,
And with her mate flew out of sight;
Southward they both their course did
    bend,
And seasons twain they there did spend:
Till after blown by southern gales,
They norward steered with filléd sails.
A prettier bird was nowhere seen,
Along the beach among the treen.
I have a third of color white,
On whom I placed no small delight;
Coupled with mate loving and true,
Hath also bid her dam adieu:
And where Aurora first appears,
She now hath perched to spend her
    years;
One to the academy flew
To chat among that learned crew:
Ambition moves still in his breast
That he might chant above the rest,
Striving for more than to do well,
That nightingales he might excel.
My fifth, whose down is yet scarce
    gone,
Is 'mongst the shrubs and bushes flown,
And as his wings increase in strength,
On higher boughs he'll perch at length.
My other three still with me nest,
Until they're grown; then as the rest,
Or here or there they'll take their flight,
As is ordained, so shall they light.
If birds could weep, then would my
    tears
Let others know what are my fears
Lest this my brood some harm should
    catch,
And be surprized for want of watch,
Whilst pecking corn and void of care,

They fall un'wares in fowler's snare:
Or whilst on trees they sit and sing,
Some untoward boy at them do fling.
Or whilst allured with bell and glass,
The net be spread, and caught alas.
Or lest by lime-twigs they be foiled,
Or by some greedy hawks be spoiled.
O would my young, ye saw my breast,
And knew what thoughts there sadly
    rest;
Great was my pain when I you bred,
Great was my care when I you fed,
Long did I keep you soft and warm,
And with my wings kept off all harm;
My cares are more, and fears than ever,
My throbs such now as 'fore were
    never:
Alas, my birds, you wisdom want,
Of perils you are ignorant;
Oft times in grass, on trees, in flight,
Sore accidents on you may light.
O to your safety have an eye,
So happy may you live and die:
Meanwhile my days in tunes I'll spend,
Till my weak lays with me shall end;
In shady woods I'll sit and sing,
And things that passed to mind I'll bring.
Once young and pleasant, as are you,
But former toys (no joys), adieu.
My age I will not once lament,
But sing, my time so near is spent.
And from the top bough take my flight
Into a country beyond sight,
Where old ones instantly grow young,
And there with seraphims set song:
No seasons cold, nor storms they see;
But spring lasts to eternity.
When each of you shall in your nest
Among your young ones take your rest,
In chirping language, oft them tell,
You had a dam that loved you well,
That did what could be done for young,
And nursed you up till you were strong,
And 'fore she once would let you fly,
She showed you joy and misery;

Taught what was good, and what was
    ill,
What would save life, and what would
    kill.
Thus gone, amongst you I may live,
And dead, yet speak, and counsel give:
Farewell, my birds; farewell, adieu,
I happy am, if well with you.

**In Memory of My Dear Grandchild
Anne Bradstreet, who Deceased June
20, 1669, Being Three Years and Seven
Months Old**

With troubled heart and trembling hand
    I write,
The heavens have changed to sorrow
    my delight.
How oft with disappointment have I
    met,
When I on fading things my hopes have
    set.
Experience might 'fore this have made
    me wise,
To value things according to their price.
Was ever stable joy yet found below?
Or perfect bliss without mixture of
    woe?
I knew she was but as a withering
    flower,
That's here today, perhaps gone in an
    hour;
Like as a bubble, or the brittle glass,
Or like a shadow turning as it was.
More fool then I to look on that was
    lent
As if mine own, when thus
    impermanent.
Farewell dear child, thou ne'er shall
    come to me,
But yet a while, and I shall go to thee;
Meantime my throbbing heart's cheered
    up with this:
Thou with thy Savior art in endless
    bliss.

5

The Small Circle of Domestic Concerns

Mary Beth Norton

Throughout the colonial period, American women lived their lives in a world dominated by men. Subject to the will of their fathers from birth until marriage, once married they became wards of their husbands with no legal rights of their own. Yet despite their subordinate status, women formed a vital and indispensable part of the family economy, as Mary Beth Norton reveals in this essay. Whether their fathers and husbands farmed, traded, or crafted manufactured goods, women spent their days near the household, cooking, cleaning, rearing children, making cloth and clothing, tending vegetables, and maintaining the pigs, chickens, and cows that supplemented the family diet.

But while domestic concerns dominated the lives of all early American women, the character of their lives varied considerably, depending upon their race and class as well as the region in which they lived. Thus Norton shows that while everyday life on the frontier was dominated by an unremitting round of daily and weekly chores with little chance for recreation and sociability, the markets and density of urban life permitted middling-class women a much greater measure of leisure and conviviality. Equally, while northern wives might have overseen the work of apprentices or household servants as part of their family duties, the wives of southern planters were veritable managers of households that extended far beyond the Great House to encompass the welfare of all those who lived on the estate. Domesticity, this essay demonstrates, took many different forms in seventeenth- and eighteenth-century America.

The household, the basic unit of eighteenth-century American society, had a universally understood hierarchical structure. At the top was the man, the lord of the fireside; next came the mistress, his wife and helpmate; following her, the children, who were expected to assist the parent of their own sex; and, finally, any servants or slaves, with the former taking precedence over the latter. Each family was represented in the outside world by its male head, who cast its single vote in elections and fulfilled its obligations to the community through service in the militia or public office. Within the home, the man controlled the finances, oversaw the upbringing of the children, and exercised a nominal supervision over household affairs. Married men understandably referred to all their dependents collectively as "my family," thereby expressing the proprietary attitude they so obviously felt.

The mistress of the household, as befitted her inferior position, consistently employed the less proprietary phrase "our family." Yet she, and not her husband, directed the household's day-to-day activities. Her role was domestic and private, in contrast to his public, supervisory functions. As the Marylander Samuel Purviance told his teenaged daughter Betsy in 1787, "the great Province of a Woman" was "Economy and Frugality in the management of [a] Family." Even if the household were wealthy, he stressed, "the meanest Affairs, are all and ought to be Objects of a womans cares." Purviance and his contemporaries would have concurred with the position taken in an article in Caleb Bingham's *The American Preceptor*, a textbook widely used in the early republic: "[N]eedle work, the care of domestic affairs, and a serious and retired life, is the proper function of women, and for this they were designed by Providence."

Of course, such statements applied only to whites, for no eighteenth-century white American would have contended that enslaved black women should work solely at domestic tasks. But the labor of female slaves too was affected by their sexual identity, for they were often assigned jobs that differed from those of male slaves, even though such tasks were not exclusively domestic. Appropriately, then, an analysis of black and white women's experiences in eighteenth-century America must begin with an examination of their household responsibilities.

I

"I have a great and longing desire to be very notable," wrote a Virginia bride in 1801, declaring her allegiance to the ideal of early American white womanhood. In this context, the adjective "notable" connoted a woman's ability to manage her household affairs skillfully and smoothly. Thus the prominent clergyman Ezra Stiles asked that his daughter be educated in such a way as to "lay a founda[tion] of a notable Woman," and a Rhode Islander wrote of a young relative that she "Sets out to be a Notable house Wife." When the Virginian Fanny Tucker Coalter exuberantly told her husband, John, "I'm the picture of bustling notability," he could have had no doubt about her meaning.

The characteristics of the notable wife were best described by Governor William Livingston of New Jersey in his essay entitled "Our Grand-Mothers," which was printed posthumously in two American magazines in the early 1790s. Decrying his female contemporaries' apparent abandonment of traditional values, Livingston presented a romanticized picture of the colonial women of the past. Such wives "placed their renown" in promoting the welfare of their families, Livingston asserted. "They were strangers to dissipation; . . . their own habitation was their delight." They not only practiced economy, thereby saving their husbands' earnings, but they also "augmented their treasure, by their industry." Most important, "they maintained good order and harmony in their empire" and "enjoyed happiness in their chimney corners," passing on these same qualities to the daughters they carefully raised to be like themselves. Their homes, in short, were "the source of their pleasure; and the foundation of their glory."

Although other accounts of the attributes of notable housewives were couched in less sentimental form, their message was the same. Ministers preaching funeral sermons for women often took as their text Proverbs 31, with its description of the virtuous woman who "looketh well to the Ways of her Household and eateth not the Bread of Idleness." So too drafters of obituaries and memorial statements emphasized the sterling housewifely talents of the women they eulogized. Such a model of female perfection did not allow a woman an independent existence: ideally, she would maintain no identity separate from that of her male-defined family and her household responsibilities. A man like James Kent, the distinguished New York lawyer, could smugly describe himself as "the independent... *Lord of my own fireside*," while women, as William Livingston had declared, were expected to tend the hearth and find "happiness in their chimney corners."

These contrasting images of autonomy and subordination were translated into reality in mid-eighteenth-century American household organization. Although the mistress directed the daily life of the household, her position within the home was secondary to that of her husband. She was expected to follow his orders, and he assumed control over the family finances. In 1750, the anonymous author of *Reflections on Courtship and Marriage*, a pamphlet long erroneously attributed to Benjamin Franklin, told men that it "would be but just and prudent to inform and consult a wife" before making "very important" decisions about monetary matters, but evidence drawn from a variety of sources indicates that few colonial husbands followed this advice. Instead, they appear to have kept the reins of financial management firmly in their own hands, rarely if ever informing their wives about even the basic details of monetary transactions.

The most comprehensive evidence of this phenomenon comes from an analysis of the claims for lost property submitted by 468 white loyalist refugee women after the Revolution.

The evidence of women's ignorance of financial affairs takes a variety of forms in the claims records. Rural wives often were unable to place a precise value on tools, lands, or harvested grain, even if they knew a farm's total acreage or the size of the harvest. Urban women frequently did not know their husbands' exact income or the cost of the houses in which they lived. The typical wealthy female was not aware of her husband's net worth because she did not know the amount of his outstanding debts or what was owed to him, and poor women occasionally failed to list any value at all for their meager possessions. Women of all descriptions, moreover, shared an ignorance of legal language and an unfamiliarity with the details of transactions concerning property with which they were not personally acquainted. The sole exceptions to their rule were a few widows who had already served several years as executrices of the family estates; some wives of innkeepers, grocers, or other shopkeepers who had assisted their husbands in business; and a small number of single women who had supported themselves through their own efforts.

Loyalist husbands, then, did not normally discuss economic decisions with their wives. The women lacked exactly that information which their husbands alone could have supplied, for they were able to describe only those parts of the property with which they came into regular contact. That the practice in these loyalist homes was not atypical is shown when one looks at patriot families as well.

American wives and widows alike repeatedly noted their lack of information about their husbands' business dealings. "I don't know anything of his affairs," a Virginian resident in London wrote in 1757; "whether his income will admit of our living in the manner we do, I am a stranger to." Elizabeth Sandwith Drinker, a Philadelphia Quaker, commented years later, "I am not acquainted with the extent of my husband's great variety of engagements," quoting an apposite poem that began,

"I stay much at home, and my business I mind." To such married women, their spouses' financial affairs were not of immediate import. But widows, by contrast, had to cope with the consequences of their ignorance. On his deathbed, a New England cleric surprised his wife with the news that she would have "many debts to pay that [she] knew nothing about," and her subsequent experience was replicated many times over—by the Marylander whose husband left no records to guide her administration of his estate, by the Virginian who had to tell her husband's employer that he had evidently neglected to maintain proper rent rolls, by the New Yorker who admitted to her son-in-law that she had known "very little" of her spouse's affairs before his death.

It might seem extraordinary that colonial men failed to recognize the potential benefits—to their children and their estates, if not to themselves—of keeping their wives informed about family finances. Yet the responsibility was not theirs alone. Married women rarely appear to have sought economic information from their husbands, whether in anticipation of eventual widowhood or simply out of a desire to understand the family's financial circumstances. On the contrary, women's statements reveal a complete acceptance of the division of their world into two separate, sexually defined spheres.

"Nature & Custom seems to have destined us for the more endearing & private & the Man for the more active & busy Walks of Life," remarked Elizabeth Willing Powel, a leader of Philadelphia society, in 1784. A similar sense of the character of the difference between male and female realms shone through the 1768 observation of a fellow Philadelphian of Mrs. Powel, the teenager Peggy Emlen, who described the men she saw hurrying about the city streets: they "all seem people of a great deal of business and importance, as for me I am not much of either." Men shared this same notion of the dichotomy between male public activity and female private passivity. In 1745, an essayist warned women that they were best "confined within the narrow Limits of Domestick Offices," for "when they stray beyond them, they move excentrically, and consequently without grace." A New Englander twelve years later worried that women might want "to obtain the other's Sphere of Action, & become Men," but he reassured himself that "they will again return to the wonted Paths of true Politeness, & shine most in the proper Sphere of domestick Life."

If women were accordingly out of place in the world beyond the household, so men were not entirely at home in the female realm of domestic affairs. The family property may have been "his" in wives' terminology, but at the same time the household furnishings were "hers" in the minds of their spouses. Wartime letters from American husbands confirm the separation of male and female spheres, more because of what they do not contain than as a result of what they do. When couples were separated by the Revolutionary War, men for the most part neglected to instruct their wives about the ordinary details of domestic life. Since they initially sent explicit directions about financial affairs, their failure to concern themselves with household management would seem to indicate that they had been accustomed to leave that realm entirely to their wives. Only if they had not previously issued orders on domestic subjects would they have failed to include such directives in their correspondence.

The evidence, then, suggests that female whites shared a universal domestic experience that differentiated their world from that of men. Their lives were to a large extent defined by their familial responsibilities, but the precise character of those obligations varied according to the nature of the household in which they resided. Although demographic historians have concentrated upon determining the size of colonial households, from the standpoint of an American woman, size—within a normal range—mattered less than composition. It meant a great deal to a housewife whether she had daughters who could assist her, whether her household contained a helpful servant or demanding elderly relative, or whether she had to contend with a resident mother-in-law for control of her own domestic affairs.

But ultimately of greater significance were differences in the wealth and location of colonial households. The chief factors that defined a white woman's domestic role arose from the family's economic status, which determined whether there would be servants or slaves, and from the household's location in a rural or urban setting. With a similarity of household roles as a basis, one can divide eighteenth-century women into four groups: poor and middling white farm women, north and south; white urban women of all social ranks; wealthy southerners who lived on plantations; and the female blacks held in bondage by those same wealthy southerners.

II

A majority of white women in eighteenth-century America resided in poor or middling farm households, and so it is reasonable to begin a discussion of female domestic work patterns with an assessment of their experience. Their heavy responsibilities are revealed most vividly in accounts left by two city families who moved to rural areas, for farm women were so accustomed to their burdensome obligations that they rarely remarked upon them.

Christopher Marshall and his wife abandoned Philadelphia when the British occupied the city in the fall of 1777, shifting their large family to Lancaster, Pennsylvania. There Marshall marveled at his wife's accomplishments, at how "from early in the morning till late at night, she is constantly employed in the affairs of the family." She not only did the cooking, baking, washing, and ironing, all of which had been handled by servants in their Philadelphia home, but she also milked cows, made cider and cheese, and dried apples. The members of the Palmer family of Germantown, Massachusetts, had a comparable experience when they moved in 1790 to Framingham, about twenty miles west of Boston. Mary Palmer, who was then fifteen and the oldest

daughter in the home, later recalled that her father had had difficulty in adjusting to the change in his womenfolk's roles. "It took years to wean him from the idea that we must be ladies," she wrote, "although he knew that we must give up all such pretensions." Mary herself thrived in the new environment. "Kind neighbors" taught her mother how to make butter and cheese, and the girls "assisted in the laborious part, keeping churn, pans, cheese-hoops and strainers nice and sweet." After she married Royall Tyler and set up housekeeping in Brattleboro, Vermont, Mary continued to practice the skills of rural housewifery she had gained as a teenager. Between managing her dairy in the summer and supervising spinning and weaving in the winter, not to mention raising five children, she observed, "I never realized what it was to have time hang heavy."

Mary Palmer's recollections disclose the seasonal nature of much of farm women's labor. Such annual rhythms and the underlying, invariable weekly routine are revealed in the work records kept by farm wives like Sarah Snell Bryant, of Cummington, Massachusetts, and Mary Cooper, of Oyster Bay, Long Island. Each week Mrs. Bryant devoted one day to washing, another to ironing, and a third at least partly to baking. On the other days she sewed, spun, and wove. In the spring she planted her garden; in the early summer she hived her bees; in the fall she made cider and dried apples; and in mid-December came hog-killing time. Mary Cooper recorded the same seasonal round of work, adding to it spring housecleaning, a mid-summer cherry harvest, and a long stretch of soap-making, boiling "souse," rendering fat, and making candles that followed the hog butchering in December. In late 1769, after two weeks of such work, she described herself as "full of freting discontent dirty and miserabel both yesterday and today."

Unlike the laconic Mrs. Bryant, who simply noted the work she had completed each day, Mrs. Cooper frequently commented on the fatiguing nature of her life. "It has been a tiresome day it is now Bed time and I have not had won minutts rest," she wrote in November 1768. One Sunday some months later she remarked, "I hoped for some rest but I am forst to get dinner and slave hard all day long." On those rare occasions when everyone else in the household was away, Mary Cooper understandably breathed a sigh of relief. "I have the Blessing to be quite alone without any Body greate or Small," she noted in late October 1768, and five years later another such day brought thanks for "some quiate moments which I have not had in weeks."

Perhaps one of the reasons why Mrs. Cooper seemed so overworked was her obsession with cleanliness. Since travelers in rural America commented frequently upon the dirt they encountered in farmhouses and isolated taverns, it seems clear either that cleanliness was not highly valued or that farm wives, fully occupied with other tasks, simply had no time to worry about sweeping floors, airing bedding, or putting things away. Mary Cooper's experience suggests that the latter explanation was more likely. Often describing herself as "dirty and distrest," she faithfully recorded her constant battle against filth. "We are cleaning the house and I am tired almost to death," she wrote in December 1768; the following spring, after seven straight days of cleaning, she complained, "O it has been a week of greate toile and no Comfort or piece to Body or mind." Another time she noted with satisfaction, "I have got some clean cloths on thro mercy some little done to clean the house," and again, "Up very late But I have got my Cloths Ironed." Obviously, if a farm woman was not willing to invest almost superhuman effort in the enterprise, keeping her household clean was an impossible task.

Mary Cooper's diary is unique in that it conveys explicitly what is only implicit in other farm wives' journals: a sense of drudgery and boredom. Sarah Snell Bryant would record that she had engaged in the same tasks for days on end, but she never noted her reaction to the repetition. This sameness was the quality that differentiated farm women's work from that performed by their husbands. No less physically demanding or difficult, men's tasks varied considerably from day to day and month to month. At most—during planting or harvest time, for example—men would spend two or three weeks at one job. But then they would move on to another. For a farmer, in other words, the basic cycle was yearly; for his wife, it was daily and weekly, with additional obligations superimposed seasonally. Moreover, men were able to break their work routine by making frequent trips to town or the local mill on business, or by going hunting or fishing, whereas their wives, especially if they had small children, were tied to the home.

Rural youngsters of both sexes were expected to assist their parents. "Their children are all brought up in industry, and have their time fully employed in performing the necessary duties of the house and farm," remarked a foreign visitor to a western Pennsylvania homestead in 1796. His inclusion of both sons and daughters was entirely accurate, for although historians have tended to emphasize the value of boys' labor to their fathers, extensive evidence suggests that girls were just as important as aides to their mothers. The fifteen-year-old Elizabeth Fuller, of Princeton, Massachusetts, for example, recorded occasionally baking pies, making candles, scouring floors, mincing meat for sausages, making cheese, and doing laundry, in addition to her primary assignments, spinning and weaving. Nabby and Betsy Foote, sisters who lived in Colchester, Connecticut, likewise noted helping their mother with housework, again in conjunction with their major chores of sewing, spinning, and weaving. When the parents of Ruth Henshaw, of Leicester, Massachusetts, called her home in mid-July 1789 after she had been visiting a relative for four days, saying, she recounted, that they "could not Subsist with out me any longer," they were only expressing what is evident in all these diaries: the labor of daughters, like that of wives, was crucial to the success of a farm household.

Brissot de Warville, an astute foreign traveler, recognized both the value of women's work and the clearly defined gender role distinctions visible in rural life in his observations upon a fellow Frenchman's Pennsylvania farm in 1788. It is a "great disadvantage," Brissot remarked, that "he does not have any poultry or pigeons and makes no cheese; nor does he have any spinning done or collect goose feathers." The reason: he was a bachelor, and "these domestic farm industries . . . can be carried on well only by women." Brissot's friend had two women indentured servants, so he did not lack female labor as such; what was missing was a wife or daughters to supervise the servants. Significantly, neither he nor Brissot seems to have considered the possibility that he could himself keep poultry or learn enough about cheesemaking to direct the servants. That was clearly "woman's work," and if there was no woman present, such work was not done, no matter how pressing the need or how great the resulting loss of potential income.

Yet in some frontier areas the gender role divisions so apparent in more settled regions did blur, although they did not break down entirely. Farmers' wives and daughters occasionally worked in the fields, especially at harvest time. Travelers from the East were unaccustomed to the sight of white female fieldworkers and wrote about it at length. In 1778, for example, a doctor from Dorchester, Massachusetts, told his wife in some amazement that he had seen Pennsylvania German women "at work abroad on the Farm mowing, Hoeing, Loading Dung into a Cart." A New Hampshire farmer, by contrast, matter-of-factly recorded in his diary his use of female relatives and neighbors for field work. In that same colony in the early 1760s the pendulum swung the other way, and men helped with women's work. In the winters, recalled one woman many years later, "the boys did as much Knitting as the Girls, and the men and boys also did the milking to spare the women."

Backcountry women had to cope with a far more rough-and-ready existence than did their counterparts to the east and south. The log cabins in which many of them lived were crudely built and largely open to the elements. Even the few amenities that brightened the lives of their poor contemporaries in areas of denser settlement were denied them; the Reverend Charles Woodmason, an Anglican missionary in western South Carolina, commented in 1768 that "in many Places they have nought but a Gourd to drink out off Not a Plate Knive or Spoon, a Glass, Cup, or any thing—It is well if they can get some Body Linen, and some have not even that." Later in the century, one woman on the Ohio frontier, lacking a churn, was reduced to making butter by stirring cream with her hand in an ordinary pail. Under such circumstances, simple subsistence would require most of a woman's energies.

How, then, did frontier women react to these primitive conditions? At least one group of pioneer men termed their wives "the greatest of Heroines," suggesting that they bore such hardships without complaint, but other evidence indicates that some women, especially those raised in genteel households, did not adapt readily to their new lives. Many, like a Pennsylvanian, must have vetoed their husbands' plans to move west because of an unwillingness to exchange a civilized life for a residence in "what she deems a Wilderness." Others must have resembled the Shenandoah Valley woman, a mother of eight, who descended into invalidism shortly after her husband moved her and their children to what their son described as a "valuable Farm but with a small indifferent house . . . & almost intirely in woods." Perhaps, like a female traveler in the west, the Virginian "felt oppress'd with so much wood towering above . . . in every direction and such a continuance of it." This was not a unique reaction: a Scottish immigrant, faced with his wife's similar response to the first sight of their new home, comforted her by promising, "[W]e would get all these trees cut down . . . [so] that we would see from house to house."

At least in this case the husband knew of his wife's discontent and reacted to it. In other instances, the lack of communication between spouses resulting from their divergent roles appears to have been heightened on the frontier, as wives deliberately concealed their unhappiness from their husbands, revealing their true feelings only to female relatives. Mary Hooper Spence, who described herself as having been beset by "misfortunes" ever since the day of her marriage, lived with her husband on the "dreary & cold" island of St. Johns (now Prince Edward Island) in the 1770s. In letters to her mother in Boston she repeatedly told of her loneliness and depression, of how she found a primitive, isolated existence "hard to bear." By contrast, her husband characterized their life as "happy" and reported to a relative that they were "comfortably" settled. Likewise, Mrs. Joseph Gilman, said by her husband to be pleased with living in the new settlement of Marietta, Ohio, in 1789, later recounted that on many occasions while milking their cows she would think of her New England home, "sob and cry as loud as a child, and then wipe her tears and appear before her husband as cheerful as if she had nothing to give her pain."

To point out the apparent dissatisfaction of many frontier women with their lives in the wilderness is not to say that they and others did not cope successfully with the trials they encountered. To cite just one example: Mrs. Hutchens, a Mississippi woman whose husband was kidnapped and whose slaves were stolen, pulled her family together in the face of adversity almost by sheer force of will alone. Her son subsequently recalled that she had told her children they could survive if they were willing to work. Accordingly, she and her three sons cultivated the fields while her daughters did the housework, spun cotton, and wove the fabric for their clothing. By the time her husband returned seven years later, she had prospered sufficiently to be able to replace all the slaves taken by the robbers.

The fact that Mrs. Hutchens put her daughters to work spinning and weaving is significant, for no household task was more time-consuming or more symbolic of the female role than spinning. It was, furthermore, a task quintessentially performed by young, single women; hence, the use of the word "spinster" to mean an unmarried female and the phrase "the distaff side" to refer to women in general. Farm wives, and especially their daughters, spent a large proportion of their time, particularly in the winter months, bending over a flax wheel or loom, or walking beside a great wheel, spinning wool. No examination of the domestic sphere can be complete without detailed attention to this aspect of household work.

Before 1765 and the subsequent rise in home manufacturing caused by colonial boycotts of British goods, spinning and weaving as ordinary chores were largely confined to rural areas of the northern and middle colonies and the backcountry South. Planters and even middling farmers who lived along the southeastern coast and city residents throughout America could usually purchase English cloth more cheaply than they could manufacture it at home, and so they bought fabric rather than asking their wives, daughters, or female slaves to spend the requisite amount of time to produce it. But rural women outside the plantation South spent much of their lives spinning. They began as girls, helping their mothers; they continued after their marriages, until their own daughters were old enough to remove most of the burden from their shoulders; and they often returned to it in old age or widowhood, as a means of supporting themselves or making use of their time. Not all farm women learned weaving, a skill open to men as well, but spinning was a nearly universal occupation among them.

Rural girls understood at an early age that spinning was "a very proper accomplishment for a farmers daughter," as the New Jersey Quaker Susanna Dillwyn put it in 1790. Susanna's niece Hannah Cox began trying to spin on an "old wheel which was in the house" when she was only seven, so her mother bought her a little new wheel, upon which Hannah soon learned to spin "very prettily." Similarly, the tutor on Robert Carter's Virginia plantation observed that his small pupils would tie "a String to a Chair & then run buzzing back to imitate the Girls spinning." Such playful fascination with the process of cloth production later turned for many girls into monotonous daily labor at wheels or looms during the months between December and May. The normal output of an experienced spinner who carded the wool herself was four skeins a day, or six if an assistant carded for her. Teenaged girls like Elizabeth Fuller, who were less practiced than their mothers, produced on the average two or three skeins a day. After a long stint of spinning tow (short coarse linen fibers) in January and February 1792, Elizabeth exploded in her diary, "I should think I might have spun up all the Swingling Tow in America by this time." Later that same year, she switched to weaving, at last completing her annual allotment on June 1. In three months she had woven 176 yards of cloth, she recorded, happily inscribing in her journal, "Welcome sweet Liberty, once more to me. How have I longed to meet again with thee."

But clothwork, which could be a lonely and confining occupation, as Elizabeth Fuller learned, could also be an occasion for socializing. Rural girls sometimes attended "spinning frolics" or quilting bees, many of which lasted for several days and ended with dancing. Even more frequently farm women "changed work," trading skills with others experienced in different tasks. Mary Palmer recalled that after her family moved to Framingham her mother would change work with other women in the area, "knitting and sewing for them while they would weave cotton and flax into cloth" for her, since as a city dweller she had never learned that skill. In a similar way Ruth Henshaw and her mother repaid Lydia Hawkins, who warped their loom for them, by helping her quilt or making her a pair of stays. Ruth regularly exchanged chores with girls

of her own age as well; in December 1789, for example, she noted, "Sally here Spining Changeing works with Me," while ten days later she was at Sally's house, carding for her.

From such trading of labor farm women could easily move on to work for pay. By 1775 Betsy and Nabby Foote had taken that step. Nabby, like Lydia Hawkins of Leicester, specialized in warping webs and making loom harnesses; her sister Betsy worked in all phases of cloth production, carding wool, hatcheling flax, and spinning, as well as doing sewing and mending for neighbors. In the rural North and South alike white women spun, wove, and sold butter, cheese, and soap to their neighbors, participating on a small scale in the market economy long before the establishment of textile factories in New England and the consequent introduction of widespread wage labor for young northern women.

Given the significance of spinning in women's lives, it is not surprising that American men and women made that occupation the major symbol of femininity. William Livingston had declared that "country girls . . . ought to be at their spinning-wheels," and when Benjamin Franklin sought a wedding present for his sister Jane, he decided on a spinning wheel instead of a tea table, concluding that "the character of a good housewife was far preferable to that of being only a pretty gentlewoman."

Compelling evidence of the link between spinning and the female role in the eighteenth-century American mind comes from the observations of two visitors to Indian villages. Confronted by societies in which women did not spin but instead cultivated crops while their husbands hunted and fished, both the whites perceived Indian sex roles as improper and sought to correct them by introducing the feminine task of spinning. Benjamin Hawkins, United States agent for the Creek tribe, admired the industrious Creek women and encouraged them to learn to spin and weave. This step, he believed, would lead to a realignment of sex roles along proper lines, because the women would be freed from dependence upon their hunter husbands for clothing, and they would also no longer have time to work on the crops. The men in turn would therefore be "obliged to handle the ax & the plough, and assist the women in the laborious task of the fields." A similar scheme was promoted by the Quaker woman Anne Emlen Mifflin, who traveled in the Seneca country as a missionary in 1803. Men should work in agriculture, she told her Indian audience, so that women would be able to learn spinning and dairy management, which were "branches suited to our sex," as opposed to "drudging alone in the labors of the field."

As Mifflin's comment shows, women, too, found spinning a necessary component of femininity, a fact best illustrated by reference to Elizabeth Graeme Fergusson's poem "The Contemplative Spinner." In 1792, Mrs. Fergusson, one of the leaders of intellectual life in republican Philadelphia, composed a poem in which she compared her spinning wheel to a wheel of fortune, leading her to a series of observations on life, death, and religion. But the wheel did more: it also reminded her of other women, linking her inextricably to "a train of Female Hands/Chearful uniting in Industrious Bands." And so, she wrote:

> In such Reflections I oft passed the Night,
> When by my Papas solitary Light
> My Wheel I turned, and thought how others toild
> To earn a morsel for a famishd Child.

To Elizabeth Graeme Fergusson, spinning symbolized her tie to the female sisterhood, just as to Benjamin Hawkins and other eighteenth-century men that occupation above all somehow appertained to femininity. It is consequently ironic that the one factor that differentiated the lives of urban women most sharply from those of their rural counterparts was the fact that they did not have to engage in cloth production. Women who had access to stores saw no point in spending hour after tedious hour at the wheel or loom. Not, at least, until doing so came to have political sig-

nificance in the late 1760s, as Americans increasingly tried to end their dependence on British manufactured goods.

III

Although urban women did not have to spin and weave, the absence of that time-consuming occupation did not turn their lives into leisured ones. Too often historians have been misled by the lack of lengthy work entries in urban women's diaries, concluding therefrom that city "ladies" contributed little or nothing to the family welfare. Admittedly, white urban women of even moderate means worked shorter hours and at less physically demanding tasks than did their rural counterparts, but this did not mean that their households ran themselves. Women still had the responsibility for food preparation, which often included cultivating a garden and raising poultry. The wives of artisans and shopkeepers also occasionally assisted their husbands in business. Furthermore, their homes were held to higher standards of cleanliness—by themselves and by their female friends—than were the homes of farm women like Mary Cooper. Even if they could afford to hire servants, they frequently complained that supervising their assistants took almost as much time and effort as doing the work themselves.

Middling and well-to-do urban women who described their daily routines in letters or diaries disclosed a uniform pattern of mornings devoted to household work, a late dinner at about two o'clock, and an afternoon of visiting friends, riding, or perhaps reading quietly at home. Although some women arose as late as eight o'clock (which one female Bostonian termed "a lazy hour"), others, including Abigail Adams, recorded that they habitually rose at five. A Pennsylvanian summed up the common practice in a poem:

> Like a notable house wife *i rise with the sun*
> Then bustle about till the business is done,
> Consult with the Cook, and *attend to the spiting*
>   [*sic*]

Then quietly seat myself down to my *knitting*—
Should a neighbour step in we *talk of the weather*
Retail all the *news* and the s*candle* together, . . .
The *tea things removed* our party disperses,
And of course puts an end to my *very fine verses*.

The chores that city women performed in the mornings resembled those of farm wives. Their diaries noted hours devoted to washing and ironing, cooking and baking, sewing and knitting. Like that of their rural counterparts, their labor was affected by the seasons, although less consistently so: in the autumn they preserved fruit and stored vegetables, and early in the winter they salted beef and pork and made sausage. Yet there were differences. Most notably, urban dwellers made daily trips to large markets, where they bought most of their meat, vegetables, cheese, and butter. Rebecca Stoddert, a Marylander who had moved to Philadelphia, marveled that her neighbors quickly killed chickens they had purchased without "think[ing] of fattening them up," a practice she deplored as wasteful and shortsighted.

Although urban women were not burdened with the major stock-tending and clothmaking chores that devolved upon farm wives, some of the time thus saved was devoted to cleaning their homes. Many of the travelers in rural areas most horrified by dirty farmhouses and taverns were themselves urban women, who had adopted standards of cleanliness for their homes, clothes, and beds that were utterly alien to farm wives. Certainly no rural woman except Mary Cooper would have written a journal entry resembling that of a Philadelphian in 1781: "As we were whitewashing & cleaning house this day I seemed anxious, I fear over anxious to have every thing clean, & in order." Another Philadelphia resident, the Quaker Sally Logan Fisher, seems to have painted, whitewashed, or wallpapered her house each spring, even though she remarked in April 1785 that it was "troublesome work indeed, the pleasure afterwards of being nice, hardly pays for the trouble." Other wives in smaller towns similarly recorded their commitment to keeping their homes neat and clean.

Cleaning, though, was perhaps the only occupation at which city dwellers of moderate means expended more energy than women living in agricultural regions. One of the benefits of residing in a city or a good-sized town was the availability of a pool of female workers who could be hired at relatively low rates. If a woman decided that she could not afford even a minimal payment, she could take a girl into her home as a sort of apprentice in housewifery, compensating her solely with room, board, and clothes. . . .

The mistresses of such [middling and wealthy] homes felt caught in a dilemma. On the one hand, servants were impertinent, lazy, untrustworthy, careless, and slovenly (to list just a few of their complaints), but on the other hand it was impossible to run a household without some help. The women who offered themselves for hire were usually either single girls or elderly widows; only in rare cases can one identify white females who spent their entire lives as servants. Instead, girls worked as maids, cooks, or laundresses for a few years before marriage, often for a series of employers. From the diaries and letters of mistresses of urban households one gains the impression of a floating population of "young Giddy Headed Girls" who did largely as they pleased, knowing that with the endemic American shortage of labor they could always find another position. Few seem to have stayed in the same household for more than a few months, or a year at most, before moving on to another post. For example, in just the five years from 1794 to 1799, Deborah Norris Logan, Sally Logan Fisher's sister-in-law, employed at least ten different female servants in fairly rapid succession. Among them were two widows, some immigrants from Ireland and Germany, a pair of sisters, and several girls.

Deborah Logan had no daughters to assist her in the home, but even if she had, she, like other urban mothers, would not have expected them to contribute as much work to the household as did their rural counterparts. City daughters from well-to-do homes were the only eighteenth-century American women who can accurately be described as leisured. The causes of their relative lack of employment have already been indicated: first, the work of an urban household was less demanding than that of a farm, so that mothers and perhaps one or two servants could do all that was necessary; and, second, city girls did not have to produce the cloth supply for the family. Accordingly, they could live at a relaxed pace, sleeping late, learning music and dancing, spending hours with male and female friends, and reading the latest novels.

This is not to say, as some historians have argued, that these young women were entirely idle and decorative, for they did extensive amounts of sewing for their families. Girls began to sew at an early age—Hannah, Sally Logan Fisher's daughter, was only eight when she made her first shirt—and they thereafter devoted many hours each day to their needles. Most of their tasks were mundane: mending and altering clothes; making shirts for their fathers and brothers; and stitching apparently innumerable aprons, caps, and shifts for themselves, their mothers, and their aunts. Such "common sewing" won a girl "no great Credit," the New Englander Pamela Dwight Sedgwick admitted in 1789, but at the same time, she pointed out to her daughter, "[I]t will be thought unpardonable negligence . . . not to doe it very nicely." Sometimes girls would work samplers or make lace, but even the wealthiest among them occasionally felt apologetic for spending a considerable amount of their time on decorative stitchery. Betsy DeLancey, a daughter of the prominent New York family, defended such evidently frivolous employment to her sister Anne in 1768 by referring to Proverbs: "I must be industrious and make myself fine with my own Hands, and who can blame me for spending some of my time in that manner when it is part of the virtuous Womans Character in the Bible."

In poor households, daughters' sewing skills could contribute significantly to family income, as may be demonstrated by reference to the Banckers of New York City. Christopher Bancker was an alcoholic, and his wife Polly tried to support the family by working as a seamstress. Yet she alone could not "du the whole," as she wrote in 1791, and so her two oldest daughters, Peggy and Betsy, also sought employment as seamstresses. Even with the girls' help the family experienced severe economic difficulties, yet the combined income of wife and daughters, coupled with charity proffered by reluctant relatives, kept the Banckers out of the poor house. Peggy and Betsy—and, by implication, other urban girls as well—thus proved to be economic assets to their families in a way that sons were not. The best that could be done with the two oldest Bancker boys was to send them out of the household to learn trades, so that they would no longer be a drag on family resources. Not until they had served apprenticeships of several years, with the expenses being borne by relatives, could they make positive contributions to the support of their parents and siblings. But their sisters had been "apprenticed" to their mother, and so they had developed salable skills at an early age. The other side of the coin was the fact that the Bancker boys' advanced training eventually paid off in higher wages, whereas the girls had little hope of ever improving their position, except through a good marriage.

Because sewing was readily portable, and because they lived so close to each other, well-to-do urban girls frequently gathered to work in sizable groups. While one of their number read, usually from a popular novel, the others would pass the afternoon or evening in sewing. Like farm girls, they created an opportunity for socializing out of the necessity for work, but as a result of their proximity they were able to meet more often, more regularly, and in greater numbers. One sewing group called itself the "Progressive Society" and confined its reading to edifying tracts. "Our design is to ameliorate, by every probable method, the morals, opinions, manners and language of each other," one of the members wrote, explaining why they excluded cardplaying, gossip, and men from their meetings.

In addition to sewing, city girls, like their rural counterparts, were taught what one of them termed "the mysteries of housewifery" by conscientious mothers. Sally Logan Fisher began to instruct her daughter Hannah in "Family affairs" when she was just ten, so that she would become "a good Housewife & an active Mistress of a Family." Daughters did some cooking, baking, and cleaning, helped to care for younger siblings, and on occasion took charge of the household. Sometimes they acquired this responsibility only when their mothers became ill, but in other cases adults deliberately adopted it as a training device. Abigail Adams, who believed it "an indispensable requisite, that every American wife, should herself know, how to order, and regulate her family," commented approvingly in 1788 that her son-in-law William Stephens Smith's four sisters were "well educated for wives as well as daughters" because "their Mamma had used them to the care of her Family by Turns. Each take it a week at a Time."

The words chosen by Mrs. Adams and Mrs. Fisher revealed a key difference in the domestic roles of urban and rural girls. Farm daughters learned to perform household tasks because their family's current well-being required their active involvement in daily work, whereas city girls acquired domestic skills primarily so that they could eventually become good wives and mothers. The distinction was crucial. Urban daughters participated sporadically in household tasks as a preparation for their own futures, but farm girls worked regularly at such chores as a direct contribution to their family's immediate welfare. The difference points up the overall contrast between the lives of urban and rural white women. In both city and farm, women made vital contributions to the success and survival of the household, but in rural areas those contributions were both more direct and more time-consuming.

IV

Wealthy southern women were directly responsible for even fewer household tasks than nor-
therners with comparable means. But northerners who moved south soon realized the falsity of an initial impression that "a mrs of a family in Carolina had nothing to doe but be waited on as their was so many negros." Anna Bowen, a young Rhode Island woman who first went to South Carolina to visit a married sister and subsequently married a planter herself, told another sister in 1790 about the problems of running a large household. Required to "think incessantly of a thousand articles of daily supply," she sometimes did not know "which way to turn," Bowen admitted, but, she added confidently, "I shall learn in time."

The daily schedules of mistresses of large plantations resembled those of wealthy urban women in the North, with the exception of the fact that social visits were confined to one or two afternoons a week because of the distance between plantations. The mornings were devoted to household affairs, although white southerners spent their time supervising the work of slaves instead of doing such chores themselves. The day began, sometimes before breakfast, with what one southern man termed "Grand Rounds from the Kitchen to the Larder, then to the Poultry Yard & so on by the Garret & Store Room home to the Parlour." After she had ascertained that the daily tasks were proceeding as planned, the mistress of the household could spend some time reading or playing music before joining her husband for dinner in early to mid-afternoon. Afterward, she would normally turn to needlework until evening, and then again to reading and writing.

The supervision of what were the largest households on the north American continent involved plantation mistresses in varied activities, almost always in the role of director rather than performer. What were small-scale operations on northern farms—running a dairy, raising poultry, tending a garden—were magnified many times on southern plantations, but they remained within the female sphere. Chores that northern women could do in a day, such as laundry, took nearly one week of every two on at least one South Carolina plantation. Food management, easily accomplished in small northern urban families with access to markets, occupied a significant amount of time and required much forethought on large plantations, where each year's harvest had to feed perhaps one hundred or more people for months. White women, it is true, did not usually make the decisions about how many hogs to kill or how many barrels of corn to set aside for food and seed, but they did manage the distribution of food once it had been stored, not to mention the supervision of its initial preservation. Furthermore, they coordinated the manufacture of the slaves' clothing, spending many hours cutting out garments or superintending that work, in addition to making, altering, and mending their families' clothes.

Such women invariably aroused the admiration of observers, who regularly commended their "industry and ingenuity," their "very able and active manner," or their character as "worthy economists" and "good managers." Surviving correspondence indicates that the praise could be completely deserved. A prime example is provided by the Marylander Hannah Buchanan, who in August 1809 returned alone to Woburn plantation while her husband remained in Baltimore on business. She reported to him in anger that the white couple they had left in charge did not have "the smallest idea of the proper economy of a Farm." Among the abuses she discovered were a misassignment of slave women to nonessential tasks, a lack of planning for the slaves' winter clothing, and extremely poor handling of food supplies, including such errors as allowing the slaves to have wheat flour, consuming all the pork, and having no vegetables at all. "This is miserable management," she declared, and set herself to correct the situation. A month later the work on winter clothes was coming along "Wonderfully," and she was filled with ideas on how to prepare and distribute the food more efficiently. Although she expressed a desire to rejoin her husband in the city, she proposed, "[L]et me direct next year

and you will spend less believe me and the people will live much better."

Appropriately, then, the primary task of girls from wealthy southern families was to gain expertise in running large estates. Like their northern counterparts, they did some cooking and baking and a fair amount of sewing, but their household roles differed from those of both farm and city girls. Whereas one New England father told his daughter, "[L]earn to work as fast as you can to make Shirts etc & assist your Mother," Thomas Jefferson advised his younger daughter, Maria, who was usually called Polly, that she should know how to "manage the kitchen, the dairy, the garden, and other appendages of the hous[e]hold." Teenaged girls like Eleanor Parke (Nelly) Custis accordingly served as "deputy Housekeeper" to the mistress of the family, who in her case was her grandmother Martha Washington. If this training was successful, parents could look with pleasure upon the accomplishments of such excellent managers as Martha Jefferson Randolph, who assured her father in 1791 that at Monticello under her direction "there is as little wasted as possible," or Harriott Pinckney Horry, whose fond mother, Eliza Lucas Pinckney, had herself managed three South Carolina plantations in the 1740s while she was still a teenager. "I am glad your little wife looks well to the ways of [her] hou[se]," Mrs. Pinckney told her new son-in-law within a month of his marriage, especially remarking upon her daughter's ability to run a "perfectly neat" dairy.

In the end, being a good plantation mistress involved very different skills from those of the usual notable housewife of northern communities. Most importantly, the well-to-do southern white woman had to know how to command and direct the activities of others, often a great many others, not just the one or two servants common to northern households. It was less essential for a wealthy female southerner to know how to accomplish tasks herself than it was for her to know how to order blacks to perform them, and to ensure that her orders were carried out. Thus when the Virginian

Elizabeth Foote Washington, who feared that she would not survive until her baby daughter reached maturity, decided to leave her a book of household advice, she devoted most of its pages to hints on the management of slaves. A mistress should behave with "steadiness," she advised; she should show the servants that she would not be "impos'd upon." The most important goal was to maintain "peace & quietness" in the household, and to this end a mistress should be careful not to complain about the slaves to her husband or her friends. Such a practice would make the servants grateful and perhaps encourage their industry, she wrote.

As it happened, both the daughters born to Mrs. Washington died in infancy, and so her detailed delineation of the way to handle house servants was not passed on as she had hoped. But other white southern girls early assumed the habit of command. A telling incident involved Anne, the daughter of James Iredell, the North Carolina attorney and eventual associate justice of the Supreme Court. At the early age of four, she showed how well she had learned her lessons by "strutting about in the yard after Susanna (whom she had ordered to do something) with her work in her hand & an Air of as much importance as if she had been Mistress of the family."

The story of Anne Iredell's behavior inevitably forces one to confront a difficult question: how did Susanna, a mature black woman, react to being ordered about by a white child? Or, to broaden the issue, what sort of lives were led by the black women who, with their husbands and children, constituted the vast majority of the population on southern plantations? Many female slaves resided on small farms and presumably worked in both field and house, but the discussion here will concentrate upon larger plantations, for it was in such households that most black women lived, since the relatively small proportion of white families who possessed slaves tended to own large numbers of them.

Significantly, the size of these plantations allowed the specialization of domestic labor.

White northern farm wives had to be, in effect, jills-of-all-trades, whereas planters often assigned slave women more or less permanently to particular tasks. A wide variety of jobs were open to black women, jobs that demanded as much skill as those performed by such male artisans as blacksmiths and carpenters. The slave list prepared by Thomas Middleton for his Goose Creek, South Carolina, plantation in 1784 included a dairymaid, a nurse, two laundresses, two seamstresses, and three general house servants. On other plantations women were also employed as cooks, spinners and weavers (after the mid-1760s), midwives, and tenders of poultry and livestock.

Female blacks frequently worked at the same job for a number of years, but they were not necessarily restricted to it for a lifetime, although practices varied from plantation to plantation. Thomas Jefferson used children of both sexes under ten as infant nurses; from the ages of ten to sixteen he assigned girls to spinning and boys to nailmaking; and then either put them into the fields or had them learn a skilled occupation. Even as adults their jobs might be changed: when Jefferson went to France as ambassador in 1784, his "fine house wench" Dinah, then twenty-three, began to work in the fields, continuing at that assignment at least until 1792. The descriptions of slaves bought or sold on other plantations likewise showed women accustomed to different occupations. Colonel Fitzgerald's Nell, aged thirty-four, was "a stout able field wench & an exceeding good Washer and Ironer"; her daughter Sophy, eighteen, was a "Stout Wench & used to both field & [hou]se Work."

All field work was not the same, of course, and women who labored "in the crop" performed a variety of functions. Evidence of work assignments from both the Jefferson and Washington plantations shows that there were some field jobs reserved for men, most notably cradling wheat and cutting and hauling timber for fences, but that women sometimes built fences. Women plowed, hoed and grubbed the land, spread manure, sowed, harrowed, and at harvest time threshed wheat or husked corn. At Landon Carter's Sabine Hall plantation in Virginia two women, Grace and Maryan, each headed a small gang of female field workers.

On outlying quarters, most women were agricultural laborers, with the occasional exception of a cook or a children's nurse. But female slaves raised at the home plantation could sometimes attain a high level of skill at conventionally "feminine" occupations. White masters and mistresses frequently praised the accomplishments of their cooks, seamstresses, and housekeepers. In a typical passage, Alice DeLancey Izard, a wealthy South Carolinian returning home after a long absence, commended her dairymaid Chloe because she found "the Dairy in excellent order, & plentifully supplied with Milk, & Butter," further observing that Chloe "has made little Chloe very useful in her line."

Mrs. Izard thereby called attention to the transmission of skills among generations of female blacks. Thomas Jefferson's censuses of his plantations demonstrate that women who were house servants tended to have daughters who also worked in the house, and the inventory of a Pinckney family plantation in 1812 similarly included a mother-daughter midwife team. Indeed, midwifery, which was most likely an occupation passed on from woman to woman rather than one taught deliberately by a master, was one of the most essential skills on any plantation. Slave midwives were often called upon to deliver white children as well as black, and masters recognized the special demands of their profession. In 1766, the midwife at Landon Carter's Fork Quarter, who was also the poultry tender, left her post to deliver a baby, an act resulting in the death of four turkeys. Even the petulant Carter realized that her midwifery duties came first, and so he did not punish her.

In this case, a conflict arose between the midwife's divergent duties within her master's household. More commonly, slave women must have had to contend with contradictory demands placed upon them by their plantation tasks and the needs of their own husbands and

children. Only a few aspects of the domestic lives led by black women within their own families can be traced in the records of white planters, for masters and mistresses did not, on the whole, concern themselves with the ways in which female slaves organized their homes. Yet occasional comments by slaveowners suggest that black women carefully made the most of what little they had and were even able to exercise some entrepreneurial initiative on occasion. Slave families occasionally maintained their own garden plots and supplemented their meager food and clothing allowances through theft or guile. Further, black women established themselves as the "general Chicken Merchants" in the plantation South. Whites often bought fowls from their female slaves instead of raising chickens themselves, as a means, Thomas Jefferson once explained, of "drawing a line between what is theirs & mine."

That some black women had a very strong sense indeed of what was "theirs" was demonstrated on Nomini Hall plantation in the summer of 1781. Robert Carter had authorized two white overseers to begin making salt, and in order to accomplish that task they commandeered an iron pot from its two female owners. Joan and Patty, the aggrieved slaves, awaited their chance and then removed the pot from the saltworks. After the whites repossessed it, the women dispatched Patty's husband, Jesse, to complain to Carter about the treatment they had received. Carter sided with the women, agreeing that their pot had been taken in an "arbitrary" manner, and he ordered it returned to them.

One could argue that Joan and Patty were emboldened to act as they did because they anticipated that Carter, a well-meaning master who eventually emancipated his slaves, would sympathize with their position. But bondwomen less favorably circumstanced also repeatedly displayed a desire to control as much of their lives as was possible under the conditions of servitude. Robert Carter's relative Landon was quick to anger, impatient with his servants and children. He frequently had recalcitrant slaves whipped, a tactic to which Robert rarely resorted, yet the women at Sabine Hall were no less insubordinate than those at Nomini. If Robert Carter's "Young & Stout" Jenny deliberately had fits "upon her being reprimanded," Landon Carter's Sarah pretended to be pregnant for a full eleven months so that she could avoid work, and Criss sent her children to milk his cows in the middle of the night in retaliation for a whipping. Similarly ingenious was James Mercer's Sall, who in August 1777 convinced her master that she had consumption and persuaded him to send her to the mountain quarter where her parents lived. That summer he ordered that she should be well fed and allowed to ride six or seven miles on horseback each day until she recovered her health, but by the following year, Mercer had concluded she was faking and directed that "she must turn out at all events unless attended with a fever."

The same willful spirit asserted itself when masters and mistresses attempted to move female slaves from their accustomed homes to other locations. A North Carolina woman who was visiting Boston wanted to have her servant Dorinda sent north to join her, but learned from a relative that Dorinda "would by no means go to Boston or North Carolina, from Cape Fear." Some years later a Pennsylvanian who had sent a slave woman to Cuba to be sold learned that she had managed to convince the white woman accompanying her that she should be returned to her Philadelphia home, because she was "Very Unhappy and always Crying." And "Miss Charlotte," an East Florida black, demonstrated her autonomy by her reaction to a dispute over who owned her. One of the two whites involved reported that she lived with neither of them, but instead "goes about from house to house," saying "now she's a free woman."

Charlotte, Sall, Dorinda, and the others gained at least a little freedom of movement for themselves, but they were still enslaved in the end. All their victories were minor ones, for they could have only limited impact upon the conditions of their bondage. White women

were subject to white men, but black women had to subordinate themselves to all whites, men, women, and children alike. The whites demanded always that their needs come first, before those of black women's own families. Female slaves' work lives were thus complicated by conflicting obligations that inflicted burdens upon them far beyond those borne by most whites.

V

White Americans did not expect their slaves to gain satisfaction from their work, for all that masters and mistresses required of their bond servants was proper behavior and a full day's labor. But white women, as already indicated, were supposed to find "happiness in their chimney corners," to return to William Livingston's striking phrase. Men certainly believed that women should enjoy their domestic role. As a Georgian told his married sister in 1796, "I am sure that those cares which duty requires to your husband, and your child—must fill up every moment of time—and leave you nothing but those sensations of pleasure—which invariably flow—from a consciousness of having left no duty unperformed." Women too anticipated happiness from achieving the goal of notable housewifery. "Domestick oeconomy . . . is the female dignity, & praise," declared Abigail Adams's younger sister, Elizabeth Smith, in the late 1760s, and a Virginian observed to a friend nearly forty years later that she had "always been taught, that within the sphere of domestic life, Woman's chief glory & happiness ought to consist."

The expectation, then, was clear: domesticity was not only a white American woman's inevitable destiny, but it was also supposed to be the source of her sense of pride and satisfaction. Regardless of the exact shape of her household role—whether she was a rural or an urban wife, or the mistress of a southern plantation—she should find fulfillment in it, and she should take pleasure in performing the duties required of her as mistress of the home.

Unsurprisingly, women rarely found the ideal as attractive in reality as it was in theory. But the reasons for their dissatisfaction with the restrictions of notable housewifery, which required them to be consistently self-effacing and constantly employed at domestic tasks, are both illuminating and unanticipated.

First, it must be noted that Mary Cooper was alone among her contemporaries in emphasizing the difficult, fatiguing nature of housework as the primary source of her complaints. Only she wrote of "the continnel cross of my famaly," only she filled her diary with accounts of weariness and endless drudgery. Women's unhappiness with their domestic lives, in other words, stemmed not from the fact that the work was tiring and demanding. Their husbands' labor was also difficult, and in eighteenth-century America there were few models of a leisured existence for either men or women to emulate. Rather, women's expressed dissatisfaction with their household role derived from its basic nature, and from the way it contrasted with their husbands' work.

As has been seen, farmers' lives were much more varied than those of their wives, not only because they rarely repeated the same chore day after day in immediate succession, but also because they had more breaks from the laboring routine. The same was true of southern planters and of urban husbands, regardless of their occupation. The diaries of planters, professional men, and artisans alike demonstrate that their weeks were punctuated by travel, their days enlivened not only by visits with friends—which their wives also enjoyed—but also by a variety of business activities that took them on numerous errands. It was an unusual week, for example, when Thomas Hazard, a Rhode Island blacksmith, worked in his shop every day without any sort of respite from his labors, or when Ebenezer Parkman, a New England clergyman, did not call on parishioners, confer with neighbors about politics, or meet with other ministers.

Against the backdrop of their husbands' diverse experiences, the invariable daily and weekly routines of housewifery seemed dull and uninteresting to eighteenth-century women, especially those who lived in urban areas, where the housework was less varied and their spouses' opportunities for socializing simultaneously greater. "The same cares and the same wants are constantly returning in domestic Life to take up my Time and attention," Pamela Dwight Sedgwick told her husband, Theodore, the Massachusetts Federalist, in words that reappeared in other women's assessments of their lives. "A continual sameness reigns throughout the Year," wrote Christian Barnes, the wife of a Marlborough, Massachusetts, merchant, and Mary Orne Tucker, a Haverhill lawyer's wife, noted in her diary that she did not record her domestic tasks in detail because "each succeeding day with very little variety would present a compleat history of the last."

New England city dwellers were not the only women who made such observations about the unchanging character of their experiences. The transplanted Rhode Islander Anna Bowen Mitchell reported from her new South Carolina home in 1793, "[T]he detail of one day . . . would be the detail of the last six months of my life," while hastening to add that her days were not "insipid," but rather filled with "heartsoothing tranquility." A Virginia planter's wife was more blunt about her situation in 1785, describing herself and her friends as "almost in a State of vegitation" because of their necessary attention to the "innumerable wants" of their large households.

She thus touched upon yet another source of housewives' discontent with their lot: the fact that their all-encompassing domestic responsibilities left them little time to themselves. In 1755, a New England woman remarked longingly to a correspondent, "[T]he little scraps of time that can be rescued from Business or Company, are the greatest cordials to my tired Spirits that I meet with." Thirty years later Pamela Sedgwick echoed her sentiments, telling her unmarried friend Betsy Mayhew, "[W]e that have connected ourselves in the famely way, find the small circle of domestic concerns engross almost all our attention." Sally Logan Fisher too commented, "[I] find so much to do in the Family that I have not all the time for retirement and improvement of my own mind in the best things that I wish," revealingly referring to her domestic duties as "these hindering things." Again, such complaints were not confined to northerners. A young Virginia wife observed in 1769 that "Domestic Business . . . even deprives thought of its Native freedom" by restricting the mind "to one particular subject without suffering it to entertain itself with the contemplation of any thing New or improving." A wry female poet made the same point in verse: "Ah yes! 'tis true, upon my Life! / No *Muse* was ever yet a *Wife*," she wrote, explaining that "Muses . . . in *poultry yards* were never seen," nor were they required "from Books and Poetry to Turn / To mark *the Labours of the Churn.*"

The point of all these remarks was the same, despite their divergent geographical and chronological origins. White American women recognized not only that their domestic obligations were never-ending, but also that their necessary concentration upon those obligations deprived them of the opportunity to contemplate "any thing New and improving." So Elizabeth Smith Shaw told her oldest sister, Mary Cranch, in 1781, several years after her marriage to the clergyman John Shaw, "[I]f Ideas present themselves to my Mind, it is too much like the good seed sown among Thorns, they are soon erased, & swallowed up by the Cares of the World, the wants, & noise of my Family, & Children." Abigail Adams in particular regretted her beloved younger sister's preoccupation with domestic concerns during her second marriage, to another clergyman, who boarded a number of students. In February 1800 she told Elizabeth (then Mrs. Stephen Peabody) that her "brilliant" talents were "encumbered" and "obstructed" by her household chores, lamenting "that the fire of imagination should be checked, that the effusions of genious should be stifled, through want of leisure to display them." Abigail's characterization of the impact of domestic responsibilities

on her sister's life bore little resemblance to William Livingston's glorification of those same activities: "The mind which is necessarily imprisoned in its own little tenement: and fully occupied by keeping it in repair: has no time to rove abroad for improvement," she observed. "The Book of knowledge is closely clasped against those who must fullfil there [*sic*] daily task of manual labour."

Even with their expressed dissatisfaction at the endless, unchanging nature of housework, one might theorize that late eighteenth-century American women could nevertheless have found their domestic lives meaningful if they and their husbands had highly valued their contributions to the family well-being. But such was not the case. Women revealed their assessments of the importance of their work in the adjectives they used to describe it: "my Narrow sphere," my "humble duties," "my little Domestick affairs."

Always the words belittled their domestic role, thereby indicating its low status in contemporary eyes. Modern historians can accurately point to the essential economic function of women within a colonial household, but the facts evident from hindsight bear little relationship to eighteenth-century subjective attitudes. In spite of the paeans to notable womanhood, the role of the household mistress in the family's welfare was understood only on the most basic level. Such minimal recognition did not translate itself into an awareness that women contributed to the wider society. Instead, just as a woman's activities were supposed to be confined to the domestic sphere, so, too, was any judgment of her importance. Americans realized that a successful household needed a competent mistress, but they failed to endow that mistress with an independent social standing or to grant to her domestic work the value it deserved. Notable housewifery was conceived to be an end in itself, rather than as a means to a greater or more meaningful goal. As such, it was an inadequate prop for feminine self-esteem.

Accordingly, it comes as no surprise to learn that women generally wrote of their household work without joy or satisfaction. They spoke only of "the discharge of the necessary duties of life," of "perform[ing] the duties that are annex'd to my Station." Even the South Carolinian Martha Laurens Ramsay, described by her husband, David, as a model wife, re-garded her "self denying duties" as "a part of the curse denounced upon Eve," as a penalty to be endured, instead of as a fulfilling experience. The usage was universal and the message unmistakable: their tasks, with rare exceptions, were "duties," not pleasures. The only Americans who wrote consistently of the joys of housewifery and notable womanhood were men like William Livingston. In contrast, Christian Barnes found the household a prison that offered no intellectual stimulation, describing it as a place where women were "Chain'd down to domestic Dutys" that "Stagnate[d] the Blood and Stupefie[d] the Senses."

Yet still women did not question the overall dimensions of the ideal domestic role. Sometimes, to be sure, they inquired about its details, as when Esther Edwards Burr, Jonathan Edwards's daughter, and her close friend Sarah Prince carried on a learned discussion about the precise meaning of the parts of Proverbs 31 that outlined the virtuous woman's daily routine. But ultimately they saw no alternative to domesticity. Many were simply resigned to the inevitable, for they had few options. Certainly some expressed the philosophy that "the height of happiness is Contentment" with one's lot, that although their life had "no great veriety . . . custom has made it agreeable . . . and to desire more would be ungreatfull." More probable, though, is the fact that the household duties women found unsatisfying were intertwined in their own minds with responsibilities from which they gained a great deal of pleasure. Their role as mistress of the household, in the end, constituted but a third of their troika of domestic duties. They were wives and mothers as well as housekeepers, and these components of domesticity gave them the emotional and psychological rewards they did not receive from running their households efficiently.

GLOSSARY

Loyalist: An adherent of the British cause during the American Revolution.

Body linen: Undergarments.

Middling: People of middle rank, neither rich nor poor.

Troika: A group of three, from the Russian troika, a carriage drawn by a team of three horses abreast.

IMPLICATIONS

In this essay, Norton depicts the differences that race, class, and region made in colonial women's lives. Yet she also points to the fundamental similarities in the roles and social expectations of women in the English colonies. If their realm was confined to the household, women nonetheless contributed significantly to the overall success of English America. Given their importance to the creation of family life and social stability in colonial America, why do you think colonial women received so little public and private recognition for the critical contributions they made?

Past Traces

The Great Awakening was noteworthy for inventing a new style of direct, extemporaneous, and emotional preaching. This reading is introduced by portions from the most famous revival sermon of the era, Jonathan Edwards' *Sinners in the Hands of an Angry God*. The power of this sermon owed a great deal to Edwards' appeal to the mainstay of traditional Puritan beliefs, the utter depravity of human beings in the sight of God. As sermons such as this one demonstrate, much of the success of the Great Awakening derived from the joining of old religion with new methods.

Jonathan Edwards, *Sinners in the Hands of an Angry God (1741)*

Your wickedness makes you as it were heavy as lead, and to tend downwards with great weight and pressure towards hell; and if God should let you go, you would immediately sink and swiftly descend and plunge into the bottomless gulf, and your healthy constitution, and your own care and prudence, and best contrivance, and all your righteousness, would have no more influence to uphold you and keep you out of hell, than a spider's web would have to stop a falling rock. Were it not for the sovereign pleasure of God, the earth would not bear you one moment; for you are a burden to it; the creation groans with you; the creature is made subject to the bondage of your corruption, not willingly; the sun does not willingly shine upon you to give you light to serve sin and Satan; the earth does not willingly yield her increase to satisfy your lusts; nor is it willingly a stage for your wickedness to be acted upon; the air does not willingly serve you for breath to maintain the flame of life in your vitals, while you spend your life in the service of God's enemies. God's creatures are good, and were made for men to serve God with, and do not willingly subserve to any other purpose, and groan when they are abused to purposes so directly contrary to their nature and end. And the world would spew you out, were it not for the sovereign hand of him who hath subjected it in hope. There are black clouds of God's wrath now hanging directly over your heads, full of the dreadful storm, and big with thunder; and were it not for the restraining hand of God, it would immediately burst forth upon you. The sovereign pleasure of God, for the present, stays his rough wind; otherwise it would come with fury, and your destruction would come like a whirlwind, and you would be like the chaff of the summer threshing floor.

The wrath of God is like great waters that are dammed for the present; they increase more and more, and rise higher and higher, till an outlet is given; and the longer the stream is stopped, the more rapid and mighty is its course, when once it is let loose. It is true, that judgment against your evil works has not been executed hitherto; the floods of God's vengeance have been withheld; but your guilt in the mean time is constantly increasing, and you are every day treasuring up more wrath; the waters are constantly rising, and waxing more and more mighty; and there is nothing but the mere pleasure of God, that holds the waters back, that are unwilling to be stopped, and press hard to go forward. If God should only withdraw his hand from the flood-gate, it would immediately fly open, and the fiery floods of the fierceness and wrath of God, would rush forth with inconceivable fury, and would come upon you with omnipotent power; and if your strength were ten thousand times greater than it is, yea, ten thousand times greater than the strength of the stoutest, sturdiest devil in hell, it would be nothing to withstand or endure it.

The bow of God's wrath is bent, and the arrow made ready on the string, and justice bends the arrow at your heart, and strains the bow, and it is nothing but the mere pleasure of God, and that of an angry God, without any promise or obligation at all, that keeps the arrow one moment from being made drunk with your blood. Thus all you that never passed under a great change of heart, by the mighty power of the Spirit of God upon your souls; all you that were never born again, and made new creatures, and raised from being dead in sin, to a state of new, and before altogether unexperienced light and life, are in the hands of an angry God. However you may have reformed your life in many things, and may have had religious affections, and may keep up a form of religion in your families and closets, and in the house of God, it is nothing but his mere pleasure that keeps you from being this moment swallowed up in everlasting destruction. However unconvinced you may now be of the truth of what you hear, by and by you will be fully convinced of it. Those that are gone from being in the like circumstances with you, see that it was so with them; for destruction came suddenly upon most of them; when they expected nothing of it, and while they were saying, Peace and safety: now they see, that those things on which they depended for peace and safety, were nothing but thin air and empty shadows. The God that holds you over the pit of hell, much as one holds a spider, or some loathsome insect over the fire, abhors you, and is dreadfully provoked: his wrath towards you burns like fire; he looks upon you as worthy of nothing else, but to be cast into the fire; he is of purer eyes than to bear to have you in his sight; you are ten thousand times more abominable in his eyes, than the most hateful venomous serpent is in ours. You have offended him infinitely more than ever a stubborn rebel did his prince; and yet it is nothing but his hand that holds you from falling into the fire every moment. It is to be ascribed to nothing else, that you did not go to hell the last night; that you was suffered to awake again in this world, after you closed your eyes to sleep. And there is no other reason to be given, why you have not dropped into hell since you arose in the morning, but that God's hand has held you up. There is no other reason to be given why you have not gone to hell, since you have sat here in the house of God, provoking his pure eyes by your sinful wicked manner of attending his solemn worship. Yea, there is nothing else that is to be given as a reason why you do not this very moment drop down into hell. O sinner! Consider the fearful danger you are in: it is a great furnace of wrath, a wide and bottomless pit, full of the fire of wrath, that you are held over in the hand of that God, whose wrath is provoked and incensed as much against you, as against many of the damned in hell. You hang by a slender thread, with the flames of divine wrath flashing about it, and ready every moment to singe it, and burn it asunder; and you have no interest in any Mediator, and nothing to lay hold of to save yourself, nothing to keep off the flames of wrath, nothing of your own, nothing that you ever have done, nothing that you can do, to induce God to spare you one moment. . . .

How dreadful is the state of those that are daily and hourly in the danger of this great wrath and infinite misery! But this is the dismal case of every soul in this congregation that has not been born again, however moral and strict, sober and religious, they may otherwise be. Oh that you would consider it, whether you be young or old! There is reason to think, that there are many in this congregation now hearing this discourse, that will actually be the subjects of this very misery to all eternity. We know not who they are, or in what seats they sit, or what thoughts they now have. It may be they are now at ease, and hear all these things without much disturbance, and are now flattering themselves that they are not the per-

sons, promising themselves that they shall escape. If we knew that there was one person, and but one, in the whole congregation, that was to be the subject of this misery, what an awful thing would it be to think of! If we knew who it was, what an awful sight would it be to see such a person! How might all the rest of the congregation lift up a lamentable and bitter cry over him! But, alas! instead of one, how many is it likely will remember this discourse in hell? And it would be a wonder, if some that are now present should not be in hell in a very short time, even before this year is out. And it would be no wonder if some persons, that now sit here, in some seats of this meeting-house, in health, quiet and secure, should be there before to-morrow morning. Those of you that finally continue in a natural condition, that shall keep out of hell longest will be there in a little time! your damnation does not slumber; it will come swiftly, and, in all probability, very suddenly upon many of you. You have reason to wonder that you are not already in hell. It is doubtless the case of some whom you have seen and known, that never deserved hell more than you, and that heretofore appeared as likely to have been now alive as you. Their case is past all hope; they are crying in extreme misery and perfect despair; but here you are in the land of the living and in the house of God, and have an opportunity to obtain salvation. What would not those poor damned hopeless souls give for one day's opportunity such as you now enjoy!

And now you have an extraordinary opportunity, a day wherein Christ has thrown the door of mercy wide open, and stands in calling and crying with a loud voice to poor sinners; a day wherein many are flocking to him, and pressing into the kingdom of God. Many are daily coming from the east, west, north and south; many that were very lately in the same miserable condition that you are in, are now in a happy state, with their hearts filled with love to him who has loved them, and washed them from their sins in his own blood, and rejoicing in hope of the glory of God. How awful is it to be left behind at such a day! To see so many others feasting, while you are pining and perishing! To see so many rejoicing and singing for joy of heart, while you have cause to mourn for sorrow of heart, and howl for vexation of spirit! How can you rest one moment in such a condition? Are not your souls as precious as the souls of the people at Suffield*, where they are flocking from day to day to Christ?

Are there not many here who have lived long in the world, and are not to this day born again? and so are aliens from the commonwealth of Israel, and have done nothing ever since they have lived, but treasure up wrath against the day of wrath? Oh, sirs, your case, in an especial manner, is extremely dangerous. Your guilt and hardness of heart is extremely great. Do you not see how generally persons of your years are passed over and left, in the present remarkable and wonderful dispensation of God's mercy? You had need to consider yourselves, and awake thoroughly out of sleep. You cannot bear the fierceness and wrath of the infinite God.-And you, young men, and young women, will you neglect this precious season which you now enjoy, when so many others of your age are renouncing all

youthful vanities, and flocking to Christ? You especially have now an extraordinary opportunity; but if you neglect it, it will soon be with you as with those persons who spent all the precious days of youth in sin, and are now come to such a dreadful pass in blindness and hardness. And you, children, who are unconverted, do not you know that you are going down to hell, to bear the dreadful wrath of that God, who is now angry with you every day and every night? Will you be content to be the children of the devil, when so many other children in the land are converted, and are become the holy and happy children of the King of kings?

And let every one that is yet out of Christ, and hanging over the pit of hell, whether they be old men and women, or middle aged, or young people, or little children, now harken to the loud calls of God's word and providence. This acceptable year of the Lord, a day of such great favours to some, will doubtless be a day of as remarkable vengeance to others. Men's hearts harden, and their guilt increases apace at such a day as this, if they neglect their souls; and never was there so great danger of such persons being given up to hardness of heart and blindness of mind. God seems now to be hastily gathering in his elect in all parts of the land; and probably the greater part of adult persons that ever shall be saved, will be brought in now in a little time, and that it will be as it was on the great out-pouring of the Spirit upon the Jews in the apostles' days; the election will obtain, and the rest will be blinded. If this should be the case with you, you will eternally curse this day, and will curse the day that ever you was born, to see such a season of the pouring out of God's Spirit, and will wish that you had died and gone to hell before you had seen it. Now undoubtedly it is, as it was in the days of John the Baptist, the axe is in an extraordinary manner laid at the root of the trees, that every tree which brings not forth good fruit, may be hewn down and cast into the fire.

Therefore, let every one that is out of Christ, now awake and fly from the wrath to come. The wrath of Almighty God is now undoubtedly hanging over a great part of this congregation: Let every one fly out of Sodom: "Haste and escape for your lives, look not behind you, escape to the mountain, lest you be consumed."

6

American Awakener

Harry S. Stout

Religion was a central focus of colonial life in seventeenth-century English America, but by the early eighteenth century ministers of all denominations were vocally complaining about their near-empty churches, the lack of respect shown to clergy in the communities they served, and a general sense of public apathy toward religion. In this, colonists were sharing in the religious doldrums that afflicted every corner of the British empire. Then, in the early 1730s, a group of young Oxford divinity students began a search for new ways to bring people back to God. The result was the creation of Methodism, a new evangelical movement within the Anglican church, and the rise of a new extemporaneous and emotional style of preaching that spoke directly to the hearts of the people at large.

The outgrowth of this new emotional approach to preaching was the rise of a powerful revival movement that swept through England's North American colonies during the 1730s and 1740s and brought tens of thousands of men and women back into colonial churches. Known collectively as the Great Awakening, these revivals were a profound restatement of American faith and religious commitment. But they were also much more. The Great Awakening was the first American undertaking to draw on the techniques of advertising and publicity that were fast developing in eighteenth-century England and were making it into the first modern nation of the Atlantic world.

In this selection, Harry S. Stout recounts the ways in which George Whitefield, the most popular preacher of the Great Awakening, organized and conducted his revivals in America. As this essay reveals, the success of the Great Awakening owed as much to the new techniques of promotion and publicity as it did to reawakened religious sentiments among colonial men and women. The Great Awakening was, according to Stout, a very complex and decidedly modern cultural affair.

From *Divine Dramatist* by Henry Stout, portions of pp. 87–106 "American Awakener," 1991. Reprinted with the permission of Eerdmann's Publishing.

Whitefield arrived in Lewes, Delaware, on October 30, 1739, almost exactly a year after his last departure. As the Georgia missionary, he had been little known to colonial audiences outside the South. But a year later, as the author of the Georgia journals, Calvinist critic of Anglicans, and tireless letter writer, he had achieved a certain fame. Moreover, the most exciting news—of the London outdoor revivals—was just reaching American newspapers when he arrived. The timing was perfect. At virtually the same moment Americans learned that Whitefield had taken London by storm, they learned he was about to preach in Philadelphia.

On the voyage over, Whitefield had developed a clearly defined plan of action for his American tour that was novel and audacious. The orphan house was only a small—if necessary—part. More ambitious was his plan to build on the techniques and momentum of the London preaching and transform his Calvinist revival into an international event with himself at the center. Such an event would have been unthinkable in the localistic, traditional culture of seventeenth-century Anglo-America. But not in 1739. All of the pieces for an international, interconnected revival were uniquely in place. In looking at the changing relationships between England and her colonies, eighteenth-century historians have described a process of "Anglicization" in which the empire was becoming increasingly more unified under British influence. The explosion of goods and trade under the comprehensive umbrella of the Navigation Acts integrated the English empire as never before. In the American colonies this economic integration was reinforced by new charters and royal governments designed to establish a political integration as well. And at the same time, American colonists were increasingly exposed to British culture and learning: intellectually and culturally they were growing more rather than less "English," as they were in matters political and economic.

In the midst of this cultural anglicization, Whitefield's plan was brilliantly simple. He would promote a religious anglicization—an integration of common religious experience around the new revivals. Just as he had adapted the marketplace to religious ends in England, so he would adapt new international linkages of transportation, trade, and communications to a self-conscious, intercolonial "Calvinist connection" built around the revival. Similar to the integrating power of Georgian politics, the East India Company, or Wedgwood pottery, Whitefield's revivals would forge a new, potentially powerful religious market around the key trading centers of Philadelphia, New York, Boston, Edinburgh, Glasgow, London, and Bristol. And from there the revivals could move inland.

Along with colonial-style imitation of English ways, Whitefield would add a wrinkle of his own to the emerging Anglo-American network. Economic and political anglicization originated in London and migrated exclusively one way. London was the core and all else the dependent periphery. Whitefield's revivals, on the other hand, could in time reverse the cultural exchange. Scotland and America could become centers of religious piety that would reverse the direction of anglicization. This was a heady enterprise that Scottish and American Calvinists were prepared to embrace and one that would endear Whitefield to his "periphery" audiences. It would reinstitute America's "Puritan errand" to a wayward Europe in the modern guise of mass revival and transdenominational, open-air appeal. To be sure, not all of this was fully clear to Whitefield in 1739. But the outline was fixed and the plan set in motion from the moment he stepped on American shores.

Whitefield selected Philadelphia as his first American stop. It was a wise choice. Although founded later than other northern cities, Philadelphia had already grown to be a major port city with a thriving market economy. The Quaker-dominated, pacifistic government was relatively untouched by the latest colonial war with France, so it was able to concentrate its energies on economic growth and the cultivation of ever-expanding markets. Its expansive mood comported well with Whitefield's energies and ambition.

Besides its geography and economic advantages, Pennsylvania also evidenced a unique cultural climate that fit Whitefield's ecumenical appeal. In its ethnic, religious, and linguistic diversity, Pennsylvania was in many ways the most American of all colonies, and Philadelphia the most cosmopolitan city. Its rich farmlands and its policy of religious toleration together attracted a heterogeneous population of Catholics, Jews, and Protestants, all of whom were tolerated and none of whom were powerful enough or, in the case of the Quaker founders, intolerant enough to stifle the others. By the same token, most of these groups had established separate islands of identity. Whitefield would strive to bring them together under the banner of revival.

If Whitefield's plan was simple in conception, it nevertheless called for tremendous human resources and intense labor. Here again, friends became important. Just as Habersham had assisted with the orphan-house ministry, so William Seward joined Whitefield on the second American trip to provide fulltime assistance with travel, funding, and above all publicity. In the early years, Whitefield relied heavily on letter writing as a crude public relations medium to spread the word of his revivals in personalized ways that both built anticipation and enlisted local helpers sympathetic to the cause of international Calvinist revival. Here Seward was essential. His job was to stay one step ahead of Whitefield. Some days he never left his lodgings, "sometimes writing a hundred letters a day." Other days he traveled by horse, spreading the word by mouth that Whitefield was coming.

Before Whitefield began in William Penn's model city of brotherly love, his way had been carefully prepared by Seward's announcements and his own meetings with local clergy of all denominations. In discussions with them he outlined his orphan house ministry and shared his vision for revival. To his great surprise, all

were enthusiastic, including Philadelphia's Anglican commissary Cummings. Indeed, Cummings was so appreciative that he turned the church over to his young colleague.

On November 6, 1739, Whitefield began his Philadelphia ministry by reading prayers and preaching at Christ Church to a "numerous congregation." Following the service, hundreds urged him "to preach in another place" that could accommodate larger crowds. With that incentive he moved out of doors, and the revival was on. On November 8, Philadelphians saw the real Whitefield preaching extemporaneously from the courtyard steps to an estimated audience of six thousand curious onlookers—nearly half of Philadelphia's urban population. The results were spectacular and ensured successes in America that would equal or exceed anything he had seen in England. Benjamin Franklin was in the audience that day, and he marveled at how far Whitefield's voice carried. No less impressive was his charismatic power. It was, Franklin later confessed, a "matter of speculation to me who was one of the Number, to observe the extraordinary Influence of his Oratory on his hearers."

Though Whitefield could not have predicted it, he and his American audiences were a perfect match. In Whitefield, American colonists found a speaker who embodied their own uncertain and highly ambitious status as English provincials. In time preacher and audience would discover many commonalities: both coveted English praise and legitimacy at the same time they chafed against authority and arbitrary powers; both were at their righteous best when challenging authority in the name of the popular audience; both craved recognition from the very authorities they loved to challenge; and, most important, both leaned toward creative, extrainstitutional solutions to entrenched problems of liberty and order—solutions that by-passed traditional authority and sought new principles of association, exchange, and order.

Pennsylvanians, like Londoners earlier, discovered that the out-of-doors location was the perfect environment for Whitefield's popularly oriented, extrainstitutional message. Indeed, in Philadelphia, where the social chasm separating rich from poor was less dramatic (there really were no rich on the level of England's aristocracy), Whitefield's appeal was even more inclusive. Outdoor preaching both expressed and encompassed social reality for Americans in a more comprehensive way than it ever could in the more stratified, hierarchical environs of England.

Whitefield's revival was peculiarly American in other ways as well. At base, his outdoor appeal and legitimacy rested on public opinion. While depending on all the local support he could get, he spoke in the name of no denomination and enjoyed no state support. His movement—if it was to become a movement—transcended traditional institutions and depended solely on the voluntary goodwill of the people. And yet the authority of public opinion was not recognized by English law. True legitimacy was conferred from above; legitimate power traveled from the top down. By the sheer location and circumstances of his ministry, Whitefield challenged these time-honored axioms of social order and hierarchy.

Every stop along Whitefield's trip from Philadelphia to New York and back was marked by record audiences, often exceeding the population of the towns in which he preached. From eight thousand in Philadelphia to three thousand in the village of Neshaminy, Pennsylvania, he won over an ever-increasing constituency. Chief among his friends and allies was the influential Tennent family, especially the elder William and his charismatic son Gilbert. They had recently begun a "New Side" Presbyterian "Log College"—over the objections of other "Old Side" Presbyterians—intended to train ministers for evangelical ministry. Soon after meeting the elder William Tennent, "an old grey-headed disciple and soldier of Jesus Christ," Whitefield identified him with the Presbyterian Erskine brothers in Scotland as part of a new Anglo-American united front of piety. Gilbert Tennent, something of an

American Howell Harris, was so enamored of Whitefield's ministry that he and another admirer, James Davenport, followed him to New York and Philadelphia, observing his manner and hoping to imitate his successes in travels of their own.

In America news traveled rapidly, and Whitefield was often surprised to discover how crowds "so scattered abroad, can be gathered at so short a warning." The advance work of Seward and the cooperation of local enthusiasts served him well. Not only were the crowds unprecedented in size, they were unusually quiet—virtually spellbound. "Even in London," Whitefield remarked, "I never observed so profound a silence."

As in England, Whitefield's field preaching relied heavily on imagination and dramatization. In one particularly favorite New World sermon, "Abraham Offering His Son," he created a series of scenes. The first scene opened with "the good old man walking with his dear child . . . now and then looking upon him, loving him, and then turning aside to weep." At this point in the narrative Whitefield himself may well have wept and momentarily halted the discourse, allowing the pathos to sink in. Then followed a second scene at the altar where Abraham was barely prevented from taking his beloved son's life in a profound moment of faith and obedience. By now the audience would be locked into Whitefield's performance and they would see with Abraham's eyes what Whitefield wanted them to see: "Fancy that you saw the aged parent standing by weeping. . . . Methinks I see the tears trickle down the patriarch Abraham's cheeks . . . adieu, my Isaac, my only Son, whom I love as my own soul; adieu, adieu." Here, as elsewhere, Whitefield's sermon in print appears melodramatic. But when performed live, with all the body language and pathos of a great actor, the lines receded into the passion and the hearer was locked into a dramatic world from which there was no easy exit. Doctrines, uses, proofs, and applications all receded into the background as the passions took over.

In the third and climactic scene, Whitefield bridged the gap separating Abraham from Christ through the passions:

> Did you weep just now when I bid you fancy that you saw the altar? Look up by faith, behold the blessed Jesus, our all-glorious Immanuel, not bound, but nailed on an accursed tree: see how he hangs crowned with thorns, and had in derision of all that are round about him: see how the thorns pierce him, and how the blood in purple streams trickles down his sacred temples! Hark! And now where are all your tears? Shall I refrain your voice from weeping? No, rather let me exhort you to look to him whom you have pierced, and mourn, as a woman mourneth for her first born.

It is not unreasonable to assume that Whitefield's dramatic mode of preaching had an even greater impact on American audiences than it did in London or Bristol for a very simple reason. Theater was a familiar—if controversial—institution in eighteenth-century England, but it had not yet reached American shores. Apart from occasional plays in Philadelphia, New York, Charleston, and Williamsburg, Americans had no organized drama. There were no professional companies or permanent stages until late in the eighteenth century. In seeing Whitefield preach, many Americans were for the first time in their lives seeing a form of theater. Until then, public performance—whether civic or religious—had been governed by classical canons of speech established by Cicero and Quintillian. Magistrates gathered on Courthouse Day in Virginia and ministers proclaiming election sermons in New England all followed models of "gravity" and "decorum" that precluded body and passion. Even New Side revivalists in the middle colonies found much to learn in the impassioned oratory of Whitefield.

Invariably audience responses were both delighted and confused. Here was someone impersonating characters, but he did not seem to be indulging in the "hypocrisy" of the stage: his characters were not fictional but real and familiar. It was biblical history in a theatrical key. After hearing Whitefield preach, New York Presbyterian minister Ebenezer Pemberton confessed, "I never saw or heard the like." In describing what he saw, Pemberton instinctively drew on dramatic terminology. Noteworthy was Whitefield's "clear and musical voice." Even more striking was his use of body: "he uses much gestures," such that "every accent of his voice, and every motion of his body, speaks, and both are natural and unaffected." All of this, moreover, was conducted in so "natural" a way that if it was the "product of art," it was "entirely concealed."

The more successful Whitefield was, the more he antagonized Anglican colleagues who shared his affiliation but invariably found themselves the butt of his biting sarcasm. If Whitefield's ministry was ecumenical, it was an all-inclusive ecumenicity that was explicitly "Calvinist" in theology and opposed to all forms of "Arminianism." In fact, Whitefield's Calvinism and anti-Arminianism became more and more strident as he traveled through Calvinist America and Scotland and met with the eagerly supportive descendants of the "old Puritans." American Anglicans were willing to meet him halfway—even South Carolina's Commissary Garden welcomed the Georgia missionary on his first visit. But Whitefield showed an obvious lack of interest. Confrontation, as Whitefield knew, aroused curiosity, and his own Anglican Church was his favorite target. Soon Anglican churchmen throughout the American colonies joined their London brethren in opposing Whitefield. And, as in England, their opposition simply fueled popular enthusiasm for the young critic who fearlessly denounced clerical "formality" and Arminian preaching.

As he traveled from Philadelphia to New York, Whitefield attracted the majority of inhabitants even as he lost Anglican support. This was the one denomination to which he was formally tied, and the one from which he had to distance himself in order to maintain his interdenominational appeal. On hearing of "a disturbance in Philadelphia," New York's

Commissary Vesey closed all Anglican pulpits to Whitefield and urged his congregations to boycott the sermons. With the battle thus joined, Whitefield had the opposition that he needed to establish "persecution" and plead for popular sympathy. Wherever he traveled, he checked the newspapers for criticism, recognizing "the advantage of the things my adversaries have inserted in the public papers: they do but excite people's curiosity, and serve to raise their attention." With characteristic bluster he excited his readers with accounts of standing the commissary off. When told his field preaching was illegal, Whitefield replied that so too was the commissary's time spent frequenting "public houses." There were times when Whitefield could be utterly enamored of authority figures, but when dealing with commissaries and bishops, he would confidently proclaim that "I was no respector of persons; if a bishop committed a fault, I would tell him of it"—though always, he added, "with a spirit of meekness."

With his own denomination closed, friends multiplied from the dissenters. In fact and spirit, most Americans were dissenters, at odds with traditional, hierarchical ways. This, combined with their historic Calvinism, elicited strong bonds of sympathy and support in response to the news of Whitefield's persecution. At each stop he found strong allies whom he integrated into his ever-expanding network of pro-revival sympathizers. Ebenezer Pemberton quickly got over his confusion and eagerly opened his meetinghouse to Whitefield's indoor preaching. A wealthy merchant, Thomas Noble of New York, agreed to work with Seward in promoting Whitefield's tours and serving as a conduit for the ever-expanding letter-writing network. These, together with the Pennsylvania New Siders, formed the nucleus of a transatlantic evangelical alliance.

When not mesmerizing audiences with his "heavenly cadence" and biblical characterizations, Whitefield was outraging Anglican clergy with his denunciations of an "unconverted ministry." In an oft-repeated sermon entitled "The Lord Our Righteousness," he launched into an attack on all clerical enemies of revival. Invariably, he used the rhetoric of the "jeremiad"—a ritual lament for lost piety, familiar to all Americans—but instead of directing it against the people, he turned it on the clerical opposition to his revival. To startled audiences he would proclaim the new orthodoxy that

> many ministers are so sadly degenerated from their pious ancestors, that the doctrines of grace, especially the personal, all-sufficient righteousness of Jesus is but too seldom, too slightly mentioned. Hence the love of many waxeth cold; and I have often thought, was it possible, that this single consideration would be sufficient to raise our venerable forefathers again from their graves; who would thunder in their ears their fatal error.

The adversarial voice, so familiar to colonial preachers, sounded quite different when directed at them.

In America, the inverted jeremiad was perfectly matched to Whitefield's novel delivery in outdoor settings. Just as the setting upset traditional social rankings and seating, so the rhetoric reversed accusations and assured the people that spiritual declension was not their fault. Through setting and rhetoric he forged a potent message capable of uniting ordinary people in a transatlantic array. Together, Whitefield and his new audiences would challenge the seats of ecclesiastical authority wherever they appeared in churches, colleges, and the press. At the same time, however, that challenge stopped short of civil authority and the "gentlemen" who embodied it. By inclination and temperament, Whitefield remained the proud Oxonian. His confrontational rhetoric was more anticlerical than antihierarchical, though popular audiences (and critics) heard both emphases in it.

On November 28, Whitefield delivered his farewell sermon to the people of Philadelphia. The meeting was to be held at Christ Church, but the audience was so large that he adjourned "to the fields," where he preached for one and a half hours from a balcony overlooking the crowd. Assembled in the audience were listeners of all classes, including local magistrates at the top and a growing cadre of slaves at the bottom. Included also was the printer-entrepreneur Benjamin Franklin, who was to become an advisor and friend of the young evangelist. Then followed a farewell dinner with the governor and proprietor Thomas Penn. Dinners like these not only boosted Whitefield's popularity and satisfied his craving for recognition among the elite but insulated him from the charge of being an incendiary bent on overturning the social order.

With the first leg of his tour a resounding success, Whitefield moved south to attend to the orphan house project that had ostensibly brought him to the New World. He had much to celebrate. He had attracted audiences that no preacher before him enjoyed. In addition, he had created a nucleus of influential contacts in Philadelphia and New York pledged to promote the cause of revival in its new outdoor setting. A new Anglo-American movement had begun to take shape. All that remained was to complete the tour and then perpetuate it with follow-up ministries and native imitators gifted with a charismatic flair for drama and spiritual sensation. Through his travels, Whitefield became the voice and symbol of a movement that transcended local boundaries and denominations and appeared poised for massive growth.

In America as in England, "revival" itself took on a new meaning as a staged, translocal event, held outdoors on weekdays in open competition with more secular entertainments and diversions. In the past, revivals were local, mysterious events that occurred once or twice in any generation and that remained within local communities. With the New Birth as his product and the promise of a transatlantic market, Whitefield introduced religion to a dawning consumer age. Wherever he encountered a "thriving place for trade," he would set up shop and market his revival.

Whitefield watched with particular interest events in Philadelphia following his tour. Since his departure in November, the forces for revival grew steadily stronger, and with them instances of confrontation and controversy. Unlike past "seasons" of renewal or "harvests" of young members, this new revival seemed to work against the churches as much as for them. Even as it threatened competing entertainments, it also threatened established churches based on traditional authority and communal norms. And in the more work-centered American context, where laborers were many and the unemployed few, it also threatened to draw workers away from their weekday labors. In the new revival, religion was becoming less a matter of family birthright or communal habit than an arena of choice based on personal preference and individual experience. Along with the intense piety of the New Birth was a rival vision of religious association and meaning that could not help but provoke confrontation.

On March 8, 1740, an incendiary sermon by Gilbert Tennent entitled "The Danger of an Unconverted Ministry" helped the Presbyterian pro-Whitefield New Siders challenge the traditional order. Tennent urged followers to leave their churches if they were not organized around the experience of the New Birth. The theme was a familiar one in Whitefield's preaching, but such rhetoric had institutional consequences. In the aftermath of Whitefield's and Tennent's blasts against an unconverted ministry, Presbyterians, Congregationalists, and Anglicans found themselves bitterly dividing over the centrality of the New Birth. A movement that had begun innocently enough outside of institutions now threatened to turn back on them and rip them apart.

Whitefield's return to Philadelphia in April coincided with the furor set in motion by Tennent's New Side manifesto. To arouse things all the more, Franklin reprinted Whitefield's blast against Tillotson in the *Pennsylvania Gazette*. Publicity and Whitefield's own charismatic and controversial presence soon made him a cause célèbre. Even Whitefield could scarce describe "the joy many felt when they saw my face again." Clearly he was well on his way to becoming an American hero, and he reveled in all the attention attending his return. He played the role of pious celebrity to perfection, careful never to offend civil authority, and invariably recording lunches and meetings with governors, proprietors, and other local dignitaries. Only the Church of England felt the sting of his criticism, and it returned the favor by closing its pulpits. Such was the case with the commissary, in contrast to their first amicable meeting. Seward explained that the change was the result "of Mr. Whitefield's writing against Archbishop Tillotson." The refusal was predictable, leading a triumphant Whitefield to gloat, "little do my enemies think what service they do me. If they did one would think, out of spite they would even desist from opposing me."

The day following his meeting with the commissary, Whitefield preached out of doors. In the morning he spoke from a scaffold built on Society Hill to an audience of five thousand. That afternoon Seward reported a sermon "from the Balcony on Society-Hill to the largest Congregation we have yet had in America, computed at Ten or Twelve thousand." The next day he traveled to Abington and preached from a horse block to three thousand. Similar crowds appeared among the Germans in Germantown and in Whitemarsh. When the commissary preached against him from James 2:8, Whitefield preached on the same text to ten times the audience. As he reported, "Religion is all the talk; and, I think I can say, the Lord Jesus hath gotten Himself the victory in many hearts."

For the most part Whitefield's outdoor sermons were ones he had perfected in England. Benjamin Franklin was in attendance at most of the Philadelphia sermons and soon learned to distinguish new creations from repeat performances:

By hearing him often I came to distinguish easily between sermons newly composed and those which he had often preached in the course of his travels. His delivery of the latter was so improved by frequent repetition, that every accent, every emphasis, every modulation of voice, was so perfectly well turned, and well placed, that without

being interested in the subject, one could not help being pleased with the discourse: a pleasure of much the same kind with that received from an excellent piece of music.

Besides the sermon on Abraham, another favorite in these months was a sermon on Zaccheus, which Seward recorded several times in his journal. The story of Zaccheus was no doubt familiar to most Philadelphians, and Whitefield's popular retelling gave it a peculiarly American flavor. Because Zaccheus was short of stature, he climbed a tree to see Jesus better. Like every insignificant person who is suddenly taken seriously, Zaccheus rejoiced when Jesus spotted him in the tree and called him by name, saying, "make haste, and come down; for to day I must abide at thy house."

With this story as his centerpiece, Whitefield delivered a sermon he turned both to social commentary and evangelical exhortation. To the wealthy of the world he warned, "let not therefore the rich glory in the multitude of their riches." For the most part, he continued, it was "the common people [who] heard our Lord gladly, and the poor [who] received the gospel." In words certain to please ordinary hearers, he pointed out not only that the rich were often insensitive to the gospel message but that sometimes they were openly hostile. For "true" gospel preachers such as himself and the Pennsylvania New Siders he warned, "let not the ministers of Christ marvel, if they meet with the [persecution] from the rich men of this wicked and adulterous generation. I should think it no scandal...to hear it affirmed, that none but the poor attended my ministry."

Having assured his hearers that "the poor are dear to my soul," Whitefield returned to Zaccheus, this time for evangelistic purposes. First he enacted a frantic Zaccheus running to hear Jesus, and then climbing the sycamore tree. Where Scripture did not record Zaccheus's thoughts, Whitefield filled in the lines with an imaginary monologue: "Surely, thinks Zaccheus, I dream: it cannot be; how should he know me? I never saw him before." Then followed the imaginative rejection: "besides I shall undergo much contempt, if I receive him under my roof." More polite "scoffers" would never demean themselves by running after Jesus; they no doubt thought he was just another "enthusiastic preacher." But Zaccheus would not be denied, and for his efforts he was rewarded with salvation. In closing, Whitefield took on the personality of Christ, urging his hearers to "come, haste away, and hide yourselves in the clefts of my wounds; for I am wounded for your transgressions; I am dying that you may live for evermore."

So caught up was Whitefield in his daily sermons, each with multiple sermonic roles, that he confessed, "I have scarce had time to eat bread from morning to evening." In Philadelphia, as in London, he was becoming lost to all but his public self in the pulpit. Once again, his experience appears more analogous to the actor on tour than to the settled preacher. Unlike ministers who preached only once or twice a week and could more easily separate their "roles" as pastor, father, husband, and community pillar, Whitefield lived in his own self-embracing world of dramatic reenactment. Just as the public self dominates his journals, so it dominated his day-to-day life in ways that were not common to other preachers.

In characterizing the nether world of the actor, Jean-Christophe Agnew observes that "he certainly never claimed to represent himself on the stage. . . . Nor, finally, did he represent his 'character.' He *was* the character as long as the action of the play went forward, and he could expect to be taken as such by his audience." In very similar ways, Whitefield *was* the biblical characters he portrayed. These characters were more than historical renditions or readings from Scripture. Through his interpretation, they took on lives of their own and became a form of revelation unique to him. In fact, in the time of the sermon he was neither Whitefield nor Zaccheus nor Herod nor Christ: he was all of them brought together in one cathartic vortex of experience and passion common to all great drama.

And so Americans discovered the Whitefield who had earlier taken London by storm. At the same time, Whitefield discovered through his preaching the passions within him and gave them true expression. He was not "acting" as he preached so much as he was exhibiting a one-to-one correspondence between his inner passions and the biblical saints he embodied. He was most complete in the pulpit, where his private and public self came together in body, voice, and gesture to be an open window into his own deepest personal response to the gospel accounts. Such performance required courage to let the self within be seen fully from without. And, like all displays of courage, it brought power and attention.

GLOSSARY

Calvinism: The religious doctrines of John Calvin, emphasizing the omnipotence of God and the salvation of the elect by God's grace alone.

Arminianism: Of or relating to the theology of Jacobus Arminius, who emphasized human free choice in achieving God's grace.

Moravian: Members of the Unitas Fratrum, an evangelical Christian communion. In 1740, the sect founded a religious colony at Bethlehem, Pennsylvania, and directed much of their energies toward converting backcountry Indians to Christianity.

"Old Side":   Anti-revival supporters of traditional religious practices.

"New Side":   Pro-revival critics of traditional religious practices.

IMPLICATIONS

The Great Awakening was marked by an unprecedented outpouring of emotional religiosity and, while it filled local churches and swelled congregations, within a year or two of a revival, church attendance generally returned to prerevival levels. From what you've read about the promotional aspects of the Great Awakening, do you think the upsurge in religious feeling was genuine? Or do you think it was a popular response to the new advertising techniques employed by Whitefield and other evangelists?

PART TWO

A Revolutionary People

The history of the American Revolution is no longer thought of simply as a story of patriotic ardour overcoming British corruption in the crucible of war. As historians have investigated the meaning of the Revolution to ordinary men and women, to Native Americans, and to African Americans (both bound and free), they have discovered a world of complexity and dispute in which people's allegiance to the patriot cause depended as much on their place in society as on abstract political or constitutional principles.

The Revolutionary War itself was a complex affair. As the essays by Alfred F. Young and James Kirby Martin reveal, ordinary artisans, farmers, laborers, and mariners had their own reasons for supporting the American cause. Like many other artisans, George Robert Twelves Hewes was attracted to the patriot cause because he found in it a way to reject the deference he had been forced to give his "superiors" during the colonial era and because it allowed him to claim an independent political voice for the first time in his life. The men who joined Washington's Continental Army, on the other hand, composed a "Most Undisciplined, Profligate Crew" of poor men from eastern North America's farms and cities. These men from the lower ranks of society risked their lives less from patriotism, Martin claims, than from the promise of the wartime pay and land bounties that might permit them to join the ranks of independent landowners after the Revolution.

American women also played crucial roles in the Revolution. From their participation in early protests and boycotts to their wartime maintenance of homes, farms, and shops—even to their work and support for the army during nearly a decade of punishing war—women's actions proved decisive in the winning of independence. Despite women's vital contribution to independence, however, their sacrifices did little to change public views about women in the post-Revolutionary era.

As Carol Berkin shows, beyond a positive reassessment of their intellectual capacities, women remained as tied to domestic duties and home-bound roles in the new republic as they had in the colonial past.

The Treaty of Paris, signed in 1783, ended the Revolutionary War and established the United States as an independent nation. At the same time, it posed many new questions to the American people. Robert E. Shalhope's essay discusses two of the most momentous of these questions: What sort of policy would the national government establish? And what sort of society would its policies promote? In the contrasting visions of Federalists and Anti-Federalists, Shalhope argues, lay the future model for American social and political development.

The Revolution had a profound impact on those outside the political realm as well. The wartime rhetoric that counterposed American liberty to British slavery brought many Americans to reconsider the institution of slavery in the new nation. Especially in the northern states, where slavery was less important economically, but in the Virginia assembly as well, state legislatures debated the question of abolition, and by the end of the eighteenth century the northern states had sent slavery on the road to extinction. In "Thomas Peters," Gary B. Nash recounts the life and labors of a young Yoruba captive who declared his own independence from slavery in 1776 by escaping to British lines. Once free, Peters became a leader of the expatriate African American community in Nova Scotia and, when discrimination and racism followed them to Canada, resettled the Nova Scotia community in Sierra Leone. In recounting Peter's lifelong struggle for personal and collective freedom, Nash underlines the vital importance of freedom to all Africans held in bondage in the American colonies.

No sooner had the Revolutionary War ended than land-hungry settlers surged over the Appalachians, claiming land in Kentucky, Tennessee, and the Northwest Territory by right of conquest. Faced with internal political divisions, wavering British support, and general white hostility, Native American leaders searched for new ways to deal with the imminent threat to their ancestral homelands. Some, like the Cherokee, chose the path of assimilation, hoping that by adopting white ways, they would be accepted into mainstream American society. Others, like the Shawnee, chose the path of pan-Indian alliance and armed resistance, arguing that whites would never permit Indian assimilation into the white republic. Whichever path they chose, however, Colin G. Calloway shows that Native Americans fashioned their own response to the changes taking place in the post-revolutionary world.

Past Traces

The Boston Tea Party of 1773 was one of the central events leading to the American Revolution. Angered by Parliament's forced sale of East India Company tea in American markets at manipulated prices that undercut local retailers, Bostonians held a public meeting about the arrival of the tea and what to do about it. Scarcely two weeks later, a group of townspeople disguised as Indians emptied three shiploads of East India tea into Boston harbor. It was Parliament's heavy-handed retribution for this protest action in 1774 that, together with memories of the Boston Massacre the previous year, led many Americans to choose the path of independence. In this document, a letter between business associates, we can see both the practical and the principled reasons behind the Tea Party protest.

John Andrews to William Barrell on the Boston Tea Party (1773)

December 18th. However precarious our situation may be, yet *such* is the present calm composure of the people that a stranger would hardly think that ten thousand pounds sterling of the East India Company's *tea* was destroy'd the night, or rather evening before last, yet its a serious truth; and if your's, together with ye other Southern provinces, should rest satisfied with *their* quota being stor'd, poor Boston will feel the whole weight of ministerial vengeance. However, its the opinion of most people that we stand an equal chance now, whether troops are sent in consequence of it or not; whereas, had it been stor'd, we should inevitably have had 'em, to enforce the sale of it.

The affair was transacted with the greatest regularity and despatch. Mr. Rotch finding he exposed himself not only to the loss of his ship but for ye value of the tea in case he sent her back with it, *without a clearance from the custom house*, as ye Admiral kept a ship in readiness to make a seizure of it whenever it should sail under *those circumstances*; therefore declin'd complying with his former promises, and absolutely declar'd his vessel should not carry it, without a *proper* clearance could be procur'd or he to be indemnified for the value of her: ⟨when a general muster was assembled, from this and all ye neighbouring towns, to the number of five or six thousand, at 10 o'clock Thursday morning in the Old South Meeting house, where they pass'd a *unanimous* vote that the *Tea* should go out of the *harbour* that afternoon, and sent a committee with Mr. Rotch to ye. Custom house to *demand* a clearance, which the collector told 'em was not in his power to give, without the duties being first paid. They then sent Mr. Rotch to Milton, to ask a pass from ye Governor, who sent for answer, that "consistent with the rules of government and his duty to the King he could not grant one without they produc'd a previous clearance from the office."— By the time he return'd with this message the candles were light in [the] house, and upon reading it, such prodigious shouts were made, that induc'd me, while drinking tea at home, to go out and know the cause of it. The house was so crouded I could get no farther than ye porch, when I found the moderator was just declaring the meeting to be *dissolv'd*, which caused another general shout, out doors and in, and three cheers. What with that, and the consequent noise of breaking up the meeting, you'd thought that the inhabitants of the infernal regions had broke loose. For my part, I went contentedly home and finish'd my tea, but was soon inform'd what was going forward: but still not crediting it without ocular demonstration, I went and was *satisfied*. They muster'd I'm told, upon Fort Hill, to the number of about two hundred, and proceeded, two by two, to Griffin's wharf, where Hall, Bruce, and Coffin lay, each with 114 chests of the *ill fated* article on board; the two former with *only* that article, but ye latter arriv'd at ye wharf only ye day before, was freighted with a large quantity of other goods, which they took the *greatest* care not to injure in the least, and before *nine* o'clock in ye evening, every chest from on board the three vessels was knock'd to pieces and flung over ye sides.

They say the actors were *Indians* from *Narragansett*. Whether they were or not, to a transient observer they appear'd as such, being cloath'd in Blankets with the heads muffled, and copper color'd countenances, being, each arm'd with a hatchet or axe, and pair pistols, nor was their dialect different from what I conceive these geniusses to *speak*, as their jargon was unintelligible to all but themselves. Not the least insult was offer'd to any person, save one Captain Conner, a letter of horses in this place, not many years since remov'd from *dear Ireland*, who had ript up the lining of his coat and waistcoat under the arms, and watching, his opportunity had nearly fill'd them with tea, but being detected, was handled pretty roughly. They not only stripp'd him of his cloaths, but gave him a coat of mud, with a severe bruising into the bargain; and nothing but their utter aversion to make any disturbance pre-vented his being tar'd and feather'd.

7

George Robert Twelves Hewes:
The Revolution and the Rise
of Popular Politics

Alfred F. Young

By the mid-eighteenth century, questions of political and social authority occupied the minds of Americans of all ranks. While the prosperous governing elites debated the nature of British parliamentary authority in the colonies, those of more humble station challenged existing social arrangements. In rural communities in which land scarcity meant that fathers could no longer offer the promise of propertied independence to their children, sons and daughters began to question the patriarchal control of their fathers and conceived children to force marriage on their own terms. In towns and cities, middling- and laboring-class people joined in questioning the customary authority that the rural gentry and urban merchants exercised. In the mobilization against Britain, these people of lower status demanded a voice in their own affairs that threatened the system of patronage and deference that had dominated social relations for generations.

In Boston, as Alfred F. Young shows, popular questioning of elite control grew in force as the Revolution approached. By following the career of George Robert Twelves Hewes, a humble shoemaker whose experiences were typical of ordinary artisans in America's pre-Revolutionary cities, Young reveals the breakdown of the system of deference that dominated much of the political and social history of colonial America. As the imperial bonds that bound British America to the mother country began to loosen following the Seven Years' War, social relations within the colonies began to change as well. Whereas in 1763 someone such as Hewes felt intimidated and socially inferior when dealing with wealthy and politically influential men such as John Hancock, fifteen years later men of Hewes's rank routinely declared themselves equal to all men, regardless of wealth or social position. The rise of this popular egalitarianism was a prominent feature of the Revolutionary era, as ordinary farmers and artisans placed their lives and livelihoods at risk for the patriot cause. By the end of the eighteenth century, these wartime sacrifices brought ordinary men such as Hewes to make unprecedented demands for social equality and popular political participation in the affairs of the new republic.

Seeing the American Revolution through the eyes of a poor shoemaker rather than from the perspective of founding fathers such as Washington, Jefferson, and John Adams has a twofold advantage. First, it enables us to see the role of ordinary people as history makers; second, it shows that a social upheaval such as the American Revolution can involve many agendas—not always shared by the various participants.

....

Late in 1762 or early in 1763, George Robert Twelves Hewes, a Boston shoemaker in the last year or so of his apprenticeship, repaired a shoe for John Hancock and delivered it to him at his uncle Thomas Hancock's store in Dock Square. Hancock was pleased and invited the young man to "come and see him on New Year's day, and bid him a happy New Year," according to the custom of the day, a ritual of noblesse oblige on the part of the gentry. We know of the episode through Benjamin Bussey Thatcher, who interviewed Hewes and wrote it up for his *Memoir* of Hewes in 1835. On New Year's Day, as Thatcher tells the story, after some urging by his master,

> George washed his face, and put his best jacket on, and proceeded straightaway to the Hancock House (as it is still called). His heart was in his mouth, but assuming a cheerful courage, he knocked at the front door, and took his hat off. The servant came:
>
> "Is 'Squire Hancock at home, Sir?" enquired Hewes, making a bow.
>
> He was introduced directly to the *kitchen,* and requested to seat himself, while report should be made above stairs. The man came down directly, with a new varnish of civility suddenly spread over his face. He ushered him into the 'Squire's sitting-room, and left him to make his obeisance. Hancock remembered him, and addressed him kindly. George was anxious to get through, and he commenced a desperate speech—"as pretty a

one," he says, "as he any way knew how,"—intended to announce the purpose of his visit, and to accomplish it, in the same breath.

> "Very well, my lad," said the 'Squire—"now take a chair, my lad."
>
> He sat down, scared all the while (as he now confesses) "almost to death," while Hancock put his hand into his breeches-pocket and pulled out a crown-piece, which he placed softly in his hand, thanking him at the same time for his punctual attendance, and his compliments. He then invited his young friend to drink his health—called for wine—poured it out for him—and ticked glasses with him,—a feat in which Hewes, though he had never seen it performed before, having acquitted himself with a creditable dexterity, hastened to make his bow again, and secure his retreat, though not till the 'Squire had extorted a sort of half promise from him to come the next New-Year's—which, for a rarity, he never discharged.

The episode is a demonstration of what the eighteenth century called deference.

Another episode catches the point at which Hewes had arrived a decade and a half later. In 1778 or 1779, after one stint in the war on board a privateer and another in the militia, he was ready to ship out again, from Boston. As Thatcher tells the story: "Here he enlisted, or engaged to enlist, on board the Hancock, a twenty-gun ship, but not liking the manners of the Lieutenant very well, who ordered him one day in the streets to take his hat off to him—

which he refused to do for any man,—he went aboard the 'Defence,' Captain Smedley, of Fairfield Connecticut." This, with a vengeance, is the casting off of deference.

What had happened in the intervening years? What had turned the young shoemaker tongue-tied in the face of his betters into the defiant person who would not take his hat off for any man? And why should stories like this have stayed in his memory sixty and seventy years later?

George Robert Twelves Hewes was born in Boston in 1742 and died in Richfield Springs, New York, in 1840. He participated in several of the principal political events of the American Revolution in Boston, among them the Massacre and the Tea Party, and during the war he served as a privateersman and militiaman. A shoemaker all his life, and intermittently or concurrently a fisherman, sailor, and farmer, he remained a poor man. He never made it, not before the war in Boston, not at sea, not after the war in Wrentham and Attleborough, Massachusetts, not in Otsego County, New York. He was a nobody who briefly became a somebody in the Revolution and, for a moment near the end of his life, a hero.

Hewes was one of the "humble classes" that made the success of the Revolution possible. How typical he was we can only suggest at this point in our limited knowledge of the "humble classes." Probably he was as representative a member of the "lower trades" of the cities and as much a rank-and-file participant in the political events and the war as historians have found. The two biographies, which come close to being oral histories (and give us clues to track down Hewes in other ways), provide an unusually rich cumulative record, over a very long period of time, of his thoughts, attitudes, and values. Consequently, we can answer, with varying degrees of satisfaction, a number of questions about one man of the "humble classes." About the "lower trades": why did a boy enter a craft with such bleak prospects as shoemaking? what was the life of an apprentice? what did it mean to be a shoemaker and a poor man in Boston? About the Revolution: what moved such a rank-and-file person to action? what action did he take? may we speak of his "ideology"? does the evidence of his loss of deference permit us to speak of change in his consciousness? About the war: how did a poor man, an older man, a man with a family exercise his patriotism? what choices did he make? About the results of the Revolution: how did the war affect him? to what extent did he achieve his life goals? why did he go west? what did it mean to be an aged veteran of the revolution? What, in sum, after more than half a century had passed, was the meaning of the Revolution to someone still in the "humble classes"?

Where one ended up in life depended very much on where one started out. George was born under the sign of the Bulls Head and Horns on Water Street near the docks in the South End. His father—also named George—was a tallow chandler and erstwhile tanner. Hewes drew the connections between his class origins and his life chances as he began his narrative for Hawkes:

My father, said he, was born in Wrentham in the state of Massachusetts, about twenty-eight miles from Boston. My grandfather having made no provision for his support, and being unable to give him an education, apprenticed him at Boston to learn a mechanical trade. . . .

In my childhood, my advantages for education were very limited, much more so than children enjoy at the present time in my native state. My whole education which my opportunities permitted me to acquire, consisted only of a moderate knowledge of reading and writing; my father's circumstances being confined to such humble means as he was enabled to acquire by his mechanical employment, I was kept running of errands, and exposed of course to all the mischiefs to which children are liable in populous cities.

Hewes's family on his father's side was "no better off than what is called in New England *moderate*, and probably not as good." The

American progenitor of the line seems to have come from Wales and was in Salisbury, near Newburyport, in 1677, doing what we do not know. Solomon Hewes, George Robert's grandfather, was born in Portsmouth, New Hampshire, in 1674, became a joiner, and moved with collateral members of his family to Wrentham, originally part of Dedham, near Rhode Island. There he became a landholder; most of his brothers were farmers; two became doctors, one of whom prospered in nearby Providence. His son—our George's father—was born in 1701. On the side of his mother, Abigail Seaver, Hewes's family was a shade different. They had lived for four generations in Roxbury, a small farming town immediately south of Boston across the neck. Abigail's ancestors seem to have been farmers, but one was a minister. Her father, Shubael, was a country cordwainer who owned a house, barn, and two acres. She was born in 1711 and married in 1728.

George Robert Twelves Hewes, born August 25, 1742, was the sixth of nine children, the fourth of seven sons. Five of the nine survived childhood—his three older brothers, Samuel, Shubael, and Solomon, and a younger brother, Daniel. He was named George after his father, Robert after a paternal uncle, and the unlikely Twelves, he thought, for his mother's great uncle, "whose Christian name was Twelve, for whom she appeared to have great admiration. Why he was called by that singular name I never knew." More likely, his mother was honoring her own mother, also Abigail, whose maiden name was Twelves.

The family heritage to George, it might be argued, was more genetic than economic. He inherited a chance to live long: the men in the Seaver line were all long-lived. And he inherited his size. He was unusually short—five feet, one inch. "I have never acquired the ordinary weight or size of other men," Hewes told Hawkes, who wrote that "his whole person is of a slight and slender texture." In old age he was known as "the little old man." Anatomy is not destiny, but Hewes's short size and long

name helped shape his personality. It was a big name for a small boy to carry. He was the butt of endless teasing jibes—George Robert what?—that Thatcher turned into anecdotes the humor of which may have masked the pain Hewes may have felt.

"Moderate" as it was, Hewes had a sense of family. Wrentham, town of his grandfather and uncles, was a place he would be sent as a boy, a place of refuge in the war, and after the war his home. He would receive an inheritance three times in his life, each one a reminder of the importance or potential importance of relatives. And he was quite aware of any relative of status, like Dr. Joseph Warren, a distant kinsman on his mother's side.

His father's life in Boston had been an endless, futile struggle to succeed as a tanner. Capital was the problem. In 1729 he bought a one-third ownership in a tannery for £600 in bills of credit. Two years later, he sold half of his third to his brother Robert, who became a working partner. The two brothers turned to a rich merchant, Nathaniel Cunningham, who put up £3,500 in return for half the profits. The investment was huge: pits, a yard, workshops, hides, bark, two horses, four slaves, journeymen. For a time the tannery flourished. Then there was the disastrous falling out with Cunningham: furious fights, a raid on the yards, debtor's jail twice for George, suits and countersuits that dragged on in the courts for years. The Hewes brothers saw themselves as "very laborious" artisans who "managed their trade with good skill," only to be ruined by a wealthy, arrogant merchant. To Cunningham, they were incompetent and defaulters. Several years before George Robert was born, his father had fallen back to "butchering, tallow chandlering, hog killing, soap, boiling &c."

The family was not impoverished. George had a memory as a little boy of boarding a ship with his mother to buy a small slave girl "at the rate of two dollars a pound." And there was enough money to pay the fees for his early schooling. But beginning in 1748, when he was six, there was a series of family tragedies. In

1748 an infant brother, Joseph, died, followed later in the year by his sister Abigail, age thirteen, and brother Ebenezer, age two. In 1749 his father died suddenly of a stroke, leaving the family nothing, it would seem, his estate tangled in debt and litigation. George's mother would have joined the more than one thousand widows in Boston, most of whom were on poor relief. Sometime before 1755 she died. In 1756 Grandfather Seaver died, leaving less than £15 to be divided among George and his four surviving brothers. Thus in 1756, at the age of fourteen, when boys were customarily put out to apprenticeship, George was an orphan, the ward of his uncle Robert, as was his brother Daniel, age twelve, each with a legacy of £2 17s. 4d. Uncle Robert, though warmly recollected by Hewes, could not do much to help him: a gluemaker, he was struggling to set up his own manufactory. Nor could George's three older brothers, whom he also remembered fondly. In 1756 they were all in the "lower" trades. Samuel age twenty-six, and Solomon, twenty-two, were fishermen; Shubael, twenty-four, was a butcher.

The reason why George was put to shoemaking becomes clearer: no one in the family had the indenture fee to enable him to enter one of the more lucrative "higher" trades. Josiah Franklin, also a tallow chandler, could not make his son Benjamin a cutler because he lacked the fee. But in shoemaking the prospects were so poor that some masters would pay to get an apprentice. In addition, George was too small to enter trades that demanded brawn; he could hardly have become a ropewalk worker, a housewright, or a shipwright. Ebenezer McIntosh, the Boston shoemaker who led the annual Pope's Day festivities and the Stamp Act demonstrations, was a small man. The trade was a sort of dumping ground for poor boys who could not handle heavy work. Boston Overseers of the Poor acted on this assumption in 1770; so did recruiting officers for the American navy forty years later. The same was true in Europe. Getting into a good trade required "connections"; the family

connections were in the leather trades, through Uncle Robert, the gluemaker, or brother Shubael, the butcher. Finally, there was a family tradition. Grandfather Shubael had been a cordwainer, and on his death in 1756 there might even have been a prospect of acquiring his tools and lasts. In any case, the capital that would be needed to set up shop of one's own was relatively small. And so the boy became a shoemaker—because he had very little choice.

Josiah Franklin had known how important it was to place a boy in a trade that was to his liking. Otherwise there was the threat that Benjamin made explicit: he would run away to sea. Hawkes saw the same thrust in Hewes's life: shoemaking "was never an occupation of his choice," he "being inclined to more active pursuits." George was the wrong boy to put in a sedentary trade that was not to his liking. He was what the Bostonians called "saucy"; he was always in Dutch. The memories of his childhood and youth that Thatcher elicited were almost all of defying authority—his mother, his teachers at dame school, his schoolmaster, his aunt, his shoemaker master, a farmer, a doctor.

Hewes spoke of his mother only as a figure who inflicted punishment for disobedience. The earliest incident he remembered could have happened only to a poor family living near the waterfront. When George was about six, Abigail Hewes sent him off to the nearby shipyards with a basket to gather chips for the fire. At the water's edge George put the basket aside, straddled some floating planks to watch the fish, fell in, and sank to the bottom. He was saved only when some ship carpenters saw the basket without the boy, "found him motionless on the bottom, hooked him out with a boat hook, and rolled him on a tar barrel until signs of life were discovered." His mother nursed him back to health. Then she flogged him.

The lesson did not take, nor did others in school with Miss Tinkum, wife of the town crier. He ran away. She put him in a dark closet. He dug his way out. The next day she put him in again. This time he discovered a jar of quince marmalade and devoured it. A new dame school with "mother McLeod" followed. Then school with "our famous Master Holyoke," which Hewes remembered as "little more than a series of escapes made or attempted from the reign of the birch."

Abigail Hewes must have been desperate to control George. She sent him back after one truancy with a note requesting Holyoke to give him a good whipping. Uncle Robert took pity and sent a substitute note. Abigail threatened, "If you run away again I shall go to school with you myself." When George was about ten, she took the final step: she sent him to Wrentham to live with one of his paternal uncles. Here, George recalled, "he spent several years of his boyhood . . . in the monotonous routine of his Uncle's farm." The only incident he recounted was of defying his aunt. His five-year-old cousin hit him in the face with a stick "without any provocation." George cursed the boy out, for which his aunt whipped him, and when she refused to do the same with her son, George undertook to "chastise" him himself. "I caught my cousin at the barn" and applied the rod. The aunt locked him up but his uncle let him go, responsive to his plea for "equal justice."

Thus when George entered his apprenticeship, if he was not quite the young whig his biographers made him out to be, he was not a youth who would suffer arbitrary authority easily. His master, Downing, had an irascible side and was willing to use a cowhide. Hewes lived in Downing's attic with a fellow apprentice, John Gilbert. All the incidents Hewes recalled from this period had two motifs: petty defiance and a quest for food. There was an escapade on a Saturday night when the two apprentices made off for Gilbert's house and bought a loaf of bread, a pound of butter, and some coffee. They returned after curfew to encounter an enraged Downing, whom they foiled by setting pans and tubs for him to trip over when he came to the door. There was an

excursion to Roxbury on Training Day, the traditional apprentices' holiday in Boston, with fellow apprentices and his younger brother. Caught stealing apples, they were taken before the farmer, who was also justice of the peace and who laughed uproariously at Hewes's name and let him go. There was an incident with a doctor who inoculated Hewes and a fellow worker for smallpox and warned them to abstain from food. Sick, fearful of death, Hewes and his friend consumed a dish of venison in melted butter and a mug of flip— and lived to tell the tale.

These memories of youthful defiance and youthful hunger lingered on for seventy years: a loaf of bread and a pound of butter, a parcel of apples, a dish of venison. This shoemaker's apprentice could hardly have been well fed or treated with affection.

The proof is that Hewes tried to end his apprenticeship by the only way he saw possible: escape to the military. "After finding that my depressed condition would probably render it impracticable for me to acquire that education requisite for civil employments," he told Hawkes, "I had resolved to engage in the military service of my country, should an opportunity present." Late in the 1750s, possibly in 1760, as the fourth and last of England's great colonial wars with France ground on and his majesty's army recruiters beat their drums through Boston's streets, Hewes and Gilbert tried to enlist. Gilbert was accepted, but Hewes was not. Recruiting captains were under orders to "enlist no Roman-Catholic, nor any under five feet two inches high without their shoes." "I could not pass muster," Hewes told Hawkes, "because I was not tall enough." As Thatcher embroiders Hawkes's story, Hewes then "went to the shoe shop of several of his acquaintances and heightened his heels by several taps[;] then stuffing his stocking with paper and rags," he returned. The examining captain saw through the trick and rejected him again. Frustrated, humiliated, vowing he would never return to Downing, he took an even more desperate step: he went down to the wharf and tried to enlist on a British ship of war. "His brothers, however, soon heard of it and interfered," and, in Thatcher's words, "he was compelled to abandon that plan." Bostonians like Solomon and Samuel Hewes, who made their living on the waterfront, did not need long memories to remember the city's massive resistance to the impressment sweeps of 1747 and to know that the British navy would be, not escape, but another prison.

About this time, shoemaker Downing failed after fire swept his shop (possibly the great fire of 1760). This would have freed Hewes of his indenture, but he was not qualified to be a shoemaker until he had completed apprenticeship. As Hewes told it, he therefore apprenticed himself "for the remainder of his minority," that is, until he turned twenty-one, to Harry Rhoades, who paid him $40. In 1835 he could tell Thatcher how much time he then had left to serve, down to the month and day. Of the rest of his "time" he had no bad memories.

Apprenticeship had a lighter side. Hewes's anecdotes give tantalizing glimpses into an embryonic apprentice culture in Boston to which other sources attest—glimpses of pranks played on masters, of revelry after curfew, of Training Day, when the militia displayed its maneuvers and there was drink, food, and "frolicking" on the Common. One may speculate that George also took part in the annual Pope's Day festival, November 5, when apprentices, servants, artisans in the lower trades, and young people of all classes took over the town, parading effigies of Pope, Devil, and Pretender, exacting tribute from the better sort, and engaging in a battle royal between North End and South End Pope's Day "companies."

Hewes's stories of his youth hint at his winning a place for himself as the small schoolboy who got the better of his elders, the apprentice who defied his master, perhaps even a leader among his peers. There are also hints of the adult personality. Hewes was punished often, but if childhood punishment inured some to pain, it made Hewes reluctant to inflict pain on others. He developed a generous streak that led him to reach out to others in trouble. When Downing, a broken man, was on the verge of leaving for Nova Scotia to start anew, Hewes went down to his ship and gave him half of the $40 fee Rhoades had paid him. Downing broke into tears. The story smacks of the Good Samaritan, of the Methodist of the 1830s counting his good deeds; and yet the memory was so vivid, wrote Thatcher, that "his features light up even now with a gleam of rejoicing pride." Hewes spoke later of the "tender sympathies of my nature." He did not want to be, but he was, a fit candidate for the "gentle craft" he was about to enter.

In Boston from 1763, when he entered his majority, until 1775, when he went off to war, Hewes never made a go of it as a shoemaker. He remembered these years more fondly than he had lived them. As Hawkes took down his story, shifting from the third to the first person:

> Hewes said he cheerfully submitted to the course of life to which his destinies directed.
>
> He built him a shop and pursued the private avocation of his trade for a considerable length of time, until on the application of his brother he was induced to go with him on two fishing voyages to the banks of New Foundland, which occupied his time for two years.
>
> After the conclusion of the French war . . . he continued at Boston, except the two years absence with his brother.
>
> During that period, said Hewes, when I was at the age of twenty-six, I married the daughter of Benjamin Sumner, of Boston. At the time of our intermarriage, the age of my wife was seventeen. We lived together very happily seventy years. She died at the age of eighty-seven.
>
> At the time when British troops were first stationed at Boston, we had several children, the exact number I do not recollect. By our industry and mutual efforts we were improving our condition.

He had his own shop—this much is clear, but the rest is surmise. There were at that time in Boston about sixty to seventy shoemakers, most of whom seem to have catered to the local market. If Hewes was typical, he would have made shoes to order, "bespoke" work; this would have made him a cordwainer. And he would have repaired shoes: this would have made him a cobbler. Who were his customers? No business records survive. A shoemaker probably drew his customers from his immediate neighborhood. Located as he was near the waterfront and ropewalks, Hewes might well have had customers of the "meaner" sort. In a ward inhabited by the "middling" sort he may also have drawn on them. When the British troops occupied Boston, he did some work for them. Nothing suggests that he catered to the "carriage trade."

Was his business "improving" or "growing better"? Probably it was never very good and grew worse. From his own words we know that he took off two years on fishing voyages with his brothers. He did not mention that during this period he lived for a short time in Roxbury. His prospects were thus not good enough to keep him in Boston. His marriage is another clue to his low fortune. Sally (or Sarah) Sumner's father was a sexton so poor that his wife and daughters had to take in washing. The couple was married by the Reverend Samuel Stillman of the First Baptist Church, which suggests that this was the church that Benjamin Sumner served. Though Stillman was respected, First Baptist was not "one of the principal churches in town," as Thatcher guessed, but one of the poorest and smallest, with a congregation heavy with laboring people, sailors, and blacks. Marriage, one of the few potential sources of capital for an aspiring tradesman, as Benjamin Franklin made clear in his autobiography, did not lift Hewes up.

Hewes stayed poor. The Boston tax records of 1771, the only ones that have survived for these years, show him living as a lodger in the house of Christopher Ranks, a watchmaker, in the old North End. He was not taxed for any property. In 1773 he and his family, which now included three children, were apparently living

with his uncle Robert in the South End; at some time during these years before the war they also lived with a brother. After almost a decade on his own, Hewes could not afford his own place. In January 1774 he inadvertently summed up his condition and reputation in the course of a violent street encounter. Damned as "a rascal" and "a vagabond" who had no right to "speak to a gentlemen in the street," Hewes retorted that he was neither "and though a poor man, in a good credit in town" as his well-to-do antagonist.

Between 1768 and 1775, the shoemaker became a citizen—an active participant in the events that led to the Revolution, an angry, assertive man who won recognition as a patriot. What explains the transformation? We have enough evidence to take stock of Hewes's role in three major events of the decade: the Massacre (1770), the Tea Party (1773), and the tarring and feathering of John Malcolm (1774).

On the night of the Massacre, March 5, Hewes was in the thick of the action. What he tells us about what brought him to King Street, what brought others there, and what he did during and after this tumultuous event gives us the perspective of a man in the street. The presence of British troops in Boston beginning in the summer of 1768—four thousand soldiers in a town of fewer than sixteen thousand inhabitants—touched Hewes personally. Anecdotes about soldiers flowed from him. He had seen them march off the transports at the Long Wharf; he had seen them every day occupying civilian buildings on Griffin's Wharf near his shop. He knew how irritating it was to be challenged by British sentries after curfew (his solution was to offer a swig of rum from the bottle he carried).

More important, he was personally cheated by a soldier. Sergeant Mark Burk ordered shoes allegedly for Captain Thomas Preston, picked them up, but never paid for them. Hewes complained to Preston, who made good and suggested he bring a complaint. A military hearing ensued, at which Hewes testified. The soldier, to Hewes's horror, was sentenced to three hundred fifty lashes. He "remarked to the court that if he had thought the fellow was to be punished so severely for such an offense, bad as he was, he would have said nothing about it." And he saw others victimized by soldiers. He witnessed an incident in which a soldier sneaked up behind a woman, felled her with his fist, and "stripped her of her bonnet, cardinal muff and tippet." He followed the man to his barracks, identified him (Hewes remembered him as Private Kilroy, who would appear later at the Massacre), and got him to give up the stolen goods, but decided this time not to press charges. Hewes was also keenly aware of grievances felt by the laboring men and youths who formed the bulk of the crowd—and the principal victims—at the Massacre. From extant accounts, three causes can be pieced together.

First in time, and vividly recalled by Hewes, was the murder of eleven-year-old Christopher Seider on February 23, ten days before the Massacre. Seider was one of a large crowd of schoolboys and apprentices picketing the shop of Theophilus Lilly, a merchant violating the anti-import resolutions. Ebenezer Richardson, a paid customs informer, shot into the throng and killed Seider. Richardson would have been tarred and feathered, or worse, had not whig leaders intervened to hustle him off to jail. At Seider's funeral, only a week before the Massacre, five hundred boys marched two by two behind the coffin, followed by two thousand or more adults, "the largest [funeral] perhaps ever known in America," Thomas Hutchinson thought.

Second, Hewes emphasized the bitter fight two days before the Massacre between soldiers and workers at Gray's ropewalk down the block from Hewes's shop. Off-duty soldiers were allowed to moonlight, taking work from civilians. On Friday, March 3, when one of them asked for work at Gray's, a battle ensued between a few score soldiers and ropewalk workers joined by others in the maritime trades. The soldiers were beaten and sought revenge. Consequently, in Thatcher's words, "quite a number of soldiers, in a word, were determined to have a row on the night of the 5th."

Third, the precipitating events on the night of the Massacre, by Hewes's account, were an attempt by a barber's apprentice to collect an overdue bill from a British officer, the sentry's abuse of the boy, and the subsequent harassment of the sentry by a small band of boys that led to the calling of the guard commanded by Captain Preston. Thatcher found this hard to swallow—"a dun from a greasy barber's boy is rather an extraordinary explanation of the origin, or one of the occasions, of the massacre of the 5th of March"—but at the trial the lawyers did not. They battled over defining "boys" and over the age, size, and degree of aggressiveness of the numerous apprentices on the scene.

Hewes viewed the civilians as essentially defensive. On the evening of the Massacre he appeared early on the scene in King Street, attracted by the clamor over the apprentice. "I was soon on the ground among them," he said, as if it were only natural that he should have turned out in defense of fellow townsmen against what was assumed to be the danger of aggressive action by soldiers. He was not part of a conspiracy; neither was he there out of curiosity. He was unarmed, carrying neither club nor stave as some others did. He saw snow, ice, and "missiles" thrown at the soldiers. When the main guard rushed out in support of the sentry, Private Kilroy dealt Hewes a blow on his shoulder with his gun. Preston ordered the townspeople to disperse. Hewes believed they had a legal basis to refuse: "they were in the king's highway, and had as good a right to be there" as Preston.

The five men killed were all workingmen. Hewes claimed to know four: Samuel Gray, a ropewalk worker; Samuel Maverick, age seventeen, an apprentice to an ivory turner; Patrick Carr, an apprentice to a leather breeches worker; and James Caldwell, second mate on a ship—all but Christopher Attucks. Caldwell, "who was shot in the back was standing by the side of Hewes, and the latter caught him in his arms as he fell," helped carry him to Dr. Thomas Young in Prison Lane, then ran to Caldwell's ship captain on Cold Lane.

More than horror was burned into Hewes's memory. He remembered the political confrontation that followed the slaughter, when thousands of angry townspeople faced hundreds of British troops massed with ready rifles. "The people," Hewes recounted, "then immediately choose a committee to report to the governor the result of Captain Preston's conduct, and to demand of him satisfaction." Actually the "people" did not choose a committee "immediately." In the dark hours after the Massacre a self-appointed group of patriot leaders met with officials and forced Hutchinson to commit Preston and the soldiers to jail. Hewes was remembering the town meeting the next day, so huge that it had to adjourn from Fanueil Hall, the traditional meeting place that held only twelve hundred, to Old South Church, which had room for five to six thousand. This meeting approved a committee to wait on officials and then adjourned, but met again the same day, received and voted down an offer to remove one regiment, then accepted another to remove two. This was one of the meetings at which property bars were let down.

What Hewes did not recount, but what he had promptly put down in a deposition the next day, was how militant he was after the Massacre. At 1:00 A.M., like many other enraged Bostonians, he went home to arm himself. On his way back to the Town House with a cane he had a defiant exchange with Sergeant Chambers of the 29th Regiment and eight or nine soldiers, "all with very large clubs or cutlasses." A soldier, Dobson, "ask'd him how he far'd; he told him very badly to see his townsmen shot in such a manner, and asked him if he did not think it was a dreadful thing." Dobson swore "it was a fine thing" and "you shall see more of it." Chambers "seized and forced" the cane from Hewes, "saying I had no right to carry it. I told him I had as good a right to carry a cane as they had to carry clubs."

The Massacre had stirred Hewes to political action. He was one of ninety-nine Bostonians who gave depositions for the prosecution that were published by the town in a pamphlet. Undoubtedly, he marched in the great funeral procession for the victims that brought the city to a standstill. He attended the tempestuous trial of Ebenezer Richardson, Seider's slayer, which was linked politically with the Massacre. ("He remembers to this moment even the precise words of the Judge's sentence," wrote Thatcher.) He seems to have attended the trial of the soldiers or Preston or both.

It was in this context that he remembered something for which there is no corroborating evidence, namely, testifying at Preston's trial on a crucial point. He told Hawkes:

When Preston, their captain, was tried, I was called as one of the witnesses, on the part of the government, and testified, that I believed it was the same man, Captain Preston, that ordered his soldiers to make ready, who also ordered them to fire. Mr. John Adams, former president of the United States, was advocate for the prisoners, and denied the fact, that Captain Preston gave orders to his men to fire; and on his cross examination of me asked whether my position was such, that I could see the captain's lips in motion when the order to fire was given; to which I answered, that I could not.

Perhaps so: Hewes's account is particular and precise, and there are many lacunae in the record of the trial (we have no verbatim transcript) that modern editors have assiduously assembled. Perhaps not: Hewes may have "remembered" his brother Shubael on the stand at the trial of the soldiers (although Shubael was a defense witness) or his uncle Robert testifying at Richardson's trial. Or he may have given pretrial testimony but was not called to the stand.

In one sense, it does not matter. What he was remembering was that he had become involved. He turned out because of a sense of kinship with "his townsmen" in danger; he stood his ground in defense of his "rights"; he was among the "people" who delegated a committee to act on their behalf; he took part in the legal process by giving a deposition, by attending the trials, and as he remembered it, by testifying. In sum, he had become a citizen, a political man.

Four years later, at the Tea Party on the night of December 16, 1773, the citizen "volunteered" and became the kind of leader for whom most historians have never found a place. The Tea Party, unlike the Massacre, was organized by the radical whig leaders of Boston. They mapped the strategy, organized the public meetings, appointed the companies to guard the tea ships at Griffin's Wharf (among them Daniel Hewes, George's brother), and planned the official boarding parties. As in 1770, they converted the town meetings into meetings of "the whole body of the people," one of which Hutchinson found "consisted principally of the Lower ranks of the People & even Journeymen. Tradesmen were brought in to increase the number & the Rabble were not excluded yet there were divers Gentlemen of Good Fortunes among them."

The boarding parties showed this same combination of "ranks." Hawkes wrote:

> On my inquiring of Hewes if he knew who first proposed the project of destroying the tea, to prevent its being landed, he replied that he did not; neither did he know who or what number were to volunteer their services for that purpose. But from the significant allusion of some persons in whom I had confidence, together with the knowledge I had of the spirit of those times, I had no doubt but that a sufficient number of associates would accompany me in that enterprise.

The recollection of Joshua Wyeth, a journeyman blacksmith, verified Hewes's story in explicit detail: "It was proposed that young men, not much known in town and not liable to be easily recognized should lead in the business." Wyeth believed that "most of the persons selected for the occasion were apprentices and journeyman, as was the case with myself, living with tory masters." Wyeth "had but a few hours warning of what was intended to be done." Those in the officially designated parties, about thirty men better known, appeared in well-prepared Indian disguises. As nobodies, the volunteers—anywhere from fifty to one hundred men—could get away with hastily improvised disguises. Hewes said he got himself up as an Indian and daubed his "face and hands with coal dust in the shop of blacksmith." In the streets "I fell in with many who were dressed, equipped and painted as I was, and who fell in with me and marched in order to the place of our destination."

At Griffin's Wharf the volunteers were orderly, self-disciplined, and ready to accept leadership.

> When we arrived at the wharf, there were three of our number who assumed an authority to direct our operations, to which we readily submitted. They divided us into three parties, for the purpose of boarding the three ships which contained the tea at the same time. The name of him who commanded the division to which I was assigned was Leonard Pitt [Lendell Pitts]. The names of the other commanders I never knew. We were immediately ordered by the respective commanders to board all the ships at the same time, which we promptly obeyed.

But for Hewes there was something new: he was singled out of the rank and file and made an officer in the field.

> The commander of the division to which I belonged, as soon as we were on board the ship, appointed me boatswain, and ordered me to go to the captain and demand of him the keys to the hatches and a dozen candles. I made the demand accordingly, and the captain promptly replied, and delivered the articles; but requested me at the same time to do no damage to the ship or rigging. We then were ordered by our commander to open the hatches, and take out all the chests of tea and throw them overboard, and we immediately proceeded to execute his orders; first cutting and splitting the chests with our tomahawks, so

as thoroughly to expose them to the effects of the water. In about three hours from the time we went on board, we had thus broken and thrown overboard every tea chest to be found in the ship; while those in the other ships were disposing of the tea in the same way, at the same time. We were surrounded by British armed ships, but no attempt was made to resist us. We then quietly retired to our several places of residence, without having any conversation with each other, or taking any measure to discover who were our associates.

As the Tea Party ended, Hewes was stirred to further action on his own initiative, just as he had been in the hours after the Massacre. While the crews were throwing the tea overboard, a few other men tried to smuggle off some of the tea scattered on the decks. "One Captain O'Connor whom I well knew," said Hewes, "came on board for that purpose, and when he supposed he was not noticed, filled his pockets, and also the lining of his coat. But I had detected him, and gave information to the captain of what he was doing. We were ordered to take him into custody, and just as he was stepping from the vessel, I seized him by the skirt of his coat, and in attempting to pull him back, I tore it off." They scuffled. O'Connor recognized him and "threatened to 'complain to the Governor.' 'You had better make your will first,' quoth Hewes, doubling his fist expressively," and O'Connor escaped, running the gauntlet of the crowd on the wharf. "The next day we nailed the skirt of his coat, which I had pulled off, to the whipping post in Charlestown, the place of his residence, with a label upon it," to shame O'Connor by "popular indignation."

A month later, at the third event for which we have full evidence, Hewes won public recognition for an act of courage that almost cost his life and precipitated the most publicized tarring and feathering of the Revolution. The incident that set it off would have been trivial at any other time. On Tuesday, January 25, 1774, at about two in the afternoon, the shoemaker was making his way back to his shop after his dinner. According to the very full account in the *Massachusetts Gazette*,

> Mr. George-Robert-Twelves-Hewes was coming along Fore-Street, near Captain Ridgway's, and found the redoubted John Malcolm, standing over a small boy, who was pushing a little sled before him, cursing, damning, threatening and shaking a very large cane with a very heavy ferril on it over his head. The boy at that time was perfectly quiet, notwithstanding which Malcolm continued his threats of striking him, which Mr. Hewes conceiving if he struck him with that weapon he must have killed him out-right, came up to him, and said to him, Mr. Malcolm I hope you are not going to strike this boy with that stick.

Malcolm had already acquired an odious reputation with patriots of the lower sort. A Bostonian, he had been a sea captain, an army officer, and recently an employee of the customs service. He was so strong a supporter of royal authority that he had traveled to North Carolina to fight the Regulators and boasted of having a horse shot out from under him. He had a fiery temper. As a customs informer he was known to have turned in a vessel to punish sailors for petty smuggling, a custom of the sea. In November 1773, near Portsmouth, New Hampshire, a crowd of thirty sailors had "genteely tarr'd and feather'd" him, as the *Boston Gazette* put it: they did the job over his clothes. Back in Boston he made "frequent complaints" to Hutchinson of "being hooted at in the streets" for this by "tradesmen"; and the lieutenant governor cautioned him, "being a passionate man," not to reply in kind.

The exchange between Malcolm and Hewes resonated with class as well as political differences:

> Malcolm returned, you are an impertinent rascal, it is none of your business. Mr. Hewes then asked him, what had the child done to him. Malcolm damned him and asked him if he was going to take his part? Mr. Hewes answered no further than this, that he thought it was a shame for him to strike the child with such a club that, if he intended to strike him. Malcolm on that damned

Mr. Hewes, called him a vagabond, and said he would let him know he should not speak to a gentleman in the street. Mr. Hewes returned to that, he was neither a rascal nor vagabond, and though a poor man was in as good credit in town as he was. Malcolm called him a liar, and said he was not, nor ever would be. Mr. Hewes retorted, be that as it will, I never was tarred nor feathered any how. On this Malcolm struck him, and wounded him deeply on the forehead, so that Mr. Hewes for some time lost his senses. Capt. Godfrey, then present, interposed, and after some altercation, Malcolm went home.

Hewes was rushed to Joseph Warren, the patriot doctor, his distant relative. Malcolm's cane had almost penetrated his skull. Thatcher found "the indentation as plainly perceptible as it was sixty years ago." So did Hawkes. Warren dressed the wound, and Hewes was able to make his way to a magistrate to swear out a warrant for Malcolm's arrest "which he carried to a constable named Justice Hale." Malcolm, meanwhile, had retreated to his house, where he responded in white heat to taunts about the half-way tarring and feathering in Portsmouth with "damn you let me see the man that dare do it better."

In the evening a crowd took Malcolm from his house and dragged him on a sled into King Street "amidst the huzzas of thousands." At this point "several gentlemen endeavored to divert the populace from their intention." The ensuing dialogue laid bare the clash of conceptions of justice between the sailors and laboring people heading the action and Sons of Liberty leaders. The "gentlemen" argued that Malcolm was "open to the laws of the land which would undoubtedly award a reasonable satisfaction to the parties he had abused," that is, the child and Hewes. The answer was political. Malcolm "had been an old impudent and mischievious [sic] offender—he had joined in the murders at North Carolina—he had seized vessels on account of sailors having a bottle or two of gin on board—he had in other words behaved in the most capricious, insulting and daringly abusive manner." He could not be trusted to justice. "When they were told the law would have its course with him, they asked what course had the law taken with Preston or his soldiers, with Capt. Wilson or Richardson? And for their parts they had seen so much partiality to the soldiers and customhouse officers by the present Judges, that while things remained as they were, they would, on all such occasions, take satisfaction their own way, and let them take it off."

The references were to Captain Preston who had been tried and found innocent of the Massacre, the soldiers who had been let off with token punishment, Captain John Wilson, who had been indicted for inciting slaves to murder their masters but never tried, and Ebenezer Richardson, who had been tried and found guilty of killing Seider, sentenced, and then pardoned by the crown.

The crowd won and proceeded to a ritualized tarring and feathering, the purpose of which was to punish Malcolm, force a recantation, and ostracize him.

> With these and such like arguments, together with a gentle crouding of persons not of their way of thinking out of the ring they proceeded to elevate Mr. Malcolm from his sled into a cart, and stripping him to buff and breeches, gave him a modern jacket [a coat of tar and feathers] and hied him away to liberty-tree, where they proposed to him to renounce his present commission, and swear that he would never hold another inconsistent with the liberties of his country; but this he obstinately refusing, they then carried him to the gallows, passed a rope round his neck, and threw the other end over the beam as if they intended to hang him: But this manoeuvre he set at defiance. They then basted him for some time with a rope's end, and threatened to cut his ears off, and on this he complied, and then they brought him home.

Hewes had precipitated an electrifying event. It was part of the upsurge of spontaneous action in the wake of the Tea Party that prompted the whig leaders to promote a "Committee for Tarring and Feathering" as an instrument of crowd control. The

"Committee" made its appearance in broadsides signed by "Captain Joyce, Jun.," a sobriquet meant to invoke the bold cornet who had captured King Charles in 1647. The event was reported in the English newspapers, popularized in three or four satirical prints, and dramatized still further when Malcolm went to England, where he campaigned for a pension and ran for Parliament (without success) against John Wilkes, the leading champion of America. The event confirmed the British ministry in its punitive effort to bring rebellious Boston to heel.

The denouement of the affair was an incident several weeks later. "Malcolm recovered from his wounds and went about as usual. 'How do you do, Mr. Malcolm?' said Hewes, very civilly, the next time he met him. 'Your humble servant, Mr. George Robert Twelves Hewes,' quoth he,—touching his hat genteely as he passed by. 'Thank ye,' thought Hewes, 'and I am glad you have learned *better manners at last.'*" Hewes's mood was one of triumph. Malcolm had been taught a lesson. The issue was respect for Hewes, a patriot, a poor man, an honest citizen, a decent man standing up for a child against an unspeakably arrogant "gentleman" who was an enemy of his country.

Hewes's role in these three events fits few of the categories that historians have applied to the participation of ordinary men in the Revolution. He was not a member of any organized committee, caucus, or club. He did not attend the expensive public dinners of the Sons of Liberty. He was capable of acting on his own volition without being summoned by any leaders (as in the Massacre). He could volunteer and assume leadership (as in the Tea Party). He was at home on the streets in crowds but he could also reject a crowd (as in the tarring and feathering of Malcolm). He was at home in the other places where ordinary Bostonians turned out to express their convictions: at funeral processions, at meetings of the "whole body of people," in courtrooms at public trials. He recoiled from violence to persons if not to property. The man who could remember the whippings of his own boyhood did not want to be the source of pain to others, whether Sergeant Burk, who tried to cheat him over a pair of shoes, or John Malcolm, who almost killed him. It is in keeping with his character that he should have come to the aid of a little boy facing a beating.

Hewes was moved to act by personal experiences that he shared with large numbers of other plebeian Bostonians. He seems to have been politicized, not by the Stamp Act, but by the coming of the troops after 1768, and then by things that happened to him, that he saw, or that happened to people he knew. Once aroused, he took action with others of his own rank and condition—the laboring classes who formed the bulk of the actors at the Massacre, the Tea Party, and the Malcolm affair—and with other members of his family: his uncle Robert, "known for a staunch Liberty Boy," and his brother Daniel, a guard at the tea ship. Shubael, alone among his brothers, became a tory. These shared experiences were interpreted and focused more likely by the spoken than the written word and as much by his peers at taverns and crowd actions as by leaders in huge public meetings.

But what ideas did Hewes articulate? He spoke of what he did but very little of what he thought. In the brief statement he offered Hawkes about why he went off to war in 1776, he expressed a commitment to general principles as they had been brought home to him by his experiences. "I was continually reflecting upon the unwarrantable sufferings inflicted on the citizens of Boston by the usurpation and tyranny of Great Britain, and my mind was excited with an unextinguishable desire to aid in chastising them." When Hawkes expressed a doubt "as to the correctness of his conduct in absenting himself from his family," Hewes "emphatically reiterated" the same phrases, adding to a "desire to aid in chastising them" the phrase "and securing our independence." This was clearly not an afterthought; it probably reflected the way many others moved toward the goal of Independence, not as a matter of original intent, but as a step made necessary when all other resorts failed. Ideology thus did not set George Hewes apart from Samuel Adams or John Hancock. The difference lies in what the Revolution did to him as a person. His experiences transformed him, giving him a sense of citizenship and personal worth. Adams and Hancock began with both; Hewes had to arrive there, and in arriving he cast off the constraints of deference.

GLOSSARY

John Hancock (1737–1793): Wealthy Boston merchant and Revolutionary leader, President of the Continental Congress (1775–1777) and first signer of the Declaration of Independence.

Dr. Joseph Warren (1741–1775): Physician and political leader in Revolutionary Boston, killed in the Battle of Bunker Hill (June 17, 1775).

Training Day: A day set aside in Massachusetts for compulsory military training.

Anti-Importation resolutions: A voluntary agreement of American merchants in the Continental Association not to trade with Britain.

Tea Party: Popular protest on December 16, 1773, directed against the British tea tax retained after the repeal of the Townshend Acts. Protesters disguised as Native Americans boarded three tea ships and threw the tea into Boston harbor.

IMPLICATIONS

Ordinary people like Hewes formed the backbone of the revolutionary movement in every American colony. The risks undertaken by non-elite men and women and the sacrifices they endured during eight long years of war brought them to expect and demand a different social and political world following the Revolution. In what ways do you think Hewes' wartime experiences changed his outlook about politics and the role that ordinary people should play in the post-Revolutionary republic?

Past Traces

The American Revolution disrupted the lives of most Americans, whether they were patriots, royalists, or neutral. Nowhere was this more true than among those living in areas where the British and American armies confronted each other. As the contending armies maneuvered for position prior to battle, no one was spared the depredations of war. In this document, an elder New Jersey farmer recounts the sufferings and losses experienced by local farmers during the Battle of Princeton in December 1776. The British Regulars, he recounts, showed little concern for noncombatants in the region and followed a policy of destruction, expropriation, and intimidation among the rural populace. In reading his account, there is little wonder that British military operations often served to cement local allegiance to the patriot cause.

A Brief Narrative of the Ravages of the British and Hessians at Princeton (1777)

I have Often Read and heard of the horror of the war but was never near it Until I was in the Eighty fifth Year of my age and I was born the 25th of September 1691 Old Stile. The regular army left Brunswick on the 7th of December 1776. The Remainder of the our men left Princetown and Marcht to Trenton (for the most of them had gone on before) and Were followed by Gen How with his army in the afternoon of the same day Within a Short time after Passing Stony Brook, our men delaying their Pursuit by Pulling up Stoney Brook Bridge. But they finding the ford past Over one of their light horsemen was shot on his horse from over the brook, and the man who shot him being on rising Ground beyond him, escaped . . . [half line].

The next Morning, having crossed the Delaware in the night, when the Regulars came to the River our men saw them and fired at the Regulars Which we heard at Princetown the Same morning, Which Prevented their crossing the River (and it is said) Killed and Wounded Several of their men.

Most of the Inhabitants of Prince Town a Day or two before [the battle] left their Dwelling Houses and went where they Could go with their Family to Escape From the Regular Army and left a Great Part of their goods behind them in their Houses for want of Carriages to take them away, Great part of Which fell into the regulars hands, and They not only Burnt up all the fire wood that the Inhabitants had Provided for Winter, but Stript Shops, out Houses and Some Dwelling houses of the boards that Covered them, and all the loose boards and Timber That the Joiners and Carpenters had in Store to work up, they Burnt with all their Fences and Garden Inclosures with in the Town & After sent their Carriages and Drew away the Farmers Fences adjoining within a mile, and laid all in Common. They also cut down Apple trees and other fruit bearing trees and burnt them, And either by Accident or Wilfully burnt a Large House lately finisht belonging to Jonathan Seargant Esq in Prince town.

And at new New Market about two short miles from thence they burnt the best Gristmill in these Parts, with a Quantity of Wheat and flower in it, and with it a Fulling mill with a large Quaintity of Cloth in it. The fuller told those Soldiers that set it on fire that he might be Accountable to the owners of the Cloth and Intreated them to let him take it out, Which they refused to do and burnt all together. They also Burnt the grist mill and a Framed dwelling House that had Six rooms in it and which Belonged to Major William Scudder and his fulling mill they burnd. These are said to be Burnt by the Regular army who took from the Neighbouring Farmhouse not only the wood but also Straw, Part of it the soldiers slept on and used in various ways to defend them from the cold and the rest they took and burnt and the wheat lost These are some of the ruins made by fire in and near Princetown contrary to that Justice which is due to all men. It is said that at a house a little out of the Western end of the Town where were a number of Regulars, for Gen[1] Sterling's Brigade belonged to the British, part of them one very cold night before the battle stripped both Wheat fields and upland Meadows setting fire not only to fire-wood and Carriages but to all sorts of

timber and specially fences, So that if they were Refenced this spring to guard their foder and feed, that that they will cost them (?). . . . [half line]. . . . and much more than this in labor and time. . . . [one line]. . . .

I am informed that they went to tanners and robbed them both of their Tanned, as well as their untanned Leather taken from their Vats. What use the latter may be to them I Know not, Unless it be to make leather Scarce in the Country and impoverish the owners. I am Also Inform'd That they have taken great Quantitys of Unbroken Flax Whether Rotted or not, To use in makeing Fortifycations and that from several they have taken all they had.

On the same day the 8th of December there followed the Regular Army a Parcel of Hessians and took away four Horses from the People to the westard of the town, One of them was said to be valued at a 100 pound, and commited Several other Outrages the same day In pulling of mens hats from their heads, Though the Regular Officers had given them Protections as they went before, In these Words or near it, Viz. Let no Man Presume to Injure A; B. In his Person or Property. Yet these men had no Regard to it But Directly to the Contrary Injured the Protected Men both in their Persons and Propertys, by Insulting their Persons and by Robing them of their Propertys. Two of these men came to David Oldens (where I then was) Mounted on Poor horses, and in an Insolent manner Demanded his Horses: But as it hapened he had sent them away, before the Regular Army came with all his Household goods and provisions Except what was absolutely Necessary for present use, and many of his Neighbours In and about Princetown had done the like and by that means Saved a good part of their Property. This Method was the very best (if not all) the Safe Protections that could be obtained so much better it is for any Man to be Protected by himself or his friends then to trust his Enemys, Yet this Method did not allways avail as I design to to show hereafter.

There went four of these Hessians to a Gentleman's House (who is called a Quaker) And after they had treated him and his Family in an Insolent Manner a Stout fellow among them laid hold of his Hat on his head and puled it of And he (though but a Smal man and between Fifty and Sixty Years of age) laid hold of their Champion and Struck up his heels and threw him on the Ground and clapt his foot on his Sword and Prevented his drawing it, And took his Hat again from him Upon that the three Other Paltroons Drew their Swords, and he was oblidged to Yield up a very good Hat Though he had a Protection several days before, which was of so little Effect that Afterwards the Regulars Robed him of a fine mare, and broke the door of his Stable to get her out, They also Robed his four Store Hogs being all he had before his face, And (as it is said) Three of their Generals were Present Cornwallice, Grant, & Leshly looking on to see how the Regular Soldiers ran After the Hogs about the Pen to Catch them. This is one Instance among many to show the Power of their Protections And Wether they are given to Protect, Or to Allure People to depend on them that they may be Plundered the Easier I shal leave to Others to Determin.

The Regulars and Hessians together Robed and Plundered two wealthy Farmers (that were brothers) of the Greatest part of their moveable Estates About four or five miles from Princetown, and not only took away their Cretures but robed their Houses and ript open their Beds and turned out the feathers and took away the Ticken and left the owners but very little to cover them, or even to live on.

They had yet some other ways to Plunder and Distress the People besides these two that I have Already Mentioned of fire and sword. They go out late in the night and Steal and Kill Sheep and cattle Even Milch Cows and skin them, leave their skins and hides and take away the meat. Another method is this their Officers Bargains with the Inhabitants for forage and other Necessarys and upon the Delivery gives the owners Receipts of the sorts and Quantitys with the Prices, but pays no money thus many Farmers are served. Others are ser'vd in a different manner the Regular Officers with their Soldiers Are by Orders boarded out at the Farmers Houses, and they take their Horses with them and take the Farmers Indian corn, Oats, and the very best of his fodder to feed them on.

At a Gentleman Farmers house the next to that where I now live There was with Officers and all one hundred and Seventy of those Genteel Unwelcome Guests. His best Rooms and beds in his House were taken up by the Officers who was fed upon the best Diet that the House afforded. In the mean time The Soldiers took and wasted what they Pleasd of his stalk tops and Oats in the sheif in Makeing sheds to keep them from the Cold when they Stood on Gaurd, besides what their Horses Devoured, And at their Departure he

Desired the Officers to give him Receipts for what they had and damage done Which they Refused and only paid him twenty shillings for fifty Pounds Damage as he Computed it.

Another officer went to another Farmers House And Imperiously Demanded two of the first Rooms in his house each with a good bed in it for him to lodge in and another to Receive in which he accordly took and the owner with his family was Oblidged to live in his Kitchen, While their horses were Eating and Destroying the very best of his Provender and hay for Which the owner never was paid a farthing.

To give a Particular Account of Every Robery and outrage comited by the Hessians and Regulars In and within five miles of Princetown (which is the Extent of these Observations of villanys done) would fill a Vollum therefore I have only Mentioned a few particulars out of a Multitude.

8

A "Most Undisciplined, Profligate Crew": Protest and Defiance in the Continental Ranks, 1776–1783

James Kirby Martin

During the first year of the Revolutionary War, the patriot cause enjoyed widespread enthusiasm and support. Expecting a short war with relatively little loss of life and damage to property, American men of all ranks joined local militia units in 1775–1776 to defend their homes and families from British "corruption" and from the red-coated army that had been sent to put down the colonial "rebellion." But as it became clear that this would be a long and costly struggle, men of middling and upper rank began to purchase substitutes or pay nominal fines for nonservice and withdrew to private life. After 1777, the bulk of military service fell to the lower ranks of American society—to poor farmers, laborers, indentured servants, slaves, and free men of color.

In this essay, James Kirby Martin recounts the struggles of these "dispensable" men as they battled not only the British army and epidemic disease but also a lack of support from the Continental Congress and the populace. Martin suggests that these men—poorly equipped and ill-fed, their pay always months in arrears—persevered less from patriotic commitment than from the Congress's promises of freedom to bondsmen and free western land to those who enlisted for the duration of the war. More than any other consideration, the prospects of escaping from the bottom of eighteenth-century society and of achieving freedom and a modest foothold on the social ladder kept Washington's army in the field during the long years of the war.

"A 'Most Undisciplined, Profligate Crew': Protest and Defiance in the Continental Ranks, 1776–1783" from *Arms and Independence: The Military Character of the American Revolution*, eds. Ronald Hoffman and Peter J. Albert (Charlottesville: Virginia, 1984), pp. 119–140. Reprinted by permission of the University Press of Virginia.

Martin's account attempts to sort out the motivations and political consciousness of ordinary people. In the heroic version of the American Revolution, men were motivated by "the Spirit of '76"—a love of liberty and a hatred of arbitrary authority. In this more sober account, ordinary people looked to their own interests and chances for advancement. In reading this essay, keep in mind the possibility that both considerations played a role in popular allegiance to the revolutionary cause.

....

A sequence of events inconceivable to Americans raised on patriotic myths about the Revolution occurred in New Jersey during the spring of 1779. For months the officers of the Jersey brigade had been complaining loudly about everything from lack of decent food and clothing to pay arrearages and late payments in rapidly depreciating currency. They had petitioned their assembly earlier, but nothing had happened. They petitioned again in mid-April 1779, acting on the belief that the legislature should "be informed that our pay is now only *minimal*, not *real*, that four months' pay of a private will not procure his wretched wife and children a single bushel of wheat." Using "the most plain and unambiguous terms," they stressed that "unless a speedy and ample remedy be provided, the total dissolution of your troops is inevitable." The Jersey assembly responded to this plea in its usual fashion—it forwarded the petition to the Continental Congress without comment. After all, the officers, although from New Jersey, were a part of the Continental military establishment.

The assembly's behavior only further angered the officers, and some of them decided to demonstrate their resolve. On May 6 the brigade received orders to join John Sullivan's expedition against the Six Nations. That same day, officers in the First Regiment sent forth yet another petition. They again admonished the assembly about pay and supply issues. While they stated that they would prepare the regiment for the upcoming campaign, they themselves would resign as a group unless the legislators addressed their demands. Complaints had now turned into something more than gentlemanly protest. Protest was on the verge of becoming nothing less than open

defiance of civil authority, and the Jersey officers were deadly serious. They had resorted to their threatened resignations to insure that the assembly would give serious attention to their demands—for a change.

When George Washington learned about the situation, he was appalled. "Nothing, which has happened in the course of the war, . . . has given me so much pain," the commander in chief stated anxiously. It upset him that the officers seemingly had lost sight of the "principles" that governed the cause. What would happen, he asked rhetorically, "if their example should be followed and become general?" The result would be the "ruin" and "disgrace" of the rebel cause, all because these officers had *"reasoned wrong about the means of obtaining a good end."*

So developed a little known but highly revealing confrontation. Washington told Congress that he would have acted very aggressively toward the recalcitrant officers, except that "the causes of discontent are too great and too general and the ties that bind the officers to the service too feeble" to force the issue. What he did promise was that he would not countenance any aid that came "in [such] a manner extorted." On the other hand, the officers had been asking the assembly for relief since January 1778, but to no avail. They, too, were not about to be moved.

The New Jersey legislature was the political institution with the ability to break the deadlock. Some of the legislators preferred disbanding the brigade. The majority argued that other officers and common soldiers might follow the First Regiment's lead and warned that the war effort could hardly succeed without a Continental military establishment. The moment was now ripe for compromise. The assemblymen agreed to provide the officers with whatever immediate relief could be mustered in return for the latter calling back their petitions. That way civil authorities would not be succumbing to intimidation by representatives of the military establishment, and the principle of subordination of military to civil authority would remain inviolate. The assembly thus provided an immediate payment of £200 to each officer and $40 to each soldier. Accepting the compromise settlement as better than nothing, the brigade moved out of its Jersey encampment on May 11 and marched toward Sullivan's bivouac at Easton, Pennsylvania. Seemingly, all now had returned to normal.

The confrontation between the New Jersey officers and the state assembly serves to illuminate some key points about protest and defiance in the Continental ranks during the years 1776–83. Most important here, it underscores the mounting anger felt by Washington's regulars as a result of their perceived (and no doubt very real) lack of material and psychological support from the society that had spawned the Continental army. It is common knowledge that Washington's regulars suffered from serious supply and pay shortages throughout the war. Increasingly, historians are coming to realize that officers and common soldiers alike received very little moral support from the general populace. As yet, however, scholars have not taken a systematic look at one product of this paradigm of neglect, specifically, protest and defiance. The purpose of this essay is to present preliminary findings that will facilitate that task.

Given that there was a noticeable relationship between lack of material and psychological support from the civilian sector and mounting protest and defiance in the ranks, it is also important to make clear that patterns of protest were very complex. A second purpose of this essay is to outline those basic patterns and to indicate why protest and defiance did not result in serious internal upheaval between army and society in the midst of the War for American Independence. To begin this assessment, we must bring Washington's Continentals to the center of the historical arena.

During the past twenty years, historians have learned that there were at least two Continental armies. The army of 1775–76 might be characterized as a republican constabulary, consisting of citizens who had respectable amounts of property and who were defending hearth and home. They came out for what they believed would be a rather short contest in which their assumed virtue and moral commitment would easily carry the day over seasoned British regulars not necessarily wedded to anything of greater concern than filling their own pocketbooks as mercenaries.

The first army had a militialike appearance. Even though phrases of commitment were high sounding, there was not much discipline or rigorous training. These early soldiers had responded to appeals from leaders who warned about "our wives and children, with everything that is dear to us, [being] subjected to the merciless rage of uncontrolled despotism." They were convinced that they were "engaged . . . in the cause of virtue, of liberty, of *God*." Unfortunately, the crushing blows endured in the massive British offensive of 1776 against New York undercut such high-sounding phrases about self-sacrifice. The message at the end of 1775 had been "Persevere, ye guardians of liberty." They did not.

The second Continental establishment took form out of the remains of the first. Even before Washington executed his magnificent turnabout at Trenton and Princeton, he had called for a "respectable army," one built on long-term enlistments, thorough training, and high standards of discipline. The army's command, as well as many delegates in Congress, now wanted soldiers who could stand up against the enemy with more than notions of exalted virtue and moral superiority to upgird them. They called for able-bodied men who could and would endure for the long-term fight in a contest that all leaders now knew could not be sustained by feelings of moral superiority and righteousness alone.

To assist in overcoming manpower shortages, Congress and the states enhanced financial promises made to potential enlistees. Besides guarantees about decent food and clothing, recruiters handed out bounty moneys and promises of free land at war's end (normally only for long-term service). Despite these financial incentives, there was no great rush to the Continental banner. For the remainder of the war, the army's command, Congress, and the states struggled to maintain minimal numbers of Continental soldiers in the ranks.

In fact, all began to search diligently for new recruits. Instead of relying on propertied freeholders and tradesmen of the ideal citizen-soldier type, they broadened the definition of what constituted an "able-bodied and effective" recruit. For example, New Jersey in early 1777 started granting exemptions to all those who hired substitutes for long-term Continental service—and to masters who would enroll indentured servants and slaves. The following year Maryland permitted the virtual impressment of vagrants for nine months of regular service. Massachusetts set another kind of precedent in 1777 by declaring blacks (both slave and free) eligible for the state draft. Shortly thereafter, Rhode Islanders set about the business of raising two black battalions. Ultimately, Maryland and Virginia permitted slaves to substitute for whites. The lower South, however, refused to do so, even in the face of a successful British invasion later in the war.

The vast majority of Continentals who fought with Washington after 1776 were representative of the very poorest and most repressed persons in Revolutionary society. A number of recent studies have verified that a large proportion of the Continentals in the second establishment represented ne'er-do-wells, drifters, unemployed laborers, captured British soldiers and Hessians, indentured servants, and slaves. Some of these new regulars were in such desperate economic straits that states had to pass laws prohibiting creditors from pulling them from the ranks and having them thrown in jail for petty debts. (Obviously, this was not a problem with the unfree.)

The most important point to be derived from this dramatic shift in the social composition of the Continental army is that few of these new common soldiers had enjoyed anything close to economic prosperity or full political (or legal) liberty before the war. As a group, they had something to gain from service. If they could survive the rigors of camp life, the killing diseases that so often ravaged the armies of their times, and the carnage of skirmishes and full-scale battles, they could look forward to a better life for themselves at the end of the war. Not only were they to have decent food and clothing and regular pay until the British had been irrevocably beaten, they had also been promised free land (and personal freedom in the cases of indentured servants, black slaves, and criminals). Recruiters thus conveyed a message of personal upward mobility through service. In exchange for personal sacrifice in the short run, there was the prospect of something far better in the long run, paralleling and epitomizing the collective rebel quest for a freer political life in the New World.

To debate whether these new Continentals were motivated to enlist because of crass materialism or benevolent patriotism is to sidetrack the issue. A combination of factors was no doubt at work in the mind of each recruit or conscript. Far more important, especially if we are to comprehend the ramifications of protest and defiance among soldiers and officers, we must understand that respectably established citizens after 1775 and 1776 preferred to let others perform the dirty work of regular, long-term service on their behalf, essentially on a contractual basis. Their legislators gave bounties and *promised* many other incentives. Increasingly, as the war lengthened, the civilian population and its leaders did a less effective job in keeping their part of the agreement. One significant outcome of this obvious civilian ingratitude, if not utter disregard for contractual promises, was protest and defiance coming from Washington's beleaguered soldiers and officers.

That relations between Washington's post-1776 army and Revolutionary society deteriorated dramatically hardly comes as a surprise to those historians who have investigated surviving records. Widespread anger among the rank and file became most demonstrable in 1779 and 1780, at the very nadir of the war effort. Pvt. Joseph Plumb Martin captured the feelings of his comrades when he reflected back on support for the army in 1780. He wrote: "We therefore still kept upon our parade in groups, venting our spleen at our country and government, then at our officers, and then at ourselves for our imbecility in staying there and starving in detail for an ungrateful people who did not care what became of us, so they could enjoy themselves while we were keeping a cruel enemy from them." Gen. John Paterson, who spoke out in March 1780, summarized feelings among many officers when he said, "It really gives me great pain to think of our public affairs; where is the public spirit of the year 1775? Where are those flaming *patriots* who were ready to sacrifice their lives, their fortunes, their all, for the public?" Such thoughts were not dissimilar from those of "A Jersey Soldier" who poured his sentiments into an editorial during May 1779 in support of those regimental officers who were trying to exact some form of financial justice from their state legislature. The army, he pointed out, had put up with "a load . . . grown almost intolerable." "It must be truly mortifying to the virtuous soldier to observe many, at this day, displaying their cash, and sauntering in idleness and luxury," he went on, including "the gentry . . . [who] are among the foremost to despise our poverty and laugh at our distress." He certainly approved the actions of his comrades because he resented "the cruel and ungrateful disposition of the people in general, in withholding from the army even the praise

and glory justly due to their merit and services," just as he resented society's failure to live up to its contract with the soldiers. These statements, which are only a representative sampling, indicate that the army had come to believe that Revolutionary civilians had taken advantage of them—and had broken their part of the contract for military services.

There were real dangers hidden behind these words. With each passing month beginning in 1777, Washington's regulars, especially that small cadre that was signing on for the long-term fight, became more professional in military demeanor. Among other things, including their enhanced potential effectiveness in combat, this meant that soldiers felt the enveloping (and reassuring) bonds of "unit cohesion." The immediate thoughts of individual soldiers, whether recruited, dragooned, or pressed into service, became attached to their respective primary units in the army, such as the particular companies or regiments in which they served. The phenomenon was nothing more than a developing comradeship in arms. Any threat or insult thus became an assault on the group, especially if that threat or insult were directed at all members of the group. The bonding effect of unit cohesion suggests that collective protest and defiance would become more of a danger to a generally unsupportive society with each passing month, unless civilians who had made grand promises started to meet their contractual obligations more effectively.

Indeed, the most readily observable pattern in Continental army protest and defiance was that it took on more and more of a collective (and menacing) character through time. At the outset, especially beginning in 1776, most protest had an individual character. Frequently it was the raw recruit, quite often anxious for martial glory but quickly disillusioned with the realities of military service once in camp, who struck back against undesirable circumstances. Protest could come through such diverse expressions as swearing, excessive drinking, assaulting officers, deserting, or bounty jumping. One source of such behavior was the dehumanizing, even brutal nature of camp life. Another had to do with broken promises about pay, food, and clothing. A third was a dawning sense that too many civilians held the soldiery in disregard, if not utter contempt.

It must be remembered that middle- and upper-class civilians considered Washington's new regulars to be representative of the "vulgar herd" in a society that still clung to deferential values. The assumption was that the most fit in terms of wealth and community social standing were to lead while the least fit were to follow, even when that meant becoming little more than human cannon fodder. Perhaps James Warren of Massachusetts summarized the social perceptions of "respectable" citizens as well as any of the "better sort" when he described Washington's troops in 1776 as "the most undisciplined, profligate Crew that were ever collected" to fight a war.

While civilians often ridiculed the new regulars as riffraff, troublemakers, or mere hirelings (while conveniently ignoring the precept that military service was an assumed obligation of all citizens in a liberty-loving commonwealth), individual soldiers did not hold back in protesting their circumstances. In many cases, they had already acknowledged the personal reality of downtrodden status before entering the ranks. Acceptance of these circumstances and the conditions of camp life did not mean, however, that these new soldiers would be passive. Thus it may be an error to dismiss heavy swearing around civilians or repeated drunkenness in camp as nothing more than manifestations of "time-honored military vices," to borrow the words of one recent student of the war period.

At least in some instances, individual soldiers could have been making statements about their sense of personal entrapment. Furthermore, protest through such methods as drunkenness (this was a drinking society but not one that condoned inebriety) was a defensive weapon. One of Washington's generals, for instance, bitterly complained in 1777 that too

many soldiers consistently made it "a practice of getting drunk . . . once a Day and thereby render themselves unfit for duty." To render themselves unfit for duty was to give what they had received—broken promises. Defiance that came in the form of "barrel fever" for some soldiers thus translated into statements about how society looked upon and treated them.

Only over time did individual acts of protest take on a more collective character. That transition may be better comprehended by considering the phenomenon of desertion. While it is true that a great many soldiers did not think of desertion as a specific form of protest, they fled the ranks with greater frequency when food and clothing were in very short supply or nonexistent, as at Valley Forge. However, primary unit cohesion worked to militate against unusually high desertion levels. Sustained involvement with a company or regiment reduced the likelihood of desertion. Hence as soldiers came to know, trust, and depend upon one another, and as they gained confidence in comrades and felt personally vital to the long-term welfare of their primary group, they were much less likely to lodge a statement of individual protest through such individualized forms as desertion.

So it appears to have been with Washington's new regulars. Thad W. Tate discovered that, in the regiments of New York, Maryland, and North Carolina, about 50 percent of all desertions occurred within six months of enlistments. Mark Edward Lender, in studying New Jersey's Continentals, also found that the rate of desertion dropped off dramatically for those soldiers who lasted through just a few months of service. The first few days and weeks in the ranks were those in which these poor and desperate new regulars asked themselves whether vague promises of a better lot in life for everyone, including themselves, in a postwar republican polity was worth the sacrifice now being demanded. Many enlistees and conscripts concluded that it was not, and they fled. Since they had little proof that they could trust the civilian population and its leaders, they chose to express their defiance through desertion. Unit cohesion, in turn, helped sustain those who read the equation differently, and it eased the pain of enduring a long war in return for the remote prospect of greater personal freedom, opportunity, and prosperity.

Then there were those individuals who neither deserted nor became hard-core regulars. By and large, this group defied civil and military authority through the practice of bounty jumping. The procedure, which Washington once referred to as "a kind of business" among some soldiers, was straightforward. It involved enlisting, getting a bounty, and deserting, then repeating the same process with another recruiting agent in another location. Some of the most resourceful bounty jumpers got away with this maneuver seven, eight, or even nine times, if not more. Most jumpers appear to have been very poor young men without family roots. The most careful of them went through the war unscathed. Bounties thus provided a form of economic aggrandizement (and survival) in a society that generally treated its struggling classes with studied neglect. To accept a bounty payment, perhaps even to serve for a short period, and then to run off, was a strongly worded statement of personal defiance.

Bounty jumping was invariably the act of protesting individuals; looting and plundering (like desertion) combined individual with collective protest. Certainly there were numerous occasions when hungry soldiers looted by themselves. Just as often, groups of starving men "borrowed" goods from civilians. Even before the second establishment took form, looting had become a serious problem. Indeed, it probably abetted unit cohesion. One sergeant, for example, described how he and his comrades, searching desperately for food, "liberated" some geese belonging to a local farmer in 1776 and devoured them "Hearty in the Cause of Liberty of taking what Came to their Hand." Next "a sheep and two fat turkeys" approached this band of hungry sol-

diers, but "not being able to give the countersign," they were taken prisoner, "tried by fire and executed" for sustenance "by the whole Division of the freebooters."

When army looting of civilian property continued its unabated course in 1777, General Washington threatened severe penalties. He emphasized that the army's "business" was "to give protection, and support, to the poor, distressed Inhabitants; not to multiply and increase their calamities." These pleas had little impact. Incident after incident kept the commander in chief and his staff buried in a landslide of civilian complaints. Threats of courts martial, actual trials, and severe punishments did not deter angry, starving, protesting soldiers. In 1780 and 1781 Washington was still issuing pleas and threats, but to little avail. Not even occasional hangings contained an increasingly defiant and cohesive soldiery that wondered who the truly poor and distressed inhabitants were—themselves or civilians ostensibly prospering because of the army's travail. To strike back at hoarding, unsupportive citizens, as they had come to perceive the populace whom they were defending, seemed only logical, especially when emboldened by the camaraderie of closely knit fellow soldiers.

Above all else, two patterns stand out with respect to common soldier protest. First, as the war effort lengthened, defiance became more of a collective phenomenon. Second, such protest had a controlled quality. While there was unremitting resentment toward civilians who were invariably perceived as insensitive and unsupportive, protest rarely metamorphosed into wanton violence and mindless destruction. Soldiers may have looted and pillaged, they may have grabbed up bounties, and they may have deserted. But they rarely maimed, raped, or murdered civilians. Pvt. Joseph Plumb Martin attempted to explain why. Even though "the monster Hunger, . . . attended us," he wrote, and the new regulars "had borne as long as human nature could endure, and to bear longer we considered folly," he insisted that his comrades had become, in the end, "truly patriotic." They were persons who "loved their country, and they had already suffered everything short of death in its cause." The question by 1779 and 1780 was whether these hardened, cohesive veterans would be willing to endure even more privation.

In reflecting positively on the loyalty of his comrades, Martin was commenting on a near mutiny of the Connecticut Line in 1780. Indeed, the specter of collective defiance in the form of line mutinies had come close to reality with the near insubordination of the New Jersey officers in 1779. They had not demonstrated in the field, but they had made it clear that conditions in the army were all but intolerable—and that civil society, when desperate to maintain a regular force in arms, could be persuaded to concede on basic demands. Washington had used the phrase "extorted"; he had also pointed out that, "notwithstanding the expedient adopted for saving appearances," this confrontation "cannot fail to operate as a bad precedent." The commander in chief was certainly right about the setting of precedents.

Among long-term veterans, anger was beginning to overwhelm discipline. There had been small-scale mutinies before, such as the rising of newly recruited Continentals at Halifax, North Carolina, in February 1776. In 1779 Rhode Island and Connecticut regiments threatened mutinies, but nothing came of these incidents. Then in 1780 another near uprising of the Connecticut Line occurred. Invariably, the issues had the same familiar ring: lack of adequate civilian support as demonstrated by rotten food, inadequate clothing, and worthless pay (when pay was available). On occasion, too, the heavy hand of company- and field-grade officers played its part. The near mutiny of the Connecticut Line in 1780 had been avoided by a fortuitous shipment of cattle and by promises from trusted officers of better treatment. In the end, the Connecticut Line calmed itself down, according to Martin, because the soldiery was "unwilling to desert the cause of our country, when in distress." Nevertheless, he explained that "we knew her cause involved our own, but what signified our perishing in the act of saving her, when that very act would inevitably destroy us, and she must finally perish with us."

By the end of 1780, there were some veterans who would have disputed Martin's reasoning. They had all but given up, let come what might for the glorious cause. On January 1, 1781, the Pennsylvania Line proved that point. Suffering through yet another harsh winter near Morristown, New Jersey, the Pennsylvanians mutinied. Some one thousand determined comrades in arms (about 15 percent of the manpower available to Washington) ostensibly wanted nothing more to do with fighting the war. On a prearranged signal, the Pennsylvanians paraded under arms, seized their artillery, and marched south toward Princeton, their ultimate target being Philadelphia. These veterans had had their fill of broken promises, of the unfulfilled contract. They maintained that they had signed on for three years, not for the duration. If they were to stay in the ranks, then they wanted the same benefits (additional bounty payments, more free land, and some pay in specie) that newer enlistees had obtained.

Formal military discipline collapsed as the officers trying to contain the mutineers were brushed aside. The soldiers killed one and wounded two other officers, yet their popular commander, Anthony Wayne, trailed along, attempting to appeal to their sense of patriotism. Speaking through a committee of sergeants, the soldiers assured Wayne and the other officers that they were still loyal to the cause, and they proved it by handing over two spies that Sir Henry Clinton had sent out from New York to monitor the situation. Moreover, the mutineers, despite their anger and bitterness, behaved themselves along their route and did not unnecessarily intimidate civilians who got in their way.

Later checking demonstrated that many of the mutineers were duration enlistees, yet that was a moot point. When the soldiers reached Trenton, representatives of Congress and the Pennsylvania government negotiated with them and agreed to discharge any veteran claiming three years in rank. Also, they offered back pay and new clothing along with immunity from prosecution for having defied their officers in leaving their posts. Once formally discharged, the bulk of the mutineers reenlisted for a new bounty. By late January 1781 the Pennsylvania Line was once more a functioning part of the Continental army.

These mutineers won because Washington was in desperate need of manpower and because they had resorted to collective defiance, not because their society wanted to address what had been grievances based on the contract for service. Unlike their officers, who had just won a major victory in driving for half-pay pensions, they were not in a position to lobby before Congress. Hence they employed one of the most threatening weapons in their arsenal, collective protest against civil authority, but only after less extreme measures had failed to satisfy their claims for financial justice. They were certainly not planning to overthrow any government or to foment an internal social revolution against better-placed members of their society. They had staked their hopes on a better life in the postwar period and had already risked their lives many times for the proposed republican polity. All told, the extreme nature of this mutiny demonstrated, paradoxically, both that Washington's long-term Continentals were the most loyal and dedicated republican citizens in the new nation, and that they were dangerously close to repudiating a dream that far too often had been a personal nightmare because of the realities of societal support and of service in the Continental army.

GLOSSARY

Six Nations:	The six nations of the Iroquois Confederacy, composed of the Mohawk, Oneida, Onondaga, Cayuga, and Seneca in 1570 and joined by the Tuscarora in 1722.
Pennsylvania Line:	The Pennsylvania contingent of Washington's Continental Army.
Continental:	A soldier in the Continental Army.
Sir Henry Clinton (1738–1795):	British general in the American Revolution who was commander in chief of British forces in North America from 1778 to 1781.

IMPLICATIONS

Martin claims that, despite general public neglect, Revolutionary soliders continued to serve in the Continental Army largely because of the of western lands they were promised as part of their enlistments. George Hewes, on the other hand, claimed that he served because of patriotism and hatred of the British. In weighing these competing claims, do you think patriotism, self-interest, or a combination of the two was the most powerful motivation among those who participated in the Revolution?

Past Traces

This reading begins with one of the most important documents of the post-Revolutionary era, Judith Sargenth Murray's *On the Equality of the Sexes*. Building on the elevation and public recognition of women's equal intellecutal capacities during the Revolutionary War, Murray makes a strong case for the acceptance of women's thinking and writing in the new republic. Written in 1790, Murray's arguments would be a continuing influence on the growth of a national women's movement in the nineteenth century.

Judith Sargent Murray, *On the Equality of the Sexes (1790)*

Is it upon mature consideration we adopt the idea, that nature is thus partial in her distributions? Is it indeed a fact, that she hath yielded to one half of the human species so unquestionable a mental superiority? I know that to both sexes elevated understandings, and the reverse, are common. But, suffer me to ask, in what the minds of females are so notoriously deficient, or unequal. May not the intellectual powers be ranged under these four heads—imagination, reason, memory and judgment. The province of imagination hath long since been surrendered up to us, and we have been crowned undoubted sovereigns of the regions of fancy. Invention is perhaps the most arduous effort of the mind; this branch of imagination hath been particularly ceded to us, and we have been time out of mind invested with that creative faculty. Observe the variety of fashions (here I bar the contemptuous smile) which distinguish and adorn the female world; how continually are they changing, insomuch that they almost render the whole man's assertion problematical, and we are ready to say, there is something new under the sun. Now, what a playfulness, what an exuberance of fancy, what strength of inventive imagination, doth this continual variation discover? Again, it hath been observed, that if the turpitude of the conduct of our sex, hath been ever so enormous, so extremely ready are we, that the very first thought presents us with an apology, so plausible, as to produce our actions even in an amiable light. Another instance of our creative powers, is our talent for slander; how ingenious are we at inventive scandal? what a formidable story can we in a moment fabricate merely from the force of a prolifick imagination? how many reputations, in the fertile brain of a female, have been utterly despoiled? how industrious are we at improving a hint? suspicion how easily do we convert into conviction, and conviction, embellished by the power of eloquence, stalks abroad to the surprise and confusion of unsuspecting innocence. Perhaps it will be asked if I furnish these facts as instances of excellency in our sex. Certainly not; but as proofs of a creative faculty, of a lively imagination. Assuredly great activity of mind is thereby discovered, and was this activity properly directed, what beneficial effects would follow. Is the needle and kitchen sufficient to employ the operations of a soul thus organized? I should conceive not. Nay, it is a truth that those very departments leave the intelligent principle vacant, and at liberty for speculation. Are we deficient in reason? we can only reason from what we know, and if opportunity of acquiring knowledge hath been denied us, the inferiority of our sex cannot fairly be deduced from thence. Memory, I believe, will be allowed us in common, since every one's experience must testify, that a loquacious old woman is as frequently met with, as a communicative old man; their subjects are alike drawn from the fund of other times and the transactions of their youth, or of maturer life, entertain, or perhaps fatigue you, in the evening of their lives. "But our judgement is not so strong— we do not distinguish so well." Yet it may be questioned, from what doth this superiority, in this determining faculty of the soul, proceed. May we not trace its source in the difference of education, and continued advantages? Will it be said that the judgment of a male of two years old, is more sage than that of a female's of the same age? I believe the reverse is generally observed to be true. But from that period what partiality! how is the one exalted and the other depressed, by the contrary modes of education which are adopted! the one is taught to aspire, and the other is early confined and limited. As their years increase, the sister must be wholly domesticated, while the brother is led by the hand through all the flowery paths of science. Grant that their minds are by nature equal, yet who shall wonder at the apparent superiority, if indeed custom becomes second nature; nay if it taketh place of nature, and that it doth the experience of each day will evince. At length arrived at womanhood, the uncultivated fair one feels a void, which the employments allotted her are by no means capable of filling. What can she do? to books she may not apply; or if she doth, to those only of the novel kind, lest she merit the appellation of a learned lady; and what ideas have been affixed to this term, the observation of many can testify. Fashion, scandal, and sometimes what is still more reprehensible, are then called in to her relief; and who can say to what lengths the liberties she takes may proceed. Meantime she herself is most unhappy; she feels the want of a cultivated mind. Is she single, she in vain seeks to fill up time from sexual employments or amusements. Is she united to a person whose soul nature made equal to her own, education hath set him so far above her, that in those entertainments which are productive of such rational felicity, she is not qualified to accompany him. She experiences a mortifying consciousness of inferiority, which embitters every enjoyment. Doth the person to whom her adverse fate hath consigned her, possess a mind incapable of improvement, she is equally wretched, in being so closely connected with an individual whom she cannot but despise. Now, was she permitted the same instructors as her brother, (with an eye however to their particular departments) for the employment of a rational mind an ample field would be opened. In astronomy she might catch a glimpse of the immensity of the Deity, and thence she would form amazing conceptions of the august and supreme Intelligence. In geography she would admire Jehova in the midst of his benevolence; thus adapting this globe to the various wants and amusements of its inhabitants. In natural philosophy she would adore the infinite majesty of heaven, clothed in condescension; and as she traversed the reptile world, she would hail the goodness of a creating God. A mind, thus filled, would have little room for the trifles with our sex are, with too much justice, accused of amusing themselves, and they would thus be rendered fit companions for those, who should one day wear them as their crown. Fashions, in their variety, would then give place to conjectures, which might perhaps conduce to the improvement of the literary world; and there would be no leisure for slander or detraction. Reputation would not then be blasted, but serious speculations would occupy the lively imaginations of the sex. Unnecessary visits would be precluded, and that custom would only be indulged by way of relaxation, or to answer the demands of consanguinity and friendship. Females would become discreet, their judgements would be invigorated, and their partners for life being circlimspectly chosen, an unhappy Hymen 1 would then be as rare, as is now the reverse.

Will it be urged that those acquirements would supersede our domestick duties. I answer that every requisite in female economy is easily attained; and, with truth I can add, that when once attained, they require no further mental attention. Nay, while we are pursuing the needle, or the superintendency of the family, I repeat, that our minds are at full liberty for reflection; that imagination may exert itself in full vigour; and that if a just foundation is early laid, our ideas will then be worthy of rational beings. If we were industrious we might easily find time to arrange them upon paper, or should avocations press too hard for such an indulgence, the hours allotted for conversation would at least become more refined and rational. Should it still be vociferated, "Your domestick employments are sufficient"—I would calmly ask, is it reasonable, that a candidate for immortality, for the joys of heaven, an intelligent being, who is to spend an eternity in contemplating the works of Deity, should at present be so degraded, as to be allowed no other ideas, than those which are suggested by the mechanism of a pudding, or the sewing [of] the seams of a garment? Pity that all such censurers of female improvement do not go one step further, and deny their future existence; to be consistent they surely ought.

Yes, ye lordly, ye haughty sex, our souls are by nature equal to yours; the same breath of God animates, enlivens, and invigorates us; and that we are not fallen lower than yourselves, let those vritness who have greatly lowered above the various discouragements by which they have been so heavily oppressed; and though I am unacquainted with the list of celebrated characters on either side, yet from the observations I have made in the contracted circle in which I have moved, I dare confidently believe, that from the commencement of time to the present day, there hath been as many females, as males, who, by the mere force of natural powers, have merited the crown of applause; who, thus assisted, have 'seized the wreath of fame. I know there are [those] who assert, that as the animal powers of the one sex are superiour, of course their mental faculties also must be stronger; thus attributing strength of mind to the transient organization of this earth born tenement. But if this reasoning is just, man must be content to yield the palm to many of the brute creation, since by not a few of his brethren of the field, he is far surpassed in bodily strength. Moreover, was this argument admitted, it would prove too much, for occular demonstration evinceth, that there are many robust masculine ladies, and effeminate gentlemen. Yet I fancy that Mr. Pope though clogged with an enervated body, and distinguished by a diminutive stature, could nevertheless lay claim to greatness of soul; and perhaps there are many other instances which might be adduced to combat so unphilosophical an opinion. Do we not often see, that when the clay built tabernacle is well nigh dissolved, when it is just ready to mingle with the parent soil, the immortal inhabitant aspires to, and even attaineth heights the most sublime, and which were before wholly unexplored. Besides, were we to grant that animal strength proved any thing, taking into consideration the accustomed impartiality of nature, we should be induced to imagine, that she had invested the female mind with superiour strength as an equivalent for the bodily powers of man. But waving this however palpable advantage, for equality only, we wish to contend.

9

Women in the American Revolution

Carol Berkin

The American Revolution marked a period full of ambiguities for American women. On the one hand, women played a prominent role in securing American independence: producing cloth, managing farms, and supporting boycotts of British goods. Yet, at the same time, women emerged from the Revolutionary era disenfranchised and denied an active public role. This seeming paradox has led some historians to argue that American women gained little from the Revolutionary experience: gender roles and women's position in society, they claim, remained little changed from colonial days. More recently, however, historians have looked beyond the issue of suffrage and found that the Revolutionary experience did indeed alter women's lives, although in small and often subtle ways.

Women played a variety of roles in the Revolutionary movement. In the pre-Revolutionary years between 1765 and 1775, women helped to enforce consumer boycotts, acted as protesters in public demonstrations against British policies, manufactured cloth and other domestic goods to replace English imports, and encouraged men to take action against the mother country. During the war years between 1775 and 1783, women supported the military as laundresses and cooks, raised money for Washington's troops, and kept their families together during months and sometimes years of wartime exile. A few, such as Deborah Sampson Gannett, even served in the Continental Army, disguised as men.

The Revolution thus expanded women's public roles in unexpected and unprecedented ways. Questions of British tyranny and American liberties were not confined to the male realm by any means, as surviving diaries and letters of a wide cross-section of American women make clear. While most Revolutionary women probably agreed with the political sentiments of their husbands, fathers, and brothers, many did not, and more than a few formed their own opinions about local and national affairs. As several historians have recently demonstrated, women even redefined the formal political discourse of the Revolutionary era to meet their own experiences and needs.

But whether or not they advanced their own political opinions, American women were forced by the actions of British and American officials to take a political stance. As the Revolutionary War progressed, even the most cautious colonists were forced to choose sides, and Whig and Tory officials alike assumed that a husband's or father's allegiance defined that of his wife or daughter. Thus, the wives and daughters of exiled patriots were maltreated by British soldiers, and the women of suspected Tory families were hounded by rebel sympathizers, irrespective of the true sentiments of the women involved. Neutrality, the evidence shows, was an impossible luxury during the Revolutionary War, for women as much as for men.

In the end, however, necessity as much as politics forced the largest number of American women into public roles. Despite the legal impediment of coverture—which placed a wife's property rights under the sole control of her husband—women were forced to take on the responsibilities of running family farms, artisan shops, and retail stores during the disruptions of the wartime years. Although some were ill-prepared for the undertaking—their husbands having shared with them little about the management of family enterprises—the overwhelming majority took on the added burdens of family direction with determination and successfully steered their families through the travails of wartime dislocation.

In the same way that Revolutionary service and personal sacrifice brought George Hewes to question traditional notions about authority and the conduct of politics, the close of the Revolution also posed the question of how their expanded wartime experiences would change the roles of American women. In this essay, Carol Berkin shows that the answer to this question stopped far short of gender equality. Instead, public sentiment granted the point that women were the intellectual equals of men but then retreated from the question of equality, granting women new roles as educators of the future citizens of the new American republic.

....

In 1750 a Pennsylvania woman in her early thirties sat for her portrait. The portrait survived two transatlantic journeys and a revolution; its subject did not. If you look at the painting, however, it is hard to believe that this imperious, confident woman then known as Grace Growden was less resilient than the canvas that has preserved her image for us. The image is striking: Grace stares boldly and directly at the viewer, her head lifted high, her posture formal but relaxed, her body clearly accustomed to the weight of brocade and velvet. Her right arm crosses the front of her body, the hand resting comfortably on her lap, while her left hand is poised, shoulder high, as if caught in the familiar act of lifting a teacup to her Lips. She offers a mild, polite smile, more in acknowledgment than welcome. Grace Growden's forehead is high and broad, her

brows arched, her nose aquiline, her eyes sharply focused. She shows the world intelligence in lieu of beauty. The woman in this portrait knows her place in society—and expects it to be acknowledged by others.

For most of her life, others did acknowledge the social superiority of Grace Growden Galloway. It was a position based first on her father's great wealth and public service and later on her wealthy husband's reputation as a lawyer and political figure. In the decade of relative political calm before the Stamp Act crisis, she reigned as one of the preeminent social figures of the mainland colonies' major city. Such preeminence did not, of course, ensure or require personal happiness. Indeed, what we know of Grace Growden's life suggests a lonely childhood and a difficult marriage, a life dominated by powerful and egotistical men. By most accounts, her father was an overbearing man and her husband, Joseph Galloway, brilliant but unstable, temperamental, argumentative, haughty, and disturbingly suspicious of others.

It was not Joseph's possible lack of affection for his wife but his politics that finally disrupted Grace's life. Throughout his career in Pennsylvania politics, Joseph Galloway viewed the British government as an ally not an enemy. Despite the shifts in Crown policy toward the colonies in the 1760s and 1770s, he never altered his opinion. On the eve of the Revolution, he argued for compromise and patience and, in the last resort, for capitulation to British wishes.

Joseph Galloway's loyalism earned him the condemnation of his colony. His service for the British army that occupied Philadelphia in 1776 ensured him his community's enmity. Fearing for his life, Galloway fled to the safety of British-occupied New York, taking with him his daughter and only child, Elizabeth.

And Grace? Grace Growden Galloway remained behind, never to see her husband or her daughter again. Why? It was certainly not a commitment to the Revolutionary movement that held her in Philadelphia. No less than Joseph Galloway, she abhorred a revolutionary cause that endangered the two things she held dear: her family and her social position. As the wife of a now notorious traitor, she could no longer claim her place in the first tier of society. And as the wife of an officially attainted property holder, she was in danger of losing the wealth on which that place had once depended. Historians usually have assumed that Joseph, like other men of property, instructed his wife to stay behind—hoping her presence might help preserve his property from confiscation. This was a tactic of many noted, or notorious, Loyalists. But Grace's diary suggests otherwise. It suggests a desire to preserve what she considered to be *her* wealth, the Growden properties, which she would pass on to her daughter as a mother's material and social legacy.

Grace Galloway sought to separate her fate from her husband's, to demand that the pun-

ishment meted out to him for his political actions fall on him alone. With the aid of lawyers, influential friends, and her own rectitude, she intended to see that the confiscating hand of revolution did not reach her daughter's legacy. And in the early months of her battle with authorities, she was confident that the names Growden and Galloway were shields strong enough to protect her in the face of a temporary political crisis.

They were not. Joseph Galloway's very political prominence, once a source of satisfaction, proved an insurmountable disadvantage. Pennsylvania rebels could not allow the wife of an officially declared traitor to win her quiet battle. Soon after Joseph departed, the Pennsylvania government moved to confiscate the extensive holdings of the Growden—Galloway union. Estates outside Philadelphia were seized; even the city mansion in which Grace Galloway resided was threatened with confiscation. Galloway's diary records her vigorous, stubborn resistance, in the courts and in the very parlors of her home. In the end, she was escorted politely but firmly out the door of her Philadelphia mansion. She had little money and few possessions with her. Her dependence on the goodwill and charity of others had begun.

During the next two years, the meanness of her circumstances filled her every thought. She meticulously recorded, and stubbornly defied, the humiliations of rented rooms and the real and imagined snubs of former friends, social equals, and eventually even her social inferiors. She watched as rebel upstarts rode by in her own confiscated carriage; she endured chilly receptions in the parlors of the elite Revolutionary families and, later, their failure to invite her at all; and she argued with lawyers and negotiated for debts from former tenants. Although she lamented to her diary that her weakness of character, her timidity and confusion, her lack of diplomacy in dealing with authorities ensured her defeat, this was far from true. It was her stubborn and intelligent resistance that prolonged these battles with the rebel government and made their simple assertion of political power so complex. There were signs that she understood this as well. For, woven into the diary, scattered among the expressions of anger, loneliness, and anxiety, were expressions of delight in a newfound independence, in a discovered capacity for autonomy.

Grace Galloway's spirit remained unbroken until she discovered that the deeds to her father's property carried only her husband's name. Marriage had made her legally invisible, just as politics had erased her social position. The woman we see in the last months of the diary bears little relationship to the woman of the 1750 portrait. She is cynical, suspicious, angry—and defeated. When she died in 1781, the war that had turned her world upside down was itself coming to an end.

Grace Galloway's experiences during the American Revolution may seem at first too extreme to be typical. Yet many colonial women would have felt a kinship with her. Like Galloway, they found that the Revolution and a protracted home-front war swept aside their ordinary life and settled expectations. Even those who did not enjoy the benefits of Galloway's social position might empathize with her intense anxiety over changes in a social order that had shaped her identity. Like Galloway, many would find themselves exercising their own judgments for the first time on legal, economic, and political matters, and testing their resources in the midst of crises, as their property was confiscated and their crops, livestock, and homes commandeered or destroyed. Some shared Grace Galloway's pleasure in this new independence and sense of competence even when their efforts ended in tragedy or personal defeat.

The impact of the Revolution on women's lives was, of course, as various as the circumstances of those lives. Social class, region, race, age, and even religion influenced what crises a women faced and the resources she might have to resolve them. For a small number, the Revolution provided opportunities that peacetime did not, opportunities that ranged from participation in meaningful activities to the promise of freedom from slavery. Yet for most women, the war was a conflict that taxed their resiliency and endangered their husbands and their family. If few of the accounts that come down to us are as bitter and despairing as Grace Galloway's, they bear, nevertheless, the familiar grim tone of war and destruction. If we see a romance in the bravery of "Molly Pitcher" or the women who served as spies for General Washington, their actual recollections speak of a dead husband lying at their feet or of a captured friend's death on a British prison ship. Only later could these women—and their historians—try to assess what positive impact the war and independence may have had on them and on their daughters as well.

In one sense, the Revolution was a victory for women. Like many upheavals, natural or social, the Revolution generated a treasure trove of sources that have allowed historians to reconstruct women's experiences. True, eighteenth-century genteel women were likely, even under stable circumstances, to leave behind the diaries and letters that earlier generations of women could not. And it is also true that African American and Indian women have left us less than the European women of the society. Yet as a society in crisis, Revolutionary America produced a vast and rich record, from newspaper accounts of women's prewar protests against British policy, to widow's petitions to the U.S. Congress regarding veteran's benefits, to claims filed by loyalist women for pensions from the British government, to books, speeches, sermons, and public debates over women's role in the Revolution and in the new republic. From the myriad of official and personal documents, individual lives can be captured in fine detail and women's collective experiences can be reconstructed. The narrative of white and black women's activities during the Revolutionary decades, for example, has been especially well told. Thus the texture of this chapter will appear richer than those that preceded it.

Although historians often write of the "coming of the American Revolution," no woman or man would have imagined such an event a dozen years before. Indeed, in 1763 colonists everywhere joined together to celebrate the English victory over the French in the great struggle for empire the Americans called the French and Indian War. The outpouring of patriotism—the parades, the bonfires, the toasts to the King, his country, and to the architect of English victory, William Pitt—may have been excessive but it was not unreasonable. The defeat of the French and the capture of Canada meant that for the first time in colonial memory warfare might cease to be a regular feature of the colonists' experience. New Englanders, in particular, rejoiced; generations of them had suffered the loss of sons and fathers and husbands in the hundred years of imperial struggle that preceded this victory. Few Massachusetts or Connecticut families had escaped burying a casualty of these wars, and if the devastation had been less extreme in Pennsylvania or South Carolina, here, too, lives had been lost and property destroyed in battle with European enemies and their Indian allies. Now, in the wake of England's crushing defeat of the French both in America and abroad, safety seemed assured.

Colonists in New England attributed Britain's victory to the hand of Providence, while in other regions people spoke of the bravery of their soldiers, the genius of William Pitt, and the military daring of General Wolfe. But everywhere colonists were in agreement that the obvious superiority of the British system of government and of its citizens was the deciding factor in the defeat of the enemy. Orators extolled the British constitution, with its system of balanced government and its delineation and protection of the "rights of Englishmen." That this civic satisfaction so quickly turned to protest must have seemed remarkable even to the protesters themselves.

American protest arose in response to Britain's postwar changes in colonial policy. In the wake of the war, the British government found itself burdened by staggering debts and the need to maintain an expensive military and naval presence. Efforts to raise funds, tighten control on colonial trade and production, and devise a workable governance for the new holdings in French Canada and the Ohio Valley brought colonial interests and imperial interests into immediate conflict. Over the 1760s and early 1770s, trade regulating measures such as the Sugar Act, revenue-raising efforts like the Stamp Act and the Townshend Acts, and provisions for the military including Quartering Acts in many colonies all eroded the colonists' confidence that their interests were synonymous with the interests of the mother country. A decade of escalating political protest and the failure of compromise eventually led to the independence movement and to a revolutionary war. Women played their role in every phase of this protest and the struggle for—or against— American independence.

Where and how women participated in these political struggles was determined by custom, coincidence, and necessity. In the decade before Lexington and Concord, the struggle between Crown and colonists was waged on four clearly defined battlefields. The first of these was the colonial governments themselves, through tests of will and skill between royal governors and the local interests of the assembly. Women were entirely absent from this arena, excluded as a sex by both law and custom. In the second arena—propaganda and the politicization of the citizens on the issues of British policy—women played a limited role. Writing for the public in newspapers or broadsides was a traditionally male activity, and women made few direct contributions to political strategy or discussions of tactics. Wives may have been present when political leaders gathered to draft their responses to new British legislation, but that presence was coincidental rather than intentional.

As with every social pattern, an exception can be found. Mercy Otis Warren was among the most famous and effective propagandists of the prewar period. She was also an active participant in the strategy sessions led by the cousins, John and Samuel, whom Loyalist governor Thomas Hutchinson disdainfully referred to as "that brace of Adamses." Warren had access to the inner circles of Massachusetts radical politics as the favored daughter and beloved sister of the James Otises, whose reputation as "trouble-makers" was transatlantic. Many a New England Loyalist's diary or post-war memoirs held these two gentlemen entirely responsible for the Revolution. Mercy Otis's access to radical circles was solidified when she married James Warren, for the leaders of Massachusetts's opposition forces met in Warren's home. Yet if gender determined her proximity to the sources of power, talent and intelligence determined her participation in their activities. Because she had a genius for satire, a flair for drama, and a willingness to use both, she became the opposition's most effective shaper of popular opinion save perhaps for Samuel Adams. Her plays and poems filled Massachusetts newspapers in the 1770s, and were widely reprinted elsewhere. In satires such as *The Defeat* and *The Group*, she gave her colony's growing crisis its cast of characters. The ambitious supporter of the Crown Thomas Hutchinson became Rapatio, Bashaw of Servia; General Timothy Ruggles was hounded by the sobriquet "Brigadier Hate-All"; and Crown propagandist Jonathan Sewall felt himself eternally marked as Beau Trumps. The heroes of her own cause, colonial resistance, were ennobled as Brutus or Cassius, reinforcing the theme that the opposition was acting to preserve rather than harm the British constitutional tradition.

A white woman had to step far outside her customary roles to participate in the realm of propaganda and strategy. But she had only to step into her kitchen or parlor to be in the center of the third arena of protest: economic sanctions. As early as 1765, the colonists' policy of nonimportation and consumer boycott of British-made goods became the most effective means to combat the Crown's new trade policies. Tins strategy reflected an awareness that the role of the colonies in Britain's

mercantile economy had shifted dramatically during the eighteenth century. Where once their value to England lay in the production of raw materials, by the 1760s the colonies had grown into an important market for British manufactured goods. Shipments of everything from cloth to tea, paint, and salt, as well as reshipments of European products from British ports, were central to the economic expansion and well-being of the mother country. A blow to this commercial link was a blow certain to be felt in the halls of Parliament. As household managers and as major consumers, white women's cooperation was vital to the success of any proposed boycott.

In 1765 New York and Boston merchants organized the first of the nonimportation movements to protest Britain's first direct tax on the colonists, the Stamp Act. The idea spread rapidly. Newspaper contributors called on colonists to give up all imported luxuries and finery and to embrace austerity until Parliament repealed this first direct tax on its colonies. When the Stamp Act was, indeed, repealed, colonists laid much of the credit for this change in policy to their boycott. Not surprisingly, they turned once again to ninimportation in the wake of the Townshend Acts and the much hated Tea Act. In both instances, boycott organizers made a conscious effort to elicit the cooperation of housewives and their daughters.

The importance of women's support for these boycotts was rarely underrated, although some leaders believed it would be difficult to arouse female patriotism or stir women to act. In 1769 Christopher Gadsden spoke frankly to his colleagues in the South Carolina assembly:

> I come now to the last, and what many say and think is the greatest difficulty of all we have to encounter, that is, to persuade our wives to give us their assistance, without which 'tis impossible to succeed . . . for 'tis well known, that none in the world are better oeconomists . . . than ours. Only let their husbands point out the necessity of such conduct; convince them, that it is the only thing that can save them and their children, from

distress, slavery, and disgrace; their affections will soon be awakened, and cooperate with their reason.

Gadsden's argument both complimented and insulted the women who were the indirect audience of his oratory. His assumption that women were politically ignorant and naturally indifferent to public matters ran side by side with his praise for their "notable housewifery." Such a view was common, particularly among the genteel classes. It was widely believed that women's political choices were, and ought to be, controlled by male relatives. This "natural" subordination based on gender was reinforced by a social subordination based on the absence of property. As every English child knew, a propertyless person could take no part in making political decisions.

Yet Gadsden was wrong. Before he issued his appeal, women of his own elite social class had been mulling over the political events of the era in their diaries and letters for several years. Furthermore, free colonial women expressed a clear understanding that their economic decisions—what to buy, what to declare a necessity, what to eschew—had become political decisions. This political awareness was dynamic, growing stronger and more widespread over the decade between the Stamp Act and the Declaration of Independence.

Thus, women who boycotted tea and wore dresses of homespun rather than imported cloth publicly defined these choices as political ones. When a group of Newport, Rhode Island, women substituted an herbal drink for imported tea, they declared it a matter of honor. When "upwards of 300 mistresses of Families, in which number the Ladies of highest rank and influence" signed a petition to abstain from tea drinking, they stated their motivation clearly: "to save their abused Country from ruin and Slavery," from dangers brought on by Parliament's "unconstitutional" attacks. These petitioners also knew how to give their tactic greater legitimacy. In the petition they linked their action to the actions of "the very respectable body of Merchants and other inhabitants" of Boston. And in Philadelphia, when Hanna Griffitts set the politics of tea drinking to verse, she established a direct relationship between housewives and the oppression of the British government.

> For the sake of Freedom's name
> (Since British Wisdom scorns repealing)
> Come, sacrifice to Patriot fame
> And give up Tea, by way of healing
> This done, within ourselves retreat.
> The Industrious arts of life to follow
> Let proud Nabobs storm and fret
> They cannot force our lips to swallow.

Even a nine-year-old like Susan Boudinot of Pennsylvania was capable of relishing a well-executed political gesture. When offered a cup of tea at the home of New Jersey's Loyalist governor, William Franklin, Susan curtsied, raised the cup to her lips, and then tossed its contents out the startled Franklin's window.

Perhaps the most widely circulated declaration of political sentiments came from Edenton, North Carolina. Here, the newspaper carried a resolution drawn up by fifty-one local women to boycott English goods. The Edenton statement was based on a sense of civic duty and responsibility. "As we cannot be indifferent on any occasion that appears to affect the peace and happiness of our country, and as it has been thought necessary for the publick good to enter into several particular resolved," wrote the Edenton women, "it is a duty we owe not only to our near and dear relations and connections, but to ourselves who are essentially interested in their welfare, to do everything as far as lies in our power to testify to our since adherence to the same." The "Edenton Resolve" prompted a broad spectrum of male response, from enthusiastic acknowledgment to satiric attack. Patriot men could hardly denounce the commitment that their own orators had urged upon the "ladies." But their Loyalist tormentors knew exactly where to aim their blows, suggesting that the colonial protest had set a sexual revolution in motion, creating aggressive women and emasculated men. Patriot ministers might continue to call on women to use their power, "to strike the Stroke, and make the Hills and Plains of America clap their hands," but American men remained ambivalent about the consequences of this political awakening. Not every man would, as the Presbyterian preacher William Tennett III promised activist women, "rise and call you blessed."

Women's response to male criticism and male approval, but especially to male "guidance," is instructive. When male writers to the newspapers suggested that patriotic women substitute rum for tea, women fired back that they did not welcome such advice. They would replace tea as they themselves saw fit, just as they would be their own judge of what to wear in place of British finery. And although the local committee men granted an ailing Salem woman an exemption, she steadfastly refused to drink tea. Nonconsumption was, she reminded them, a matter of personal principle. Historians can find similar evidence that by the 1770s women of all ages and regions had a well-developed sense of their own political agency. Even a thirteen-year-old could speak confidently in her diary of her independent political choices. "As I am (as we say) a daughter of liberty," she wrote in the early 1770s, "I chuse to war [wear] as much of our own manufactory as pocible."

The fourth arena for protest was the streets. For many centuries the crowd had been a recognized form of political expression for those without access to formal political power in English society. In England and the colonies, protests against rising food prices, onerous taxes, and infractions of popularly held moral standards were a tradition among the poor. Not surprisingly, opposition to British policy took to the streets as well. Sometimes these mass demonstrations were organized and led by elite politicians and businessmen who saw their value as propaganda and who recognized the need to mobilize broad popular support. But the sailors, dockworkers, and servants who participated in what critics called "riots" and supporters called "demonstrations" were just as often the agents of their own political acts.

Few of these crowds were exclusively male. If women did not take an active part in acts of destruction such as the raid on Thomas Hutchinson's Cambridge home, they did not shy away from acts of physical violence. Generally, crowd actions organized by elites conformed to genteel notions of respectability and discouraged female participation. But the more spontaneous the demonstration, the more likely the participation of women. Women joined in the tarring and feathering of local merchants who continued to import British goods, and sometimes organized their own intimidation efforts against perceived enemies of either sex. In 1775, when a Massachusetts woman expressed her politics indirectly by naming her newborn son in honor of the British commander Thomas Gage, a crowd of patriot women attacked her house, fully prepared to tar and feather both mother and child.

Even when they did not participate directly, evidence of women's solidarity with the demonstrators' cause was considered critical. Women were valued as spectators or witnesses, in part because workingmen often couched their protest against British policy in terms of its devastating impact on "widows" and "fatherless" children. But the women of their class did not need to be told where their interests lay. Many felt the impact of British policy directly, especially the wives and daughters of Boston and New York dockworkers, who suffered when moonlighting British soldiers took their men's jobs away. Thus, throughout the 1760s and early 1770s, working-class women, attended ritual events such as commemorations of the Stamp Act repeal, the hanging of political enemies in effigy, and funeral marches for protesters killed by British soldiers. On the evening that British tea was dumped into the murky waters of Boston Harbor in 1774, the silent witnesses lining the wharfs and docks included several women and children.

Women who supported the American protest did not hold a monopoly, of course, on activism or on an emerging political consciousness. Political involvement was evident among the wives and daughters of Crown officials and supporters who were often the earliest victims, if not the intended targets, of their neighbors' protests. Indeed, attacks on their male relatives served to sharpen the political awareness of these women and to force them to follow political developments more closely than many of their neighbors. Terrifying experience was a strong impetus to political awareness for a woman like Anne Hulton, who watched her brother, Customs Commissioner Henry Hulton, flee a jeering Boston mob. By 1774, attacks on the homes of known Crown sympathizers had become common, and while the men fled to safety, their wives often found themselves facing an angry and sometimes drunken crowd.

Women shopkeepers or merchants who supported Crown policy were directly challenged to conform with the boycott regulations or suffer the consequences. Gender was no protection for Anne and Betsy Cumming when they were accused of breaking the nonimportation agreement in 1768. When members of the local boycott committee entered her shop, Betsy defended herself firmly and directly. "I told them we have never entered into eney agreement not to import for it was verry trifling our Business," she later explained to her aunt. She reprimanded the men for trying to "inger two industrious Girls who ware Striving in an honest way to Git their Bread."

And like Grace Galloway, many Loyalist women developed a sense of the price of political commitment before their Revolutionary neighbors were forced to do so. In October 1775, a Virginia woman was called before a local Committee of Safety to answer accusations that she was engaged in Loyalist activities. When she refused to cooperate with this extra-legal Revolutionary committee, they declared her "insolent, scandalous, and indecent," judged her "an enemy of her Country," and instructed her neighbors "to break off all kinds of intercourse and connection with her." Thus, even before independence was declared, social isolation for some had begun.

As the likelihood of war grew stronger, women's activism intensified. In New England, where fighting preceded a formal declaration of war, observers on both sides remarked on women's enthusiasm for the conflict. In early September 1774, local militias were mustered in response to a false report that Boston-based British troops planned to attack neighboring Cambridge. The women, recorded one eyewitness, "surpassed the Men for Eagerness & Spirit in the Defense of Liberty by Arms." He marveled that "at every house Women and Children [were] making Cartridges, running Bullets, making Wallets, baking Biscuit, crying and bemoaning & at the same time animating their Husbands & Sons to fight for their liberties, tho not knowing whether they should ever see them again." The observer's amazement is more surprising than the behavior of these Massachusetts women. For these women knew, as did most colonial women, that the approaching war would be a home-front war. Loyalist or patriot, Indian, African, or European, American women understood that such a war allowed no civilians. Even if a family was to attempt strict neutrality, the effects of war—scarcity, inflation, danger, and dislocation—would find them.

The women of Lexington and Concord were among the first to experience the terrible realities of war. "We were roused from the benign Slumbers of the season," wrote Hannah Winthrop to Mercy Warren on April 19, 1775, "by beat of drum and ringing of Bell, with the dire alarm that a thousand of the Troups of George the third were gone forth to murder the peaceful inhabitants of the surrounding villages . . . It seemed necessary to retire to some place of safety til the calamity passed." There proved to be few places of safety. As the battle reached the outskirts of Cambridge, Winthrop saw "the glistening instruments of death, proclaiming by an incessant fire, that much blood must be shed, that many widow'd & orphan'd ones be left."

Like the "crying," "bemoaning," and "animating" women of Cambridge, colonial women of every region moved quickly to aid in the mobilization for war. Their cooperation was vital, for the newly constituted continental government had few resources and would rely heavily in the beginning on popular contributions to equip its army. Patriot women found that several areas of household production shifted easily into wartime production. Sewing circles redirected their efforts, causing fancy embroidery on fancy linen to give way to the plain stitching necessary for soldiers' shirts. As a result, continental soldiers, most of them farmers and laborers, could be seen parading in uniforms made of rich fabrics originally intended for Sunday suits or ladies' gowns. Girls and their mothers took up knitting, producing stockings and gloves for the soldiers. Acting as a sort of volunteer quartermaster corps, women of all ranks mounted drives to collect basic, essential materials, asking other housewives to contribute pewter plate, candlesticks, and ordinary window weights to be melted down for cannonballs and shot. One New England woman, eager to contribute metal for bullets, melted down not only her pewter tableware and her clockweights but all the nameplates from her family's tombstones.

As always, the most assertive efforts by women proved disconcerting to some men. While the Philadelphia physician Dr. Benjamin Rush applauded the fund-raising efforts of his wife and her genteel friends, praising them for "at last becom[ing] principals in the glorious American controversy," the newly appointed commander in chief, General George Washington, was less enthusiastic. Washington's personal vision of female patriotism belonged to those who could be passive and admiring, and who could quietly suffer through the turbulence of war. When Philadelphia's Julia Stockton Rush, Sally Bache, and Esther DeBerdt forwarded to Washington the money they had collected, he felt obligated to thank them graciously. He refused, however, to acknowledge their accompanying letter, which audaciously instructed him on the allocation of those funds.

Soon, however, the growing shortage of essential household supplies began to absorb women's energies. As Britain moved to cut off the colonies' regular channels of trade, sugar began to disappear from tables, and salt, pins, molasses, and medicine vanished. The problems were exacerbated by merchants who took advantage of the situation and began to hoard their stock, hoping to charge higher prices as the scarcity increased. Women responded angrily. In East Hartford, Connecticut, twenty women marched in "martial array & excellent order" on a shop where a store of sugar was being kept. Although the owner insisted that the sugar was being held for the American Army, the protesters were unconvinced. They "requisitioned" 218 pounds of his supply. Similar stories followed from across the regions. In 1777 a Poughkeepsie, New York, merchant was rumored to be hoarding sugar. When his wife tried to avoid a confrontation by offering to sell the cache at four dollars a pound, local women were unsatisfied. Accompanied by two continental soldiers, a crowd of twenty-two women demanded entry to the merchant's home, saying that they would have the sugar "at their own price." Armed with a hammer and scales, they proceeded to weigh the sugar they wanted and to leave behind a far smaller sum than the anxious woman had suggested. The following year, almost a hundred women assembled with a cart and marched to the warehouse of a wealthy Boston merchant suspected of hoarding coffee. When he refused to turn over the keys to his storerooms, the women seized him by the neck and tossed him into the cart. They quickly relieved him of the keys, opened the warehouse, hoisted out the coffee, loaded it into the cart, and drove off. As Abigail Adams reported, "A large concourse of Men stood amazed silent Spectators."

In the long run, attacks on shops and warehouses proved useless, for merchants' supplies rapidly dwindled. In these circumstances, women's ability to improvise proved more important than their "oeconomy." The most serious threat was the absence of a salt supply, since colonial families relied on salt to preserve meat over the winter. Experimentation proved that a lye extracted from walnut ashes could be used as a preservative, although it did little to improve the taste of the food. Other substitutes followed, including sage and herb teas and an ersatz rum made from corn syrup for local army use.

In the end, of course, it was the absence of men, not of supplies, that taxed women's resourcefulness. Some had encouraged that absence. As one Philadelphia woman proudly wrote: "I will tell you what I have done . . . My only brother I have sent to the American camp with my prayers and blessings. I hope he will not disgrace me . . . and had I twenty sons and brothers they should go." Others were filled with regret. But whether they had resisted the military service of husband or father or encouraged it, the war left women alone with the responsibilities of home, farm, or shop and family in circumstances that were daunting. Inflation quickly ate up the ordinary family's savings, and a soldier's pay, though faithfully sent home whenever it was actually received, could not support that family. By 1778 it was said that four months' pay could not purchase a single bushel of wheat. Enlisted men received letters daily, demanding or pleading for their return. In a rush of words, one such desperate wife poured out a litany of grievances: "I am without bread, and cannot get any, the Committee will not supply me, my children will starve, or if they do not, they must freeze, we have no wood, neither can we get any— *Pray Come Home*." Faced with such realities, men often deserted, slipping out of camp as harvest time approached or disappearing at night as winter set in.

Not every husband would—or could— return home, however. Nor did every woman

left to manage her husband's or father's affairs find the experience disastrous. There were, after all, profits to be made in wartime—armies to be fed and shortages of food to be overcome in the regions where fighting was concentrated. Especially in New England, where the fighting ended almost as soon as the war officially began, some women were able to turn a profit from a farm. For many more, there was satisfaction in simply preserving the family's farm or business through the long economic crisis. As one historian discovered, subtle changes in pronouns in the correspondence between wife and husband reflected larger changes in women's sense of their familiar role. At first, thinking of herself as a surrogate, or deputy husband, a woman might report to her husband on the condition of "his" farm or "his" crops. As months or years passed, that same woman slipped into a discussion of "our" farm and "our" crops. Not a few of them made the transition to a sense of hard-earned ownership that the young Eliza Lucas had made, that is, to "my" farm and "my" crop.

Throughout the war, the destruction of property wrought by an army on the move amazed civilians. The usually unflappable Eliza Lucas Pinckney was shaken by the ruin she saw around her in 1780–81 in the wake of British troop movements. Suffering was universal, she wrote, "crops, stock, boats, carts, etc all gone taken or destroyed." Circumstances were the same in Georgia. "Property of every kind has been taken from its inhabitants," wrote one survivor, "their Negros, Horses, & Cattle drove and carried away." And the demand that women open their homes to the quartering of troops meant further damage. A Long Island woman recorded the daily destruction of her property by the Hessian troops she had been forced to house. The soldiers "take the fence rails to burn, so that the fields are all left open, and the cattle stray away and are often lost; burn fires all night on the ground, and to replenish them, go into the woods and cut down all the young saplings, thereby destroying the growth of ages." When the soldiers, some of them living in her kitchen, received their monthly rations of rum, "we have trying and grievous scenes to go through, fighting, brawls, drumming and fifing, and dancing the night long." Friendly armies did as much damage as the enemy, as Loyalist Elizabeth Drinker discovered when a British officer commandeered her home. He put his own horses in her stable, moved into the front parlors, took over an upstairs room and the kitchen, and gave noisy dinner parties at her expense.

The loss of property was not the only thing to be feared when an army was near. Civilians, women in particular, felt so vulnerable to physical violence and to fatal disease that sometimes the mere rumor of an approaching army was enough to produce panic. In 1776 word that the British were sailing up the Chesapeake led to frantic efforts both to flee and to defend the city of Annapolis. "What with the darkness of night, thunder, lightning, and rain," wrote one woman, added to the "cries of women and children, people hurrying their effects into the country, drums beating to arms," the arrival of ships could be no more terrible than the preparation for it.

Such fears were well grounded. Smallpox and dysentery spread through Boston during the British occupation in 1775 and moved quickly into the surrounding countryside, killing women and children as well as soldiers and militiamen. Fires during the battle for New York City in 1776 left a quarter of the civilian population homeless. Although many of these civilians were women and children, gender was not the defining factor where disease or raging fires were concerned. But being female did make women vulnerable to rape. From the large-scale rapes documented in Fairfield and New Haven, Connecticut, in July of 1779 to the individual attacks reported in New Jersey or New York, the threat of physical violence against women was a persistent fear and a historical reality. Women of all ages were victims, from the thirteen-year-old raped by six soldiers to the backcountry matrons raped by Europeans disguised as Indians.

Women who had been raped were often reluctant to report the attack. The price for public disclosure was too high. As one Princeton man conceded, "Against both Justice and Reason We Despise these Poor Innocent Sufferers . . . Many virtuous women have suffered in this Manner and kept it Secret for fear of making their lives miserable." At times the women's reluctance was based on the futility of the disclosure rather than its potential damage to their reputation. In the fall and winter of 1776, for example, officers of the British occupying forces based on Staten Island and in New Jersey did little to halt the systematic and brutal rapes of local women reported to them. Indeed, cavalry commander Lord Rawdon preferred to cast the situation in lighthearted terms. "The fair nymphs of this isle [Staten Island] are in wonderful tribulation," he wrote to his uncle. "A girl cannot step into the bushes to pluck a rose without running the most imminent risk of being ravished." The results amused him greatly, he added, for "we have the most entertaining court-martials every day."

Women's impulse to flee from the military's presence was understandable, but many commented on its futility. The lesson Margaret Livingston learned when she fled New York only to reencounter the British in Connecticut was to "never move from the place providence has placed me in come what Foe that will." A North Carolinian echoed these sentiments: "The English are certainly at Halifax but I suppose they will be every where & I will fix myself here it is as safe as anywhere else & I can be no longer tossed about." A Pennsylvania woman put it bluntly to John Adams, in tennis Grace Galloway would surely understand. "If the two opposite Armys were to come alternately ten times," Adams recalled her saying, "she would stand by her Property untill she should be kill'd. If she must be a Beggar, it should be where she was known."

The presence of the army did not, of course, strike every woman with apprehension or fear. There was a benign aspect to military occupation that was as real in the experiences of some women as rape was for others. Young women from Winchester, Virginia, to Newport, Rhode Island, to Philadelphia recorded with pleasure the presence of an occupying army whose officer corps provided dancing partners, dinner guests, and opportunities for flirtation. One young woman admitted that "she wishe[d] there was to be [more war] if it were not for the shedding of blood. The war, as she understood it, was a seasonal ebb and flow of discomfort and delight: "They had a little fighting, to be sure, in the summer, but when winter came they forgot all the calamities of war and drowned their cares in assemblies, concerts, card parties, etc."

For African American women, the impact of military occupation was equally unpredictable. For some, the opportunity for freedom arose from the disruption of white society's daily life. But in many cases, military occupation separated black families. As white families fled an enemy, they took their slaves with them—dividing black husbands and wives, parents and children in the process. In New York City, for example, few enslaved wives and husbands shared the same master. When rebel families fled from the city and Loyalists from the surrounding countryside fled to it, many black families were thus broken apart.

Not all wartime damage was due to the demands of the military or to its thoughtless abuse. As Grace Galloway could testify, Loyalist women suffered the loss of property and the fall into poverty at the hands of former neighbors. Their houses were plundered, their shops destroyed, their families sometimes ejected naked from their homes. For these women, the enemy never broke camp and moved on.

If the Revolutionary War came to the majority of women, it is also true that a sizable minority went to it. Well over 20,000 wives, lovers, fiancées, and prostitutes filled both the American and the British army camps throughout the war, transforming these sites into bustling towns. The motives of these "camp followers" were various: some feared starvation if they remained at home, others Indian attack; some could not bear the loneliness or anxiety of not knowing their husband's fate; and some saw profit to be made from both sex and theft. Black women, sometimes accompanied by their children, came to the British army camps in a bid for freedom from their rebel masters. British officials encouraged these desertions by Southern slaves, offering sanctuary less out of humanitarian motives than in hopes of demoralizing rebel planters and disrupting the Southern economy.

Camp followers were considered necessary evils by British commanders, who understood the value of women. Their mercenary soldiers were less likely to desert if their wives and families came to war with them. Thus, the British institutionalized camp following, especially among their German troops, and allowed female civilians rations and supplies to bring aboard their transport ships. In their ledger books, ship officers carefully recorded the women and the expenses they accrued as "baggage."

The American commanders liked camp followers no better than their enemies did, although they, too, acknowledged their usefulness. A wife in camp could promise a reliable soldier. Indeed, American commanders were not above keeping enslaved African American women hostage in the camps to ensure that their soldier-husbands did not desert. And women in the camps could be enlisted as nurses, cooks, launderers, and food foragers—a menial labor force skilled in domestic arts and also willing to take on the unpleasant duty of stripping the enemy dead for useful items. Despite women's service to the army, supply sergeants begrudged the extra rations, skimpy though they were, that they doled out to women. Their concerns were not entirely unreasonable, of course. Supplies at winter camps such as Valley Forge were scarce and women and children were unwelcome extra mouths. In addition, army officers had to grapple with the very real problems caused by campsite prostitution: disease, theft, and black-market sales of soldiers' liquor to the Indians in exchange for supplies. The prostitutes who flocked to Washington's army in New York reached alarming proportions, and several soldiers were killed at or near their reputed meeting grounds. The colonel responsible for breaking up fights between soldiers and women called his mission "Hell's work." Frustrated by the endless trouble, he railed against, the "bitchfoxy jades, jills, haggs, [and] strums" who defied his regulation.

General Washington, in particular, fumed about camp followers, regularly complaining that pregnant women, small children, chickens, dogs, and domestic paraphernalia drastically diminished his army's mobility. On occasion, his orders that women march separately from men and through a city's back streets and alleys sparked resistance. One Philadelphia observer reported that the women and children were "spirited off into the quaint, dirty little alleyways and side streets. But they hated it. The army bad barely passed through the main thoroughfares before these camp followers poured after their soldiers again, their hair flying, their brows beady with the heat, their belongings slung over one shoulder, chattering and yelling in sluttish shrills as they went and spitting in the gutters."

This observer, like many commentators, saw the camp followers through a biased lens of gentility. As many soldiers were drawn from the working or impoverished ranks of society, their wives were unlikely to exhibit the social graces of the eighteenth-century lady. And the presence of prostitutes among their ranks marked the soldiers' wives as "sluttish" by association. When the wives of high-ranking officers, including General Washington's Martha, arrived to spend the winter camp months with their husbands, these ladies were treated far differently than the wives of enlisted men.

Enlisted men, on the other hand, and sometimes their immediate officers, developed an admiration for camp followers. A soldier's wife asked no special treatment—and received none. Her rations were sparer, her blanket no warmer, and she was expected to endure the misery of lice, dysentery, and long marches without complaint. When a woman proved more durable than her husband, the soldiers readily acknowledged her fortitude. A sergeant's wife won the admiration of one observer as they crossed a swamp on Benedict Arnold's harrowing march to Canada. "Now Mrs. Grier," he recalled, "had got before me. My mind was humbled, yet astonished, at the exertions of this good woman. Her clothes more than waist high, she waded before me to firm ground." Despite the lifting of her skirts, this camp follower remained "a virtuous and respectable woman" in the eyes of the soldiers she accompanied.

Many of the Mrs. Griers saw combat and did battle. As water and ammunition carriers, the wives of soldiers sometimes observed the moment of their widowhood and took up their dead or dying husband's place on the battle-field or beside the cannon. Known generically as "Molly Pitchers," because of the water they carried to cool the cannons and to quench the men's thirst, a number of these women filed for pensions from the government for their service. Among them were invalids left crippled by their war wounds. Few were compensated, although in July 1779, Congress did grant a military pension to Margaret Corbin, who had been hit by grapeshot at her husband's post, captured by the British, and left completely disabled by her injuries.

Wives like Margaret Corbin, Mrs. Grier, and Mary "Molly Pitcher" Ludwig may have participated in the Revolution out of loyalty to, or dependence on, their husbands rather than out of a political commitment to national independence. They also may have entered the military camp with loyalty to a political cause as well articulated and elaborated as their husband's. Since they have not left a record of their personal motives, we cannot be certain. Women's applications for military pensions, and the many petition received from women by local, state, and national governments requesting compensation for requisitioned property or relief from poverty suggest that women were deeply conscious of the services given and sacrifices made to the creation of an independent nation. Whether patriotism is synonymous with political consciousness is perhaps the question. What can be said is that these women had made direct individual contributions to the public good, to the larger commonwealth rather than to the "little commonwealth" of family, and they wished their role to be acknowledged.

Some women found other ways to serve the military. A few set aside their society's gender boundaries completely, donning men's clothing—assuming a male identity—to enlist in the American Army. The most famous of these women, Deborah Sampson Gannett, saw active service as Robert Shirtliffe until she was revealed as a woman by a physician tending to her fever. Gannett slipped with similar ease back into a female rote, marrying in the postwar years and bearing several children. How many other white women saw battle as men is unknown.

A significant number of white women chose to use their society's gender-based assumptions to advance the cause they supported. As spies and saboteurs, some women used their femininity as a disguise to gather intelligence and convey sensitive information. Their stories are numerous and frequently told. Some of these spies acted spontaneously, seizing the opportunity to obtain critical information about the enemy in their midst. In South Carolina, for example, a fifteen-year-old farmer's daughter named Dicey Langston outwitted the Loyalist troops who had camped beside her family's farm. As she went about her daily chores, she took careful note of the troops' number, their supplies, and even their morale. She conveyed this information to American force in the neighboring county. It was several months before the Loyalists realized who the spy among them was. And in Philadelphia, Lydia

Darragh made similar use of the enemy's short-sightedness to serve General Washington. Officers of the British occupying army paid little attention to Darragh as she served their evening meals. While they talked strategy and made plans for their spring campaign. Darragh listened and remembered. She passed along almost verbatim accounts to George Washington, smuggling messages past unsuspecting British soldiers by sewing them into the linings of her pockets.

Sometimes it was a girl's youth, sometimes a woman's old age that made her invisible to an enemy who assumed that women, being women, were passive onlookers rather than Revolutionary participants. Not infrequendy, however, American forces made the same mistake. One of General Henry Clinton's most dependable spies, Ann Bates, spent three years visiting American army camps as a peddler, counting men, supplies, and artillery as she sold her wares.

Most of these women spies acted on their own initiative, unable to resist or to avoid the opportunity and what they saw as their obligation to sabotage the enemy. But there were organized spy rings as well. The most elaborate of these, the Culper Ring, was based in New York, where fighting in the first year of war was fierce and the British occupation of the area was long. The ring established itself in 1778 on the strategically located Long Island Sound, which linked Connecticut and New York. At the center of the operation was a Mrs. Anna Strong, whose property, at Strong's Neck, Long Island, lay near several inlets where supply boats from American-held Connecticut might land and remain overnight undetected. Mrs. Strong acted as a signal woman, employing the most mundane domestic chores to fulfill her assignments. When the coast was clear of British patrols, she went to her clothesline and hung her black petticoat along with an agreed-upon number of white handkerchiefs. Although the head of the ring was a man, the majority of its operatives were women, for they were better able to enter and leave occupied New York City without raising suspicion. The domestic tenor of the Culper Ring activities—its baskets of fruit and food carried to city relatives, its laundry-line messages—belied the dangers of participation. In 1779 one of the women, known to us only by her code number, 355, was captured and imprisoned on the British prison ship *Jersey*. Like most of the prisoners of war crammed into the ship's hold, agent 355 did not survive.

In 1781, General Lord Cornwallis surrendered to General George Washington and the British abandoned their efforts to restore the rebellious colonies to the empire. Sporadic fighting continued for months, but Americans and their former rulers understood that independence had been won. If defeat was a blow to English pride and to British power at home, it was far more intimately experienced by Loyalist women and men, whether European, African American, or Indian.

Throughout the war, much of white Loyalist women's experience was a mirror image of patriot women's experience. During the pre-Revolutionary protests, some Loyalist women had been drawn into political activism, defending their rights to sell or consume British goods as they saw fit. Some had stood beside the windows of their homes, watching patriot crowds gather, waiting to see if their houses would be destroyed, their possessions looted, their husbands and fathers harmed. When the war began, Loyalist women served as spies, saboteurs, and couriers for the British; they flocked to British army camps; and they died or were wounded during battle. Like patriot women, some made self-conscious and autonomous choices to preserve their political loyalty. Among them were the newspaper editors Margaret Draper and Anne Catherine Greene, who fully and publicly asserted their loyalism, and three New York property owners—Margaret Inglis, Susannah Robinson, and Mary Morris—who were cited in the 1779 New York Act of Attainder and who lost their entire estates as a result. Some came to

Loyalism as a consequence of their familial or marital ties. Even then, a woman might feel the pull of conflicting loyalties. Esther Sewall, for example, was a daughter of the patriotic Quincy family and sister-in-law to John Hancock, but the wife of Massachusetts's leading Crown propagandist. Marital loyalty carried her into exile in 1775.

For African American women, the choice of loyalties was based on different considerations than those of white women. In a search for their own freedom, enslaved women took advantage of any opportunity the divisions between patriot and loyalist offered. Some supported an American victory, in hopes that the confiscation of their Loyalist master's estate might make their emancipation possible. But Loyalism was more often the best choice. The British had courted black support from the beginning of the war, promising freedom to all slaves who deserted rebel masters and benefits to black men willing to enlist with the British Army. With conscious irony, black Loyalist troops had marched to battle under the banner "Liberty to Slaves." Thus, when the British evacuated Loyalists from New York City at the end of the war, 3,000 African Americans boarded the transport ships headed for Canada. Over 900 were women, usually accompanied by children. Most of these former servants or slaves did not think of their departure as an exile but as a chance for a new beginning. Yet for many the costs were high: permanent separation from family members who had not won their freedom, who had been captured or seized as booty by Revolutionary forces, or whose Loyalist masters took them to another location. When Phillis Halstead, for example, boarded a transport in New York Harbor, she carried with her a two-year-old daughter born free behind British lines, but if this thirty-five-year-old woman had a husband or older children they did not make the journey with her.

Native American women of the coastal regions also participated in a struggle to retain their independence that intersected with but was not joined to the colonists' struggle for nationhood. The conflict between Crown and colonies left the Indians few and limited choices: American independence meant certain and immediate white expansion into tribal territories, while a British victory promised only a delay, a pause in the struggle to preserve their own autonomy. Most tribes chose to support the British, although some, like the Cherokee and two tribes of the Iroquois Confederation, cast their lot with the colonists. Thus, Indian women became Loyalists through diplomacy rather than direct commitment to the Crown.

The defeat of the British drove both white and black Loyalist women from their homes in the newly independent nation. War veterans of both races were given land grants in Canada, and British transports carried the refugees to Newfoundland and Nova Scotia. Here, African Americans experienced such intense racism, including physical violence and abuse of their legal rights, that a contingent left their land behind and relocated in Liberia. Other African Americans were less fortunate; viewed as captured booty by the officers and crew of the transport ships they boarded, these men and women were frequently resold into slavery in the Caribbean.

For white Loyalists, Canada was not refuge but exile. Leaving behind family, friends, neighbors, and familiar landscape and climate, they started new lives in the sparsely populated, forbidding land they called "Nova Scarcity." Their despair was captured in the words of one woman, who wrote: "I climbed to the top of Chipman's Hill and watched the sails disappear in the distance, and such a feeling loneliness came over me that though I had

not shed a tear through all the war, I sat clown on the damp moss with my baby on my lap and cried bitterly."

The women who took refuge in England fared no better. Even the wealthiest and most prominent Loyalist men and women who began their exiles in England soon found themselves struggling to make ends meet. As their money or credit ran out, families moved frequently, each time to smaller, shabbier quarters. Husbands and fathers grew melancholy or morose, for they realized that their exile was permanent and their careers disrupted forever. Like Grace Galloway, these Loyalists had lost their place in society.

Loyalist, widows in both England and Canada faced the complex and confusing task of filing claims with the British government for their pensions and for compensations for their husbands' loyalty or service and often for their own. These claims are riddled with worries of poverty and isolation, and the same anxiety over their children's futures that Grace Galloway felt. If widowhood left one Boston woman unhappy, she was certain that "what adds to my affliction is, my fears for my Daughter, who may soon be left a Stranger and friendless." And begging assistance from the British treasury, a New Jersey woman wrote of "the inexpressible mortification of seeing my children in want." For these women, and for all those like them, the struggle continued long after peace was declared.

Had the war ended for patriot women? In the decades after the Peace Treaty of 1783, the answer appeared to be this: The war was over, but the impact of the Revolution upon the roles, behaviors, expectations, and identity of American women was just beginning.

GLOSSARY

Attainted:	Loyalist property confiscated by local and state patriot officials.
Samuel Adams (1722–1803):	American Revolutionary leader whose agitations spurred Bostonians toward rebellion against British occupation and rule. He was a member of the First and Second Continental Congresses, signed the Declaration of Independence, and served as governor of Massachusetts (1794–1797).
Thomas Hutchinson (1711–1780):	American colonial official who was unpopular as governor of Massachusetts (1771–1774) because of his elitism and support of British policies.
Benjamin Rush (1745–1813):	American physician, politician, and educator. A signer of the Declaration of Independence, he was involved in nearly every reform movement in the early United States. He is especially known for promoting the abolition of slavery and the humane treatment of the mentally handicapped.

IMPLICATIONS

If men, such as George Hewes in the previous essay, could draw on their Revolutionary experiences to claim complete political inclusion in the new nation, what do you believe accounts for the failure of women to gain the same inclusion? What impediments did women continue to encounter in the post-Revolutionary world that men did not?

The idea of a strong, centralized government was repugnant to most Americans in the post-Revolutionary era. In most people's minds, strong government meant arbitrary and self-interested rule by an elite over the people at large. This reading begins with one of the most powerful statements against centralized government represented in the Constitution of 1787. Although the identity of Brutus is unknown, the sixteen essays penned under that pseudonym are a classic statement of the Anti-Federalist position. In this essay, Brutus makes the case for a Bill of Rights that would protect ordinary citizens against the potential powers of a centralized national government.

Brutus, *Second Essay Opposing the Constitution (1787)*

To the Citizens *of the* State *of* New-York.

I flatter myself that my last address established this position, that to reduce the Thirteen States into one government, would prove the destruction of your liberties.

But lest this truth should be doubted by some, I will now proceed to consider its merits.

Though it should be admitted, that the argument against reducing all the states into one consolidated government, are not sufficient fully to establish this point; yet they will, at least, justify this conclusion, that in forming a constitution for such a country, great care should be taken to limit and define its powers, adjust its parts, and guard against an abuse of authority. How far attention has been paid to these objects, shall be the subject of future enquiry. When a building is to be erected which is intended to stand for ages, the foundation should be firmly laid. The constitution proposed to your acceptance, is designed not for yourselves alone, but for generations yet unborn. The principles, therefore, upon which the social compact is founded, ought to have been clearly and precisely stated, and the most express and full declaration of rights to have been made—But on this subject there is almost an entire silence.

If we may collect the sentiments of the people of America, from their own most solemn declarations, they hold this truth as self evident, that all men are by nature free. No one man, therefore, or any class of men, have a right, by the law of nature, or of God, to assume or exercise authority over their fellows. The origin of society then is to be sought, not in any natural right which one man has to exercise authority over another, but in the united consent of those who associate. The mutual wants of men, at first dictated the propriety of forming societies; and when they were established, protection and defence pointed out the necessity of instituting government. In a state of nature every individual pursues his own interest; in this pursuit it frequently happened, that the possessions or enjoyments of one were sacrificed to the views and designs of another; thus the weak were a prey to the strong, the simple and unwary were subject to impositions from those who were more crafty and designing. In this state of things, every individual was insecure; common interest therefore directed, that government should be established, in which the force of the whole community should be collected, and under such directions, as to protect and defend every one who composed it. The common good, therefore, is the end of civil government, and common consent, the foundation on which it is established. To effect this end, it was necessary that a certain portion of natural liberty should be surrendered, in order, that what remained should be preserved: how great a proportion of natural freedom is necessary to be yielded by individuals, when they submit to government, I shall not now enquire. So much, however, must be given up, as will be sufficient to enable those, to whom the administration of the government is committed, to establish laws for the promoting the happiness of the community, and to carry those laws into effect. But it is not necessary, for this purpose, that individuals should relinquish all their natural rights. Some are of such a nature that they cannot be surrendered. Of this kind are the rights of conscience, the right of enjoying and defending life, &c. Others are not necessary to be resigned, in order to attain the end for which government is instituted, these therefore

ought not to be given up. To surrender them, would counteract the very end of government, to wit, the common good. From these observations it appears, that in forming a government on its true principles, the foundation should be laid in the manner I before stated, by expressly reserving to the people such of their essential natural rights, as are not necessary to be parted with. The same reasons which at first induced mankind to associate and institute government, will operate to influence them to observe this precaution. If they had been disposed to conform themselves to the rule of immutable righteousness, government would not have been requisite. It was because one part exercised fraud, oppression, and violence on the other, that men came together, and agreed that certain rules should be formed, to regulate the conduct of all, and the power of the whole community lodged in the hands of rulers to enforce an obedience to them. But rulers have the same propensities as other men; they are as likely to use the power with which they are vested for private purposes, and to the injury and oppression of those over whom they are placed, as individuals in a state of nature are to injure and oppress one another. It is therefore as proper that bounds should be set to their authority, as that government should have at first been instituted to restrain private injuries.

This principle, which seems so evidently founded in the reason and nature of things, is confirmed by universal experience. Those who have governed, have been found in all ages ever active to enlarge their powers and abridge the public liberty. This has induced the people in all countries, where any sense of freedom remained, to fix barriers against the encroachments of their rulers. The country from which we have derived our origin, is an eminent example of this. Their magna charta and bill of rights have long been the boast, as well as the security, of that nation. I need say no more, I presume, to an American, than, that this principle is a fundamental one, in all the constitutions of our own states; there is not one of them but what is either founded on a declaration or bill of rights, or has certain express reservation of rights interwoven in the body of them. From this it appears, that at a time when the pults of liberty beat high and when an appeal was made to the people to form constitutions for the government of themselves, it was their universal sense, that such declarations should make a part of their frames of government. It is therefore the more astonishing, that this grand security, to the rights of the people, is not to be found in this constitution.

It has been said, in answer to this objection, that such declaration of rights, however requisite they might be in the constitutions of the states, are not necessary in the general constitution, because, "in the former case, every thing which is not reserved is given, but in the latter the reverse of the proposition prevails, and every thing which is not given is reserved." It requires but little attention to discover, that this mode of reasoning is rather specious than solid. The powers, rights, and authority, granted to the general government by this constitution, are as complete, with respect to every object to which they extend, as that of any state government—It reaches to every thing which concerns human happiness—Life, liberty, and property, are under its controul. There is the same reason, therefore, that the exercise of power, in this case, should be restrained within proper limits, as in that of the state governments. . . .

10

The Constitution and the Competing Political Cultures of Late-Eighteenth-Century America

Robert E. Shalhope

The men who met in 1787 to consider how best to reform the national government were of a variety of minds. Northerners and southerners, from cities and the countryside, these men represented the diverging interests that marked early America. Yet whatever their differences, these men shared a common concern: As leaders of the world's newest republic, how could they prevent the inevitable slide into decline and despotism that marked the history of all previous republics? To these men, schooled in the classical doctrine that republics required a virtuous people who could put self-interest aside, the competing interests of class, region, and party were sure signs of decay and impending doom. How, then, could they act to prevent these social divisions from developing in America?

As Robert E. Shalhope demonstrates, political thought at the close of the eighteenth century offered two answers. Localists—mostly small farmers and rural artisans with few connections to the commercial world—saw the answer in a continuation of America as a decentralized republic of small property holders. With every American a small holder of property, there would be no large accumulations of wealth to challenge the virtuous government of the republic, and every citizen would have a stake—and thus an interest—in society.

A different and more modern view was offered by Alexander Hamilton, who thought the entire Republican conception of government, upon which so much of contemporary thought rested, misconceived. A cosmopolitan Federalist, Hamilton envisioned America as a great commercial and industrial empire on the model of Great

From *The Roots of Democracy: American Thought and Culture, 1760–1800* by Robert E. Shalhope (Boston: Twayne Publishers, 1990), pp. 94–111. Reprinted by permission.

Britain. For him, the creation of classes and competing interests was both inevitable and ultimately desirable. Much like modern-day conservatives, Hamilton saw capitalists as the creators of national wealth and sought to link the state with these men of wealth, augmenting their power and influence in society and ensuring American economic development. In this way, Hamilton hoped to move America away from the agrarian republic of Franklin and Jefferson and make it into a modern industrial state.

As Shalhope shows, it was ultimately these two notions of national development that competed in the mind of James Madison, principal architect of the Constitution, and came to structure American politics for a half-century following the Constitutional Convention of 1787.

In each state legislature two relatively well-defined opposing political blocs emerged to contest the issues. These groups did not form systematic organizations, nor did they extend into the electorate through institutional forms or organized electioneering. Rather they provided political expression within the legislatures to socioeconomic and cultural tensions that had been building for several decades. While no party labels or appellations appeared during the period, the terms *localist* and *cosmopolitan* best capture the essential nature of these opposing legislative blocs.

The opposing perspectives of cosmopolitans and localists resulted from their contrasting experiences. Cosmopolitans resided along the Atlantic coast or major navigable streams in long-established counties and townships, as well as the urban and more heavily populated districts. Cosmopolitanism thrived in those areas that had been most thoroughly Anglicized. The cosmopolitan delegate pursued an occupation—merchant, trader, laywer, commercial farmer—that compelled him to deal with a broader world and permitted him to share in the cultural and social activities of his community. He enjoyed wealth, or at least comfortable circumstances. He very likely owned slaves or employed servants, had assets well beyond his debts, had served as a Continental officer during the war or in an important civil capacity, and had the benefit of formal education. His view of the world, particularly when compared to his localist colleagues, was extensive.

Localists represented isolated, independent, and relatively egalitarian communities scattered through the inland regions of the nation located far from or inaccessible to established trade routes. The localist delegate was very likely a farmer and might also, like most of his constituents, be in debt. If he had seen military service, it was as a militia officer, and so the experience was brief and likely did not take him far from home. Few localist delegates had held previous civil office, and if they had, it entailed only local responsibilities. They had little if any formal education and, given their restricted experiences, had difficulty perceiving a world much larger than their own neighborhoods or counties. Their goal was to represent the needs of their own people—their fellow debtors, small property holders, and newly emergent market farmers.

These divergent cultural backgrounds were reflected in the voting patterns that emerged in the state legislatures. Localists worked constantly to reduce governmental expenses. They did not fill newly created governmental offices or hold redeemable state certificates or notes. By and large localists took care of their own needs. They built roads, paid their ministers' salaries, supported what schools they had, and took care of their poor. In essence they wanted to be left alone. Consequently they resented having to pay taxes on land and other necessaries when that tax revenue seemed to benefit others. Localist delegates pressed for many forms of debtor relief. They consistently supported inflationary policies that eased the conditions of debtors, provided relief for tax-payers, and supplied publicly supported money or credit at low interest to promote economic expansion and prevent foreclosures. Above all, they demanded a plentiful supply of money that would be considered legal tender in the payment of debts and taxes.

Localist representatives took negative stands on a number of other issues. They opposed the creation of banks and legislation to aid businessmen in urban areas. They resisted the unimpeded return of loyalists, who, once they had regained their property, would support the cosmopolitan cause. They were cynical about state-supported colleges and systems of public education, hesitant to support congressional demands for enlarged powers, and violently opposed to the idea of strengthening the central government. These people, trusting no one but their own kind, supported a simple egalitarian form of democracy that left them in control of their own affairs and free from hostile and corrupt outside forces.

In contrast, cosmopolitans believed most governmental activity fostered the greater good of society. This was particularly true if they themselves exercised political power. They supported payment of the debt in full, not merely because they held most of the state certificates and would thus benefit directly but also because they believed that government must, in order to maintain a good reputation, create solvent economic substructures with an outstanding basis of credit among the world at large. As the personal beneficiaries of good government, they supported higher salaries for public officials.

Cosmopolitans also supported a solid judicial system, improved transportation, subsidies to promote economic expansion, a stable monetary system, and the maintenance of good order. Never hesitating to pay their portion to receive such benefits, they demanded that all residents of the state share in these expenses by paying their taxes promptly, and preferably in specie. All private debts as well should also be paid promptly and in full. To these men, paper

money and debtor relief schemes appeared ill conceived and dangerously irresponsible. Cosmopolitans supported the authority and majesty of government. They consistently voted in favor of granting requests from the Confederation government for greater powers and looked favorably upon the creation of a stronger national government. Being broad-minded, urbane individuals, they quickly forgave loyalists, favored state-supported colleges, and endorsed the cultural and economic development of towns. Therefore the sort of democracy the localists advocated seemed like no government at all. It meant the domination of rational, educated, and propertied men by those of little property and even less insight into what responsible government was all about. Localism, to the cosmopolitan, meant narrow, selfish interests being pressed by ambitious provincials with little regard for order, decorum, station, and morals. It stood, in short, for the destruction of the sort of government that gentlemen had known—and controlled—for ages.

Beneath the tension within the legislatures coursed a deep cultural antagonism that repeatedly surfaced in newspaper essays, pamphlets, and public orations. In the minds of cosmopolitans, American society faced a crisis resulting from a combination of licentiousness and excessive democracy. Legislatures should be composed of men of property, independence of mind, firmness, education, and a wide knowledge of history, politics, and the laws of their society. Unfortunately, according to a Boston newspaper, such "men of sense and property" were being rapidly displaced in the legislative halls of the states by "blustering ignorant men." A Massachusetts gentlemen claimed that government was increasingly falling into the hands of those who, though perhaps honest, "yet from the contractedness of their Education, and whose views never extended further than a small farm or a bond of 50 or 100£ cannot, from long habit, be persuaded to view Matters on a large or national scale." Such men, "being unacquainted with the nature of Commerce view the Merchants as real positive Evils hence as well from Obstinacy as Ignorance, Trade, by which only a Nation can grow rich, is neglected." Cosmopolitans worried over the future, "when almost every office is in the hands of those who are not distinguished by property, family, education, manners or talents."

For their part localists remained suspicious of gentlemen who constantly assumed it to be their privilege to draw power into their hands at the expense of the common people. An incident in South Carolina in 1784, involving an alleged insult to John Rutledge by a tavern keeper, William Thompson, became a *cause célèbre* and led to a clear articulation of localist resentments—resentments that had festered for years. When the state legislature threatened to banish Thompson for his indiscretion against one of its own, the tavern keeper and ex-captain in the Revolutionary service struck back. His public address of April 1784, a classic articulation of the resentment building against social superiority, spoke out on behalf of the people, or "those more especially, who go at this day, under the opprobrious appellation of, the *Lower Orders of Men*." Thompson not only attacked those aristocratic "Nabobs" attempting to humiliate him but upended the predominant eighteenth-century belief that only a natural aristocracy was peculiarly qualified to rule. He argued that the "persons and conduct" of Rutledge and other "Nabobs" of South Carolina "in *private* life, may be unexceptionable, and even amiable, but their pride, influence, ambition, connections, wealth and political principles, ought, in *public* life, ever to exclude them from *public confidence*." All that republican leadership required was "being *good, able, useful*, and *friends to social quality*," because in a republican government "consequence is from the *public opinion*, and not from *private fancy*." Then, in tones heavy with irony, Thompson related how he, a tavern keeper, "a *wretch* of no higher rank in the Commonwealth than that of Common-Citizen," was debased by "those *self-exalted*

characters, who affect to compose the *grand hierarchy* of the State, ... for having dared to dispute with a *John Rutledge*, or any of the NABOB *tribe*." No doubt, Thompson exclaimed, Rutledge had "conceived me his inferior." However, the tavern keeper, like so many others in similar circumstances, could no longer "comprehend the *inferiority*." The animosity between those considering men like Thompson as their inferiors and those like Thompson who would no longer accept such treatment underlay the social ferment that boiled just beneath the surface of the legislatures and throughout American society in the 1780s.

DEMOCRATIC EXCESSES

Within this environment many cosmopolitan gentlemen became convinced that their society faced a social crisis. For men well versed in eighteenth-century political theory, it was not difficult to diagnose the illness plaguing their society. If British rule twenty years previously had degenerated into a perversion of power, the excesses of the people now had become a perversion of liberty. By this the gentry did not necessarily mean mob violence, although Shays' Rebellion in the winter of 1786–87 shocked them; rather they meant the quite legal democratic actions of the state legislatures. The delegates, elected in as fair a manner and based upon as equal a representational scheme as the world had ever seen, openly perpetrated the excesses that so disturbed the gentry. In those assemblies paper money schemes, the confiscation of property, and the whole panoply of debtor-relief legislation that undercut creditors and violated property rights achieved legitimacy.

James Madison's experience in the Virginia legislature from 1784 through 1787 epitomized the unease cosmopolitans throughout the nation endured. Madison quickly discovered that not all of his fellow legislators were gentlemen. In his opinion most cared little for public honor or honesty and seemed intent upon serving only narrow, local interests. Calm reason and order gave way to clamorousness and chaos. Lawmakers during Madison's tenure appeared to him to scramble to secure the demands of their constituents with little regard for consistency or the systematic creation of a body of laws to promote the overall interests of the state. Government, in the hands of "Individuals of extended views, and of national pride," could enlighten, but that standard would never be served by "the multitude," who could rarely conceive of issues except in terms of their own pocketbooks and their own neighborhoods.

Such a perception was by no means unique to Madison. Gentlemen everywhere grew increasingly disillusioned with the "characters too full of Local attachments and Views to permit sufficient attention to the general interest" who disgraced the state legislatures by ceaselessly advancing particular causes and pandering "to the vulgar and sordid notions of the populace." For Madison and his gentlemanly colleagues, the legislative branch of state governments, long considered the expression of the people's will as well as the best protector of their liberties, now seemed to have become a democratic despot. A tremendously important shift occurred in their thoughts; the fear and suspicion of political power long associated with the executive now became fixed upon the individual state assemblies.

Again James Madison offered the most cogent insights into the matter: "Wherever the real power in a Government lies, there is the danger of oppression. In our Governments the real power lies in the majority of the Community, and the invasion of private rights is chiefly to be apprehended, not from acts of Government contrary to the sense of its constituents, but from acts in which the Government is the mere instrument of the major number of the constituents." The people were just as capable of becoming despotic as any king or prince. Consequently the classical perception, in which the people's liberties faced a constant threat from the power of their rulers, made little sense. In America, rather than the many fearing the few, "It is much more to be dreaded that the few will be unnecessarily sacrificed to the many." This fear of the power of the majority, when combined with the gentry's growing apprehension regarding the character of the American people, created the most profound despair for men like Madison and his colleagues. In Madison's mind Americans must discover "a republican remedy for the diseases most incident to republican government."

Others agreed with Madison and set about reforming the state constitutions that had been written in 1776–77, adopting the Massachusetts Constitution of 1780 as their model. With a legislature balanced between a House that embodied the people and a Senate apportioned according to property valuation, a strong executive, and a judiciary appointed by the governor, this constitution represented a check on the unrestrained power of the people. A bill of rights spelled out the principle of the separation of powers in great detail. Some genteel reformers wanted to go beyond the Massachusetts Constitution as a model. They hoped to change the very character of the lower houses, first by decreasing the number of delegates so as to make the assembly more stable and energetic, and second by reducing their powers.

These efforts did not go unnoticed. Localists, who had welcomed changes in their state governments wrought by the Revolution, became apprehensive. For them the Revolution, by granting greater powers to much-enlarged legislatures, had been a success. From their perspective, the Revolution was just beginning to achieve its goals: a more equitable republican society where each individual and locale could gain autonomy and control.

By 1786–1787, the reformation of the central government became the primary concern of those worried about America's ability to sustain republican governments and a prosperous republican society. As a result, when the Constitutional Convention gathered in Philadelphia in 1787, it represented the culmination of reform efforts to curb the democratic excesses of the state legislatures and to provide an institutional framework that could safely accommodate the dynamic changes taking place within American society.

THE CONSTITUTION

The convention that met in Philadelphia throughout the summer of 1787, attended almost entirely by men of a cosmopolitan frame of mind, effected a political revolution as great as the one that gained independence from Great Britain. The delegates scrapped the Articles of Confederation and created a truly national government, a single continental republic that penetrated the state governments to the people themselves. At its head stood a powerful executive with broad appointive powers within the executive and judicial branches, who also served as commander in chief of armed forces and exercised virtual control over the nation's diplomatic affairs. Chosen by electors elected by the people rather than by the legislature, the president gained further independence during his four-year term of office, and he was eligible for perpetual reelection. The Constitution also created a separate, potentially powerful national judiciary branch, whose justices would hold office during good behavior and so gained immunity from the vagaries of popular election. The legislative branch consisted of a House of Representatives elected by the people and apportioned according to population and a Senate selected by the individual states composed of two senators from each state, each with one vote. Both houses of Congress enjoyed extensive legislative prerogatives, and Congress gained wide powers under the Constitution that had been denied it by the Articles. Most important, it now had the power to tax and to regulate commerce. In addition the new document specifically denied certain prerogatives to the states; they could no

longer print paper money, impair the obligation of contracts, be involved in foreign affairs, or lay imposts or duties on imports and exports. The Constitution, unlike the Articles, created a true national state with extensive coercive powers.

The new government reflected the central cosmopolitan tenets of its authors. According to Alexander Hamilton, it suited "the commercial character of America"; John Jay felt that it mirrored the true "manners and circumstances" of the nation, which were "not strictly democratical." The new arrangement must control the democratic excesses of the states by insulating the federal government from the populist forces that had sprung up with the Revolution. In addition, it should restore political influence to selfless gentlemen of broad vision and education. Madison believed that the best way to ensure this was to create "such a process of elections as will most certainly extract from the mass of Society the purest and noblest characters which it contains; such as will at once feel most strongly the proper motives to pursue the end of their appointment, and be most capable to devise the proper means of attaining it." This desire to attract the best men to the government and then to allow them to exercise independent judgment resulted in the complexity of separate constituencies, staggered terms of office, and elaborate mechanisms of election created by the new form of government. Only such a filtration of talent and modification of the undiluted expression of the people could safeguard the hierarchical world of America's gentlemen.

At the same time the creation of an active, energetic government promised to unleash the commercial potential of the nation that had been inhibited by state control over commerce. With a national framework within which to work, the entrepreneurial interests of the gentry could develop the tremendous economic potential of the young republic. The new government, empowered to deal aggressively with foreign powers and to control the nation's commercial activities, could now actively promote national prosperity. Geographical expansion, commercial development, and the consolidation and mobilization of mercantile capital seemed a real possibility at last.

JAMES MADISON AND THE CONSTITUTION

These two impulses—to control democratic excesses and to create a more beneficial commercial environment—lay at the heart of the cosmopolitan's view of the good society; yet they also constituted the source of his greatest tension and frustration. Backward looking in his political beliefs—desperate in his desire to hang on to the neoclassical political and social world of the eighteenth century—and yet modern in his economic outlook, the cosmopolitan became a victim of his own success. The capitalistic practices of his economic world fostered an individualistic ethos that eroded his neoclassical world of hierarchy and deference from which he derived his sense of identity and security.

James Madison's intellectual search for a way to preserve republican government and society from its own worst excesses led him to a careful reconsideration of what American society had become by the mid-1780s. Struggling to comprehend the changes that were transforming the new republic, he caught glimpses of the weaknesses in the conflicting sources of authority—hierarchy and localism—that struggled for dominance. Out of his effort to think through the work accomplished at Philadelphia, he arrived at the conclusion that the Constitution provided a framework for government and society resting on entirely different principles of authority than any previous governmental system. He presented this new understanding of political science, as well as his still inchoate perceptions of America's changing culture, in his contributions to the *Federalist* essays, published with those of Hamilton and Jay to support the ratification of the Constitution.

In these essays Madison spoke to the tension emerging in American society between the individual and the community. He attempted to find a system to oblige self-interested, self-governing men to respect the rights of others and to promote the interests of the larger community. He thus explored a middle ground between the potential tyranny of unrestrained majorities and the potential oppression of a hierarchy of centralized power. "The practicable sphere of a republic," he reasoned, must be large enough to "break and control the violence of faction," but it should never be so large as to sever the democratic bond between governors and the governed. While republican government should restrain the undiluted will of the people, that will must never be denied. In Madison's view governments existed solely to protect and enlarge the freedom of the people as well as their equality of opportunity. The best guarantee of such a purpose was to be certain that governmental power and authority rested on the consent of the governed. This constituted the most vital republican principle to which all just government must adhere. Therefore Madison's primary intent became to discover the proper mechanism that would provide such insurance while at the same time maintaining order and integrity in government.

Madison believed this mechanism existed in the federal structure created by the Constitution. That system would be able to refine and purify the will of the majority by causing it to pass through the successive filters of state and national governments while simultaneously guaranteeing that government at either level, however purified, always rested upon the will of the people. State authorities would attend to issues requiring a particular understanding of the parochial needs of local situations, while federal representatives would handle national issues requiring broader vision and scope. Because each level of government had been carefully balanced, no separate branch of either the state or federal government would be able to operate in opposition to the interest of the whole people. In addition, the state and national governments acted as checks upon one another. Given the creation of these safeguards, future generations of Americans would be able to enjoy as much self-government as human nature would allow.

Within this system Madison could constantly seek the middle ground. If the heedless pursuit of local interests threatened to overwhelm national authority or erode republican principles, Madison could throw his support to the central government and emphasize majority rule. Such was the case in 1787. If, however, a group of power-hungry leaders were to capture the central government at some future time and thereby threaten to destroy republican government through an oppressive oligarchy, he could emphasize anticentralist, libertarian principles and organize the countervailing powers of the state governments. For Madison, such a shifting of forces to achieve a proper equilibrium was necessary in order to ensure a lasting American republic.

In *Federalist* No. 10, Madison offered his clearest statement of the diseases that most commonly threatened a republic and their proper remedies. Sensing the emergence of a diverse individualism within the new republic, Madison knew that to gain legitimacy within this society government must rest upon the sacredness of the individual and each citizen's right to the fullest and freest expression of that individuality. He knew also that "as long as the reason of man continues fallible, and he is at liberty to exercise it, different opinions will be formed." Such "diversity in the faculties of men" must always be given free reign. Indeed, for Madison, "the protection of these faculties is the first object of government." In making such a commitment, however, Madison realized full well that a diverse society composed of self-interested individuals must inexorably result in the creation of fiercely competitive antagonistic factions. Such factions naturally resulted from the liberties cherished in a republican society. To remove their causes was to destroy the very essence of a republican society. Thus, since the causes of faction could not be eliminated, "relief is only to be sought in the means of controlling, its *effects*." This meant creating a governmental structure that simultaneously protected the peoples' liberties from the emergence of a single oppressive power and vitiated the power of factions themselves.

In Madison's mind, the Constitution accomplished this by dispersing power between state and central authorities and by dividing and balancing it among the executive, legislative, and judicial branches of the national government. While nearly every element of government at both the state and federal levels was elected by the people, these elections took place at different times and within such a variety of diverse electoral districts as to make it extremely difficult for one self-interested faction to gain simultaneous control of all branches of government throughout the nation. If a faction did control several state legislatures and gained a majority in the federal House, the Senate, the president, and the judiciary still stood as checks upon its excesses.

The surest means to control the effects of faction, however, lay in extending the geographic extent of government. The larger the republican government is, contrary to Montesquieu's dictums, the more secure the republican society is. Thus, "The influence of factious leaders may kindle a flame within their particular states, but will be unable to spread a general conflagration through the other states: a religious sect may degenerate into a political faction in a part of the confederacy; but the variety of sects dispersed over the entire face of it, must secure the national councils against any danger from that source: a rage for paper money, for an abolition of debts, for an equal division of property, or for any other improper or wicked project, will be less apt to pervade the whole body of the union than a particular member of it."

Madison's view of American society rested on the realization that a self-interested and diverse population had emerged within the young republic. No longer could an outmoded hierarchy or a localism based upon majoritarian sentiments offer entirely legitimate bases of authority. The one smacked entirely too much of aristocracy, and the other promised only chaos. For Madison, then, the Constitution fostered a diverse individualistic society, but at the same time it produced a checked and balanced government of real authority and power. The Constitution had indeed designed a government to protect a republican society from itself.

THE FEDERALISTS

Like Madison, the great bulk of Federalists —the name assumed by the cosmopolitan supporters of the Constitution—believed that the new government could preserve American republicanism from the democratic excesses they saw all around them. Republicanism to these gentlemen meant mobility, equality of opportunity, and careers open to men of talent. Such a perception of equality, however, was not incompatible with their commitment to hierarchy. In their minds all societies consisted of gradations of social orders held together by the deference owed to individuals in higher stations by those in lower ones. In a republic any person of ability should be free to move upward, but Federalists naturally assumed that individuals who rose in a republican society would first acquire the requisites of social superiority—property, education, social connections, broad experiences—before they took on the responsibilities of political authority. For this reason respectable people stood aghast as they witnessed men "whose fathers they would have disdained to have sit with the dogs of their flocks, raised to immense wealth, or at least to carry the appearance of a haughty, supercilious and luxurious spendthrift." Worse, state legislatures, the traditional Whig bastions of liberty, filled up with "men without reading, experience, or principle." Authority rested in "the Hands of those whose ability or situation in Life does not entitle them to it."

In spite of, or perhaps because of, the changes taking place in their society,

Federalists clung desperately to classical traditions of disinterested public leadership. For them the Constitution promised a last hope to preserve the republican ideal of a government in the hands of the "worthy" rather than the "licentious."

Many Federalists accepted Madison's argument in *Federalist* No. 10. The "better sort" might be overpowered by localists in the many small electoral districts required by state legislatures, but in enlarged congressional districts men of broad contacts and experience would surely gain election and thus control of the national government, which, with its enhanced powers, now had the opportunity to shape American society. Thus, the Constitution offered a filtration of talent that seemed to promise the reassertion of genteel authority.

To accept the logic of *Federalist* No. 10, however, enmeshed the Federalists in several paradoxes. First, by recognizing that American society had become fragmented into a multiplicity of conflicting interests—interests that could become overbearing local majorities in particular state legislatures—they accepted a conception of society that undermined the traditional social justification for a natural aristocracy and an elitist style of politics. The notion of the organic unity of society had always undergirded the existence of a disinterested natural aristocracy. Now Federalists seemed to believe that such a society no longer existed.

Also, by depending upon the new governmental structure to solve the social and political problems arising from the Revolution, Federalists acquiesced to the very democratic politics that they blamed for the ills of their society. Indeed democratic elections became the basis for the perpetuation of the natural elite's continued domination of politics. So long as constituencies could be made large enough to stifle the opportunities for social upstarts to gain office, the popular vote would elect natural leaders. Democracy could be made to support an elitist style of politics, and, Federalists hoped, an ordered society as well.

Federalists had little difficulty in presenting the Constitution as continuing the libertarian tradition of republicanism and the embodiment of the people's interests. This was possible because since 1776, political ideals had taken on new meanings, and republican principles had undergone subtle transformations. In their effort to defend the Constitution, Federalists drew together the disparate strands of thought that had emerged throughout the previous decade. Gradually, still not always aware of the consequences, the Federalists created an entirely new conception of politics out of these previously disconnected republican ideas.

At the heart of their emerging persuasion lay the idea of federalism. Here Federalists had to wrestle with the paradoxical idea of simultaneous jurisdiction by two legislative bodies—a clear contradiction of the fixed idea of supreme and indivisible sovereignty. James Wilson, a prominent Pennsylvania jurist, solved this problem at his state's ratification convention. There he claimed that those who argued that competing independent taxing powers—Congress and the state legislatures—could not exist within the same community had entirely misunderstood the nature of sovereignty in America. For Wilson, sovereignty was indeed indivisible, but it did not rest in either the state or the national legislature. Supreme power in America emanated from the people; they were the source of government. The people never surrendered this sovereignty. They merely dispensed portions of it to the various branches and levels of government as they saw fit.

Once sovereignty had been located in the people, the new system of government made perfect intellectual sense, and the Federalists could not restrain their enthusiasm for introducing the power and control of the people into every aspect of the newly created governmental structure. To attack the Constitution now meant to attack the people themselves. "We the People" assumed a transcendent new meaning. Indeed, given the fundamentally different principle upon which the new Constitution rested, it became entirely logical for the Federalists to defend the absence of a bill of rights. Since all power resided in the people, what they did not specifically delegate to Congress they reserved to themselves. Therefore it was not within the national government's power to grant specific rights to the people. For the government to do so would have meant that it comprised the fountain of all power, just as it did in the decadent and despised societies of Europe.

Such contentions revealed the gradually emerging assumptions about government and society that made up the Federalist system. The traditional libertarian division of rulers and people into separate and opposing interests became irrelevant. Instead the old spheres of power and liberty had been fused. The people now held all power; their representatives in the various branches of the government became their servants. Consequently the government itself became the shield of the people's liberties, not a potentially dangerous threat requiring constant scrutiny. Governmental power became, in Federalist literature, indistinguishable from that of the people. Once this view had been established, the Confederation government no longer made any sense. With all power lodged in a single unchecked branch of the government, what was to keep a combination of men from oppressing the very people they were supposed to serve?

The clearest theme that ran through Federalist arguments in the ratification conventions was the need to distribute and separate traditionally mistrusted governmental power. The old conception of a mixed polity no longer made any sense. America, the Federalists argued, was a new, unique republican society of talent and ability with no distinct social orders, only the people. To create a government in which all branches represented the people made perfect sense. All that was necessary was to separate power into distinct executive, judicial, and legislative branches and to balance them against one another. In this way, the entire government, not just the legislature, became a democracy. Thus the Federalists presented the new government as a thoroughly democratic entity based on the needs and desires of the people. The Constitution, in their rhetoric, epitomized traditional republican maxims and represented the culmination of the popular thrust of the Revolution itself.

THE ANTI-FEDERALISTS

Opponents of the Constitution, the Anti-Federalists, did not see it that way. Indeed if any central theme coursed throughout their arguments, it was that the Federalists meant to erect an oppressive aristocracy that would stifle the democratic tendencies fostered by the Revolution. In the New York ratification convention Melancton Smith warned that the new government "will fall into the hands of the few and the great." A Marylander, Timothy Bloodworth, exclaimed that "the great will struggle for power, honor and wealth, the poor become a prey to avarice, insolence, and oppression." A newspaper essay claimed that the Philadelphia convention had created "a monstrous aristocracy" that would "swallow up the democratic rights of the union, and sacrifice the liberties of the people to the power and domination of a few."

Such observations revealed that Anti-Federalists opposed the Constitution for the very reasons that Federalists supported it. They recognized that the new governmental structure would prevent ordinary individuals from gaining election to Congress and would thereby exclude local interests from actual representation in that body. Samuel Chase objected that "the government is not a government of the people" because only the rich and well born would gain election to Congress. Members of the minority in the Pennsylvania ratifying convention recognized that because of the election process, "men of the most elevated rank in life will alone be chosen. The other orders in the society, such as farmers, traders, and mechanics, who all ought to have a competent number of their best informed men in the legislature, shall be totally unrepresented."

Melancton Smith in New York remained convinced "that this government is so constituted that the representatives will generally be composed of the first class in the community, which I shall distinguish by the name of the *natural aristocracy* of the country."

These feelings of resentment sprang from a widespread sense of suspicion, hostility, and fear of a hierarchy of outsiders that permeated Anti-Federalism. The Constitution instituted a government of strangers; worse, those strangers were gentlemen who not only had no fellow feeling with simple folk but felt superior to them. Old Amos Singletary during the Massachusetts ratification convention voiced the defiant hostility and deep insecurities of localists: "These lawyers, and men of learning and moneyed men, that talk so finely, and gloss over matters so smoothly, to make us poor illiterate people swallow down the pill, expect to get into Congress themselves; they expect to be managers of this Constitution, and get all the power and all the money into their own hands, and then they will swallow all us little folks like the great *Leviathan*; yes, just as the whale swallowed up Jonah."

These attitudes—antagonism toward aristocracy, commitment to the most intimate participation in government by the widest possible variety of people, devotion to the egalitarian impulses of the Revolution—spawned majoritarian attitudes toward state legislatures but not toward the proposed new Congress.

Although the leadership of the Anti-Federalists included a number of prominent gentlemen—Rawlins Lowndes, George Mason, Richard Henry Lee, George Clinton—these men opposed the Constitution out of a philosophical and intellectual commitment to state government. Anti-Federalism itself emerged from much more visceral emotions. As much a social and a cultural phenomenon as a political movement, it sprang from a reactionary localism that pervaded American society. In the mid-1780s Anti-Federalism was handicapped because its ideas had yet to coalesce into a coherent political ideology. Consequently, in one state convention after another, Anti-Federalists found themselves bullied and embarrassed by their polished, articulate, unified Federalists opponents.

While the Anti-Federalist cause floundered, some individual adherents displayed a keen understanding of the social and political world emerging in America. This was particularly true of William Findley of Pennsylvania, a man who was far more representative of Anti-Federalist thought than gentlemen such as Mason or Clinton. Findley, an Irish immigrant who began life in America as an apprenticed weaver, had risen to become a spokesman for the debtor–paper money interests in the Pennsylvania legislature by the mid-1780s. A self-made man, Findley had never assumed the refinements of gentility—education, affluence, sophistication in speech and dress. Instead he remained an outspoken advocate of middling aspirations, achievements, and resentments. Indeed, he felt a special antagonism toward members of the gentry who looked down upon him and his kind.

Findley never denied serving the interests of his constituents. Indeed, he prided himself upon it and declared that whenever an individual had "a cause of his own to advocate, interest will dictate the propriety of canvassing for a seat" in the legislature. Findley saw nothing wrong with this. To him self-interest was the driving force within American society: "The human soul is affected by wealth, in almost all its faculties. It is effected by its present interests, by its expectations, and by its fears." Findley freely admitted to being self-interested, but he belligerently refused to believe gentlemen were any different. He had no patience with the argument of the genteel that they served in political positions simply to promote the common good. Throughout his terms in the Pennsylvania legislature, Findley had intimate contact with the gentry; the mystique of disinterested aristocratic authority had no power over him. He knew that for all their claims of superiority emanating from knowledge, experience, education, and extensive connections,

gentlemen differed from their neighbors only in having more money.

In Findley's mind American society was a heterogeneous mixture composed of "many different classes or orders of people, Merchant, Farmer, Planter Mechanic and Gentry or wealthy Men"; each group with equal claim to the rights and privileges of government. In such a disparate and egalitarian society, no group or class or men could possibly represent the interests of the entire community: "No man when he enters into society, does it from a view to promote the good of others, but he does it for his own good." Consequently the only fair system of representation must be one in which "every order of men in the community . . . can have a share in it." Each local interest must be directly represented in order for the pluralistic society emerging in America to be embodied fully and completely within the government. This belief, combined with their conviction that the Constitution would keep ordinary individuals out of the national government, fed the antagonism Findley and his Anti-Federalist colleagues felt toward the Federalists.

Findley's attacks upon deference and the ability of gentlemen to govern in the interest of a common good was part of an entirely new perception of politics and society. Rather than a harmonious unity that solidified all orders into an organic whole, he saw society divided into disconnected and antagonistic interests. Whether he realized the implications of what he was saying or not, when he and other Anti-Federalists attacked the traditional idea of a natural aristocracy governing in the interest of all, they also indirectly undermined the belief in an organic social order that underlay their own localist brand of republicanism.

Not all of the Anti-Federalists sensed the changes taking place in their society as clearly as Findley, but all expressed an eighteenth-century libertarian distrust of hierarchy that came from a traditional local sense of community. They knew no other language. As they stumbled toward a new understanding of their world, they remained dependent on an anachronistic vocabulary. Bred upon the hostility believed to exist between the spheres of power and liberty, they felt certain that a republican government could exist only in a small geographic region of homogeneous interests and that they must distrust all executive and aristocratic power. Now, however, they watched in horror as the Federalists turned each weapon in their republican arsenal against them. When Anti-Federalists attacked a powerful executive or an independent Senate as potential sources of oppression by rulers set against the people, Federalists scoffed at them and replied that the president and senators were only agents of the people, not a separate and potentially oppressive interest at all. Whenever Anti-Federalists attacked the Constitution on the grounds that it divided sovereignty, they met the rebuff that sovereignty lay with the people and that to attack the Constitution was to attack the people. When Anti-Federalists demanded a bill of rights—the essence of libertarian republicanism—their opponents made them appear foolish by asking how a government could guarantee rights to the people when the sovereign people themselves limited and restricted the government. Everywhere Anti-Federalists found their own arguments turned back upon them. Republicanism, democracy, the sovereignty of the people—all seemed to have found a home in the Federalist camp.

As long as the powerful localism that permeated American society remained disparate, inchoate, and disconnected from its natural roots within the New World environment, it could not overcome the well articulated ideology of the Federalists. Still, the Anti-Federalist cause enjoyed tremendous popularity. Even without many brilliant debaters, clever parliamentarians, newspaper editors, or men of great individual prestige within their ranks and little, if any, organization, the Anti-Federalists suffered only the narrowest of defeats.

A CHANGING CULTURE

The struggle over the Constitution produced a number of paradoxes and ironic consequences. The Federalists, elitists who wished to create a powerful centralized government controlled by the rich and the well born, constantly spoke in terms of the sovereignty of the people; they presented their case in the most democratic and radical language. Under this guise they managed to create a government that answered their needs—or so they imagined. In 1787 they had little reason to believe that the Constitution might also provide a national framework that could, under changed circumstances, just as easily accommodate the rise of a national democracy. The Anti-Federalists, on the other hand, who wished to create a decentralized government with direct participation by all classes of people, employed an archaic and anachronistic libertarian language of communalism. Yet, in actuality, their behavior belied such an ideal.

An embryonic individualism was tearing at both the hierarchical and localist bases of authority represented by the Federalists and the Anti-Federalists. On the one hand, capitalistic economic practices of the Federalists eroded the social foundation underlying their traditional perception of a natural aristocracy. On the other, the egalitarianism characteristic of localism became increasingly manifested in an individualistic, self-interested behavior that fragmented the communal substructure of localism. As Federalists looked backward to an eighteenth-century ideal of politics and society, Anti-Federalists groped toward a new conception of society and politics more consonant with the transformations taking place within American society. Both groups exhibited thought and behavior characteristic of the newly emerging culture of the American republic.

GLOSSARY

Articles of Confederation:	First American national constitution, adopted by the Continental Congress at York, Pennsylvania, November 15, 1777.
Shays' Rebellion:	Rural protest movement in central Massachusetts during the winter of 1786–1787, directed against harsh state tax payments that led to repeated farm foreclosures.
James Madison (1751–1836):	A member of the Continental Congress (1780–1783) and the Constitutional Convention (1787) who strongly supported ratification of the Constitution and was a contributor to *The Federalist Papers* (1787–1788), which argued the effectiveness of the proposed Constitution; later became the fourth president of the United States (1809–1817).
Alexander Hamilton (1755?–1804):	The first U.S. secretary of the treasury (1789–1795), who established the national bank and public credit system and was author of several of *The Federalist Papers*.
John Jay (1745–1829):	American diplomat and jurist who served in both Continental Congresses and helped negotiate peace with Great Britain (1782–1783), was the first chief justice of the U.S. Supreme Court (1789–1795) and author of several of *The Federalist Papers*.

IMPLICATIONS

Only recently have historians begun to take the Anti-Federalist position seriously, not as a collection of backward-looking sentiments against modern politics, but as a principled set of arguments concerning the relationship between the state and its citizens. Reading this essay, why do you think the majority of Americans were "localists," that is, supporters of the Anti-Federalist position, during the 1780s?

Past Traces

Widely considered as intellectually inferior before the American Revolution, women and African Americans faced similar impediments in their quest for equal status and inclusion in the new nation. But while women could turn to their successful wartime conduct of family affairs to advance their claim for intellectual parity, African Americans had to follow a different path. Beginning in the 1780s, African American leaders began to develop public arguments designed to demonstrate the equality of the African American intellect. This reading begins with one of these documents, Benjamin Banneker's letter to Thomas Jefferson, advancing the case for African American intellectual capacities. Faced with a growing intellectual movement that posited the natural, biological inferiority of some "races"—including people of African descent—Banneker's arguments fell on deaf ears. Not until well into the twentieth century would Banneker's points become widely accepted in America.

Benjamin Banneker, *Letter to Thomas Jefferson on the African American Intellect (1791)*

Sir, I am fully sensible of the greatness of that freedom which I take with you on the present occasion; a liberty which Seemed to me Scarcely allowable, when I reflected on that distinguished, and dignifying station in which you Stand; and the almost general prejudice and prepossession which is so previlent in the world against those of my complexion. . . .

Sir I freely and Chearfully acknowledge, that I am of the African race, and, in that colour which is natural to them of the deepest dye: and it is under a Sense of the most profound gratitude to the Supreme Ruler of the universe, that I do now confess to you, that I am not under that State of tyrannical thralldom, and inhuman captivity, to which too many of my brethren are doomed; but that I have abundantly tasted of the fruition of those blessings which proceed from that free and unequalled liberty with which you are favoured and which I hope you will willingly allow you have received from the immediate Hand of that Being from whom proceedeth every good and perfect gift.

Sir, Suffer me to recall to your mind that time in which the Arms and tyranny of the British Crown were exerted with powerful effort, in order to reduce you to a State of Servitude; look back I entreat you on the variety of dangers to which you were exposed, reflect on that time in which every human aid appeared unavailable, and in which even hope and fortitude wore the greatful Sense of your miraculous and providential preservation; You cannot but acknowledge, that the present freedom and trenquility which you enjoy you have mercifully received, and that it is the peculiar blessing of Heaven.

This, Sir, was a time in whch you clearly saw into the injustice of a State of Slavery, and in which you have Just apprehension of the horrors of its condition, it was now Sir, that your abhorrence thereof was so excited, that you publickly held forth this true and invaluable doctrine, which is worthy to be recorded and remembered in all Succeeding ages. "We hold these truths to be Self evident, that all men are created equal, and that they are endowed by their creator with certain inalienable rights, that amongst them are life, liberty, and the persuit of happiness." . . .

Sir, I suppose that your knowledge of the situation of my brethern is too extensive to need a recital here; neither shall I presume to prescribe methods by which they may be relieved, otherwise than by recommending to you, and all others, to wean yourselves from those narrow prejudices which you have imbibed with respect to them, and as Job proposed to his friends, "Put your Souls in their Souls' stead," thus shall your hearts be enlarged with kindness and benevolence towards them, and thus shall you need neither the direction of myself or others in what manner to proceed herein.

And now. Sir, altho my Sympathy and affection for my brethern hath caused my enlargement thus far, I ardently hope that your candour and generosity will plead with you in my behalf, when I make known to you, that it was not originally my design; but that having taken up my pen in order to direct to you as a present, a copy of an Almanack which I have calculated for the Succeeding year, I was unexpectedly and unavoidably led there to. . . .

11

Thomas Peters:
Millwright and Deliverer

Gary B. Nash

It was Edmund Burke who most forcefully raised the issue of the hypocrisy of American revolutionaries who, he declared before Parliament, "Whelped for liberty while holding a half-million fellow human beings in bondage." As Burke understood, slavery was the great contradiction of the American Revolution—how, indeed, was it possible for a people to rise up in rebellion against British "slavery" while maintaining chattel slavery as an institution for their own economic benefit?

In the course of the Revolution, growing numbers of white northerners answered the challenge that slavery posed to their Revolutionary ideals by electing officials who passed immediate and gradual abolition laws. But official manumission was a slow and uneven process that often kept Africans and African Americans in bondage until middle- or old-age. And in the South, calls for abolition where quickly drowned by the overwhelming voices of self-interested planters. A more immediate and effective pathway to freedom was taken by tens of thousands of African American slaves who declared their independence during the Revolution, not in formal public pronouncements, but by individually and collectively walking away from slavery. As the Revolution disrupted the normal course of American society, slaves used the breakdown of discipline and surveillance to escape their masters and mistresses. Some fled to live among Native American societies to the west, while others sought emancipation by serving as substitutes for their white owners in local militia units and in Washington's army. But most cast their lots for freedom by accepting the British wartime promise of freedom to any bondsman who deserted his master and served in the British cause. By war's end, more than 3000 former slaves evacuated America with the British, making the American Revolution the nation's largest and most successful slave rebellion.

In this essay, Gary B. Nash traces the life of one of these self-freed men, Thomas Peters. Captured in Africa in his early twenties, Peters spent the remainder of his life seeking freedom. As Nash shows, Peters' struggle did not end with the close of the American Revolution. Instead he faced discrimination, exploitation, and budding racism in British Canada and had to struggle yet again for freedom, finally achieving it in the British-led resettlement of Sierra Leone. In the end, Peters' struggle for freedom was one of the most poignant and persistent of the Revolutionary era.

....

Historians customarily portray the American Revolution as an epic struggle for independence fought by several million outnumbered but stalwart white colonists against a mighty England between 1776 and 1783. But the struggle for "life, liberty, and the pursuit of happiness" also involved tens of thousands of black and Native American people residing in the British colonies of North America. If we are to understand the Revolution as a chapter in their experience, we must attach different dates to the process and recast our thoughts about who fought whom and in the name of what liberties. One among the many remarkable freedom fighters whose memory has been lost in the fog of our historical amnesia was Thomas Peters.

In 1760, the year in which George III came to the throne of England and the Anglo-American capture of Montreal put an end to French Canada, Thomas Peters had not yet heard the name by which we will know him or suspected the existence of the thirteen American colonies. Twenty-two years old and a member of the Egba branch of the Yoruba tribe, he was living in what is now Nigeria. He was probably a husband and father; the name by which he was known to his own people is unknown to us. In 1760 Peters was kidnapped by African slave traders and marched to the coast. His experience was probably much like that described by other Africans captured about this time:

As the slaves come down . . . from the inland country, they are put into a booth or prison,

built for that purpose, near the beach . . . and when the Europeans are to receive them, they are brought out into a large plain, where the [ships'] surgeons examine every part of every one of them to the smallest member, men and women being all stark naked. Such as are allowed good and sound are set on one side, and the others by themselves; which slaves are rejected are called Mackrons, being above thirty-five years of age, or defective in their lips, eyes, or teeth, or grown gray; or that have the venereal disease, or any other imperfection.

It was Peters' lot to be sold to the captain of a French slave ship, the *Henri Quatre*. But it mattered little whether the ship was French, English, Dutch, or Portuguese, for all the naval architects of Europe in the eighteenth century were intent on designing ships that could pack in slaves by the hundreds for the passage across the Atlantic. Brutality was systematic, in the form of pitching overboard any slaves who fell sick on the voyage and of punishing offenders with almost sadistic intensity as a way of creating a climate of fear that would stifle any insurrectionist tendencies. Even so, suicide and mutiny were not uncommon during the ocean crossing, which tells us that even the extraordinary force used in capturing, branding, selling, and transporting Africans from one continent to another was not enough to make the captives submit tamely to their fate. So great was this resistance that special techniques of torture had to be devised to cope with the thousands of slaves who were determined to starve themselves to death on the middle passage rather than reach the New World in chains. Brutal whippings and hot coals applied to the lips were frequently used to open the mouth of recalcitrant slaves. When this did not suffice, a special instrument, the *speculum oris,* or mouth opener, was employed to wrench apart the jaws of a resistant African.

Peters saw land again in French Louisiana, where the *Henri Quatre* made harbor. On his way to the New World, the destination of so many aspiring Europeans for three centuries, he had lost not only his Egba name and his family and friends but also his liberty, his dreams of happiness, and very nearly his life. Shortly thereafter, he started his own revolution in America because he had been deprived of what he considered to be his natural rights. He needed neither a written language nor constitutional treatises to convince himself of that, and no amount of harsh treatment would persuade him to accept his lot meekly. This personal rebellion was to span three decades, cover five countries, and entail three more transatlantic voyages. It reveals him as a leader of as great a stature as many a famous "historical" figure of the revolutionary era. Only because the keepers of the past are drawn from the racially dominant group in American society has Peters failed to find his way into history textbooks and centennial celebrations.

Peters never adapted well to slavery. He may have been put to work in the sugarcane fields in Louisiana, where heavy labor drained life away from plantation laborers with almost the same rapidity as in the Caribbean sugar islands. Whatever his work role, he tried to escape three times from the grasp of the fellow human being who presumed to call him chattel property, thus seeming to proclaim, within the context of his own experience, that all men are created equal. Three times, legend has it, he paid the price of unsuccessful black rebels: first he was whipped severely, then he was branded, and finally he was obliged to walk about in heavy ankle shackles. But his French master could not snuff out the yearning for freedom that seemed to beat in his breast, and at length he may have simply given

up trying to whip Peters into being a dutiful, unresisting slave.

Some time after 1760 his Louisiana master sold Peters to an Englishman in one of the southern colonies. Probably it was then that the name he would carry for the remainder of his life was assigned to him. By about 1770 he had been sold again, this time to William Campbell, an immigrant Scotsman who had settled in Wilmington, North Carolina, located on the Cape Fear River. The work routine may have been easier here in a region where the economy was centered on the production of timber products and naval stores—pine planking, barrel staves, turpentine, tar, and pitch. Wilmington in the 1770s contained only about 200 houses, but it was the county seat of New Hanover County and, as the principal port of the colony, a bustling center of the regional export trade to the West Indies. In all likelihood, it was in Wilmington that Peters learned his trade as millwright, for many of the slaves (who made up three-fifths of the population) worked as sawyers, tar burners, stevedores, carters, and carpenters.

The details of Peters' life in Wilmington are obscure because nobody recorded the turning points in the lives of slaves. But he appears to have found a wife and to have begun to build a new family in North Carolina at this time. His wife's name was Sally, and to this slave partnership a daughter, Clairy, was born in 1771. Slaveowners did not admit the sanctity of slave marriages, and no court in North Carolina would give legal standing to such a bond. But this did not prohibit the pledges Afro-Americans made to each other or their creation of families. What was not recognized in church or court had all the validity it needed in the personal commitment of the slaves themselves.

In Wilmington, Peters may have gained a measure of autonomy, even though he was in bondage. Slaves in urban areas were not supervised so strictly as on plantations. Working on the docks, hauling pine trees from the forests outside town to the lumber mills, ferrying boats and rafts along the intricate waterways, and marketing various goods in the town, they achieved a degree of mobility—and a taste of freedom—that was not commonly experienced by plantation slaves. In Wilmington, masters even allowed slaves to hire themselves out in the town and to keep their own lodgings. This practice became so common by 1765 that the town authorities felt obliged to pass an ordinance prohibiting groups of slaves from gathering in "Streets, alleys, Vacant Lots" or elsewhere for the purpose of "playing, Riotting, Caballing." The town also imposed a ten o'clock curfew for slaves to prevent what later was called the dangerous practice of giving urban slaves "uncurbed liberty at night, [for] night is their day."

In the 1770s, Peters, then in his late thirties, embarked on a crucial period of his life. Pamphleteers all over the colonies were crying out against British oppression, British tyranny, British plans to "enslave" the Americans. Such rhetoric, though designed for white consumption, often reached the ears of black Americans whose own oppression represented a stark contradiction of the principles that their white masters were enunciating in their protests against the mother country. Peters' own master, William Campbell, had become a leading member of Wilmington's Sons of Liberty in 1770; thus Peters witnessed his own master's personal involvement in a rebellion to secure for himself and his posterity those natural rights which were called inalienable. If inspiration for the struggle for freedom was needed, Peters could have found it in the household of his own slave master.

By the summer of 1775 dread of a slave uprising in the Cape Fear area was widespread. As the war clouds gathered, North Carolinians recoiled at the rumor that the British intended, if war came, "to let loose the Indians on our Frontiers, [and] to raise the Negroes against us." In alarm, the Wilmington Committee of Safety banned imports of new slaves, who might further incite the black rebelliousness that whites recognized was growing. As a further precaution, the Committee dispatched patrols to disarm all blacks in the Wilmington area. In July, tension mounted further, as the British commander of Fort Johnston, at the mouth of the Cape Fear River below Wilmington, gave "Encouragement to Negroes to Elope from their Masters" and offered protection to those who escaped. Martial law was imposed when slaves began fleeing into the woods outside of town and the word spread that the British had promised "every Negro that would murder his Master and family that he should have his Master's plantation." For Thomas Peters the time was near.

In November 1775 Lord Dunmore, the royal governor of Virginia, issued his famous proclamation offering lifelong freedom for any American slave or indentured servant "able and willing to bear arms" who escaped his master and made it to the British lines. White owners and legislators threatened dire consequences to those who were caught stealing away and attempted to squelch bids for freedom by vowing to take bitter revenge on the kinfolk left behind by fleeing slaves. Among slaves in Wilmington the news must have caused a buzz of excitement, for as in other areas the belief now spread that the emancipation of slaves would be a part of the British war policy. But the time was not yet ripe because hundreds of miles of pine barrens, swamps, and inland waterways separated Wilmington from Norfolk, Virginia, where Lord Dunmore's British forces were concentrated, and slaves knew that white patrols were active throughout the tidewater area from Cape Fear to the Chesapeake Bay.

The opportune moment for Peters arrived four months later, in March 1776. It was then that he struck his blow for freedom. On February 9 Wilmington was evacuated as word arrived that the British sloop *Cruizer* was proceeding up the Cape Fear River to bombard the town. A month later twenty British ships arrived from Boston, including several troop transports under Sir Henry Clinton. For the next two months the British controlled the river, plundered the countryside, and set off a wave of slave desertions. Peters seized the moment, broke the law of North Carolina, redefined himself as a man instead of a piece of William Campbell's property, and made good his escape. Captain George Martin, an officer under Sir Henry Clinton, organized the escaped slaves from the Cape Fear region into the company of Black Pioneers. Seven years later, in New York City at the end of the war, Peters would testify that he had been sworn into the Black Pioneers by Captain George Martin along with other Wilmington slaves, including his friend Murphy Steel, whose fortunes would be intertwined with his own for years to come.

For the rest of the war Peters fought with Martin's company, which became known as the Black Guides and Pioneers. He witnessed the British bombardment of Charleston, South Carolina, in the summer of 1776, and then moved north with the British forces to occupy Philadelphia at the end of the next year. He was wounded twice during subsequent action and at some point during the war was promoted to sergeant, which tells us that he had already demonstrated leadership among his fellow escaped slaves.

Wartime service places him historically among the thousands of American slaves who took advantage of wartime disruption to obtain their freedom in any way they could. Sometimes they joined the American army, often serving in place of whites who gladly gave black men freedom in order not to risk life and limb for the cause. Sometimes they served with their masters on the battlefield and hoped for the reward of freedom at the war's end. Sometimes they tried to burst the shackles of slavery by fleeing the war altogether and seeking refuge among the trans-Allegheny Indian tribes. But most frequently freedom was sought by joining the British whenever their regiments were close enough to reach. Unlike the dependent, childlike Sambos that some historians have described, black Americans took up arms, as far as we can calculate, in as great a proportion to their numbers as did white Americans. Well they might, for while white revolutionaries were fighting to protect liberties long enjoyed, black rebels were fighting to gain liberties long denied. Perhaps only 20 percent of the American slaves gained their freedom and survived the war, and many of them faced years of travail and even reenslavement thereafter. But the Revolution provided them with the opportunity to stage the first large-scale rebellion of American slaves—a rebellion, in fact, that was never duplicated during the remainder of the slave era.

At the end of the war Peters, his wife Sally, twelve-year-old Clairy, and a son born in 1781 were evacuated from New York City by the British along with some three thousand other Afro-Americans who had joined the British during the course of the long war. There could be no staying in the land of the victorious American revolutionaries, for America was still slave country from north to south, and the blacks who had fought with the British were particularly hated and subject to reenslavement. Peters understood that to remain in the United States meant only a return to bondage, for even as the articles of peace were being signed in Paris southern slaveowners were traveling to New York in hopes of identifying their escaped slaves and seizing them before the British could remove them from the city.

But where would England send the American black loyalists? Her other overseas possessions, notably the West Indian sugar islands, were built on slave labor and had no place for a large number of free blacks. England itself wished no influx of ex-slaves, for London and other major cities already felt themselves burdened by growing numbers of impoverished blacks demanding public support. The answer to the problem was Nova Scotia, the easternmost part of the frozen Canadian wilderness that England had acquired at the end of the Seven Years War. Here, amidst the sparsely scattered old French settlers, the remnants of Indian tribes, and the more recent British settlers, the American blacks could be relocated. Thousands of British soldiers being discharged after the war in

America ended were also choosing to take up life in Nova Scotia rather than return to England. To them and the American ex-slaves the British government offered on equal terms land, tools, and rations for three years.

Peters and his family were among the 2,775 blacks evacuated from New York for relocation in Nova Scotia in 1783. But Peters' ship was blown off course by the late fall gales and had to seek refuge in Bermuda for the winter. Not until the following spring did they set forth again, reaching Nova Scotia in May, months after the rest of the black settlers had arrived. Peters found himself leading his family ashore at Annapolis Royal, a small port on the east side of the Bay of Fundy that looked across the water to the coast of Maine. The whims of international trade, war, and politics had destined him to pursue the struggle for survival and his quest for freedom in this unlikely corner of the earth.

In Nova Scotia the dream of life, liberty, and happiness turned into a nightmare. The refugee ex-slaves found that they were segregated in impoverished villages, given scraps of often untillable land, deprived of the rights normally extended to British subjects, forced to work on road construction in return for the promised provisions, and gradually reduced to peonage by a white population whose racism was as congealed as the frozen winter soil of the land. White Nova Scotians were no more willing than the Americans had been to accept free blacks as fellow citizens and equals. As their own hardships grew, they complained more and more that the blacks underbid their labor in the area. Less than a year after Peters and the others had arrived from New York, hundreds of disbanded British soldier-settlers attacked the black villages—burning, looting, and pulling down the houses of free blacks.

Peters and his old compatriot Murphy Steel had become the leaders of one contingent of the New York evacuees who were settled at Digby, a "sad grog drinking place," as one visitor called it, near Annapolis Royal. About five hundred white and a hundred black families, flotsam thrown up on the shores of Nova Scotia in the aftermath of the American Revolution, competed for land at Digby. The provincial governor, John Part, professed that "as the Negroes are now in this country, the principles of Humanity dictates that to make them useful to themselves as well as Society, is to give them a chance to Live, and not to distress them." But local white settlers and lower government officials felt otherwise and soon bent the governor to their will. The promised tracts of farm land were never granted, provisions were provided for a short time only, and racial tension soared. Discouraged at his inability to get allocations of workable land and adequate support for his people, Peters traveled across the Bay to St. John, New Brunswick, in search of unallocated tracts. Working as a millwright, he struggled to maintain his family, to find suitable homesteads for black settlers, and to ward off the body snatchers, who were already at work reenslaving blacks whom they could catch unawares, selling them in the United States or the West Indies.

By 1790, after six years of hand-to-mouth existence in that land of dubious freedom and after numerous petitions to government officials, Peters concluded that his people "would have to look beyond the governor and his surveyors to complete their escape from slavery and to achieve the independence they sought." Deputized by more than two hundred black families in St. John, New Brunswick, and in Digby, Nova Scotia, Peters composed a petition to the Secretary of State in London and agreed to carry it personally across the Atlantic, despite the fearsome risk of reenslavement that accompanied any free black on an oceanic voyage. Sailing from Halifax that summer, Peters reached the English capital with little more in his pocket than the plea for fair treatment in Nova Scotia or resettlement "wherever the Wisdom of Government may think proper to provide for [my people] as Free Subjects of the British Empire."

Peters' petition barely disguised the fact that the black Canadians had already heard of the plan afoot among abolitionists in London to establish a self-governing colony of free blacks on the west coast of Africa. Attempts along these lines had been initiated several years before and were progressing as Peters reached London. In the vast city of almost a million inhabitants Peters quickly located the poor black community, which included a number of ex-slaves from the American colonies whose families were being recruited for a return to the homeland. He searched out his old commanding officer in the Black Guides and Pioneers and obtained letters of introduction from him. It is also possible that he received aid from Ottobah Cugoano, an ex-slave whose celebrated book, *Thoughts and Sentiments on the Evil and Wicked Traffic of Slavery and Commerce of the Human Species,* had made him a leader of the London black community and put him in close contact with the abolitionists Granville Sharp, Thomas Clarkson, and William Wilberforce. Once in touch with these men, Peters began to see the new day dawning for his people in Canada.

Peters had arrived in London at a momentous time. The abolitionists were bringing to a climax four years of lobbying for a bill in Parliament that would abolish the slave trade forever; and the ex-slave was on hand to observe the parliamentary struggle. The campaign was unsuccessful in 1791 because the vested interests opposed to it were still too powerful. But it was followed by the introduction of a bill to charter the Sierra Leone Company for thirty-one years and to grant it trading and settlement rights on the African coast. That bill passed. The recruits for the new colony, it was understood, were to be the ex-slaves from America then living in Nova Scotia. After almost a year in London, working out the details of the colonization plan, Peters took ship for Halifax. He was eager to spread the word that the English government would provide free transport for any Nova Scotian blacks who wished to go to Sierra Leone and that on the African coast they would be granted at least twenty acres per man, ten for each wife, and five for each child. John Clarkson, the younger brother of one of England's best-known abolitionists, traveled with him to coordinate and oversee the resettlement plan.

This extraordinary mission to England, undertaken by an uneducated, fifty-four-year-old ex-slave, who dared to proceed to the seat of British government without any knowledge that he would find friends or supporters there, proved a turning point in black history. Peters returned to Nova Scotia not only with the prospect of resettlement in Africa but also with the promise of the secretary of state that the provincial government would be instructed to provide better land for those black loyalists who chose to remain and an opportunity for the veterans to reenlist in the British army for service in the West Indies. But it was the chance to return to Africa that captured the attention of most black Canadians.

Peters arrived in Halifax in the fall of 1791. Before long he understood that the white leaders were prepared to place in his way every obstacle they could devise. Despised and discriminated against as they were, the black Canadians would have to struggle mightily to escape the new bondage into which they had been forced. Governor Parr adamantly opposed the exodus for fear that if they left in large numbers, the charge that he had failed to provide adequately for their settlement would be proven. The white Nova Scotians were also opposed because they stood to lose their cheap black labor as well as a considerable part of their consumer market. "Generally," writes our best authority on the subject, "the wealthy, and influential, class of white Nova Scotians was interested in retaining the blacks for their own purposes of exploitation."

So Peters, who had struggled for years to burst the shackles of slavery, now strove to break out of the confinements that free blacks suffered in the Maritime Provinces. Meeting with hostility and avowed opposition from Governor Parr in Halifax, he made the journey of several hundred miles to the St. John valley in New Brunswick, where many of the people he represented lived. There too he was harassed by local officials; but as he spread word of the opportunity, the black people at St. John were suffused with enthusiasm and about 220 signed up for the colony. With his family at his side, Peters now recrossed the Bay of Fundy to Annapolis. Here he met with further opposition. At Digby, where he had first tried to settle with his wife and children some eight years before, he was knocked down by a white man for daring to lure away the black laborers of the area who worked for meager wages. Other whites resorted to forging indentures and work contracts that bound blacks to them as they claimed; or they refused to settle back wages and debts in hopes that this would discourage blacks from joining the Sierra Leone bandwagon. "The white people . . . were very unwilling that we should go," wrote one black minister from the Annapolis area, "though they had been very cruel to us, and treated many of us as though we had been slaves."

Try as they might, neither white officials nor white settlers could hold back the tide of black enthusiasm that mounted in the three months after John Clarkson and Thomas Peters returned from London. Working through black preachers, the principal leaders in the Canadian black communities, the two men spread the word. The return to Africa soon took on overtones of the Old Testament delivery of the Israelites from bondage in Egypt. Clarkson described the scene at Birchtown, a black settlement near Annapolis, where on October 26, 1791 some three hundred and fifty blacks trekked through the rain to the church of their blind and lame preacher, Moses Wilkinson, to hear about the Sierra Leone Company's terms. Pressed into the pulpit, the English reformer remembered that "it struck me forcibly that perhaps the future welfare and happiness, nay the very lives of the individuals then before me might depend in a great measure upon the words which I should deliver. . . . At length I rose up, and explained circumstantially the object, progress, and result of the Embassy of Thomas Peters to England." Applause burst forth at frequent points in Clarkson's speech, and in the end the entire congregation vowed its intent to make the exodus out of Canada in search of the promised land. In the three days following the meeting 514 men, women, and children inscribed their names on the rolls of prospective emigrants.

Before the labors of Clarkson and Peters were finished, about twelve hundred black Canadians had chosen to return to Africa. This represented "the overwhelming majority of the ones who had a choice." By contrast, only fourteen signed up for army service in the British West Indies. By the end of 1791 all the prospective Sierra Leonians were making their way to Halifax, the port of debarkation, including four from Peters' town of St. John, who had been prohibited from leaving with Peters and other black families on trumped-up charges of debt. Escaping their captors, they made their way around the Bay of Fundy through dense forest and snow blanketed terrain, finally reaching Halifax after covering 340 miles in fifteen days.

In Halifax, as black Canadians streamed in from scattered settlements in New Brunswick and Nova Scotia, Peters became John Clarkson's chief aide in preparing for the return to Africa. Together they inspected each of the fifteen ships assigned to the convoy, ordering some decks to be removed, ventilation holes to be fitted, and berths constructed. Many of the 1,196 voyagers were African-born, and Peters, remembering the horrors of his own middle passage thirty-two years before, was determined that the return trip would be of a very different sort. As the ships were being prepared, the Sierra Leone recruits made the best of barracks life in Halifax, staying together in community groups, holding religious services, and talking about how they would soon "kiss their dear Malagueta," a reference to the Malagueta pepper, or "grains of paradise," which grew prolifically in the region to which they were going.

On January 15, 1792, under sunny skies and a fair wind, the fleet weighed anchor and stood out from Halifax harbor. We can only imagine the emotions unloosed by the long-awaited start of the voyage that was to carry so many ex-slaves and their children back to the homeland. Crowded aboard the ships were men, women, and children whose collective experiences in North America described the entire gamut of slave travail. Included was the African-born ex-Black Pioneer Charles Wilkinson with his mother and two small daughters. Wilkinson's wife did not make the trip, for she had died after a miscarriage on the way to Halifax. Also aboard was David George, founder of the first black Baptist church to be formed among slaves in Silver Bluff, South Carolina, in 1773. George had escaped a cruel master and taken refuge among the Creek Indians before the American Revolution. He had reached the British lines during the British occupation of Savannah in 1779, joined the exodus to Nova Scotia at the end of the war, and become a religious leader there. There was Moses Wilkinson, blind and lame since he had escaped his Virginia master in 1776, who had been another preacher of note in Nova Scotia and was now forty-five years old. Eighty-year-old Richard Herbert, a laborer, was also among the throng, but he was not the oldest. That claim fell to a woman whom Clarkson described in his shipboard journal as "an old woman of 104 years of age who had requested me to take her, that she might lay her bones in her native country." And so the shipboard lists went, inscribing the names of young and old, African-born and American-born, military veterans and those too young to have seen war-time service. What they had in common was their desire to find a place in the world where they could be truly free and self-governing. This was to be their year of jubilee.

The voyage was not easy. Boston King, an escaped South Carolina slave who had also become a preacher in Nova Scotia, related that the winter gales were the worst in the memory of the seasoned crew members. Two of the fifteen ship captains and sixty-five black emigrés died en route. The small fleet was scattered by the snow squalls and heavy gales; but all reached the African coast after a voyage of about two months. They had traversed an ocean that for nearly three hundred years had carried Africans, but only as shackled captives aboard ships crossing in the opposite direction, bound for the land of their misery.

Legend tells that Thomas Peters, sick from shipboard fever, led his shipmates ashore in Sierra Leone singing, "The day of jubilee is come; return ye ransomed sinners home." In less than four months he was dead. He was buried in Freetown, where his descendants live today. His final months were ones of struggle also, in spite of the fact that he had reached the African shore. The provisions provided from England until the colony could gain a footing ran short, fever and sickness spread, the distribution of land went slowly, and the white councilors sent out from London to superintend the colony acted capriciously. The black settlers "found themselves subordinate to a white governing class and subjected to the experiments of nonresident controllers." Racial resentment and discontent followed, and Peters, who was elected speaker-general for the black settlers in their dealings with the white governing council, quickly became the focus of the spreading frustration. There was talk about replacing the white councilors appointed by the Sierra Leone Company with a popularly elected black government. This incipient rebellion was avoided, but Peters remained the head of the unofficial opposition to the white government until he died in the spring of 1792.

Peters lived for fifty-four years. During thirty-two of them he struggled incessantly for personal survival and for some larger degree of freedom beyond physical existence. He crossed the Atlantic four times. He lived in French Louisiana, North Carolina, New York, Nova Scotia, New Brunswick, Bermuda, London, and Sierra Leone. He worked as a field hand, millwright, ship hand, casual laborer, and soldier. He struggled against slavemasters, government officials, hostile white neighbors, and, at the end of his life, even some of the abolitionists backing the Sierra Leone colony. He waged a three-decade struggle for the most basic political rights, for social equity and for human dignity. His crusade was individual at first, as the circumstances in which he found himself as a slave in Louisiana and North Carolina dictated. But when the American Revolution broke out, Peters merged his individual efforts with those of thousands of other American slaves who fled their masters to join the British. They made the American Revolution the first large-scale rebellion of slaves in North America. Out of the thousands of individual acts of defiance grew a legend of black strength, black struggle, black vision for the future. Once free of legal slavery, Peters and hundreds like him waged a collective struggle against a different kind of slavery, one that while not written in law still circumscribed the lives of blacks in Canada. Their task was nothing less than the salvation of an oppressed people. Though he never learned to write his name, Thomas Peters articulated his struggle against exploitation through actions that are as clear as the most unambiguous documents left by educated persons.

GLOSSARY

Millwright:	A skilled maker of wooden machinery, especially flour mills.
Sawyers:	Carpenters.
Committee of Safety:	Local Revolutionary government.
Sir Henry Clinton (1738–1795):	British general and commander in chief of British forces in North America during the American Revolution.

IMPLICATIONS

The story of Thomas Peters raises one of the most profound questions in American history: the place of ethnic outsiders and people of color in a nation economically, politically, and culturally dominated by those who traced their ancestry to English and northeastern European roots. Peters struck his vote for freedom by escaping to British lines and later by leading Canadian Blacks to Sierra Leone. Do you think his fate would have been different if he had served in the American army and lived in the North? Would African repatriation have been an acceptable alternative to northern free blacks, who faced discrimination and disfranchisement in the New Republic?

One of the first acts of the new United States government was to declare the Native Americans living in the trans-Appalachian West a defeated people whose lands and lives were now under the control of the national government. Following this, government policy quickly turned to coerced treaties that forced Native Americans to relinquish large portions of their ancestral lands to the United States. While many tribal elders acceded to this policy, hoping to avoid war and maintain something of their patrimony, younger warriors bristled at the idea of land cessions and increasingly called for armed resistance to white incursions on their land. This reading begins with two statements of the warriors' position, the first by Little Turtle of the Miami and the second by Tecumseh of the Shawnee. As both statements make clear, Native Americans sought to maintain an independent path in the new nation.

Little Turtle on the Treaty of Greenville (1795)

Elder Brother [U.S. negotiator], and all you present: I am going to say a few words, in the name of Pottawatamies, Weas and Kickapoos. It is well known to you all, that people are appointed on those occasions, to speak the sentiments of others; therefore am I appointed for those three nations.

Elder Brother: You told your younger brothers, when we first assembled, that peace was your object; you swore your interpreters before us, to the faithful discharge of their duty, and told them the Great Spirit would punish them, did they not perform it. You told us, that it was not you, but the President of the Fifteen Fires [states] of the United States, who spoke to us; that, whatever he should say, should be firm and lasting; that it was impossible he should say what was not true. Rest assured, that your younger brothers, the Miamis, Ottawas,

Chippewas, Pottawatamies, Shawnees, Weas, Kickapoos, Piankeshaws, and Kaskaskias, are well pleased with your words, and are persuaded of their sincerity. You have told us to consider of the boundaries you showed us; your younger brothers have done so, and now proceed to give you their answer.

Elder Brother: Your younger brothers do not wish to hide their sentiments from you. I wish to be the same with those of the Wyandottes and Delawares; you have told us that most of the reservations you proposed to us belonged to our fathers, the French and the British. Permit your younger brothers to make a few observations on this subject.

Elder Brother: We wish you to listen with attention to our words. You have told your younger brothers that the British imposed falsehoods on us when they said the United States wished to take our lands from us, and that the United States had no such designs. You pointed out to us the boundary line, which crossed a little below Loromie's Store and struck Fort Recovery and runs from thence to the Ohio, opposite the mouth of the Kentucky River.

Elder Brother: You have told us to speak our minds freely, and we now do it. This line takes in the greater and best part of your brothers' hunting ground. Therefore, your younger brothers are of the opinion you take too much of their lands away and confine the hunting of our young men within the limits too contracted. Your brothers, the Miamis, the proprietors of those lands, and all your younger brothers present, wish you to run the lines as you mentioned to Fort Recovery and to continue it along the road; from thence to Fort Hamilton, on the great Miami River. This is what your brothers request you to do, and you may rest assured of the free navigation of that river, from thence to its mouth, forever.

Brother: Here is the road we wish to be the boundary between us. What lies to the east we wish to be yours; that to the west, we would desire to be ours.

Elder Brother: In speaking of the reservations, you say they are designed for the same purpose as those for which our fathers, the French and English, occupied them. Your younger brothers now wish to make some observations on them.

Elder Brother: Listen to me with attention. You told us you discovered on the Great Miami traces of an old fort. It was not a French fort, brother; it was a fort built by me. You perceived another at Loromies. "Tis true a Frenchman once lived there for a year or two. The Miami villages were occupied as you remarked, but it was unknown to your younger brothers until you told them that we had sold the land there to the French or English. I was much surprised to hear you say that it was my fore-fathers had set the example to other Indians in selling their lands. I will inform you in what manner the French and English occupied those places.

Elder Brother: These people were seen by our forefathers first at Detroit. Afterwards we saw then at the Miami village—that glorious gate, which your younger brothers had the happiness to own, and through which all the good words of our chiefs had to pass, from the north to the south, and from the east to the west, Brothers, these people never told us they wished to purchase our lands from us.

Elder Brother: I now give you the true sentiment of your younger brothers the Miamis, with respect to the reservation at the Miami villages. We thank you for kindly contracting the limits you at first proposed. We wish you to take this six miles square on the side of the river where your fort now stands, as your younger brothers wish to inhabit that beloved spot again. You shall cut hay for your cattle wherever you please, and you shall never require in vain the assistance of your younger brothers at that place.

Elder Brother: The next place you pointed to was the Little River, and said you wanted two miles square at that place. This is a request that our fathers, the French or British, never made us. It was always ours. This carrying place [portage] has heretofore proved in a great degree the subsistence of your younger brothers. That place has brought us in the course of one day the amount of one hundred dollars. Let us both own this place and enjoy in common the advantages it affords. You told us at Chicago the French possessed a fort. We have never heard of it. We thank you for the trade you promised to open in our country, and permit us to remark that we wish our former traders may be continued and mixed with yours.

Elder Brother: On the subject of hostages, I have only to observe that I trust all my brothers present are of my opinion with regard to peace and our future happiness. I expect to be with you every day when you settle on your reservations, and it will be impossible for me or my people to withhold from you a single prisoner. Therefore, we don't know why any of us should remain here. These are the sentiments of your younger brothers present, on these particulars.

Tecumseh on Land Cessions (1810)

. . . It is true I am a Shawnee. My forefathers were warriors. Their son is a warrior. From them I only take my existence; from my tribe I take nothing. I am the maker of my own fortune; and oh! that I could make that of my red people, and of my country, as great as the conceptions of my mind, when I think of the Spirit that rules the universe. I would not then come to Governor Harrison, to ask him to tear the treaty, and to obliterate the landmark; but I would say to him. Sir, you have liberty to return to your own country. The being within, communing with the past ages, tells me, that once, nor until lately, there was no white man on this continent. That it then all belonged to red men, children of the same parents, placed on it by the Great Spirit that made them, to keep it, to traverse it, to enjoy its production, and to fill it with the same race. Once a happy race. Since made miserable by the white people, who are never contented, but always encroaching. The way, and the only way to check and stop this evil, is, for all the red men to unite in claiming a common and equal right in the land, as it was at first, and should be yet; for it never was divided, but belongs to all, for the use of each. That no part has a right to sell, even to each other, much less to strangers; those who want all, and will not do with less. The white people have no right to take the land from the Indians, because they had it first; it is theirs. They may sell, but all must join. Any sale not made by all is not valid. The late sale is bad. It was made by a part only. Part do not know how to sell. It requires all to make a bargain for all. All red men have equal rights to the unoccupied land. The right of occupancy is as good in one place as in another. There cannot be two occupations in the same place. The first excludes all others. It is not so in hunting or travelling; for there the same ground will serve many, as they may follow each other all day; but the camp is stationary, and that is occupancy. It belongs to the first who sits down on his blanket or skins, which he has thrown upon the ground, and till he leaves it no other has a right.

12

The Revolution in Indian Country

Colin G. Calloway

The American Revolution disrupted the lives of all Americans, but few felt the disruption as acutely as the Indians of the Eastern Woodlands. Weakened by the French loss of their North American territories in the recent Seven Years' War (1754–1763) and unable to revive the play-off system that had allowed them to sustain their independence since the early seventeenth century, the people of the Eastern Woodlands faced their worst prospects since the beginning of European contact. During the Revolutionary War, Indian Country became a battleground in which contending armies fought, but also in which American soldiers sought to take Indian land and settle old scores. In the end, the Revolutionary War ended with an American victory that turned the full weight of the new nation against Indian sovereignty and in many cases, survival.

But, as Colin Calloway argues in this essay, in truth Indians did not simply drift away in silence in the aftermath of the Revolution. Instead, individual Indians, families, and whole nations created new adaptations to the unwelcome circumstances of the post-Revolutionary era. While their paths varied, some choosing armed resistance while others opted for assimilation to white ways, all Indians continued to adjust, adapt, and forge an independent world for themselves in the New Nation. As Calloway reveals, Indians were as much active and conscious players as their white counterparts in the complex drama of the American Revolution.

From *Native American and the Early Republic*, edited by Fredrick E. Hoxie, Ronald Hoffman, and Peter J. Albert, pages 3–33 "The Continuing Revolution in Indian Country" by Collin Calloway, copyright © 1999. Reprinted by permission of Colin Calloway.

The "world turned upside down" for American Indians long before it did for Lord Cornwallis, and many Indian nations were already shadows of their former selves by 1775. European emigration, European diseases, European firearms, and European imperial ambitions had produced political upheaval, economic dislocation, and demographic disaster throughout Indian country. Generations of contact had seen precedents established, attitudes ingrained, and patterns of coexistence worked out and fall apart. Indian communities in colonial America struggled to survive in a chaotic new world, and yet despite massive inroads in Indian country and Indian cultures, Indian people were still virtually everywhere in colonial America.

The forces that had inverted their world intensified with the outbreak of the Revolution. At first the American Revolution had looked very much like an English civil war to Indian eyes, and most Native Americans tried to avoid becoming entangled in it. Throughout the eastern woodlands, and throughout the war, British and American agents solicited Indian support. An Abenaki woman in western Maine said her tribe was being constantly courted. "O, straing [strange] *Englishmen* kill one another," she said. "I think the world is coming to an end." In the spring of 1777 British agent William Caldwell warned the Senecas not to "regard anything the Bigknife [Americans] might say to them for tho he had a very smooth Oily Tongue his heart was not good." Two years later American commander Daniel Brodhead warned the Shawnees that the British would tell them fine stories but had come three thousand miles only "to rob & Steal & fill their Pockets."

Such competition produced confusion and division in Indian communities as people wrestled with how best to proceed in perilous and uncertain times. Fernando de Leyba told Governor of Louisiana Bernardo de Galvez in the summer of 1778 that the war was "causing a great number of Indian tribes to go from one side to the other without knowing which side to take." Discourse and discord were part of the normal process by which most eastern woodland societies reached consensus, but the issues raised by the Revolution were such that consensus could not always be reached. The divisions of colonial society that John Adams summarized as one-third patriot, one-third loyalist, and one-third neutral were replicated with numerous variations in countless Indian communities in North America, and, as elsewhere on the frontier, the pressures imposed by the Revolution revealed existing fissures as well as creating new ones. The Delawares in 1779 asked Congress to distinguish between their nation as a whole, which was still friendly, and the actions of a few individuals who, like the loyalists in the states, sided with the British and had been obliged to leave the nation. As provocations increased, however, neutrality became increasingly precarious, even impossible, forcing Indians to choose sides.

The national mythology has assigned Indians a minimal and one-dimensional role in the Revolution: they chose the wrong side and they lost. But commitment was never unanimous, and in Indian country the American Revolution often translated into an American civil war. The League of the Iroquois—the confederacy of the Mohawks, Oncidas, Onondagas, Cayugas, Senecas, and Tuscaroras that stretched across upper New York state—had managed to maintain a pivotal position in North American affairs by preserving formal neutrality and essential unity of action in previous conflicts, but was unable to do so now. Samuel Kirkland, the New England Presbyterian missionary who himself generated significant divisions in Oneida society, heard Indians say that "they never knew a debate so warm & contention so fierce to have happened between these two Brothers, Oneidas & Cayugas, since the commencement of their union." The bitter divisions the Revolution produced *within* the Oneidas were "not yet forgotten" by 1796. In 1775 both the Oneidas and Senecas took a neutral stance; two years later they were killing each other at the Battle of Oriskany and the league's central council fire at Onondaga was ritually extinguished. Pro-British warriors burned Oneida crops and houses in revenge; Oneidas retaliated by burning Mohawk homes. Most Tuscaroras also supported the Americans while the Cayugas lent their weight to the British. The Onondagas maintained a precarious neutrality until American troops burned their towns in 1779. For the Iroquois the Revolution was a war in which, in some cases literally, brother killed brother.

In Massachusetts the Stockbridge Indians, a community of Christian Mohican and neighboring groups, had their own scores to settle against the British, having been deprived of lands while warriors were away fighting *for* the Crown in earlier wars and having tried in vain to seek redress. They volunteered at the outbreak of the Revolution and assisted the Americans steadfastly, despite suffering heavy losses. William Apess, a Pequot Indian writing in the next century, said that the small Indian town of Mashpee on Cape Cod furnished twenty-six men for the patriot service, all but one of whom "fell martyrs to liberty in the struggle for Independence." Pequots and Mohegans from Connecticut suffered similar high casualties. Indian women widowed by the war were forced to look outside their communities for husbands, intermarrying with Anglo-American and African-American neighbors.

The situation elsewhere in New England and eastern Canada was less simple. The Abenakis, for generations the shock troops of New France against the New England frontier, displayed ambivalence, despite considerable British coercion. Some served the British; others offered their services to George Washington. About forty-five Abenaki families took up residence near American settlements on the upper Connecticut and supplied scouts and soldiers for the American army. Those who remained in Canada became deeply divided, and some appeared to play both sides of the street. Most Abenakis seem to have restricted their role to watching the woods. Other Canadian tribes displayed similar reluctance and ambivalence, while the village of Caughnawaga (Kahnawake) near Montreal

became a hotbed of intrigue in the contest for Indian allegiance in the north. In Maine and Nova Scotia the Passamaquoddies, Micmacs, and Maliseets were not eager to become involved in a war that had little to do with them or to offer them. Many sided with the Americans but then split as British power and British goods exerted increasing influence.

In the strategically crucial Ohio country, the Indians were the prize in a diplomatic tug of war between Henry Hamilton, the British commander at Detroit, and George Morgan, the American Indian agent at Fort Pitt. The Delawares, neutral at the outbreak of the war, soon came under pressure from American and British agents and from other tribes, particularly the pro-British Wyandots under Half King to the north. A group of young Delaware warriors defected, but even General Hand's infamous "squaw campaign" did not destroy the tribe's commitment to peace. The United States signed a treaty with the Delawares in 1778 in an effort to secure their neutrality and right of passage across their lands, but many Delawares complained they had been deceived into taking up the hatchet for the United States. White Eyes and John Killbuck of the Turtle clan displayed continued pro-American sympathies, but Captain Pipe and the Wolf clan moved to the Sandusky River, closer to the Wyandots and the British. The American murder of White Eyes, their strongest supporter in the Delaware National Council, and their failure to provide the trade goods the Delawares needed, allowed Pipe to gain influence among his hungry and disillusioned people.

A detachment of Delawares served the United States through the final years of the war, but in 1780 Daniel Brodhead declared the Delawares had "acted a double part long enough." American troops, guided by Killbuck and his men, burned the Delaware capital at Coshocton. Killbuck's followers took refuge at Fort Pitt, where they not only suffered hunger and hardship but were exposed to danger at the hands of American frontiersmen to whom all Indians were the same. Those Delawares

who lived in separate villages under the guidance of Moravian missionaries also clung to a
neutrality that cost them dearly. In 1782
American militia marched to the Moravian
Delaware town of Gnadenhutten, rounded up
the inhabitants, and bludgeoned to death
ninety-six men, women, and children.

The neighboring Shawnees had been
involved in long resistance against encroachment on their lands and had just fought a
costly war against Lord Dunmore and Virginia.
Shawnee emissaries were active in efforts to
form a confederacy against American expansion, but the Shawnees themselves were
divided over the question of further resistance
and many migrated west of the Mississippi.
The Shawnee chief Cornstalk tried to preserve
his people's fragile neutrality but confessed he
was unable to restrain his "foolish Young
Men." Moreover, the Americans displayed
their peculiar penchant for murdering key
friends at key moments. After Cornstalk was
killed under a flag of truce at Fort Randolph in
1777, his Maquachake peace party joined the
still-neutral Delawares at Coshocton, but most
of the Shawnees now made common cause
with King George.

In the South the Cherokees had already had
grim experience of the consequences of becoming involved in the wars of their non-Indian
neighbors, but, with settlers encroaching on
their lands, they fought this war for their own
reasons. While the older chiefs watched in
silent dejection, Dragging Canoe and younger
Cherokees accepted a war belt from the northern nations and threw themselves into the
fighting early in the Revolution. After expeditions from Virginia and North and South
Carolina destroyed Cherokee towns and crops,
the older chiefs sued for peace, and refugees
fled to the Creeks, the Chickasaws, and to
Pensacola. The nation split along generational
lines as many younger warriors followed the
lead of Dragging Canoe, seceding to form new
communities at Chickamauga, which became
the core of Cherokee resistance until 1795.
Other Cherokees suffered as a result of
Chickamauga resistance; some helped the

Americans, and the Revolution assumed the
look of a civil war in Cherokee country.

Elsewhere in the South, Choctaw towns
were divided between Britain and Spain; the
majority supported King George, but British
agents always feared losing them. The
Chickasaws were basically pro-British, while
the Catawbas, surrounded by settlers, supported the Americans. At the beginning of the
Revolution, the Creeks were at war with the
Choctaws, and though the British now took
measures to end a conflict they had previously
encouraged, the Cherokee experience gave
them ample reason to drag their feet. British
Indian superintendent John Stuart complained
they were "a mercenary People, Conveniency
& Safety are the great Ties that Bind them."
Most eventually sided with the British and
about 120 Creeks and over 700 Choctaws
fought alongside the British in the defense of
Pensacola against Spanish attack early in 1781.
But the war divided the Creeks into bitter
factions.

Any overview of Indian dispositions and
allegiances is difficult and hazardous. Most
tribes fluctuated in their sentiments, intertribal
alliances formed at the cost of increased intra-
tribal disunity, and participation was usually
cautious and often relatively brief. One of
the first communities to wage war against
the Americans was Pluggy's Town, where
Chippewas, Wyandots, and Ottawas joined
Mingoes (Ohio Iroquois), and where Americans found it was often "difficult to tell what
Nation are the Offenders." Pluggy's Mingoes
caused consternation among neighboring tribes
who blamed them for corrupting their young
men and threatening to embroil everyone in
the war. In June 1778 Congress found that
the nations at war against them in the West
included "the Senecas, Cayugas, Mingoes and
Wiandots in general, a majority of the Onondagas and a few of the Ottawas, Chippewas,
Shawnese & Delawares, acting contrary to the
voice of their nations," but the situation was
not that simple and was constantly changing.
A month later, delegates from the Shawnees,
Ottawas, Mingoes, Wyandots, Potawatomis,

Delawares, Mohawks, and Miamis accepted a war belt from Henry Hamilton at Detroit. While Delawares, Oneidas, Tuscaroras, and other Indians friendly to the United States gathered "to guard against the impending Storm" and called on the Americans for protection, Thomas Jefferson and others advocated using friendly tribes to wage war against hostile ones.

The American Revolution was not only a civil war for Indian people; it also amounted to a world war in Indian country, with surrounding nations, Indian and non-Indian, at war, on the brink of war, or arranging alliances in expectation of war. American history has paid little attention to the impact of this war on the Indians' home front. American campaign strategy aimed to carry the war into Indian country, destroy Indian villages, and burn Indian crops late in the season when there was insufficient time for replanting before winter. American troops and militia tramped through Indian country, leaving smoking ruins and burned cornfields behind them. American soldiers and militia matched their British and Indian adversaries in the use of terror tactics. George Rogers Clark declared that "to excel them in barbarity was and is the only way to make war upon Indians and gain a name among them," and he carried his policy into effect at Vincennes by binding and tomahawking Indian prisoners within sight of the besieged garrison. Pennsylvania offered $1,000 for every Indian scalp; South Carolina £75 for male scalps, and Kentucky militia who invaded Shawnee villages dug open graves to scalp corpses.

Barely had the Cherokees launched their attacks on the backcountry settlements than the colonists carried fire and sword to their towns and villages, bringing the nation to its knees. Even Dragging Canoe's villages were not invulnerable to attack: Evan Shelby burned eleven of them in 1779, forcing the Chickamaugas to relocate in safer locations. John Sevier burned fifteen Middle Cherokee towns in March 1781, and the following summer destroyed new Lower Cherokee towns on the Coosa River. American armies marching through Cherokee country in pursuit of Chickamauga raiders did not always distinguish between Cherokee friends and Cherokee foes, thereby swelling Dragging Canoe's ranks with new recruits. A Cherokee headman summed up the cost of the Revolution for his people: "I . . . have lost in different engagements six hundred warriors, my towns have been thrice destroyed and my corn fields laid waste by the enemy." British reports claimed Cherokee women and children were butchered in cold blood and burned alive.

In the spring of 1779, Col. Goose Van Schaick marched against the Onondaga settlements, laying waste their towns and crops, slaughtering cattle and horses, and carrying off thirty-three prisoners. In the fall Gen. John Sullivan led his famous expedition into Iroquois country on a campaign of destruction that burned forty towns, 160,000 bushels of corn, as well as beans, squash, orchards, and cattle. Meanwhile, Daniel Brodhead devastated the Seneca and Munsee towns on the Allegheny. The Americans spent whole days systematically destroying Iroquois fields and food supplies. The Iroquois pulled back and sustained minimal casualties, but an Onondaga chief later claimed that when the Americans attacked his town, "they put to death all the Women and Children, excepting some of the Young Women, whom they carried away for the use of their Soldiers & were afterwards put to death in a more shameful manner."

Deprived of food and shelter, Iroquois women and children faced starvation as one of the coldest winters on record gripped North America. Refugees fled to British posts for support, and thousands of Indian men, women, and children huddled in miserable shelters around Fort Niagara. Fearing retaliation from their relatives, many Oneidas abandoned their villages and placed themselves under American protection near Schenectady where, living in wretched refugee camps, they endured the prejudice of the American garrison.

Thomas Jefferson wanted the Shawnees exterminated or driven from their lands, and American invasions of Shawnee country became a regular feature of the war. In 1779 Col. John

Bowman attacked the town of Chillicothe on the Little Miami River. In 1780 the Shawnees burned Chillicothe as George Rogers Clark approached and fought a major engagement at Piqua. Clark returned two years later, burning Shawnee villages and orchards. The pattern continued in 1786 when Kentucky militia attacked Maquachake villages—murdering Molunthy as the old chief clutched an American flag and a copy of the treaty he had signed with the Americans just months before—and with Gen. Josiah Harmar's expedition in 1790. Chillicothe was destroyed four times in this period, but the Shawnees rebuilt it each time in different locations.

American soldiers were impressed by the cornucopia they destroyed in Indian fields and villages; by eighteenth-century frontier standards, Indian communities were rich in agricultural foodstuffs when not disrupted by the ravages of war. Moreover, many Indian towns provided material comforts that were the envy of frontier whites. The Oneidas later submitted to Congress claims for compensation for their losses that included sheep, horses, hogs, turkeys, agricultural implements, wheat, oats, corn, sugar, linen, calico, kettles, frying pans, pewter plates, "10 tea-cups & sawcers," "6 punch bowls," tablespoons, wampum, candlesticks, silver dollars, harness, sleighs, plows, "a very large framed house [with a] chimney at each end [and] painted windows," a teapot, ivory combs, white flannel breeches, silk handkerchiefs, mirrors, and scissors. The wealth they found in Indian country gave Americans an economic incentive to go on campaigns and made them eager to seize fertile Indian lands once the war was over.

Even when the war was not fought on the Indians' home ground, it produced disruption and misery in Indian communities. Men who fell in battle were not only warriors. They were "part-time soldiers" who were also husbands, fathers and sons, providers and hunters. Warriors who were out on campaign could not hunt or clear fields; women who were forced to flee when invasion threatened could not plant and harvest. Indians still tried to wage war with the seasons: warriors preferred to wait

until their corn was ripe before they took up the hatchet, and according to one observer "quit going to war" when hunting season came. But war now dominated the activities of the community and placed tremendous demands on the people's energy at the expense of normal economic and social practices. Even before Sullivan's campaign, there were food shortages in Iroquois longhouses as "the Young Men were already either out at War, or ready to go," and many Mohawks became sick from eating nothing but salt meat. At a time when the need for food increased greatly, Indians could not cultivate the usual quantities of corn and vegetables, and what they did grow was often destroyed before it could be harvested. Crops also suffered from natural causes in time of war. The late 1770s marked the beginning of a period of "sporadically poor crops" among southeastern tribes. Partial failure of the Creek corn crop in 1776 produced near famine at a time when the influx of Cherokee refugees placed additional demands on food supplies. Choctaw crops failed in 1782, increasing the people's reliance on deer hunting. Hunting became vital to group survival, but fewer hunters were available, and hunting territories could be perilous places in time of war.

As a result, Indian communities became increasingly dependent on British, American, or Spanish allies to provide them with food, clothing, and trade. Rival powers waged economic warfare to compel Indian allegiance, and harsh economic realities increasingly curtailed the tribes' freedom of action and governed their decisions. Dependency on outside supplies of food and clothing rendered the end of the war all the more catastrophic, when allies deserted and supplies dried up.

Those tribes who supported the Americans or remained neutral suffered as much as those who fought with the British. In the spring of 1782, those Cherokees who remained friendly to the Americans were "in a deplorable situation, being naked & defenceless for want of goods and ammunition," besides being caught between loyalists and patriots who assumed they were hostile. In December a group of

Cherokees en route to Richmond elicited the sympathy of William Christian, one of the generals who had carried devastation to their towns in the summer of 1776: "The miseries of those people from what I see and hear seem to exceed description; here are men, women & children almost naked; I see very little to cover either sex but some old bear skins, and we are told that the bulk of the nation are in the same naked situation." To make matters worse, Cherokee crops that year had been "worse than ever was known." The next month the Cherokee chief Oconastota begged Col. Joseph Martin for trade at low prices, adding: "All the old warriors are dead. There are now none left to take care of the Cherokees, but you & myself, & for my part I am become very old."

Disease took an additional toll. Smallpox raged at Onondaga in the winter of 1776–77, among the Creeks and Cherokees in the fall of 1779, and among the Chickamaugas and Georgia Indians in the spring of 1780. It struck the Oneida refugees at Schenectady in December 1780 and hit the Genesee Senecas in the winter of 1781–82. Cold and disease killed 300 Indians in the refugee camps at Niagara in the winter of 1779–80.

The Revolution dislocated thousands of Indian people. Mobility was a fundamental feature of Indian life, but seasonal migration for social or subsistence purposes now gave way to flight from the horrors of war. Indian villages relocated to escape American assault; communities splintered and reassembled, sometimes amalgamating with other communities. Many Shawnees migrated from Ohio to Missouri where they took up lands under the auspices of the Spanish government. By the end of the Revolution, those Shawnees who remained in Ohio were crowded into the northwestern reaches of their territory, and in time they joined other Indians in creating a multitribal, multivillage community centered on the Auglaize. Indian refugees flooded into Niagara and Schenectady, Detroit and St. Louis, St. Augustine and Pensacola; Iroquois loyalists relocated to new homes on the Grand River in Ontario. Stockbridge Indians, unable to secure relief from their former allies after the Revolution, joined other Christian Indians from New England in moving to lands set aside for them by the Oneidas. By 1787 "there was a vast concourse of People of many Nations" at New Stockbridge. Hundreds of refugee Indians drifted west of the Mississippi and requested permission to settle in Spanish territory. Abenaki Indians, dispersed by previous wars from northern New England into the Ohio Valley, turned up in Arkansas after the Revolution. Nor were Indian people the only migrants in Indian country. Micmacs in Nova Scotia suffered from the inroads of Loyalist settlers fleeing the Revolution to the south; English refugees fleeing Spanish reprisals following the Natchez rebellion took refuge in Chickasaw country.

Escalating warfare and concomitant economic dislocation reached even into ritual and ceremonial life. Eastern woodland Indians tried to maintain their social and ceremonial calendar tied to the rhythm of the seasons: in 1778 the Creeks frustrated the British by refusing to take the warpath until after the Green Corn Ceremony. But the endemic warfare of the Revolution threw many traditional religious practices and sacred observances into disarray. Not only did the ancient unity of the Iroquois league crumble but many of the ceremonial forms that expressed that unity were lost. Preparatory war rituals were neglected or imperfectly performed, and the Cayuga leader Kingageghta lamented in 1789 that a "Great Part of our ancient Customs & Ceremonies have, thro' the Loss of Many of our principal men during the War, been neglected & forgotten, so that we cannot go through the whole with our ancient Propriety." The traditional Cherokee year was divided into two seasons, with the winter reserved for war, and returning warriors underwent ritual purification before reentering normal village life. Now war was a year-round activity and Chickamauga communities existed on a permanent war footing. In addition, the Cherokees' six major religious festivals of the year became telescoped into one— the Green Corn festival. Many Cherokees remembered the 1780s as marking the end of the old ways. The loss of sacred power threatened the Indians' struggle for independence, and, according to historian Gregory Evans Dowd, Indian resistance movements of the Revolutionary and post-Revolutionary era drew strength from the recognition that they "could and must take hold of their destiny by regaining sacred power." Indians in the new republic sought to recover through ritual, as well as through war and politics, some of what they had lost. New religious practices also suffered in the Revolution. Missionary work was disrupted and Christian Mohawks devoted less time to their observances because war occupied their attention. Delaware Moravian communities endured forced relocation at the hands of the British and destruction at the hands of Americans.

For all the devastation they suffered, Indians remained a force to be reckoned with during and after the Revolution. Most survived the destruction of their villages and cornfields. The Shawnees, for example, sustained minimal casualties when the Americans invaded their country, withdrew before the invaders, then returned and rebuilt their villages when the enemy retreated. Untouched food sources beyond the enemy's reach and support from the British at Detroit sustained the Shawnee war effort in the face of repeated assaults. George Rogers Clark recognized the limitations of the American search-and-destroy strategy so long as the Indians could resort to the British supplies at Detroit. Sullivan's campaign too was more effective in burning houses and crops than in killing Iroquois: as one American officer noted, "The nests are destroyed but the birds are still on the wing."

GLOSSARY

"The World Turned Upside Down": The tune played at British general Lord Cornwallis's surrender at Yorktown on October 19, 1781, marking the end of the Revolutionary War. The tune came from the popular 1775 London musical, *Maid of the Oaks*.

John Adams (1735–1826): The first Vice President (1789–1797) and second President (1797–1801) of the United States. Adams played a major role in the American Revolution, the drafting of the Declaration of Independence, and the debate on the Constitution of 1787.

New France: The possessions of France in North America that included much of southeast Canada, the Great Lakes region, and the Mississippi Valley.

George Rogers Clark (1752–1818): American military leader who led numerous raids on British troops and American Indians in the Northwest Territory during the Revolutionary War.

Green Corn Festival: A three-day corn harvest festival that included dancing and initiation rituals.

IMPLICATIONS

As Calloway reveals in this essay, the American Revolution dealt devastating blows to Indian peoples, no matter whether they allied with the Americans, sided with the British, or attempted to remain neutral. What do you think accounts for the unusual ferocity of warfare in Indian Country during the Revolution?

PART THREE

An Expanding People

In the 40 years leading to the Civil War, the United States grew in many dramatic ways. The population more than doubled between 1820 and 1860 and—equally important—the mixture of peoples who made up the country's population became more diverse. Mexicans and new groups of Native Americans were annexed by the expanding nation, while German, Irish, and Chinese immigrants flocked to its coastal cities and inland farms. The nation grew physically as well. Of the 23 states that made up the union in 1820, only Louisiana lay west of the Mississippi River; by the beginning of the Civil War, the nation counted 11 new states, all but three of them in the trans-Mississippi West. In 1860, the United States stretched from the Atlantic to the Pacific.

Not only did the nation's economy grow during the antebellum years, but the Northeast developed into an early industrial center. In the northern states, what had been a region of independent farmers, artisans, and shopkeepers became increasingly a region of employers and their dependent employees. In the southern states, the international demand for cotton rejuvenated the system of plantation slavery that led the two regions along increasingly divergent courses.

The forces of agrarian change that drove tens of thousands of eastern farmers to seek better fortunes in the West are the subject of Robert A. Gross's essay "Culture and Cultivation." The growing penetration of national and international markets into rural Concord, Massachusetts, transformed the lives of its residents, Gross argues, forcing them to balance their family- and community-oriented lives against the impersonal forces of the marketplace. In Concord, as in the rest of the United States, the Revolution set in motion social, economic, and political forces that would transform everyday life in the early nineteenth century.

The human side of northern economic transformation is analyzed in essays by Ronald Schultz and Christine Stansell. Looking at the dynamic religious culture of Philadelphia artisans at a time when their craft system was under unrelenting assault by sweatshops and competition from cheaper and less-skilled immigrant labor, Schultz shows that religion played a central role in craftsmen's response to their economic predicament. In New York City, on the other hand, the concerns of poor women—especially those who were heads of households—involved more than maintaining their families. By the middle of the nineteenth century, these women also had to deal with middle- and upper-class reformers who used charity as a form of social engineering, granting aid to those whom they judged "respectable" and denying it to those who clung to the culture of the streets. As Stansell argues, the conflict over the "uses of the streets" was as much a struggle over the proper role of women in the new industrial order as a confrontation between women of different social classes.

As the northern states industrialized and pioneers settled the western states, the South experienced an economic renaissance based not on industry but on a new staple crop: cotton. In "Gouge and Bite, Pull Hair and Scratch," Elliott J. Gorn analyzes the culture of ordinary white male southerners. Violence was endemic in a society that relied on physical coercion to maintain discipline among its slave labor force, and, as abolitionists often claimed, the ubiquitousness of violence distorted all of white society, slaveholder and non-slaveholder alike.

The California Gold Rush was one of the central events of the nineteenth century, drawing tens of thousands of men and women from around the world to seek their fortunes in the United States' far western territory. While the prospect of quick wealth has long played a central role in explaining the rush to California, more recent historical accounts have emphasized the cultural motivations that impelled thousands of middle-class American men to leave their wives and families in the East and Midwest for the Sierra gold fields. In "No Boy's Play," Malcolm Rohrbough explores the motivations of these middle-class men and recounts their experiences in the Gold Rush. While almost none returned home with the fortunes they sought, they all treasured the unstructured, frontier experience for the remainder of their lives.

The Civil War has long occupied a privileged place in American history. The spectacle of American fighting American, of family pitted against family, has fired the imagination of generations of Americans, beginning as soon as the war ended. Historians, too, have felt the urgency of conflict and the importance of the issues involved, but their professional concerns turn more to explaining the causes and impact of the war. In "Husbands and Wives," Drew Gilpin Faust examines the impact that the war had on southern plantation mistresses. As she reveals, the wives of southern plantation owners lived in a world of privilege, but they also lived in a limited world dominated by their husbands. When the war took their husbands (and often their slaves) away, plantation mistresses found themselves adrift in an unfamiliar world of self-reliance. While some adjusted, many more hungered for the prewar days of affluent dependence.

Past Traces

As America moved from being a regional, agricultural society to one increasingly dominated by commerce, manufacturing, and markets, the vast majority of Americans continued to earn their living by tilling the soil. These farmers retained their traditional agrarian goals of relative self-sufficiency, independence, and family provision. Yet the commercial trends that were transforming America also touched American farmers, drawing them increasingly into the national and international marketplace. This reading begins with an excerpt from an essay by Hector St. John de Crèvecoeur, a French immigrant and perceptive commentator on American life. In this essay, Crèvecoeur tells a somewhat idealized story about the life of an American farmer and, in the process, depicts the continued relevance of traditional American agrarian ideals in a time of rapid economic and social change.

Hector St. John de Crèvecoeur, *The American Belisarius (c. 1790s)*

In the township of —— lived S. K., the son of a Dutch father and of an English mother. These mixtures are very frequent in this country. From his youth he loved and delighted in bunting, and the skill he acquired confirmed his taste for that manly diversion. In one of the long excursions which he took in the mountains of —— (which he had never before explored), mixing the amusements of the chase with those of more useful contemplation, and viewing the grounds as an expert husbandman, he found among the wilds several beautiful vales formed by Nature in her most indulgent hours when, weary with the creation of the surrounding cliffs and precipices, she condescended to exhibit something on which Man might live and flourish—a singular contrast which you never to meet with in the mountains of America: the more rocky, barren, and asperous are the surrounding ridges, the richer and more fertile are the intervales and valleys which divide them. Struck with the singular beauty and luxuriance of one of these spots, he returned home, and soon after patented it. I think it contained about one thousand acres.

With cheerfulness he quitted the paternal estate he enjoyed, and prepared to begin the world anew in the bosom of this huge wilderness, where there was not even a path to guide him. He bad a road to make, some temporary bridges to make, overset trees to remove, a house to raise, swamps to convert into meadows and to fit for the scythe, upland fields to clear for the plough— such were the labours he had to undertake, such were the difficulties he had to overcome. He surmounted every obstacle; he was young, healthy, vigorous, and strong-handed. In a few years this part of the wilderness assumed a new face and wore a smiling aspect. The most abundant crops of grass, of fruit, and grain soon succeeded to the moss, to the acorn, to the wild berry, and to all the different fruits, natives of that soil. Soon after these first successful essays, the fame of his happy beginning drew abundance of inferior people to that neighbourhood. It was made a county, and in a short time grew populous, principally with poor people, whom some part of this barren soil could not render much richer. But the love of independence, that strong attachment to wives and children which is so powerful and natural, will people the tops of cliffs and make them even prefer such settlements to the servitude of attendance, to the confinement of manufactories, or to the occupation of more menial labours.

There were in the neighbourhood two valuable pieces of land, less considerable indeed, but in point of fertility as good as his own. S. K. purchased them both and invited his two brothers-in-law to remove there; generously making them an offer of the land, of his teams, and every other necessary assistance; requiring only to be paid the advanced capital whenever they should be enabled; giving up all pretensions to interest or any other compensation. This handsome overture did not pass unaccepted. They removed to the new patrimony which they had thus easily purchased, and in this sequestered situation became to S. K. two valuable neighbours and friends. Their prosperity, which was his work, raised no jealousy in him. They all grew rich very fast. The virgin earth abundantly repaid them for their labours and advances, and they

soon were enabled to return the borrowed capital which they had so industriously improved. This part of the scene is truly pleasing, pastoral, and edifying: three brothers, the founders of three opulent families, the creators of three valuable plantations, the promoters of the succeeding settlements that took place around them. The most plentiful crops, the fattest cattle, the greatest number of hogs and horses, raised loose in this wilderness, yearly accumulated their wealth, swelled their opulence; and rendered them the most conspicuous families in this corner of the world. A perfect union prevailed not only from the ties of blood, but cemented by those of the strongest gratitude.

Among the great number of families which had taken up their residence in that vicinage, it was not to be expected that they could all equally thrive. Prosperity is not the lot of every man; so many casualties occur that often prevent it. Some of them were placed, besides, on the most ungrateful soil, from which they could barely draw a subsistence. The industry of Man, the resources of a family, are never tried in this cold country, never put to the proof, until they have undergone the severity of a long winter. The rigours of this season generally require among this class of people every exertion of industry, as well as every fortunate circumstance that can possibly happen. A cow, perhaps, a few sheep, a couple of poor horses, must be housed, must be fed through the inclement season; and you know that it is from the labour of the summer, from collected grasses and fodder, this must proceed. If the least accident through droughts, sickness, carelessness or want of activity happens, a general calamity ensues. The death of any one of these precious animals oversets the well-being of the family. Milk is wanting for the children; wood must be hauled; the fleeces of sheep cannot be dispensed with. What providence can replace these great deficiencies?

Happily S. K. lived in the neighbourhood. His extreme munificence and generosity had hitherto, like a gem, been buried, for he had never before lived in a country where the needy and the calamitous were so numerous. In their extreme indigence, in all their unexpected disasters, they repair to this princely farmer. He opens to them his granary; he lends them hay; he assists them in whatever they want; he cheers them with good counsel; he becomes a father to the poor of this wilderness. They promise him payment; he never demands it. The fame of his goodness reaches far and near. Every winter his house becomes an Egyptian granary where each finds a supply proportioned to his wants. Figure to yourself a rich and opulent planter situated in an admirable vale, surrounded by a variety of distressed inhabitants, giving and lending, in the midst of a severe winter, cloaks, wool, shoes, etc., to a great number of unfortunate families; relieving a mother who has not perhaps wherewithal to clothe her new-born infant; sending timely succour, medicines, victuals a valetudinarian exhausted with fatigues and labours; giving a milch cow to a desolated father who has just lost his in a quagmire as she went to graze the wild herbage for want of hay at home; giving employment; directing the labours and essays of these grateful but ignorant people towards a more prosperous industry. Such is the faithful picture of this man's conduct, for a series of years, to those around him. At home he was hospitable and kind, an indulgent father a tender husband, a good master. This, one would imagine, was an object on which the good genius of America would have constantly smiled.

Upon an extraordinary demand of wheat from abroad, the dealers in this commodity would often come to his house and solicit from him the purchase of his abundant crops. "I have no wheat," said he, "for the rich; my harvest is for the poor. What would the inhabitants of these mountains do were I to divest myself of what superfluous grain I have?" "Consider, sir, you will receive your money in a lump, and God knows when you are to expect it from these needy people, whose indolence you rather encourage by your extreme bounty. "Some do pay me very punctually. The rest wish and try to do it, but they find it impossible; and pray, must they starve because they raise less grain than I do?" Would to God I were acquainted with the sequel of this humane conversation! I would recapitulate every phrase; I would dwell on every syllable. If Mercy herself could by the direction of the Supreme Being assume a visible appearance, such are the words which this celestial Being would probably utter for the example, for the edification of mankind. 'Tis really a necessary relief and a great comfort to find in human society some such beings, lest in the crowd, which through experience we find so different, we should wholly lose sight of that beautiful original and of those heavenly dispositions with which the heart of Man was once adorned.

One day as he was riding through his fields, he saw a poor man carrying a bushel of wheat on his back. "Where now, neighbour?"

"To mill, sir."

"Pray, how long since you are become a beast of burthen?"

"Since I had the misfortune of losing my jade."

"Have you neither spirit nor activity enough to catch one of my wild horses?"

"I dare not without your leave."

"Hark ye, friend, the first time I see you in that servile employment whilst I have so many useless ones about my farm, you shall receive from me a severe reprimand." The honest countryman took the hint, borrowed a little salt and a halter, and soon after appeared mounted on a spirited mare, which carried him where he wanted to go and performed for him his necessary services at home.

In the fall of the year it was his usual custom to invite his neighbours in, helping him to hunt and to gather together the numerous heads of swine which were bred in his woods that he might fat them with corn which he raised in the summer. He made it a rule to treat them handsomely and to send them home each with a good hog as a reward for their trouble and attendance. In harvest and haying he neither hired nor sent for any man but, trusting to the gratitude of the neighbourhood, always found his company of reapers and hay-makers more numerous than he wanted. It was truly a patriarchal harvest gathered for the benefit of his little world. Yet, notwithstanding his generosity, this man grew richer every crop; every agricultural scheme succeeded. What he gave did not appear to diminish his stores; it seemed but a mite, and immediately to be replaced by the hand of Providence. I have known Quakers in Pennsylvania who gave annually the tenth part of their income, and that was very great; but this man never counted, calculated, nor compared. The wants of the year, the calamities of his neighbourhood, were the measure by which he proportioned his bounty. The luxuriance of his meadows surpassed all belief; I have heard many people say, since his misfortunes, that they have often cut and cured three tons and a half per acre. The produce of his grain was in proportion; the blessings of heaven prospered his labours and showered fertility over all his lands. Equally vigilant and industrious, he spared neither activity nor perseverance to accomplish his schemes of agriculture. Thus he lived for a great number of years, the father of the poor and the example of this part of the world. He aimed at no popular promotion, for he was a stranger to pride and arrogance. A simple commission as a militia-captain was all that distinguished him from his equals.

13

Culture and Cultivation: Agriculture and Society in Thoreau's Concord

Robert A. Gross

For the first three hundred years of its existence, the United States was predominantly a land of farmers. As late as 1800, more than nine out of ten people lived in agrarian towns and villages, where most of them were members of small, independent farming families. Regulated by the yearly cycle of the seasons and the daily rhythms of the field and barnyard, life on these farms changed little between the seventeenth and early nineteenth centuries. Life in these pastoral communities centered on land and family, and even such apparently economic transactions as the purchase of land and the borrowing of money were family affairs undertaken in the spirit of neighborliness. But as regional and international commerce expanded after the American Revolution and new markets in the trans-Appalachian South and West fostered the beginnings of industrialization, farmers found themselves dealing with a rapidly changing world in which contracts and money were valued more than neighborliness and community.

In this essay, Robert A. Gross explores the transformation of northern agriculture between the Revolution and the Civil War by focusing on the well-known town of Concord, Massachusetts. As markets expanded in post-Revolutionary America, they placed an ever-increasing number of new products within the reach of farmers and rural artisans, who had previously produced by themselves most of the goods their families needed. It was this intense contact with a growing market in manufactured goods and agricultural products, a market in which local merchants played a defining role, that transformed social and economic relationships in rural Massachusetts, increasing farmers' independence of their neighbors while at the same time undermining the social and economic basis of traditional community life. But, as Gross

"Culture and Cultivation: Agriculture and Society in Thoreau's Concord." *Journal of American History*, 69, pp. 42–61. Copyright © 1982 by The Organization of American Historians. Reprinted by permission of the *Journal of American History*.

reminds us, this rural transformation was a slow and uneven process that took generations—not years—to complete. Despite the growing importance of market relationships, many of the family and community values of 1800 continued to direct everyday
life there as late as the Civil War.

Gross's account of rural Massachusetts entering a new age reminds us of one of
the historian's greatest concerns: tracing both change and continuity. New England
farms changed—sometimes dramatically—in the early nineteenth century, but as
Gross also shows, much in rural life remained untouched by the new system of
agrarian capitalism as late as the Civil War.

....

The town of Concord, Massachusetts, is
usually thought of as the home of minutemen and transcendentalists—the place where
"the embattled farmers" launched America's
war for political independence on April 19,
1775, and where Ralph Waldo Emerson and
Henry David Thoreau, more than a half-
century later, waged their own struggles for
intellectual independence, both for themselves
as writers and for American culture as a whole.
But in the late nineteenth century, Concord
acquired a distinction it never possessed in the
years when it was a seedbed of revolutionary
scholars and soldiers. It became a leading
center of agricultural improvement. Thanks to
the coming of the railroad in 1844, Concord
farmers played milkmen to the metropolis
and branched out into market gardening and
fruit raising as well. Concord was nursery to
a popular new variety of grape, developed
by a retired mechanic-turned-horticulturist
named Ephraim Bull. And to crown its reputation, the town called the cultural capital of
antebellum America by Stanley Elkins became
the asparagus capital of the Gilded Age.
Concord was, in short, a full participant in yet
another revolution: the agricultural revolution
that transformed the countryside of New
England in the middle decades of the nineteenth century.

The progress of that agricultural revolution
forms my central theme. The minutemen of 1775
inhabited a radically different world from that
of their grandchildren and great-grandchildren on
the eve of the Civil War. We know the general
outlines of how things changed—that farmers

gradually abandoned producing their own food,
clothing, and tools and turned to supplying
specialized, urban markets for a living. In the
process, they rationalized their methods and
altered the ways they thought about their work.
Theirs was a new world in which modern science
was wedded to agricultural capitalism. But the
process by which that world came into being is
little known. Historians have given their attention
chiefly to more dramatic events—to the rise of
cities and factories, to the story of Boston and
Lowell. No less important was the revolution in
the countryside. Without it, the creation of an
urban-industrial society would have been
impossible.

Together, the city and the country underwent a great transformation. The years from
around 1800 to 1860 comprise what Emerson
called an "age of Revolution"—a time "when
the old and the new stand side by side and
admit of being compared; when the energies
of all men are searched by fear and by hope;
when the historic glories of the old can be compensated by the rich possibilities of the new
era." What could be a better time to be alive,
Emerson asked. That is essentially the inquiry
I am undertaking—an inquiry into what it
was like to make and to experience the great
transition to modern agricultural capitalism in
Concord.

The agricultural revolution did not come
suddenly in an irresistible wave of change. The
process was a slow and uneven one, proceeding by fits and starts and sometimes encounter-
ing setbacks along the way. Some things never
really changed at all, and not until the end of

the period, with the coming of the railroad, had a new world truly been born.

All of this, of course, can be said only with the historian's benefit of hindsight. To the participants in the process, who did not know the outcomes, the transition must have been at times a deeply unsettling experience. It challenged old habits and practices, demanded new responses while promising only uncertain rewards, and swept up those who wanted only to be left alone, comfortably carrying on their fathers' ways. Even those farmers and entrepreneurs who successfully rode the tide must have had their doubts. Those who resisted or just plain failed said little about their fate, succumbing to what Thoreau saw as lives of "quiet desperation." In the effort to reconstruct the experience of the transition, Thoreau's observations bear close reading. Thoreau was the most powerful and articulate critic of agricultural capitalism that America produced in the decades before the Civil War.

Had a visitor come to Concord around 1800 and lived through the 1850s, he would certainly have been unprepared for the ways things changed. At the opening of a new century, the agricultural economy was very much tied to the past. In the size of their farms, in the crops and livestock they raised, in the ways they used the land, farmers still carried on as their fathers had.

For one thing, the number of farms was the same in 1800 as it had been in 1750 and 1771: about 200. And the average size of a farm was no bigger in 1800 than it had been before: around sixty acres. These were unchanging facts of life in eighteenth-century Concord; nothing—not even revolution, war, and depression—would alter them in the slightest.

This fundamental stability in the number and size of farms was no accident, no haphazard outcome of social evolution. It was a deliberate creation, a rational adaptation to the conditions of farming and family life in the preindustrial, household economy. This arrangement of farms on the landscape arose in response to a basic dilemma Concord began to encounter as early as the 1720s: there were too many young people in town and not enough land for them all—not enough, at least, for them to support families in the usual way. Markets did not exist to sustain comfortable livings on very small farms. Nor would the farming methods of the day have enabled the yeomen of Concord to produce substantial surpluses had the demand for them suddenly appeared. As a result, so long as families continued to be fruitful and multiply as successfully as they did and so long as death continued to stalk New Englanders less relentlessly than it did people in the Old World, the people of Concord would have to face up to the inevitable outcome. There was a fundamental imbalance between numbers and resources. Something would have to give.

As it turned out, what gave was the aspiration of colonial patriarchs to settle all their sons close by on family lands. As early as the 1720s, it was becoming clear that some estates in Concord could not be split up "without Spoiling the Whole." Instead, increasingly, one son—often, but not invariably, the eldest—would inherit the homestead intact. The other children would have to go into trade, take portions and dowries in cash, or, in what was commonly the case, move away and settle on frontier lands. In effect, a continuing exodus of young people to new lands underwrote the stability of Concord's farms. Emigration was the key to the future, to insuring that old patterns would go on unchanged. That mechanism worked so successfully that the colonial framework of farming in Concord—some 200 farms of about sixty acres on the average—survived intact not just until 1800 but until the eve of the Civil War. No matter how much things changed, young people growing up on farms in nineteenth-century Concord had in common with their eighteenth-century forebears the expectation that most would move away and make new lives in another town.

For those who stayed behind on the homesteads around 1800, farming went on in traditional ways. In the household economy of Concord the needs of the family and the labor it supplied largely determined what was produced and in what amounts. This does not mean that farms were self-sufficient. Farmers normally strove to obtain a surplus of goods to exchange with neighbors and to enter into the stream of trade. Given the limited markets and the constraints on production in the eighteenth century, surpluses were necessarily small. Most farmers lacked the incentive or the capacity to participate extensively in trade.

Indeed, most farmers even lacked the ability to be fully self-sufficient. Historians have been led astray by the image of the independent yeoman, wholly dependent on his own resources, that eighteenth-century writers like J. Hector St. John Crèvecoeur have handed down to us. What we would think of as the basic necessities of colonial husbandry—plows, oxen, pastures, sheep—were absent on a great many farms. A third of Concord's farmers did not own oxen, and if they were like the farmers in the towns of Groton, Marlborough, and Dedham, whose inventories have been examined by Winifred Rothenberg at Brandeis University, half of them did not possess a plow and three-quarters (72 percent) had no harrow (this was the case down to 1840). Nor were farmers in Concord any more self-sufficient in the production of textiles. Almost half had no sheep in 1771, and in 1750 some 56 percent raised no flax at all.

What did people do, then, for basic necessities? They borrowed from neighbors or kin, exchanged goods or labor with others, or resorted to the store. Perhaps most often, they made do with what they had. This was a world of scarcity in which expectations were modest and always circumscribed. People had to accept the fact that labor and capital were required to supply all one's necessities "from within." It was the rich—the large landholders and the men who combined farming with a profitable trade—who could aspire to independence. It was they who produced most of the flax in Concord in 1750, planting about one-fourth to one-half an acre on the average, which is what the books say the ordinary farmer usually had. And it was they who could provide a wise variety of their own foods. The wealthy were able to take care of these needs precisely because they were engaged in trade, thereby acquiring the resources to hire labor and diversify livestock and crops. Market participation and self-sufficiency were not at opposite ends of a spectrum. Rather, market dependence without facilitated independence within. So when we read about the self-sufficient farmer, we should be skeptical: he was the exceptional man, uniquely favored by fortune. The editor of *Old Farmer's Almanack*, Robert Bailey Thomas, spoke for a good many readers when he remarked that "there is a great satisfaction derived from living as much as possible upon the produce of one's own farm." But it was a satisfaction that only a few farmers ever enjoyed. Although independence was the general ambition, interdependence was the inescapable fact of life.

The world of trade, then, offered a way out of the pervasive dependency of farmers on one another—out of the constant borrowing back and forth, the necessity of exchanging work, the endless keeping of accounts to ascertain one's standing in the community-wide network of credits and debts. And trade in agricultural surpluses played an important role in colonial Concord, shaping the principal uses to which people put their lands. Throughout the second half of the eighteenth century, farmers in Concord and elsewhere in eastern Massachusetts kept most of their improved land in grass. In Ipswich, over 90 percent of the improved land in 1771 was in meadows and pasture; in Concord that year, 80 percent. In a sense, farmers were doing what came naturally; the soil was well suited to raising grass. But it was the pull of urban markets that prompted farmers to emphasize their mowing and grazing lands. Concord was beef country in the late colonial era. The agricultural economy was based on cereals—mainly rye and corn—for home consumption and beef for market.

This was an extensive agricultural regime, where farmers saved on labor by exploiting land. The trouble was that by the eve of the Revolution, the land was losing its capacity to support livestock. Between 1749 and 1771, cattle holdings increased by a fifth, but to feed them farmers had to expand their pasturage by 84 percent, even though sheep raising was declining sharply. Concord was starting to experience a serious agricultural decline. Indeed, so poor was the town's farming reputation that it blighted the marriage prospects of a young cabinet maker and farmer named Joseph Hosmer. It is said that when he asked for the hand of a wealthy farmer's daughter in Marlborough, Massachusetts, in 1759, he was rejected out of hand. "Concord plains are sandy," complained the father. "Concord soil is poor; you have miserable farms there, and no fruit. There is little hope that you will ever do better than your father, for you have both farm and shop to attend to, *and two trades spoil one.* Lucy shall marry her cousin John; he owns the best farm in Marlboro', and you must marry a Concord girl, who cannot tell good land from poor." Joseph Hosmer ultimately won the girl, but he had to pasture his cattle outside of Concord—in Rutland and Princeton, Massachusetts.

By 1801, though still very much bound to the past, Concord was beginning to feel the stirrings of agricultural change. Markets were opening up everywhere for farmers, thanks to the extraordinary prosperity the United States enjoyed during the era of the Napoleonic wars. The port cities—merchants to the world in the 1790s and early 1800s—boomed, and so, in turn, did their hinterland. Concord farmers began to raise substantial surpluses of rye, wood, and hay for the market. They met the needs not only of Boston and Charlestown but also of the rapidly growing non-farming popu-

lation at home. Between 1771 and 1801, the share of Concord's population engaged in crafts and trade doubled, from 15 percent to 33 percent.

The agricultural economy remained essentially what it had been: an economy based on cereals, grasses, and cattle. It would stay that way up through 1840. That year 86 percent of the improved land lay in meadows and pasture. But within that framework, farmers steadily devoted more and more of their energies to producing for market. They raised three principal commodities for sale: oats, hay, and wood. The production of oats was clearly geared to city markets; it far outstripped the growth in the numbers of horses in Concord, and it clearly paralleled the periods of most rapid increase for Boston and Lowell. Expanded hay production came as a result of the increasing conversion of pastures and unimproved land to what were called "English and upland meadows," land plowed and seeded with clover, timothy, and herd's-grass. Adoption of English hay was the major agricultural improvement of the era, and Concord farmers took it up with zeal. They cultivated meadowlands for cash, while relying on the natural river meadows of the Concord and Assabet rivers to feed their own livestock. As a result, the average farmer doubled his production of English hay from 4 to 8 tons between 1801 and 1840, while his output of fresh meadow hay barely increased from about 8 to 8.5 tons. For the most part, the land converted to English hay was made available by the clearing of vast woodlands for market.

At the same time as farmers were concentrating on these staples, they also sought out new crops. They experimented with teasels, broomcorn, and silk, none of which worked. They added potatoes for both family use and sale. A few wealthy farmers engaged in commercial wool growing on a large scale, raising flocks of one thousand or so sheep before the entire business collapsed in the 1830s from cheap western competition. Far more typical were the small-scale efforts of men like "Uncle Ben" Hosmer—Joseph's younger brother—to assemble surpluses for sale.

By 1840 wagons and roads had so improved that a good deal of butter was being made and sold in Concord. But it was not until the coming of the railroad that large-scale production of milk, eggs, fruits, and garden vegetables became truly profitable in Concord. Before then, small farmers like Ben Hosmer had to concentrate on bulky goods—oats, hay, and wood—supplemented by whatever other surpluses they could get. And note that it was Dinah Hosmer, not Ben, who put up the butter and eggs.

In these circumstances, it is not surprising that farmers continued the effort to supply their own necessities, even as they sought new products for market. To be sure, they were quick to abandon raising their own cloth when cheap textiles started streaming out of the new mills. But a great many farmers never had been able to furnish their own linen or wool. When it came to foodstuffs, they still did as much as they could for themselves. Rye steadily declined in relative importance from 1800 to 1840, but even in 1840 three-quarters of the farmers in town still raised enough for their bread. The same holds true for fodder crops. English hay went to market; the fresh meadows fed livestock at home.

This combination of production for both markets and home use meant, in practice, that farmers were adding greatly to the burdens of their work. One crop was not substituted for another. Farmers simply exploited themselves more intensively than ever. Once they had spread their labor over the land, plowing shallowly, manuring thinly, and cultivating infrequently, with the result that yields were low. That was acceptable when farmers chiefly raised grain crops for family use and the profits came from grazing livestock. But now farmers depended for a living on far more intensive work: chopping wood, reclaiming land for English hay, digging potatoes, making butter, and occasionally even nursing mulberry bushes.

Farmers not only labored more intensively than ever. They did so in a radically new setting. By the mid-1820s, the evidence strongly suggests that hired labor had come to supplant family labor on the farm. Between 1801 and 1826 the ranks of landless men in Concord expanded from around 150 to 250, even as opportunities in crafts and trade stagnated and the number of farms remained unchanged. Those laborers must have been doing something for a living. Since farmers' sons were continuing the exodus out of Concord—but at an earlier age and to lands farther and farther from home—it is likely the laborers were taking their place. The hired hand had become a commonplace figure on the farm as early as 1815. Thomas's "Farmer's Calendar" for May of that year assumed that farmers had already "hired a man for a few months, to help along with your work," and it offered this advice: "If you have a good faithful one, then set store by him and treat him well, and, mind me now, don't you fret.—*Steady, boys, steady*, is the song for a farmer—If you get yourself into a habit of continually fretting, as some do, then it is ten to one if you can get good men to work for you. But some prefer a dull, lazy lubber, because he is cheap! but these *cheap* fellows I never want on my farm."

Thomas's comments suggest that a calculating, even suspicious spirit dominated the relations between farmers and their help. Where once farm boys had labored for their fathers out of duty, love, and an expectation that they would inherit land of their own someday, now it was money—and money alone—that kept help working on the farm. The social relations of production were imbued with the ethos of agricultural capitalism.

The same rationalizing, economizing impulse transformed the work customs of the community. As late as 1840, many farmers still lacked basic resources to do their work, even as they added to the demands on themselves. Nonetheless, they gave up cooperative practices like the huskings and apple bees of old. These were now condemned as uneconomical and wasteful "frolics," given over to heavy drinking and coarse entertainment. When one writer in the *Concord Gazette* of 1825 wistfully lamented the disappearance of bundling, country dances, and "the joyous huskings" of the past, he was roundly denounced by another for peddling immorality in the press. Neighborly sharing and cooperation probably diminished in another way as well. Agricultural reformers urged farmers to be as sparing as possible in "changing works." Again the *Old Farmer's Almanack* tells the changing sentiment. "There are some," Thomas complained in 1821, "who cannot bear to work alone. If they have a yard of cabbages to hoe, they must call in a neighbour to change work. Now this is very pleasant, but it tends to lounging and idleness and neglect of business; for we cannot always have our neighbours at work with us." Concord farmers likely took such advice; in *Walden*, Thoreau assumes that the farmer characteristically works alone and is starved for company by the time he comes back from the fields. An era had come to an end: farmers now relied on the claims of cash rather than the chain of community to do their work.

Edward Jarvis, a prominent nineteenth-century medical reformer who grew up in Concord, celebrated this development as a positive force in social life. "The people of Concord are none the less kind, sympathetic and generous than their fathers, but they are stronger in body and in beast. They are more self-sustaining, and it is better that each should do his own work, with his own hands or by such aid as he can compensate in the ordinary way. . . . The world's work is now as well and completely done as ever and people both individually and socially are as happy and more prosperous, and are loving, generous and ready to aid in distress, poverty, and sickness, wherever these shall present themselves, in any family or neighborhood."

Jarvis wrote in 1878, at the end of the long transition, and he summarized as progress what small farmers at the time may have experienced as a very mixed blessing. Huskings

may have wasted corn; changing works may have been a bother; and the exchange of goods and labor among farmers could sometimes end up in hard feelings and lawsuits on both sides. Still, the farmer who lacked money to hire all the help he needed had no alternative but to depend on his neighbors or exploit himself to the hilt.

Even before the railroad era, then, Concord farmers had entered the world of modern capitalism, with its characteristic institutions of money and markets. Producing for market had not, however, wholly displaced traditional activities on the farm; men still tried to furnish their food from within. This attempt to combine new demands with old ones added significantly to the burden of farm work; it amounted to a speed-up: more output in less time.

The intensification of farm work accelerated even more sharply after the railroad linked Concord more tightly and speedily to Boston market. The goods that the city demanded were those that required long hours of unremitting toil. Dairying was probably to become the most important. Between 1800 and 1840, as farmers turned to making butter for sale, the average herd of cows on a farm rose slightly from $4\frac{1}{2}$ to 5. The next decade saw that figure increase again to 6. More dramatically, the proportion of men owning ten cows or more doubled from 11 to 22 percent. It was in the 1840s, too, that farmers began on a large scale to reclaim the many acres of boggy meadow in town for English hay. This was immensely costly and labor-intensive work. Those who could afford it hired Irish laborers to do the job; increasingly, cheap foreign labor displaced native help. Finally, the demand for wood boomed in these years; so vigorously did farmers respond to the market that by 1850 they had reduced the forests of Concord to a mere tenth of the town. Some people were already alarmed at the prospect of timber running out. In short, the steady chopping of the ax; the bustle of men spading up meadows, hauling gravel, and raking hay; the clanging of milk pails—these were the dominant sounds on Concord's farms in the 1840s. These sounds reverberate through *Walden*, and all of them finally were orchestrated to the movements of that locomotive whose piercing whistle as it swept into town announced the triumph of a new order of things.

GLOSSARY

Ralph Waldo Emerson (1803–1882): One of America's most renowned writers and a central figure of American transcendentalism, whose poems, orations, and especially his essays are regarded as landmarks in the development of American thought and literary expression.

Henry David Thoreau (1817–1862): A seminal figure in the history of American thought who spent much of his life in Concord, Massachusetts, where he became associated with the New England transcendentalists; bestknown for his "Civil Disobedience" (1849) and *Walden* (1854).

Napoleonic Wars: European wars fought between Britain and France, 1799–1815. The need for provisions caused by the wars provided American farmers with exceptionally lucrative markets for their produce.

IMPLICATIONS

In this essay, Gross suggests that many farmers embraced the new, more impersonal, relationships that accompanied the rise of commerce and commercial values in nineteenth-century America. From your reading of his essay, why do you think American farmers embraced these values? Do you think they were looking for ways to adapt new means to achieve old ends?

Past Traces

One of the most profound economic changes in early nineteenth-century America was the transformation of the traditional craft system into early capitalist production. At the center of this change was the transformation of independent craftsmen into the newly formed ranks of employers and employees. This reading begins with two documents that directly reflect this transformation, petitions from journeymen (employees) and masters (employers) explaining their positions in an 1845 strike. In adopting old craft terms for masters and journeymen and in issuing public declarations of their positions, these resolutions remind us that much of the old craft world remained intact in early capitalist relationships.

Resolutions of the Journeymen Carpenters/Resolutions of the Master Carpenters (1845)

Resolutions of Journeymen Carpenters

Notice to house carpenters and housewrights in the country. An advertisement having appeared in the papers of this city, giving information that there is at this time a great demand for workmen in this branch of mechanical business in this city, it is considered a duty to state for the benefit of our brethren of the trade that we are not aware of any considerable demand for labor in this business, as there is, at this time, a very considerable number of journeymen carpenters who are out of employ, and the probable inducement which led to the communication refereed to arises from a disposition manifested on the part of the builders in this city to make their own terms as to the price of labor and the number of hours labor which shall hereafter constitute a day's work. It being a well-known fact that the most unreasonable requirements have been hitherto extracted with regard to the terms of labor of journeymen mechanics in this city; and it is further well known that in the cities of New York, Philadelphia, Baltimore, and most of the other cities of much more liberal and equitable course of policy has been adopted by the master-builders, on this subject, giving to their journeymen that fair and liberal support to which they are unquestionably entitled. It is an undoubted fact that, on the present system, it is impossible for a journeyman housewright and house carpenter to maintain a family at the present time with the wages which are now usually given to the journeymen house carpenters in this city.

Resolutions of Master Carpenters

Resolved, That we learn with surprise and regret that a large number of those who are employed as journeymen in this city have entered into a combination for the purpose of altering the time of commencing and terminating their daily labor from that which has been customary from time immemorial, thereby lessening the amount of labor each day in a very considerable degree.

Resolved, That we consider such a combination as unworthy of that useful and industrious class of the community who are engaged in it; that it is fraught with numerous and pernicious evils, not only as respect their employers but the public at large, and especially themselves; for all journeymen of good character and of skill may expect very soon to become masters and, like us, the employers of others; and by the measure which they are now inclined to adopt they will entail upon themselves the inconvenience to which they seem desirous that we should not be exposed?

Resolved, That we consider the measure proposed, as calculated to exert a very unhappy influence on our apprentices—by seducing them from that course of industry and economy of time to which we are anxious inure them. That it will expose the journeymen themselves to many temptations and improvident practices from which they are happily secure; while they attend to that wise and salutary maxim of mechanics, "Mind your business." That we consider idleness as the most deadly bane to usefulness and honorable living; and knowing (such is human nature that, where there is no necessity, there is no exertion, we fear and dread the con-sequences of such a measure upon the morals and well-being of society).

Resolved, That we cannot believe this project to have originated with many of the faithful and industrious sons of new England but are compelled to consider it an evil of foreign growth, and one which, we hope and trust, will not take root in the favored soil of Massachusetts. And especially that our city, the early rising and industry of whose inhabitants are universally proverbial, may not be infested with the unnatural production.

Resolved, That if such a measure were ever to be proper and necessary, the time has not yet arrived when it is so; if it would ever be just, it cannot be at a time like the present, when builders have generally made their engagements and contracts for the season, having predicated their estimates and prices upon the original state of things in reference to journeymen. And we appeal therefore to the good sense, the honesty, and justice of all who are engaged in this combination, and ask them to review their doings, contemplate their consequences, and then act as becomes men of sober sense and of prudence.

Resolved, finally, That we will make no alteration in the manner of employing journeymen as respects the time of commencing and leaving work and that we will employ no man who persists in adhering to the project of which we complain.

14

God and Workingmen: Popular Religion and the Formation of Philadelphia's Working Class, 1790–1830

Ronald Schultz

The growth of factories in the first half of the nineteenth century was the most visible aspect of American industrialization. The creation of large three- and four-story buildings housing hundreds of operatives who worked to the rhythm of steam- or water-driven machinery presented a striking contrast to the predominantly rural scale and pace of American life.

But while the factory system has long been the hallmark of America's transformation from an agrarian to an industrial nation, the most important industrial changes took place not in the factory but in the small artisan shops that dominated the American economy before the Civil War. In these shops, skilled craftsmen, who had learned their trades through long years of apprenticeship and journeyman training, controlled their daily output, the quality of their products, and the rhythm of work itself following long-established craft rules and customs.

Beginning in the early nineteenth century, however, growing numbers of merchants and master craftsmen began to view the slow pace of craft production as a hindrance in their quest to supply large quantities of cheap manufactured goods to rapidly expanding western and southern markets. Breaking craft skills into simple, easily learned tasks and hiring semiskilled and unskilled workers to perform them, these

"God and Workingmen: Popular Religion and the Formation of Philadelphia's Working Class, 1790–1830," reprinted from *Religion in a Revolutionary Age*, eds. Ronald Hoffman and Peter J. Albert. (Charlottesville, VA: University Press of Virginia), pp. 125–155. Reprinted with the permission of the University Press of Virginia.

early manufacturers undercut the craft system and placed all aspects of production under their control. The demise of the craft system meant more than changes in work regimes, however; it announced the end of an ancient culture and way of life as well.

Artisans responded to the demise of their way of life in numerous ways. Some accepted their fate with resignation while others attempted to escape the downward slide into dependency by joining the ranks of manufacturing employers. But for many artisans, the answer to their plight lay in the organization of craft unions. Beginning in the 1820s, skilled artisans in New York City, Philadelphia, and other American production centers formed themselves into craft unions that attempted to restore the artisan voice to the workplace and to stem their declining social and economic fortunes. In this study of Philadelphia artisans at the cusp of industrialization, Ronald Schultz explores the role that religion played in the organization of the nation's first workingmen's movement. Organized religion proved to be a double-edged sword for Philadelphia craftsmen, Schultz tells us, for it could demand personal rejection of worldly concerns and lead to the acceptance of new industrial conditions as easily as it could reinforce artisan values and serve as an ally in the struggle to restore the artisans' independent position in American society. This tension between worldly and otherworldly religious concerns would never be fully reconciled and would continue to mark the relationship between religion and the American labor movement well into the twentieth century.

....

In ways we are only beginning to understand, the age of the American Revolution was also the formative age of America's working class. Between the mobilization for Independence of the mid-1770s and the final political resolution of the Revolution in the 1820s, laboring-class Americans experienced a profound transformation in their personal and working lives.

As the nation's economy turned from colonial dependence to embrace industrial independence, the give-and-take of the small shop and the uneven rhythms of craft production gave way to the increasing regularity and limited autonomy of manufactories and the putting-out system. In the process of confronting the rise of manufacturing and the declining fortunes of their unique way of life, American artisans and less skilled workingmen forged a working-class movement from the raw material of craft traditions, popular politics, and rational religion.

Post-Revolutionary Philadelphia was a religious battleground. Responding to what the Rev. Robert Adair described as "a moral wilderness" of unchurched apprentices, journeymen, and poor working people, representatives of small sects and major denominations combed the city for laboring-class converts. In meeting halls, on street corners, from storefront churches—even in an occasional tavern—urban itinerants preached, cajoled, and exhorted "plain and unlettered" Philadelphians to join the ranks of the pious. City ministers embarked on this search for new souls because they were concerned and anxious. As they walked the back streets and alleys of laboring-class neighborhoods, they drew back from what they described as the "ignorance and vice" and the "moral degradation" of laboring-class parents and their "poor and ignorant children prowling the streets" without the "wholesome restraints" of religion. For the new breed of itinerants, laboring-class Philadelphia was both a test of their moral courage and an unparalleled opportunity for redemption on a massive scale.

Philadelphia's urban itinerants shared with many of their clerical contemporaries a middle-class disdain for the unruliness of laboring-class life. Yet the rough-hewn lifestyles they witnessed on their daily rounds were stubbornly real and thriving, for post-Revolutionary Philadelphia was a city in the midst of enormous social change. To begin with, there were simply more people. On the eve of the Revolution the city was already the largest in America with a population of more than 25,000. Postwar prosperity and the growth of cloth and iron manufacturing in the early nineteenth century brought thousands of new immigrants from Britain to join a flood of migrants from rural Pennsylvania and other seaboard states. By 1800 Philadelphia contained 81,000 inhabitants, nearly half living in the rapidly growing laboring-class suburbs of the Northern Liberties and Southwark. The 1810 federal census enumerated more than 111,000 residents, and when the workingmen's movement peaked in 1830, the city held nearly 189,000 people.

This influx of people changed the scale of social relations in Philadelphia. No longer did craftsmen, merchants, and shopkeepers live side by side along the same street or lane as they had in the colonial city. Instead, by the turn of the nineteenth century, affluent and laboring-class Philadelphians lived in separate neighborhoods with their own distinctive ways of life. As a result, after 1800 the "better" and "poorer" sort saw and knew each other less well than at any previous time in the city's history. Increasingly isolated in their own neighborhoods, middle- and upper-class men and women gradually came to view their working-class counterparts with suspicion—as an alien and potentially dangerous people.

This growing distance between the everyday experiences and the diverse cultures of the city's upper, middling, and lower ranks ultimately became one of the engines of nineteenth-century urban evangelicalism and helped thrust Philadelphia into the forefront of post-Revolutionary benevolence. But if the growing rift in the city's class structure troubled urban itinerants, it was the changing nature of the city's work force that worried them more. Throughout the colonial era

Philadelphia's reputation as a manufacturing center rested on the output of hundreds of small shops housing a working master, one or two journeymen, and a like number of apprentices, indentured servants, or slaves. Only comparatively large enterprises like shipyards and ropewalks required a greater number of craftsmen and laborers, and the city never supported more than a handful of these highly capitalized establishments.

By 1820, however, Philadelphia was no longer a craftsman's city. Now manufactories and putting-out concerns began to appear among the small shops that continued to dot the urban landscape. Employing young, half-trained apprentices and career-stalled journeymen, these early industrial enterprises divided tasks, increased hours, and, in the process, drove production up and prices down in ruinous competition with Philadelphia's small masters. The eclipse of the traditional craft system was evident as early as 1820 when more than a third of the city's workers labored in medium- and large-scale manufactories and uncounted others earned their livelihoods as dependent outworkers.

Even in the remaining smaller shops work relations were vastly different from those of colonial times. By the end of the Revolution, lifelong journeymen and apprentices working on wage contracts had already begun to replace traditionally independent craftsmen. This trend accelerated after the turn of the century, as mushrooming southern and western markets along with growing competition from larger and better capitalized manufacturers drove independent masters to cut costs the only way they could—by cheapening the price of labor. By hiring boys as laborers rather than apprentices, and by working them alongside journeymen increasingly trapped in a downward cycle of wage labor and dependence, small masters cut their costs and weakened craft traditions as well. By 1820 apprentice and journeyman had become nostalgic atavisms for what were, in fact, simply younger and older wage workers.

Immigration added a final note of change to the city's burgeoning manufacturing economy. Soon after the postwar economy stabilized in the mid-1790s, low-paid Irish laborers, artisans, and handloom weavers flocked to Philadelphia, swelling the already substantial ranks of the city's laboring poor. Coming at a time when even British- and American-born mariners, laborers, and tailors could support their families only by periodic resort to private and public poor relief, the arrival of the Irish only lowered already minimal wages and placed greater strain on a rudimentary relief system.

Viewing the human costs of this rapidly disintegrating craft economy at close range, urban proselytizers set about the task of social reconstruction, armed with a mixture of religious zeal, personal determination, and a deep sense of moral righteousness. The Methodists were the first onto the field, attempting as early as the 1760s to revive the laboring-class enthusiasm that had lain dormant in Philadelphia since George Whitefield's enormously successful revivals of the 1740s and 1750s. Directing their urban efforts from a sail loft along the Delaware riverfront, Thomas Webb, a British soldier turned itinerant, Edward Evans, a ladies' shoemaker, and James Emerson, a seller of orange-lemon shrubs, created Philadelphia Methodism with a distinctively plebeian cast. The church retained this laboring-class identification during the uncertain years of the Revolution and into the 1780s and 1790s. By 1794 slightly more than half the city's white male Methodists were workingmen, and by 1801 that proportion had grown to 68 percent.

The rapid growth of American Methodism in the post-Revolutionary era owed much to the denomination's characteristic expectation that proselytes would confirm their conversion by becoming active bearers of their newfound faith. The Methodist discipline encouraged the creation of a lay ministry, and while only a handful might advance from class leader to full-fledged itinerant, many more took on missionary efforts closer to home. In 1803, to cite but one example, a group of Philadelphia craftsmen, most of them cordwainers, created the Hospitable Society as a vehicle for missionary work among the city's laboring poor. Traveling door to door, the visiting committee braved the "frequent insults and abuse" that greeted them at many laboring-class homes to bring a message of "relief" and personal salvation "to their fellow creatures." Although apparently much more successful in converting wives than workingmen, the intensive campaign of the Hospitable Society did reap its share of male converts, some of whom spread the word among their mates. In this way, Methodism expanded its laboring-class membership until, between 1830 and 1840, independent churches existed in each of Philadelphia's working-class suburbs and four of every five male members worked for his living.

The success of the Methodists in attracting working-class members elicited two sorts of reactions from the city's other denominations. The Quakers, Anglicans, and Lutherans were for the most part comfortable with the social composition of their existing congregations. Although Anglicans and Quakers were prominent among the city's many benevolent organizations, some of which touched the lives of the laboring poor, their churches made no direct attempts to recruit among working people. Other denominations were less complacent and organized themselves to follow the Methodist example. The Presbyterians, especially, trod close to the heels of the Methodists. Heirs, with the Methodists, of the Great Awakening, New Side Presbyterianism claimed a humble following through the Revolution and into the post-Revolutionary decades. In 1804, well before Methodist itinerants moved from the city into the laboring-class suburbs, the Presbyterians built a church in the Northern Liberties to accommodate the sailors and maritime craftsmen who were coming to dominate the district. If they met with only modest success in the early years—the 1804 subscription listed nearly as many merchants as workingmen—within a decade almost half the membership of the Northern Liberties church came from the district's working class.

The Rev. James Patterson was elected pastor of the Northern Liberties church in September 1813. Finding that "the number that regularly attended upon religious instruction . . . was not very encouraging," Patterson borrowed a technique from local Methodists and began visiting door-to-door in the narrow streets and back alleys of the Liberties. Unlike the reception accorded the members of the Methodist Hospitable Society a decade earlier, Patterson found the district more cordial, and before long his church was too small for his expanding congregation. Part of his success stemmed from his open distaste for deference and moralistic priggishness, attitudes he shared with many workingmen. As his successor in the Northern Liberties pulpit noted, Patterson possessed a "perfect disrelish of everything that savoured of affected dignity," and he frankly pitied any man who "had nothing but his clerical robes to entitle him to the confidence and respect of men."

Patterson was clearly the right man for his "plain and unlettered" congregation of workingmen and their families. His popularity was confirmed when, in January 1816, he inaugurated a seven-month-long revival. Preaching to overflow crowds, initially for seventy-six consecutive nights and then, after a brief respite, for another ninety, Patterson beat on the themes of Presbyterian doctrine: the total depravity of the heart, salvation through the sacrifice of the Son of God, and the dreadful doom awaiting those who rejected the gospel. By the end of his spiritual marathon, Patterson lay ill and exhausted, but his Northern Liberties church counted 180 new communicants and many more were said to have joined neighboring congregations because of his preaching.

The powerful effect of Patterson's preaching on his predominantly young working-class audience is preserved in a journal entry he made late in the revival. In it Patterson recounts the story of a young journeyman who experienced conversion the day after attending the revival. "While sitting on his work-bench," the entry begins, "he was powerfully convicted by reading the well known hymn, 'Alas, and did my Saviour bleed.' He fell upon his knees beside his work-bench, and cried aloud for mercy. This was the means of awakening four of his shop-mates to see and feel their danger as sinners, and to plead for salvation. They continued in supplication til mid-night, when they began to rejoice in hope, and to praise God for redeeming love."

In James Patterson the Presbyterians had their best hope for victory in the competition for laboring-class souls. Yet neither Patterson's determined oratory nor the Methodists' self-expanding system of converts managed to capture more than a minority of Philadelphia workingmen for the militias of Christ. Even as he enjoyed the satisfaction of a successful revival, Patterson endured the street corner taunts of young journeymen and apprentices who called after him mockingly, "brimstone, fire and brimstone." Nor could Patterson or the Methodists stop the growing number of masters and employers who worked their apprentices and journeymen on Sunday. And what could anyone do with the master baker who forbade his fourteen-year-old apprentice to read the New Testament, warning him that "it will fill your head with foolish freaks"?

Working-class religiosity ran in many veins, and active proselytizing and enthusiastic revivals could not hope to tap them all. Again, it was the Rev. James Patterson who, unknowingly, demonstrated this. In an 1819 journal entry, Patterson considered his failure to convert a mariner whose wife was about to join the Presbyterian Church. Forcing his wife to accompany him on a country excursion the very Sunday she was to join Patterson's church, the mariner, apparently ill with tuberculosis, suffered a pulmonary lesion and was carried back to the city nearly dead. It was a weak and ashen-faced man whom Patterson confronted when he visited the couple's home shortly afterward. Realizing the gravity of the man's illness, the parson asked him whether he had made peace with God and was prepared to die. With that, the mariner flew into a rage and bellowed at Patterson, "I want no popish stuff, and no pope about me when I am going to die." Calming somewhat, he continued, "I am very weak, I don't wish you to talk to me." Undaunted, Patterson declined to leave and instead asked the mariner whether he believed the scriptures to be the word of God. By now incredulous, the sailor sprang from his sofa and turned to Patterson exclaiming, "I am astonished that you would ask any one such a question in an enlightened land." He then looked about the room for his pistols and threatened to shoot Patterson if he did not leave. Patterson departed unharmed and the mariner died a few months later, but not before calling a Universalist minister to his side.

This small glimpse of working-class life reveals another aspect of popular religion in the post-Revolutionary era. Like the beleaguered mariner, many workingmen viewed the missionary impulses of the Methodists and Presbyterians as an invasion of their world and an imposition on their way of life. This explains both the rough reception accorded the Hospitable Society's visiting committee in 1803 and the taunts that James Patterson endured fifteen years later. If they wanted religion, many laboring-class Philadelphians seemed to be saying, they would find it for themselves.

And so many did, finding a religion that fit with their views, often in surprising places. The dying mariner of Patterson's memoir found his religion with a Universalist minister. Likewise, Joe Holden, a New York blacksmith, thought that Universalism "may not be so bad after all" and undertook his own study of the matter. Large numbers of Philadelphia craftsmen followed suit. As early as 1796, Benjamin Rush, an early convert to Universalism, noted the laboring-class appeal of Elhanan Winchester's Sunday evening lectures on universal salvation. Rush's observation is confirmed by the 1793 subscription list of Winchester's First

Universalist Church, in which nearly two-thirds of the identifiable signers were workingmen. If we add the 8 percent who were shopkeepers, grocers, and innkeepers—men with close ties to the city's craftsmen—fully 71 percent of the church's subscribers were members of Philadelphia's still amorphous working class.

If Universalism was primarily a region that attracted craftsmen, small shopkeepers, and a handful of liberal intellectuals in the late eighteenth century, it was even more so during the first three decades of the following century. A tally of the surviving pew books for the years 1814–25 reveals a membership dominated by the city's *menu peuple*. In this crucial period of working-class formation, 91 percent of the identifiable members fell within this plebeian group, while fully 78 percent listed working-class occupations. Here, then, was a religion that spoke to the needs and desires of city workingmen. While the numerical strength of Universalism's plebeian appeal is remarkable in itself, it is made even more so by the fact that the Universalists, unlike the Methodists and Presbyterians, did not proselytize or mount revivals but attracted their following by simple lectures delivered in a moderate-sized church situated in Lombard Street, some distance from the city's largest working-class neighborhoods. That Philadelphia craftsmen and small shopkeepers were willing to tramp across the city on Sunday evenings to attend lectures and services speaks eloquently for the powerful attraction that drew the city's working classes to Universalism.

There were thus many paths that Philadelphia workingmen might walk in search of salvation. Some followed lay preachers into the Methodist connection and took their religion from the intimacy and fellowship of weekly class meetings. Others ran with open hearts to the message of emotional revelation that sputtered from fiery Presbyterians. Still others marked out their own path and moved with measured gait to embrace the democratic salvation offered by Universalism. But knowing the paths taken is not yet to understand the place of religion in the formation of Philadelphia's working class. What did Methodism, Presbyterianism, or Universalism offer workingmen? Was it hope for a better future, respite from the swift flow of social change, or strength to forge new collective identities in a rising manufacturing economy? An answer to these questions can only be found by placing the appeal of these plebeian denominations against the backdrop of Philadelphia's emerging working-class movement and the popular moral tradition that informed it.

Philadelphia's working-class movement developed over the course of a century, beginning with the political mobilization of city craftsmen during the 1720s and ending with the creation of distinctive working-class organizations at the close of the 1820s. In the course of this long and complex history, only the outlines of which can be sketched here, a unique set of popular intellectual traditions powerfully shaped the making of the city's working class.

More a group of closely connected attitudes about work, community, and social justice than a fully articulated ideology, the small-producer tradition was the moral code by which artisans lived out their productive lives. At its core was a simple statement of the labor theory of value, or as it was more commonly rendered before the nineteenth century, the social value of labor. Beginning with the rise of urban guilds to political prominence in the twelfth century, English and European craftsmen asserted the linked claims that their labor alone was responsible for the transformation of nature into socially useful goods and that this social usefulness entitled them to respect and well-being within their communities. By the time of the English Civil War, this simple idea had developed into what would become the typical artisan claim of the eighteenth and nineteenth centuries: that labor represented the basis of community life and the foundation of all collective wealth.

From the artisan's claim that civil society rested on the foundation of his labor, it was a short distance to the corollary notion that the craftsmen's collective contribution to the commonwealth placed them on an equal footing with other members of the community. Thus, it was no accident that artisans and small farmers were notorious advocates of democratic political reforms from at least the time of the English Civil War. Claiming the rights of "free-born Englishmen," small producers defended their rights to jury trial by their peers, to due process of law, and, if not the right to vote, then at least their right to be heard on the hustings. In the American context, artisan struggles during and after the Revolution would expand these rights to include manhood suffrage and the right of ordinary citizens to hold elective office. Whether encountered in England or America, however, artisan notions of free-born rights ran at odds with the prevailing notions of political rights and privileges propounded by large property holders and their political supporters. Against the claim that only the possession of substantial property provided a man with a true interest in society, artisans countered that the attainment of a skill and the social indispensability of productive labor combined to give all workingmen at least as great a stake in society as that claimed by the wealthy landowner or merchant.

In the end, however, artisans derived their notion of equality from practice rather than high political theory. Since the Middle Ages, membership in a trade conferred upon craftsmen the right to voice their opinions, to vote, and to hold formal office or informal positions of authority within their trade organizations. In short, it gave them the right to determine the affairs of their trade in conjunction with their fellow craftsmen. Thus, in drawing together popular notions of free-born rights with the rough democracy of the shop and informal trade society, artisans came to view themselves as equals, not only with other workingmen, but also with the wealthiest and most powerful members of society.

The third pillar of the small-producer tradition was competency. Few terms were as ubiquitous among artisans and other small producers as this. In its most basic form, competency was the lifelong ability of an artisan to provide a comfortable existence for his family through his own labor. A competency was the promise of moderate well-being and financial independence purchased through the early acquisition of a skill and the lifelong practice of a trade. For Anglo-American craftsmen, entry into a trade meant entering into a covenant with the community, a covenant in which the artisan offered a life of productive labor to the community in return for the respect of his peers and an independent life free from protracted want.

A sense of community-mindedness completed the small-producer tradition. Artisanal notions of community derived from the internal structure of the trades as well as from the local nature of craft production itself. Petty production in early America was typically production for a local market where producers and customers not only knew each other but were bound by intimate ties of custom and clientage. Under these conditions, in which artisans depended upon personal goodwill for their livelihood, the maintenance of community bonds was crucial to the smooth operation of the craft system.

But beyond the nature of small production itself, artisanal ideas about community developed from the communal organization of the craft workshop. Almost all artisans worked in small establishments with a handful of other craftsmen and apprentices. Even in larger enterprises like shipyards and metal works, craftsmen worked in gangs or crews that were seldom composed of more than a dozen men. Human relationships in these small-scale conditions were intimate and characterized by a norm of mutuality and cooperation. The shop was a little community where work rules, the pace of production, and personal relationships were governed to a considerable degree by the workers themselves. When artisans turned

their attention to the larger community around them, they naturally referred to the daily operations of their shops as a guide. Much as earlier craft guilds looked to the operations of the workshop when they sought to create regulations for the conduct of their trades, artisans relied upon the world of the shop when they sought a model for the proper functioning of the community in which they lived.

Artisans, then, viewed community, like their craft, as an association of individuals who labored together for the benefit of all. A well-run society, like a well-regulated trade, required the subordination of individual self-interest and acquisitiveness to the collective well-being of its members. Just as artisans arranged shop tasks and the pace of production to ensure that there was work enough for all, so craftsmen saw a proper community as one in which labor and its rewards were shared with fairness and equality and in which no productive member lacked in essentials while others had a more than ample supply. What craftsmen could not abide was a society where a few men lived on the fruits of the workingmen's labor and deprived producers of their just recompense.

These qualities—the value of labor, equality, competency, and community—made up the small-producer tradition. Together they represented the intellectual and moral standard against which Philadelphia artisans measured the religious appeals of Methodist class leaders, Presbyterian evangelists, and Universalist ministers. As events were to prove, those appeals led city workingmen along two, very different, paths.

Blessed are the poor in spirit for they,
Towards heav'ns kingdom are far on the way.

In lowly rev'rence let me come,
And bow in heart before thy awful throne.

The words are those of John Cox, a humble Philadelphia shoemaker, amateur poet, and ardent spokesman for working-class piety. His seven hundred-odd lines of uneven verse represent one of the few direct statements of laboring-class religiosity that have come down to us and reveal the unmistakable accents of the evangelical appeal among the working classes.

In England, as E. P. Thompson noted long ago, Methodism and other evangelical confessions offered solace and spiritual recompense to the victims of industrial change, albeit at the price of a lifelong obedience and servility that extended well beyond the spiritual kingdom into the texture of everyday life. In Philadelphia the evangelical message was more complex and equivocal, and the conditions of its auditors were altogether different. Unlike England, where the crushing weight of state repression joined with severe industrial dislocation to make of Methodism a "chiliasm of despair," laboring-class Philadelphians faced a more gradual industrial transformation with the power of manhood suffrage securely in their hands. Accordingly, evangelical religion offered craftsmen a more positive, if ultimately limiting, message. In their simple theology as well as in their spontaneous and democratic style, urban itinerants appealed to a working class that had successfully thrown off the bonds of colonial deference and had begun to demand a politics as plain and direct as their small-producer ethos. In this sense, evangelicalism was part of the larger cultural emergence of artisans and lesser workingmen into the public life of the post-Revolutionary era.

But in the wider view, the evangelical appeal touched something deeper than the Revolutionary political experiences of ordinary men and women. In the postwar years, Methodist and Presbyterian evangelists opened the doors of Christian brotherhood to Philadelphia's working people. In its early stages, post-Revolutionary evangelicalism held forth the prospect of a religion that could encompass both searing emotionality and traditional notions of artisanal respectability. Under the cover of institutional legitimacy provided by their class meetings and shoestring congregations, workingmen and their families found the freedom to express the mutual release of emotion that was an essential part of working-class culture, a culture that the city's more established churches eschewed and condemned. Unlike the city's more staid clerics, urban itinerants exhorted their congregations to *feel* the power of God's grace and their own shared religiosity. At the same time they provided their parishioners with institutional channels—churches, class meetings, and love feasts—that cloaked their expressive emotionality with a measure of public respectability.

What ordinary Philadelphians sought in evangelical religion was collective commitment and shared experience, the mutual validation of belief and community that comes from rituals of collective catharsis and experiential piety. A nineteenth-century mariner described this evangelical appeal with great poignancy: "What I likes along o'preachin'," he told a traveling evangelist, is "when a man is a-preachin' at me I want him to take somert hot out of his heart and shove it into mine,—that's what I calls preachin'." It was by taking "somert hot" from their hearts and sharing it with their congregations that urban evangelists created the electric waves of piety that washed over their rough-hewn flocks. From the end of the Revolution until well into the next century, these plebeian proselytizers provided a respectable venue for those who thought, as did an anonymous Boston sailor, that "faith is suth'n like Tinder: shut it up and it will go out, but give it vent and it will burn." Urban evangelicalism blew across a smoldering working-class piety that had long been ignored by more conventional churches and ignited flames of enthusiasm that would shape the lives of large numbers of working people for generations to come.

The shared experiences of conversion, prayer, and public testimony built powerful and lasting bonds between preachers, class leaders, and rank-and-file believers. At the same time, the evangelical emphasis on the individual's responsibility for salvation, nurtured and confirmed within the circle of collective fellowship, conveyed a sense of self-worth and community esteem that paralleled traditional craft feelings and norms. For many craftsmen and deskilled workingmen, the competency and self-respect that was lost in the decline of the craft system might be redeemed in the class meeting and evangelical congregation. In the end, it was this combined search for secular redemption, personal recognition, and spiritual salvation that brought floods of working-class converts into Philadelphia's Methodist and Presbyterian churches in the years following the Revolution.

But for all its positive attributes—its democratic inclusiveness, its fostering of personal and collective worth, its promise of spiritual redemption—evangelicalism carried with it the heavy baggage of its Calvinist heritage. Despite its evident humanism and the genuine concern of street preachers and class leaders to bring religion to the poor, urban evangelicalism was haunted by the notion of the depravity of man. In the final analysis, urban itinerants brought religion to the working-class as a way of tempering the sin and meanness that they saw as inherent in human nature, especially as it was manifested among the nation's lower orders. In the evangelists' eyes, mankind was by nature evil, and righteous living was, for all men and women, the labor of Sisyphus. Once unremitting depravity was accepted as the essence of human nature, asceticism and fear became the only pathways to salvation. Herein lay the central tension in the evangelical message to the working class: accept God's love and you may regain your competency and self-respect, but involve yourself too much with worldly concerns and you face eternal damnation from a wrathful, punishing God.

John Cox's *Rewards and Punishments* captures this tension exactly, in its title as well as its verse. Cox begins by offering the promise of restored competency and general prosperity that would be God's reward to a regenerate Philadelphia:

> Filled with God's grace, our city will shine bright,
> And over the world will cast resplendent light;
> Our enemies shall never do us harm,
> For he will help us with outstretched arm.

All that is required to achieve this urban millennium is for the men and women of the city to bridle their passions and learn the lesson of humility:

> Let us arise and shake ourselves from dust,
> And he will help us overcome our lust;
> His goodness he will extend to every soul,
> If they will subject be to his control.

This is the message of a loving God, a God ever ready to "help us with outstretched arm." But, let human pridefullness and arrogance triumph, and the project fails. Here Cox's God takes on a more ominous countenance:

> With base ingratitude ye did despise
> My statutes, and from me did turn your eyes,
> And for this thing I on you will send terror,
> As long as you will still persist in error.

The path is clearly marked: this way, reward; that way, punishment. Like Christian, John Bunyan's archetypal seeker, Philadelphians are offered choices and a moral road map. One path leads to the postmillennial Celestial City, all others lead to urban poverty and degrading dependency. Aware of the uncertainty of the human heart, Cox closes his promise with a characteristic evangelical warning wrapped within a threat: "If that we his blessed task forsake, / He'll on our heads his dreadful anger shake."

For John Cox and workingmen who thought like him, the evangelical message of repressive deliverance promised the resurrection of a world of small producers, a world in which their labor would lead not only to competency but to simple respect. Most artisans in post–Revolutionary Philadelphia shared these aspirations and many spent their lives searching for a way to redeem what they saw as the lost promise of the American Revolution. Some, like Cox, found that way in an evangelical religion that traded laboring-class solidarity for the fellowship of the class meeting and, perhaps, a small measure of worldly success.

By rejecting the solidarity of the emerging labor movement for the consolation of faith, submission, not struggle became the center of Cox's religion:

> Let us with pleasure bear each dispensation,
> In ev'ry rank of life and ev'ry station;
> Let us become as clay in [a] potter's hand
> To mould in any form at his command.

In the end, it was submission rather than organization that would finally yield both temporal and spiritual rewards:

> Let us in all things to his will submit,
> With patience undergo all he thinks fit:
> And if unto the end we him adore,
> We will receive of him a heav'nly store.

This was one side of working-class religion; restraint, repression, and self-denial operating through submission and fear to produce a life of satisfaction and self-esteem. All that was required was to reject the tavern, the Sunday excursion, the camaraderie of games and gambling, and, along with it, the journeymen's society and mutuality, the integument of working-class culture. What would be left in the end was not a working class but "respectable" workingmen indistinguishable in sentiment from their middle-class employers.

There was, of course, another side to working-class religion and it was, in many ways, the more important of the two. It was the side that empowered rather than diminished working-class life. Unlike Methodism and evangelical Presbyterianism, both of which still bore the marks of Puritanical Calvinism in their message of denial and submission, this alternative to overweening piety offered democratic salvation as well as an open acceptance of the working-class way of life. In Philadelphia, this brighter side of working-class religion found its most forceful expression in the doctrines and organizations of the Universalist Church.

Part of a widespread reaction to predestinarian doctrines in the years following the Revolution, Universalism embraced the notion of salvation for everyone. Against John Cox's paradoxical image of a benevolent yet ultimately vengeful God, Universalists counterposed the God of pure love—a God who, in the end, understood human frailties and forgave human transgressions. The message of the Universalists was thus a simple but powerful one: all will be saved.

Translated from doctrine into practice, Universalism took on a distinctively laboring-class voice as early as the 1790s in the form of didactic hymns. Written to instruct as well as entertain, hymnody became the vehicle for Universalism's popular appeal. Something of this plebeian appeal can be sensed in Abner Kneeland's "Invitation to the Gospel," with its imagery of plenty and social leveling:

> Hear ye that starve for food,
> By feeding on the wind,
> Or vainly strive with earthly good,
> To fill an empty mind.
>
> The Lord of Love has made,
> A soul reviving feast,
> And lets the world, of every grade,
> To rich provision taste.

Universalist hymnody also contained more direct appeals, as in Elhanan Winchester's paean to "America's Future Glory and Happiness," which focused on the central theme of the craftsman's creed, a life of competency:

> No more the labour'r pines, and grieves,
> For want of plenty round;
> His eyes behold the fruitful sheaves,
> Which makes his joys abound.

Such working-class themes ran through many Universalist hymns, but their appeal to city workingmen ran deeper still. In their hymns and preaching, Universalists often spoke of a community of love in ways that echoed the solidarity of tight-knit journeymen's societies and the mutuality of the larger working-class community:

How sweet is the union of souls,
In harmony, friendship and love;
Lord help us, this union to keep,
In *union* God grant we may meet.

This was written in 1808, a time when masters and journeymen were being relentlessly driven apart by the new manufacturing economy, a time during which the Democratic-Republican party was dividing itself into opposing manufacturing and working-class wings. Reading these lines against the evidence of an emerging working-class movement, it would have been difficult for many Philadelphia workingmen to separate the union of Christian fellowship from early craft unions.

In the end, this was the most remarkable aspect of the Universalist–working-class connection. While the Universalist credo mirrored traditional artisan values better than the doctrines of any other denomination, it was not beliefs that ultimately mattered. It was organization. From its inception, the Universalist Church was a meeting ground for the leaders (and at least some of the rank-and-file) of Philadelphia's working-class movement.

We can date the beginnings of the post–Revolutionary workers' movement from the formation of the Democratic Society of Pennsylvania in 1793. Organized by old Antifederalists and a new generation of opposition politicians, the Democratic Society brought Philadelphia craftsmen into organized politics for the first time since the 1770s. The political connection of Philadelphia Universalism was evident the same year, when 39 percent of the church's subscribers were also listed as members of the Democratic Society.

As the Democratic Society broadened into the Democratic-Republican party and, early in the nineteenth century, the party began to organize workingmen into neighborhood political clubs, the Universalist Church continued to play an informal organizing role. Not only did the church count such Democratic-Republican luminaries as Alexander James Dallas and Matthew Clarkson among its members, but, more importantly, it also included two of the city's most prominent working-class leaders on its rolls. Anthony Cuthbert, a mastmaker and member of one of Philadelphia's most prominent artisan families, and Israel Israel, an innkeeper and political champion of the early nineteenth-century workingmen's movement, were both active Universalists from the 1790s through the 1820s. Israel, who first earned his reputation among craftsmen for his selfless efforts in laboring-class neighborhoods during the yellow fever epidemic of 1794, became one of the most important popular leaders of the early nineteenth century.

The paucity of church records for the first two decades of the nineteenth century limits our understanding of the church's organizing role in those years, but the continued presence of popular leaders such as Cuthbert and, especially, Israel, coupled with the increasing working-class presence in the church itself, strongly suggests the church's importance to the emerging working-class movement. This importance was underlined when the workers' movement took on an institutional structure during the late 1820s. The creation of the Mechanics' Union of Trade Associations in 1827 and the Workingmen's party the following year marked the formation of America's first working class. Led by William Heighton, a local shoemaker of English birth, the Mechanics' Union and the Workingmen's party forged artisan intellectual traditions and popular politics into a powerful working-class presence in Philadelphia. Universalism played more than a minor role in this process, for not only was Heighton a follower of Universalist doctrines, he also organized the Mechanics' Union through a series of meetings held in the city's Universalist churches.

Religion played an important part in Heighton's ambitious and multifaceted plan to restore the producing classes—farmers, mechanics, and laborers—to their rightful place in American society. In an address delivered at the newly gathered Second Universalist Church, located near the working-class suburb of the Northern Liberties, Heighton outlined his plan. The cause of the continuing economic and social decline of Philadelphia's working classes, he declared, was the growing dominance of the "avaricious accumulators and ungenerous employers" of the city. This class of "aristocratic accumulators," Heighton told his working-class audience, consisted of social and economic parasites who obtained their livelihoods solely from the fruits of other men's labor. The degraded condition of Philadelphia workingmen, he explained, came not from human moral failings or the wrath of a displeased God, but from the unrestrained greed of men who lived by exploiting the city's working classes.

In time, Heighton hoped to set the united working classes of the city against this growing class of accumulators. In the meantime, he maintained that it was the duty of Philadelphia's "legislative, judicial, and theological classes" to exercise "their influence to remedy [the workers'] degraded condition." Yet, as Heighton painstakingly pointed out, none of these classes had thus far brought any degree of social justice to the workingman's door, and the clergy had failed most egregiously of all.

In the course of his public indictment of Philadelphia's reforming clergy, Heighton outlined the proper role of religion in a future republic of labor. As he saw it, the social and moral obligation of the clergy was not simply to "teach evangelical truths" but "to teach the absolute necessity of undeviating justice between man and man." While he thought that true Christian ministers ought to be living "imitators of those primitive Christians who had 'all things in common,'" Heighton found instead that most Philadelphia clerics remained blind to the "legalized extortion" practiced on the city's working classes. "Why do they not point out the enormous injustice of one class of

men possessing legal authority to take advantage of the necessities of another?" he asked. And why had the denominational clergy not directed "the power of their reasoning, and the thunders of their eloquence against the unjust and vice-creating system of conflicting interest—a system so directly opposed to that adopted by . . . the Prince of Peace?"

If the established clergy were shameless in their failure to speak out against this pernicious evil, the evangelists were, for Heighton, the most culpable of all. Taking aim at the city's Methodist and evangelical Presbyterian ministers, he pointed to the futility of their quest for working-class redemption in a world structured by industrial capitalism. With barely disguised contempt Heighton warned his listeners that "not all the fervent intercessions of prayer, not all the influence of pathetic exhortation, nor all the declarations of divine denunciation, can ever arrest the progress of sin while the system of individual interest and competition is supported." For Heighton, the only hope for redemption lay not in working-class piety within the present system but in a united effort by clergy and workingmen alike to overturn that system in the name of social justice.

Religion, then, was closely bound up with Heighton's vision of a republic of independent producers; the competition and individual interest of the wage-labor market was a moral injustice, to be sure, but it was also a sin. The interest of the clergy and the interest of workingmen were consequently the same: the creation of a moral society founded in social justice. "If the clergy would arrest the fatal march of vice," Heighton advised, "let them direct their attacks on its fountain head." "The grand nursery of sin must be destroyed," he added, "before they can cherish any reasonable hopes of a general and permanent reformation in our country." Thus the republic of labor would be more than a society of loosely associated producers; it would be God's true community.

In the broadest sense, then, religion occupied a prominent place in Philadelphia's working-class movement because that movement went well beyond a simple strengthening of workers' market capacities. Heighton's aim, whether in the Mechanics' Union or the Workingmen's party, was to reform American society, to make America into the moral community that both clergy and workingmen saw as the nation's brightest promise. As husbandmen of public and private morality, the American clergy could do much to bring about this reformation, if only they would direct "their talents, their learning, and their influence . . . against the mainspring of all evil, and source of every crime." If all of America's clerics would follow the example of their Universalist brethren and unite with the nation's working people in the project of labor reform, "religion [would] extend, and flourish in all its sublime and harmonious beauties" throughout the entire nation.

Popular religion thus played an important role in the formation of Philadelphia's working class. While some workingmen retreated into the quiescence of evangelical piety and finally turned their backs on the working-class movement, many others turned to religion as a moral force that underwrote their own traditions and pointed toward a more hopeful future. While much, much more remains to be done before we can fully understand the place of religion in early working-class life, the case of the Universalists and Philadelphia's workingmen's movement suggests that religion could be a powerful ally in the workingmen's quest for economic and social justice.

GLOSSARY

Benevolence: A middle-class movement that originated in the nation's churches and which sought to dispense aid and religious ideas to the poor.

Evangelicalism: A form of religious exhortation that emphasizes direct emotional experience on the part of both minister and congregation.

Plebeian: Nonelite men and women.

George Whitefield (1714–1770): Follower of John Wesley in England who preached widely in the American colonies and was a central figure in the Great Awakening of the mid-eighteenth century instrumental in establishing Methodism in America.

Benjamin Rush (1745–1813): American physician, politician, and educator; a signer of the Declaration of Independence, involved in nearly every reform movement in the early Unite States, and especially known for promoting the abolition of slavery and the humane treatment of the mentally handicapped.

John Bunyan (1628–1688): English Baptist preacher and author of *Pilgrim's Progress*, the most popular religious tract after the Bible in America. *Pilgrim's Progress* is an allegorical tale of Christian's journey from the City of Destruction to the Celestial City.

IMPLICATIONS

Historians have often viewed religious commitment as an alternative to unionization in the early nineteenth century, arguing that workers turned to God or unions, but never both, to resolve the personal conflicts they felt in the early industrial era. In this essay, Schultz suggests a different approach: that organized religion could serve as an important support of the fledgling union movement. In what ways do you think religion was a retreat from unionization and the problems of economic transformation? In what ways could religion form the basis for criticism of the new industrial order?

Past Traces

The early textile factories that began to dot the landscape of the rural northeast in the late eighteenth and early nineteenth centuries brought forth a divided response from Americans at large as well as from the women who worked there. While some saw the mills in a positive light, as ways of adding to the number of scarce jobs in the countryside or as a means to make the United States a self-sufficient manufacturing nation, others saw in the mills a reflection of contemporary England, where similar mills had ushered in a regime of poverty, ill health, and low morals. In this document, Lucy Larcom, an early worker in the Lowell, Massachusetts, cotton mills and a fledgling poet, recounts her experiences at the power loom with a degree of ambivalence that was characteristic of early women mill operatives. What did it mean that mill workers were viewed as mere "hands" rather than as individuals? And what effect did the monotonous routine of factory work have on women's minds? Larcom offers no solutions here but instead points to a set of problems that occupied the minds of many Americans in early industrial America.

Lucy Larcom, *An Idyll of Work* (1884)

But this was waste,—this woman-
  faculty
Tied to machinery, part of the machine.
That wove cloth when it might be
  clothing hearts
And minds with queenly raiment. She
  foresaw
The time must come when mind itself
  would yield
To the machine, or leave the work to
  hands
Which were hands only.
. . . These [women] counted but as
  "hands!" named such! . . .
It must not be at all, or else their toil
Must be made easier, larger its
  reward! . . .
Here was a problem, then,
For the political theorist: how to save

Mind from machinery's clutches.
The rumbling wheels and rattling bands
All in succession roll,
The regulator swiftly moves;
And regulates the whole . . .

The bales of cotton soon are brought,
And from the Picker flows
Swift through the cards and breakers
  come,
And to the Speeder goes.

With rapid flight the Speeder flies
T'is pleasing to behold,
The roping round the bobins wind,
One half can near be told.

The next we know the spinners call
For roping to be brought,

It's carried from the carding room,
And on their spindles caught.
Come, listen friends, and you, I tell
What spinners they can do,
The roping they will quick convert,
To warp and filling to.

Another sight I now behold,
It is a pleasing scene,
The warp is taken soon as spun,
And wound around the beam.

Then soon it's carried out of sight,
Into the dressing room,

It's warped and dressed all complete,
And fitted for the loom.
The slaie and harness is prepared,
Each thread for to convene,
The looms are placed in rows
   throughout,
The weavers stand between.

The shuttle now is swiftly thrown,
It flies from end to end
And they stand ready all the while,
Each broken thread to mend. . . .

15

Women, Children, and the Uses of the Streets: Class and Gender Conflict in New York City, 1850–1860

Christine Stansell

The years between 1820 and 1860 witnessed the development of an intensive campaign to redefine the proper place of women in American society. Coming at a time of intense social and cultural change, the impulse to create a distinctively American conception of womanhood and definition of female virtue spread rapidly throughout America. Depicting the home as a domestic haven in an increasingly competitive and commercial world, the "Cult of True Womanhood" attributed to women a vital function in maintaining republican virtue during a threatening period of industrialization and urbanization. This "Cult of True Womanhood" prescribed a series of characteristics for women, as guardians of national virtue, to cultivate. Of these, the most important were religious piety, moral purity, submissiveness to men, and the maintenance of the home as place of comfort and moral education.

While many women embraced the virtues of "true womanhood," a life of domesticity was never a real possibility for poor and working-class women. Forced to work in order to maintain their families and lacking the resources and leisure necessary to maintain a middle-class household, these working women carved out lives regulated by their own distinctive social and cultural values. But, as Christine Stansell reveals in this essay, this working-class women's culture came into increasing conflict with the domestic ideal of middle- and upper-class women reformers in the course of the nineteenth century. Offering moral advice and economic aid to working-class women through a growing network of benevolent organizations, Bible societies, and temper-

"Women, Children, and the Uses of the Streets: Class and Gender Conflict in New York City, 1850–1860." *Feminist Studies*, 8:2, (1982) pp. 309–335. Reprinted by permission of the publisher, Feminist Studies, Inc., c/o Women's Studies Program, University of Maryland, College Park, MD 20742.

ance associations, these middle-class women sought to force working-class women from the public world of the streets and tenements into the private world of domesticity. By granting assistance only to those women who would adopt their notions of respectable living, these reforming women attempted to make the domestic ideal a universal reality in antebellum America.

....

On a winter day in 1856, an agent for the Children's Aid Society (CAS) of New York encountered two children out on the street with market baskets. Like hundreds he might have seen, they were desperately poor—thinly dressed and barefoot in the cold—but their cheerful countenances struck the gentleman, and he stopped to inquire into their circumstances. They explained that they were out gathering bits of wood and coal their mother could burn for fuel and agreed to take him home to meet her. In a bare tenement room, bereft of heat, furniture, or any other comforts, he met a "stout, hearty woman" who, even more than her children, testified to the power of hardihood and motherly love in the most miserable circumstances. A widow, she supported her family as best she could by street peddling; their room was bare because she had been forced to sell her clothes, furniture, and bedding to supplement her earnings. As she spoke, she sat on a pallet on the floor and rubbed the hands of the two younger siblings of the pair from the street. "They were tidy, sweet children," noted the agent, "And it was very sad to see their chilled faces and tearful eyes." Here was a scene that would have touched the heart of Dickens, and seemingly many a chillier mid-Victorian soul. Yet in concluding his report, the agent's perceptions took a curiously harsh turn.

> Though for her pure young children too much could hardly be done, in such a woman there is little confidence to be put . . . it is probably, some cursed vice has thus reduced her, and that, if her children be not separated from her, she will drag them down, too.

Such expeditions of charity agents and reformers into the households of the poor were common in New York between 1850 and 1860. So were such harsh and unsupported judgments of working-class mothers, judgments which either implicitly or explicitly converged in the new category of the "dangerous classes." In this decade, philanthropists, municipal authorities, and a second generation of Christian evangelicals, male and female, came to see the presence of poor children in New York's streets as a central element of the problem of urban poverty. They initiated an ambitious campaign to clear the streets, to change the character of the laboring poor by altering their family lives, and, in the process, to eradicate poverty itself. They focused their efforts on transforming two elements of laboring-class family life, the place of children and the role of women.

There was, in fact, nothing new about the presence of poor children in the streets, nor was it new that women of the urban poor should countenance that presence. For centuries, poor people in Europe had freely used urban public areas—streets, squares, courts, and marketplaces—for their leisure and work. For the working poor, street life was bound up not only with economic exigency, but also with childrearing, family morality, sociability, and neighborhood ties. In the nineteenth century, the crowded conditions of the tenements and the poverty of great numbers of metropolitan laboring people made the streets as crucial an arena as ever for their social and economic lives. As one New York social investigator observed, "In the poorer portions of the city, people live much and sell mostly out of doors."

How, then, do we account for this sudden flurry of concern? For reformers like the agent from CAS, street life was antagonistic to ardently held beliefs about childhood, womanhood, and, ultimately, the nature of civilized urban society. The middle class of which the reformers were a part was only emerging, an economically illdefined group, neither rich nor poor, just beginning in the antebellum years to assert a distinct cultural identity. Central to its self-conception was the ideology of domesticity, a set of sharp ideas and pronounced opinions about the nature of a moral family life. The sources of this ideology were historically complex and involved several decades of struggles by women of this group for social recognition, esteem, and power in the family. Nonetheless, by midcentury, ideas initially developed and promoted by women and their clerical allies had found general acceptance, and an ideology of gender had become firmly embedded in an ideology of class. Both women and men valued the home, an institution which they perceived as sacred, presided over by women, inhabited by children, frequented by men. The home preserved those social virtues endangered by the public world of trade, industry, and politics; a public world which they saw as even more corrupting and dangerous in a great city like New York.

Enclosed, protected, and privatized, the home and the patterns of family life on which it was based thus represented to middle-class women and men a crucial institution of civilization. From this perspective, a particular geography of social life—the engagement of the poor in street life rather than in the enclave of the home—became in itself evidence of parental neglect, family disintegration, and a pervasive urban social pathology. Thus in his condemnation of the impoverished widow, the CAS agent distilled an entire analysis of poverty and a critique of poor families: the presence of her children on the streets was synonymous with a corrupt family life, no matter how disguised it might be. In the crusade of such mid-Victorian reformers to save poor children from their parents and their class lie the roots of a long history of middle-class intervention in working-class families, a history which played a central part in the making of the female American working class.

Many historians have shown the importance of antebellum urban reform to the changing texture of class relations in America, its role in the cultural transformations of urbanization and industrialization. Confronted with overcrowding, unemployment, and poverty on a scale theretofore unknown in America, evangelical reformers forged programs to control and mitigate these pressing urban problems, programs which would shape municipal policies for years to come. Yet their responses were not simply practical solutions, the most intelligent possible reactions to difficult circumstances; as the most sensitive historians of reform have argued, they were shaped by the world view, cultural affinities, conceptions of gender, class prejudices, and imperatives of the reformers themselves. Urban reform was an interaction in which, over time, both philanthropists and their beneficiaries changed. In their experience with the reformers, the laboring poor learned—and were forced—to accommodate themselves to an alien conception of family and city life. Through their work with the poor, the reformers discovered many of the elements from which they would forge their own class and sexual identity, still ill-defined and diffuse in 1850; women, particularly, strengthened their role as dictators of domestic and familial standards for all classes of Americans. The reformers' eventual triumph in New York brought no solutions to the problem of poverty, but it did bring about the evisceration of a way of urban life and the legitimation of their own cultural power as a class.

The conflict over the streets resonated on many levels. Ostensibly the reformers aimed to rescue children from the corruptions and dangers of the city streets; indeed the conscious motives of many, if not all, of these well-meaning altruists went no further. There were many unquestioned assumptions, however, on which their benevolent motives rested, and it is in examining these assumptions that we begin to see the challenge which these middle-class people unwittingly posed to common practices of the poor. In their cultural offensive, reformers sought to impose on the poor conceptions of childhood and motherhood drawn from their own ideas of domesticity. In effect, reformers tried to implement their domestic beliefs through reorganizing social space, through creating a new geography of the city. Women were especially active; while male reformers experimented, through a rural foster home program, with more dramatic means of clearing the streets, middle-class ladies worked to found new working-class homes, modeled on their own, which would establish a viable alternative to the thoroughly nondomesticated streets. Insofar as the women reformers succeeded, their victory contributed to both the dominance of a class and of a specific conception of gender. It was, moreover, a victory which had enduring and contradictory consequences for urban women of all classes. In our contemporary city streets, vacated, for the most part, of domestic life yet dangerous for women and children, we see something of the legacy of their labors.

CHILDREN'S USES OF THE STREETS

Unlike today, the teeming milieu of the New York streets in the mid-nineteenth century was in large part a children's world. A complex web of economic imperatives and social mores accounted for their presence there, a presence which reformers so ardently decried. Public life, with its panoply of choices, its rich and varied texture, its motley society, played as central a role in the upbringing of poor children as did private, domestic life in that of their more affluent peers. While middle-class mothers spent a great deal of time with their children (albeit with the help of servants), women of the laboring classes condoned for their offspring an early independence—within bounds—on the streets. Through peddling, scavenging, and the shadier arts of theft and prostitution, the streets offered children a way to earn their keep, crucial to making ends meet in their households. Street life also provided a home for children without families—the

orphaned and abandoned—and an alternative to living at home for the especially independent and those in strained family circumstances.

Such uses of the streets were dictated by exigency, but they were also intertwined with patterns of motherhood, parenthood, and childhood. In contrast to their middle- and upper-class contemporaries, the working poor did not think of childhood as a separate stage of life in which girls and boys were free from adult burdens, nor did poor women consider mothering to be a full-time task of supervision. They expected their children to work from an early age, to "earn their keep" or to "get a living," a view much closer to the early modern conceptions which Philippe Ariès describes in *Centuries of Childhood*. Children were little adults, unable as yet to take up all the duties of their elders, but nonetheless bound to do as much as they could. To put it another way, the lives of children, like those of adults, were circumscribed by economic and familial obligations. In this context, the poor expressed their care for children differently than did the propertied classes. Raising one's children properly did not mean protecting them from the world of work; on the contrary, it involved teaching them to shoulder those heavy burdens of labor which were the common lot of their class, to be hardworking and dutiful to kin and neighbors. By the same token, laboring children gained an early autonomy from their parents, an autonomy alien to the experience of more privileged children. But there were certainly generational tensions embedded in these practices: although children learned independence within the bounds of family obligation, their self-sufficiency also led them in directions that parents could not always control. When parents sent children out to the streets, they could only partially set the terms of what the young ones learned there.

Streetselling, or huckstering, was one of the most common ways for children to turn the streets to good use. Through the nineteenth century, this ancient form of trade still flourished in New York alongside such new institutions of mass marketing as A.T. Stewart's department store. Hucksters, both adults and children, sold all manner of necessities and delicacies. In the downtown business and shopping district, passers-by could buy treats at every corner: hot sweet potatoes, bake-pears, teacakes, fruit, candy, and hot corn. In residential neighborhoods, hucksters sold household supplies door to door: fruits and vegetables in season, matchsticks, scrub brushes, sponges, strings, and pins. Children assisted adult hucksters, went peddling on their own, and worked in several low-paying trades which were their special province: crossing-sweeping for girls; errandrunning, bootblacking, horseholding, and newspaperselling for boys. There were also the odd trades in which children were particularly adept, those unfamiliar and seemingly gratuitous forms of economic activity which abounded in nineteenth-century metropolises; one small boy whom a social investigator found in 1859 made his living in warm weather by catching butterflies and peddling them to canary owners.

Younger children, too, could earn part of their keep on the streets. Scavenging, the art of gathering useful and salable trash, was the customary chore for those too small to go out streetselling. Not all scavengers were children; there were also adults who engaged in scavenging full-time, ragpickers who made their entire livelihoods from "all the odds and ends of a great city." More generally, however, scavenging was children's work. Six- or seven-year-olds were not too young to set out with friends and siblings to gather fuel for their mothers. Small platoons of these children scoured neighborhood streets, ship and lumber yards, building lots, demolished houses, and the precincts of artisan shops and factories for chips, ashes, wood, and coal to take home or peddle to neighbors. "I saw some girls gathering cinders," noted Virginia Penny, New York's self-styled Mayhew. "They burn them at home, after washing them."

The economy of rubbish was intricate. As children grew more skilled, they learned how to turn up other serviceable cast-offs. "These gatherers of things lost on earth," a journal had called them in 1831. "These makers of something out of nothing." Besides taking trash home or selling it to neighbors, children could peddle it to junk dealers, who in turn vended it to manufacturers and artisans for use in industrial processes. Rags, old rope, metal, nails, bottles, paper, kitchen grease, bones, spoiled vegetables, and bad meat all had their place in this commercial network. The waterfront was especially fruitful territory: there, children foraged for loot which had washed up on the banks, snagged in piers, or spilled out on the docks. Loose cotton shredded off bales on the wharves where the southern packet ships docked, bits of canvas and rags ended up with paper- and shoddy-manufacturers (shoddy, the cheapest of textiles, made its way back to the poor in "shoddy" ready-made clothing). Old rope was shredded and sold as oakum, a fiber used to caulk ships. Whole pieces of hardware—nails, cogs, and screws—could be resold: broken bits went to iron- and brass-founders and coppersmiths to be melted down; bottles and bits of broken glass, to glassmakers. The medium for these exchanges were the second-hand shops strung along the harbor which carried on a bustling trade with children despite a city ordinance prohibiting their buying from minors. "On going down South Street I met a gang of small Dock Thieves . . . had a bag full of short pieces of old rope and iron," William Bell, police inspector of second-hand shops, reported on a typical day on the beat in 1850. The malefactors were headed for a shop like the one into which he slipped incognito, to witness the mundane but illegal transaction between the proprietor and a six-year-old boy, who sold him a glass bottle for a penny. The waterfront also yielded trash which could be used at home rather than vended: tea, coffee, sugar, and flour spilled from sacks and barrels, and from the wagons which carried cargo to nearby warehouses.

The growth of the street trades meant that increasing numbers of children worked on their own, away from adult supervision. This situation magnified the opportunities for illicit gain, the centuries-old pilfering and finagling of apprentices and serving-girls. When respectable parents sent their children out to scavenge and peddle, the consequences were not always what they intended: these trades were an avenue to theft and prostitution as well as to an honest living. Child peddlers habituated household entryways, with their hats and umbrellas and odd knickknacks, and roamed by shops where goods were often still, in the old fashion, displayed outside on the sidewalks. And scavenging was only one step removed from petty theft. The distinction between gathering spilled flour and spilling flour oneself was one which small scavengers did not always observe. Indeed, children skilled in detecting value in random objects strewn about the streets, the seemingly inconsequential, could as easily spot value in other people's property. As the superintendent of the juvenile asylum wrote of one malefactor, "He has very little sense of moral rectitude, and thinks it but little harm to take small articles." A visitor to the city in 1857 was struck by the swarms of children milling around the docks, "scuffling about, wherever there were bags of coffee and hogshead of sugar." Armed with sticks, "they 'hooked' what they could." The targets of pilfering were analogous to those of scavenging: odd objects, unattached to persons. The prey of children convicted of theft and sent to the juvenile house of correction in the 1850s included, for instance, a bar of soap, a copy of the *New York Herald*, lead and wood from demolished houses, and a board "valued at 3¢." Police Chief George Matsell reported that pipes, tin roofing, and brass doorknobs were similarly endangered. Thefts against persons, pickpocketing and mugging, belonged to another province, that of the professional child criminal.

Not all parents were concerned about their children's breaches of the law. Reformers were not always wrong when they charged that by sending children to the streets, laboring-class parents implicitly encouraged them to a life of crime. The unrespectable poor did not care to discriminate between stolen and scavenged goods, and the destitute could not afford to. One small boy picked up by the CAS told his benefactors that his parents had sent him out chip picking with the instructions "you can take it wherever you can find it"—although like many children brought before the charities, this one was embroidering his own innocence and his parents' guilt. But children also took their own chances, without their parents' knowledge. By midcentury, New York was the capital of American crime, and there was a place for children, small and adept as they were, on its margins. Its full-blown economy of contraband, with the junk shops at the center, allowed children to exchange pilfered and stolen goods quickly and easily: anything, from scavenged bottles to nicked top hats could be sold immediately.

As scavenging shaded into theft, so it also edged into another street trade, prostitution. The same art of creating commodities underlay both. In the intricate economy of the streets, old rope, stray coal, rags, and sex all held the promise of cash, a promise apparent to children who from an early age learned to be "makers of something out of nothing." For girls who knew how to turn things with no value into things with exchange value, the prostitute's act of bartering sex into money would have perhaps seemed daunting, but nonetheless comprehensible. These were not professional child prostitutes; rather, they turned to the lively trade in casual prostitution on occasion or at intervals to supplement other earnings. One encounter with a gentleman, easy to come by in the hotel and business district, could bring the equivalent of a month's wages in domestic service, a week's wages seamstressing, or several weeks' earnings huckstering. Such windfalls went to pay a girl's way at home or, more typically, to purchase covertly some luxury—pastries, a bonnet, cheap jewelry, a fancy gown—otherwise out of her reach.

Prostitution was quite public in antebellum New York. It was not yet a statutory offense, and although the police harassed streetwalkers and arrested them for vagrancy, they had little effect on the trade. Consequently, offers from men and inducements from other girls were common on the streets, and often came a girl's way when she was out working. This is the reason a German father tried to prevent his fourteen-year-old daughter from going out scavenging when she lost her place in domestic service. "He said, 'I don't want you to be a rag-picker. You are not a child now—people will look at you—you will come to harm,'" as the girl recounted the tale. The "harm" he feared was the course taken by a teenage habitué of the waterfront in whom Inspector Bell took a special interest in 1851. After she rejected his offer of a place in service, he learned from a junk shop proprietor that, along with scavenging around the docks, she was "in the habit of going aboard the Coal Boats in that vicinity and prostituting herself." Charles Loring Brace, founder of the CAS, claimed that "the life of a swill-gatherer, or coal-picker, or chiffonier [ragpicker] in the streets soon wears off a girl's modesty and prepares her for worse occupation," while Police Chief Matsell accused huckster-girls of soliciting the clerks and employees they met on their rounds of counting houses.

While not all girls in the street trades were as open to advances as Brace and Matsell implied, their habituation to male advances must have contributed to the brazenness with which some of them could engage in sexual bartering. Groups of girls roamed about the city, sometimes on chores and errands, sometimes only with an eye for flirtations, or being "impudent and saucy to men," as the parents of one offender put it. In the early 1830s, John R. McDowall, leader of the militant Magdalene Society, had observed on fashionable Broadway "females of thirteen and fourteen walking the streets without a protector, until some pretended gentleman gives them a nod, and takes their arm and escorts them to houses of assignation." McDowall was sure to exaggerate, but later witnesses lent credence to his description. In 1854, a journalist saw nearly fifty girls soliciting one evening as he walked a mile up Broadway, while diarist George Templeton Strong referred to juvenile prostitution as a permanent feature of the promenade in the early 1850s: "no one can walk the length of Broadway without meeting some hideous troop of ragged girls." But despite the entrepreneurial attitude with which young girls ventured into prostitution, theirs was a grim choice, with hazards which, young as they were, they could not always foresee. Nowhere can we see more clearly the complexities of poor children's lives in the public city. The life of the streets taught them self-reliance and the arts of survival, but this education could also be a bitter one.

The autonomy and independence which the streets fostered through petty crime also extended to living arrangements. Abandoned children, orphans, runaways, and particularly independent boys made the streets their home: sleeping out with companions in household areas, wagons, marketplace stalls, and saloons. In the summer of 1850, the *Tribune* noted that the police regularly scared up thirty or forty boys sleeping along Nassau and Ann streets; they included boys with homes as well as genuine vagabonds. Police Chief Matsell reported that in warm weather, crowds of roving boys, many of them sons of respectable parents, absented themselves from their families for weeks. Such was Thomas W., who came to the attention of the CAS; "sleeps in stable," the case record notes. "Goes home for clean clothes; and sometimes for his meals." Thomas's parents evidently tolerated the arrangement, but this was not always the case. Rebellious children, especially boys, evaded parental demands and discipline by living on the streets full-time. Thus John Lynch left home because of some difficulty with his father: he was sent on his parents' complaint to the juvenile house of correction on a vagrancy charge.

Reformers like Matsell and the members of the CAS tended to see such children as either orphaned or abandoned, symbols of the misery and depravity of the poor. Their perception, incarnated by writers like Horatio Alger in the fictional waifs of sentimental novels, gained wide credibility in nineteenth-century social theory and popular thought. Street children were essentially "friendless and homeless," declared Brace. "No one cares for them, and they care for no one." His judgment, if characteristically harsh, was not without truth. If children without parents had no kin or friendly neighbors to whom to turn, they were left to fend for themselves. Such was the story of the two small children of a deceased stonecutter, himself a widower. After he died, "they wandered around, begging cold victuals, and picking up, in any way they were able, their poor living." William S., fifteen years old, had been orphaned when very young. After a stay on a farm as an indentured boy, he ran away to the city, where he slept on the piers and supported himself by carrying luggage off passenger boats: "William thinks he has seen hard times," the record notes. But the testimony garnered by reformers about the "friendless and homeless" young should also be taken with a grain of salt. The CAS, a major source of these tales, was most sympathetic to children who appeared before the agents as victims of orphanage, desertion, or familial cruelty; accordingly, young applicants for aid sometimes presented themselves in ways which would gain them the most favor from philanthropists. The society acknowledged the problem, although it claimed to have solved it: "runaways frequently come to the office with fictitious stories . . . Sometimes a truant has only one parent, generally the mother, and she is dissipated, or unable to control him. He comes to the office . . . and tells a fictitious story of orphanage and distress." Yet in reality, there were few children so entirely exploited and "friendless" as the CAS believed.

Not surprisingly, orphanage among the poor was a far more complex matter than reformers perceived. As Carol Groneman has shown, poor families did not disintegrate under the most severe difficulties of immigration and urbanization. In the worst New York slums, families managed to keep together and to take in those kin and friends who lacked households of their own. Orphaned children as well as those who were temporarily parentless—whose parents, for instance, had found employment elsewhere—typically found homes with older siblings, grandparents, and aunts. The solidarity of the laboring-class family, however, was not as idyllic as it might seem in retrospect. Interdependence also bred tensions which weighed heavily on children, and in response, the young sometimes chose—or were forced—to strike out on their own. Step-relations, so common in this period, were a particular source of bad feelings. Two brothers whom a charity visitor found sleeping in the streets explained that they had left their mother when she moved in with another man after their father deserted her. If natural parents died, step-parents might be particularly forceful about sending children "on their own hook." "We haven't got no father nor mother," testified a twelve-year-old wanderer of himself and his younger brother. Their father, a shoemaker, had remarried when their mother died; when he died, their stepmother moved away and left them, "and they could not find out anything more about her."

Moreover, the difficulties for all, children and adults, of finding work in these years of endemic underemployment created a kind of half-way orphanage. Parents emigrating from New York could place their boys in apprenticeships which subsequently collapsed and cast the children on their own for a living. The parents of one boy, for example, left him at work in a printing office when they moved to Toronto. Soon after they left, he was thrown out of work; to support himself he lived on the streets and worked as an errand boy, news boy, and bootblack. Similarly, adolescents whose parents had left them in unpleasant or intolerable situations simply struck out on their own.

A widow boarded her son with her sister when she went into service; the boy ran away when his aunt "licked him." Thus a variety of circumstances could be concealed in the category of the street "orphan."

All these customs of childhood and work among the laboring poor were reasons for the presence of children, girls and boys, in the public life of the city, a presence which reformers passionately denounced. Children and parents alike had their uses for the streets. For adults, the streets allowed their dependents to contribute to their keep, crucial to making ends meet in the household economy. For girls and boys, street life provided a way to meet deeply ingrained family obligations. This is not to romanticize their lives. If the streets provided a way to meet responsibilities, it was a hard and bitter, even a cruel one. Still, children of the laboring classes lived and labored in a complex geography, which reformers of the poor perceived only as a stark tableau of pathology and vice.

To what degree did their judgments of children redound on women? Although reformers included both sexes in their indictments, women were by implication more involved. First, poverty was especially likely to afflict women. To be the widow, deserted wife, or orphaned daughter of a laboring man, even a prosperous artisan, was to be poor; female self-support was synonymous with indigence. The number of self-supporting women, including those with children, was high in midcentury New York: in the 1855 census report for two neighborhoods, nearly 60 percent of six hundred working women sampled had no adult male in the household. New York's largest charity reported in 1858 that it aided 27 percent more women than men. For women in such straits, children's contributions to the family income were mandatory. As a New York magistrate had written in 1830: "of the children brought before me for pilfering, nine out of ten are those whose fathers are dead, and who live with their mothers." Second, women were more responsible than men for

children, both from the perspective of reformers and within the reality of the laboring family. Mothering, as the middle class saw it, was an expression of female identity, rather than a construction derived from present and past social conditions. Thus the supposedly neglectful ways of laboring mothers reflected badly not only on their character as parents, but also on their very identity as women. When not depicted as timid or victimized, poor women appeared as unsavory characters in the annals of reformers: drunken, abusive, or, in one of the most memorable descriptions, "sickly-looking, deformed by over work . . . weak and sad-faced." Like prostitutes, mothers of street children became a kind of half-sex in the eyes of reformers, outside the bounds of humanity by virtue of their inability or unwillingness to replicate the innate abilities of true womanhood.

REFORMERS AND FAMILY LIFE

In the 1850s, the street activities of the poor, especially those of children, became the focus of a distinct reform politics in New York. The campaign against the streets, one element in a general cultural offensive against the laboring classes which evangelical groups had carried on since the 1830s, was opened in 1849 by Police Chief Matsell's report to the public on juvenile delinquency. In the most hyperbolic rhetoric, he described a "deplorable and growing evil" spreading through the streets. "I allude to the constantly increasing number of vagrants, idle and vicious children of both sexes, who infest our public thoroughfares." Besides alerting New York's already existing charities to the presence of the dangerous classes, Matsell's expose affected a young Yale seminarian, Charles Loring Brace, just returned from a European tour and immersed in his new vocation of city missionary. Matsell's alarmed observations coalesced with what Brace had learned from his own experiences working with boys in the city mission. Moved to act, Brace in 1853 founded the CAS, a charity which concerned itself with all poor children, but especially with street "orphans." Throughout the 1850s, the CAS carried on the work Matsell had begun, documenting and publicizing the plight of street children. In large measure because of its efforts, the "evil" of the streets became a central element in the reform analysis of poverty and a focus of broad concern in New York.

Matsell, Brace, and the New York philanthropists with whom they associated formed— like their peers in other northeastern cities —closely connected network of secular and moral reformers. Unlike philanthropists in the early nineteenth century, who partook of an older attitude of tolerance to the poor and of the providential inevitability of poverty, mid-Victorians were optimistic that poverty could be abolished by altering the character of their almoners as workers, citizens, and family members. The reformers of the streets were directly concerned with the latter. In their efforts to teach the working poor the virtues of the middle-class home as a means of self-help, they laid the ideological and programmatic groundwork for a sustained intervention in working-class family life.

There were, then, greater numbers of children in the New York streets after 1845, and their activities were publicized as never before. Faced with an unprecedented crisis of poverty in the city, reformers fastened on their presence as a cause rather than a symptom of impoverishment. The reformers' idea that the curse of poor children lay in the childrearing methods of their parents moved toward the center of their analysis of the etiology of poverty, replacing older notions of divine will. In the web of images of blight and disease which not only reflected but also shaped the midcentury understanding of poverty, the tenement house was the "parent of constant disorders, and the nursery of increasing vices," but real parents were the actual agents of crime. In opposition to the ever more articulate and pressing claims of New York's organized working men, this first generation of "experts" on urban poverty

averred that familial relations rather than industrial capitalism were responsible for the misery which any clear-headed New Yorker could see was no transient state of affairs. One of the principal pieces of evidence of "the ungoverned appetites, bad habits, and vices" of laboring-class parents was the fact that they sent their offspring out to the streets to earn their keep.

The importance of domesticity to the reformers' own class identity fostered this shift of attention from individual moral shortcomings to the family structure of a class. For these middle-class city dwellers, the home was not simply a place of residence; it was a focus of social life and a central element of class-consciousness, based on specific conceptions of femininity and childrearing. There, secluded from the stress of public life, women could devote themselves to directing the moral and ethical development of their families. There, protected from the evils of the outside world, the young could live out their childhoods in innocence, freed from the necessity of labor, cultivating their moral and intellectual faculties.

From this vantage point, the laboring classes appeared gravely deficient. When charity visitors, often ladies themselves, entered the households of working people, they saw a domestic sparseness which contradicted their deepest beliefs about what constituted a morally sustaining family life. "[Their] ideas of domestic comfort and standard of morals, are far below our own," wrote the Association for Improving the Condition of the Poor (AICP). The urban poor had intricately interwoven family lives, but they had no *homes*. Middle-class people valued family privacy and intimacy: among the poor, they saw a promiscuous sociability, an "almost fabulous gregariousness." They believed that the moral training of children depended on protecting them within the home; in poor neighborhoods, they saw children encouraged to labor in the streets. The harshness and intolerance with which midcentury reformers viewed the laboring classes can be partly explained by the disparity between these two ways of family life. "Homes—in the better sense—they never know," declared one investigating committee; the children "graduate in every kind of vice known in that curious school which trains them—the public street." The AICP scoffed at even using the word: "Homes . . . if it is not a mockery to give that hallowed name to the dark, filthy hovels where many of them dwell." To these middle-class women and men, the absence of home life was not simply due to the uncongenial physical circumstances of the tenements, nor did it indicate the poor depended upon another way of organizing their family lives. Rather, the homelessness of this "multitude of half-naked, dirty, and leering children" signified an absence of parental love, a neglect of proper childrearing which was entwined in the habits and values of the laboring classes.

MIDDLE-CLASS WOMEN AND THE CHILDREN'S AID SOCIETY

Rather than encouraging girls to break away from their families, the ladies sought the opposite: to create among the urban laboring classes a domestic life of their own. They aimed to mold future wives and mothers of a reformed working class: women who would be imbued with a belief in the importance of domesticity and capable of patterning their homes and family lives on middle-class standards.

It was this strategy of change which would eventually dominate attempts to reform working-class children. The ladies envisioned homes which would reorganize the promiscuously sociable lives of the poor under the aegis of a new, "womanly" working-class woman. In the CAS industrial schools and Lodging-House, girls recruited off the streets learned the arts of plain sewing, cooking, and housecleaning, guided by the precept celebrated by champions of women's domestic mission that "nothing was so honorable as industrious *house-work*." These were skills which both

prepared them for waged employment in seamstressing and domestic service and outfitted them for homes of their own: as the ladies proudly attested after several years of work, their students entered respectable married life as well as honest employment. "Living in homes reformed through their influence," the married women carried on their female mission reformers by proxy.

Similarly, the women reformers instituted meetings to convert the mothers of their students to a new relationship to household and children. Classes taught the importance of sobriety, neat appearance, and sanitary housekeeping: the material basis for virtuous motherhood and a proper home. Most important, the ladies stressed the importance of keeping children off the streets and sending them to school. Here, they found their pupils particularly recalcitrant. Mothers persisted in keeping children home to work and cited economic reasons when their benefactresses upbraided them. The CAS women, however, considered the economic rationale a pretense for the exploitation of children and the neglect of their moral character. "The larger ones were needed to 'mind' the baby," lady volunteers sardonically reported, "or go out begging for clothes . . . and the little ones, scarcely bigger than the baskets on their arms, must be sent out for food, or chips, or cinders." The Mother's Meetings tried, however unsuccessfully, to wean away laboring women from such customary practices to what the ladies believed to be a more nurturant and moral mode of family life: men at work, women at home, children inside.

In contrast to the male reformers [of the CAS], the women of the society tried to create an intensified private life within New York itself, to enclose children within tenements and schools rather than to send them away or incarcerate them in asylums. There is a new, optimistic vision of city life implied in their work. With the establishment of the home across class lines, a renewed city could emerge, its streets free for trade and respectable promenades, and emancipated from the inconveniences of pickpockets and thieves, the affronts of prostitutes and hucksters, the myriad offenses of working-class mores and poverty. The "respectable" would control and dominate public space as they had never before. The city would itself become an asylum on a grand scale, an environment which embodied the eighteenth-century virtues of reason and progress, the nineteenth-century virtues of industry and domesticity. And as would befit a city for the middle class, boundaries between public and private life would be clear: the public space of the metropolis would be the precinct of men, the private space of the home, that of women and children.

GLOSSARY

Magdalene Society: A middle-class reform society which sought to reform prostitutes, provide them with alternative occupations, and thus end prostitution in the early United States.

Charles Dickens (1812–1870): English novelist noteworthy for his portrayal of the lives of the poor.

IMPLICATIONS

Many historians have argued that middle-class men and women of the antebellum era engaged in a wide range of reform movements because they were fearful of the poverty and lack of "morality" that seemed rampant in American society. In order to protect themselves and their position in society, middle-class reformers attempted to impose their own values on working- and lower-class Americans. Why do you think middle-class reformers were so unconcerned about the views of working-class mothers? What do you see as the basic conflict between middle-class women and their working-class counterparts in the antebellum era?

Past Traces

Violence was an integral part of antebellum American life, and governments as well as reformers fought a constant battle to contain the use and spread of violence in America. This reading begins with an account of one form of antebellum violence, the first duel fought in the new state of Illinois in 1819. The Stuart-Bennett duel became a widely cited example of government attempts to attenuate violence, in this case through the successful use of murder changes in state courts.

The Stuart-Bennett Duel (1819)

The origin of the quarrel between the two men was a very trivial matter, growing out of Bennett's horse trespassing on Stuart's cornfield. The horse was a "breachy" animal, and repeatedly broke into Stuart's cornfield, which greatly enraged the latter, and he told Bennett if he didn't keep his horse out of his field he would shoot the horse. This threat was disregarded by Bennett, and the horse continued to break into the field, until one day Stuart carried his threat into execution—that is, he induced his hired man to shoot the horse with a gun loaded with powder and coarse salt, which he did, and the animal ran home bleeding and smarting with pain. Bennett became greatly enraged over the shooting of his horse, though the wound was but slight, and when he learned that Stuart was responsible for the shooting he was disposed to seek revenge. The animal was a great favorite with Bennett and the more he thought of how it had been treated the more his anger grew. While in this frame of mind he met with Jacob Short

and Nathaniel Fike I a pair of young Bacchanalians, who made their haunt, and hibernated, at Tannehill's tavern, which then occupied the southwest corner of the public square on Main street, the site of the present National Hotel.

Short and Fike, thinking to have some sport out of the affair, advised Bennett to seek satisfaction from Stuart by challenging him to mortal combat. They told him that Stuart had grievously injured and insulted him, and that the only proper course for him to pursue was to challenge him to fight a duel. Bennett really assented to this, and the challenge was sent. In the meantime Short and Fike saw Stuart and told him of their plan to have some sport out of Bennett, and they at once arranged for a sham duel. Short and Fike, who were to act as seconds, promised Stuart that the guns should be loaded with powder only. Although Stuart understood that it was to be a sham duel, and was only intended to enliven the monotony of life in the then small village,

Bennett did not so understand it, and with him it was to be no mockery, as the sequel proved.

The arrangements for the duel were made in the court house, where the parties all met. The court house was then located on the southwest corner of Main and Illinois streets, in front of James Tannelill's tavern, with whom the writer was then living and continued to live for eight or nine years thereafter. The young men of the town teased and plagued Bennett a good deal about the proposed duel by telling him that he would take the "Duck ague" and couldn't shoot with accuracy; and Bennett, to show them that he was a sure shot, loaded his rifle and shot the head off a chicken that was in the yard close by.

After the parties had made all arrangements for the duel, and were pretty full of Tannehill's whiskey, they repaired to the duelling ground, which was located about midway between Main street and the present mansion of the late Adam W. Snyder. The ground in that vicinity was all vacant then with only a few scattering trees. The principals were placed about twenty five steps apart, and just as the word "Fire," which was agreed on as the signal was uttered, Bennett fired and Stuart fell, face downward, to the ground shot in the region of the heart. He fell on his gun and immediately expired.

Fike, his second, went to him, and turning him over, took the rifle he had dropped and discharged it in the air, so that it was never known whether it contained a ball or not. There was a suspicion with many that the crack of the gun was that of one containing a ball. Bennett and both seconds were arrested immediately and committed to jail, the latter, however, soon being released on bail. The State had but lately (in 1818) been admitted into the Union, and, it appears from the records, that the State had neither law, nor officials, to try prisoners in St. Clair county. The Legislature being in session at the time, it proceeded at once to enact laws for the emergency, and to appoint officials. A special term of court was called, and a bill of indictment was returned against all three for murder. On the eve of the trial Bennett succeeded in escaping from the jail, a log structure, by boring a series of holes in one of the lop, which he forced from its place and thus made his way out. Such was the sheriffs report when directed to bring the prisoner into court. Bennett fled into the wilds of Arkansas Territory, and was not heard from by the authorities for two and a half years. At the end of that time it was learned that he had been in communication with his wife; that he was at St. Genevieve, Missouri, and that he had arranged for her to meet and join him there, having sent a team and wagon for her and the children. A reward was still standing for his apprehension at that time.

James Tannehill and others followed the team and family, and on arriving at the Mississippi river met Bennett, and arresting him brought him back to Belleville. He was again indicted, tried and convicted, and sentenced to death by hanging. The execution took place on September 3, 1821, in a vacant field on which a part of West Belleville is now located. The execution was public, and was witnessed by one of the largest assemblages ever brought together in this county.

Poor Bennett! he lost his life for the love he had for his family. He stated on the scaffold that he was willing to risk his life for the pleasure of once more greeting his wife and children. He also denied that he had put the bullet in the gun that killed Stuart.

16

"Gouge and Bite, Pull Hair and Scratch": The Social Significance of Fighting in the Southern Backcountry

Elliott J. Gorn

Violence was an integral part of everyday life in antebellum America. In the nation's cities, members of competing fire companies routinely fought one another for the right to put out fires, local sporting matches often turned into general brawls, and bearbaiting and cockfighting continued to be favorite popular pastimes. On the western frontier, white encroachment and Indian resistance regularly led to the shedding of blood, and in every community court dockets recorded an alarming number of assaults, batteries, and other forms of criminal violence. As antebellum reformers never tired of pointing out, unrestrained violence seemed to be an essential component of the American character.

But while violence was endemic to antebellum society, nowhere did it play such a crucial social role as in the American South. Since the colonial era, southern men were notorious for the frequency and ferocity with which they fought one another, often for seemingly insignificant reasons. To call someone a "Scotsman" or a "rogue" was enough to provoke a fray that might cost a combatant his eye, his ear, or even his life. In this essay, Elliott J. Gorn surveys the ubiquitous violence of the American South and attempts to explain this peculiar regional trait by pointing to three interrelated characteristics. According to Gorn, the undeveloped state of the market economy emphasized fierce loyalties to kin and locality while the hard life of the backcountry promoted drinking, joking, and fighting as forms of personal release. Status and reputation in this rough-and-tumble world accrued to those who took personal risks lightly and were willing to inflict pain and permanent injury without flinching. In the southern backcountry, Gorn suggests, violence was truly the measure of a man.

....

"I would advise you when You do fight Not to act like Tygers and Bears as these Virginians do—Biting one anothers Lips and Noses off, and *gowging* one another—that is, thrusting out one anothers Eyes, and kicking one another on the Cods, to the Great damage of many a Poor Woman." Thus, Charles Woodmason, an itinerant Anglican minister born of English gentry stock, described the brutal form of combat he found in the Virginia backcountry shortly before the American Revolution. Although historians are more likely to study people thinking, governing, worshiping, or working, how men fight—who participates, who observes, which rules are followed, what is at stake, what tactics are allowed—reveals much about past cultures and societies.

The evolution of southern backwoods brawling from the late eighteenth century through the antebellum era can be reconstructed from oral traditions and travelers' accounts. As in most cultural history, broad patterns and uneven trends rather than specific dates mark the way. The sources are often problematic and must be used with care; some speculation is required. But the lives of common people cannot be ignored merely because they leave few records. "To feel for a feller's eyestrings and make him tell the news" was not just mayhem but an act freighted with significance for both social and cultural history.

As early as 1735, boxing was "much in fashion" in parts of Chesapeake Bay, and forty years later a visitor from the North declared that, along with dancing, fiddling, small swords, and card playing, it was an essential skill for all young Virginia gentlemen. The term "boxing," however, did not necessarily refer to the comparatively tame style of bare-knuckle fighting familiar to eighteenth-century Englishmen. In 1746, four deaths prompted the governor of North Carolina to ask for legislation against "the barbarous and inhuman manner of boxing which so much prevails among the lower sort of people." The colonial assembly responded by making it a felony "to cut out the Tongue or pull out the eyes of the King's Liege People." Five years later the assembly added slitting, biting, and cutting off noses to the list of offenses. Virginia passed similar legislation in 1748 and revised these statutes in 1772 explicitly to discourage men from "gouging, plucking, or putting out an eye, biting or kicking or stomping upon" quiet peaceable citizens. By 1786 South Carolina had made premeditated mayhem a capital offense, defining the crime as severing another's bodily parts.

Laws notwithstanding, the carnage continued. Philip Vickers Fithian, a New Jerseyite serving as tutor for an aristocratic Virginia family, confided to his journal on September 3, 1774:

> By appointment is to be fought this Day near Mr. *Lanes* two fist Battles between four young Fellows. The Cause of the battles I have not yet known; I suppose either that they are lovers, and one has in Jest or reality some way supplanted the other; or has in a merry hour called him a *Lubber* or a *thick-Skull*, or a *Buckskin*, or a *Scotsman*, or perhaps one has mislaid the other's hat, or knocked a peach out of his Hand, or offered him a dram without wiping the mouth of the Bottle; all these, and ten thousand more quite as trifling and ridiculous are thought and accepted as just Causes of immediate Quarrels, in which every diabolical Strategem for Mastery is allowed and practiced.

The "trifling and ridiculous" reasons for these fights had an unreal quality for the matter-of-fact Yankee. Not assaults on persons or property but slights, insults, and thoughtless gestures set young southerners against each other. To call a man a "buckskin," for example, was to accuse him of the poverty associated with leather clothing, while the epithet "Scotsman" tied him to the low-caste Scots-Irish who settled the southern highlands. Fithian could not understand how such trivial offenses caused the bloody battles. But his incomprehension turned to rage when he realized that spectators attended these "odious and filthy amusements" and that the fighters allayed their spontaneous passions in order to fix convenient dates and places, which allowed time for rumors to spread and crowds to gather. The Yankee concluded that only devils, prostitutes, or monkeys could sire creatures so unfit for human society.

Descriptions of these "fist battles," as Fithian called them, indicate that they generally began like English prize fights. Two men, surrounded by onlookers, parried blows until one was knocked or thrown down. But there the similarity ceased. Where as "Broughton's Rules" of the English ring specified that a round ended when either antagonist fell, southern bruisers only began fighting at this point. Enclosed not inside a formal ring—the "magic circle" defining a special place with its own norms of conduct—but within whatever space the spectators left vacant, fighters battled each other until one called enough or was unable to continue. Combatants boasted, howled, and cursed. As words gave way to action, they tripped and threw, gouged and butted, scratched and choked each other. "But what is worse than all," Isaac Weld observed, "these wretches in their combat endeavor to their utmost to tear out each other's testicles."

Around the beginning of the nineteenth century, men sought original labels for their brutal style of fighting. "Rough-and-tumble" or simply "gouging" gradually replaced "boxing" as the name for these contests. Before two bruisers attacked each other, spectators might demand whether they proposed to fight fair—according to Broughton's Rules—or rough-and-tumble. Honor dictated that all techniques be permitted. Except for a ban on

weapons, most men chose to fight "no holts barred," doing what they wished to each other without interference, until one gave up or was incapacitated.

The emphasis on maximum disfigurement, on severing bodily parts, made this fighting style unique. Amid the general mayhem, however, gouging out an opponent's eye became the sine qua non of rough-and-tumble fighting, much like the knockout punch in modern boxing. The best gougers, of course, were adept at other fighting skills. Some allegedly filed their teeth to bite off an enemy's appendages more efficiently. Still, liberating an eyeball quickly became a fighter's surest route to victory and his most prestigious accomplishment. To this end, celebrated heroes fired their fingernails hard, honed them sharp, and oiled them slick. "You have come off badly this time, I doubt?" declared an alarmed passerby on seeing the piteous condition of a renowned fighter. " 'Have I,' says he triumphantly, shewing from his pocket at the same time an eye, which he had extracted during the combat, and preserved for a trophy."

As the new style of fighting evolved, its geographical distribution changed. Leadership quickly passed from the southern seaboard to upcountry counties and the western frontier. Although examples could be found throughout the South, rough-and-tumbling was best suited to the backwoods, where hunting, herding, and semisubsistence agriculture predominated over market-oriented, staple crop production. Thus, the settlers of western Carolina, Kentucky, and Tennessee, as well as upland Mississippi, Alabama, and Georgia, became especially known for their pugnacity.

The social base of rough-and-tumbling also shifted with the passage of time. Although brawling was always considered a vice of the "lower sort," eighteenth-century Tidewater gentlemen sometimes found themselves in brutal fights. These combats grew out of challenges to men's honor—to their status in patriarchal, kin-based, small-scale communities—and were woven into the very fabric of daily life. Rhys Isaac has observed that the Virginia gentry set the tone for a fiercely competitive style of living. Although they valued hierarchy, individual status was never permanently fixed, so men frantically sought to assert their prowess—by grand boasts over tavern gaming tables laden with money, by whipping and tripping each other's horses in violent quarter-races, by wagering one-half year's earnings on the flash of a fighting cock's gaff. Great planters and small shared an ethos that extolled courage bordering on foolhardiness and cherished magnificent, if irrational, displays of largess.

Piety, hard work, and steady habits had their adherents, but in this society aggressive self-assertion and manly pride were the real marks of status. Even the gentry's vaunted hospitality demonstrated a family's community standing, so conviviality itself became a vehicle for rivalry and emulation. Rich and poor might revel together during "public times," but gentry patronage of sports and festivities kept the focus of power clear. Above all, brutal recreations toughened men for a violent social life in which the exploitation of labor, the specter of poverty, and a fierce struggle for status were daily realities.

During the final decades of the eighteenth century, however, individuals like Fithian's young gentlemen became less inclined to engage in rough-and-tumbling. Many in the planter class now wanted to distinguish themselves from social inferiors more by genteel manners, gracious living, and paternal prestige than by patriarchal prowess. They sought alternatives to brawling and found them by imitating the English aristocracy. A few gentlemen took boxing lessons from professors of pugilism or attended sparring exhibitions given by touring exponents of the manly art. More important, dueling gradually replaced hand-to-hand combat. The code of honor offered a genteel, though deadly, way to settle personal disputes while demonstrating one's elevated status. Ceremony distinguished antiseptic duels from lower-class brawls. Cool restraint and customary decorum proved a man's ability to shed blood while remaining emotionally detached, to act as mercilessly as the poor whites but to do so with chilling gentility.

Slowly, then, rough-and-tumble fighting found specific locus in both human and geographical landscapes. We can watch men grapple with the transition. When an attempt at a formal duel aborted, Savannah politician Robert Watkins and United States Senator James Jackson resorted to gouging. Jackson bit Watson's finger to save his eye. Similarly, when "a low fellow who pretends to gentility" insulted a distinguished doctor, the gentleman responded with a proper challenge. "He had scarcely uttered these words, before the other flew at him, and in an instant turned his eye out of the socket, and while it hung upon his cheek, the fellow was barbarous enough to endeavor to pluck it entirely out." By the new century, such ambiguity had lessened, as rough-and-tumble fighting was relegated to individuals in backwoods settlements. For the next several decades, eye-gouging matches were focal events in the culture of lower-class males who still relished the wild ways of old.

"The indolence and dissipation of the middling and lower classes of Virginia are such as to give pain to every reflecting mind," one anonymous visitor declared. "Horse-racing, cock-fighting, and boxing-matches are standing amusements, for which they neglect all business; and in the latter of which they conduct themselves with a barbarity worthy of their savage neighbors." Thomas Anburey agreed. He believed that the Revolution's leveling of class distinctions left the "lower people" dangerously independent. Although Anburey found poor whites usually hospitable and generous, he was disturbed by their sudden outbursts of impudence, their aversion to labor and love of drink, their vengefulness and savagery. They shared with their betters a taste for gaming, horse racing, and cockfighting, but "boxing matches, in which they display such barbarity, as fully marks their innate ferocious disposition," were all their own. Anburey concluded that an English prize fight was humanity itself compared to Virginia combat.

Another visitor, Charles William Janson, decried the loss of social subordination, which caused the rabble to reinterpret liberty and equality as licentiousness. Paternal authority—the font of social and political order—had broken down in America, as parents gratified their children's whims, including youthful tastes for alcohol and tobacco. A national mistrust of authority had brought civilization to its nadir among the poor whites of the South. "The lower classes are the most abject that, perhaps, ever peopled a Christian land. They live in the woods and deserts and many of them cultivate no more land than will raise them corn and cabbages, which, with fish, and occasionally a piece of pickled pork or bacon, are their constant food. . . . Their habitations are more wretched than can be conceived; the huts of the poor of Ireland, or even the meanest Indian wig-wam, displaying more ingenuity and greater industry." Despite their degradation—perhaps because of it—Janson found the poor whites extremely jealous of their republican rights and liberties. They considered themselves the equals of their best-educated neighbors and intruded on whomever they chose. The gouging match this fastidious Englishman witnessed in Georgia was the epitome of lower-class depravity:

We found the combatants . . . fast clinched by the hair, and their thumbs endeavoring to force a passage into each other's eyes; while several of the bystanders were betting upon the first eye to be turned out of its socket. For some time the combatants avoided the *thumb stroke* with dexterity. At length they fell to the ground, and in an instant the uppermost sprung up with his antagonist's eye in his hand!!! The savage crowd applauded, while, sick with horror, we galloped away from the infernal scene. The name of the sufferrer was John Butler, a Carolinian, who, it seems, had been dared to the combat by a Georgian; and the first eye was for the honor of the state to which they respectively belonged.

Janson concluded that even Indian "savages" and London's rabble would be outraged by the beastly Americans.

While Janson toured the lower South, his countryman Thomas Ashe explored the territory around Wheeling, Virginia. A passage, dated April 1806, from his *Travels in America* gives us a detailed picture of gouging's social context. Ashe expounded on Wheeling's potential to become a center of trade for the Ohio and upper Mississippi valleys, noting that geography made the town a natural rival of Pittsburgh. Yet Wheeling lagged in "worthy commercial pursuits, and industrious and moral dealings." Ashe attributed this backwardness to the town's frontier ways, which attracted men who specialized in drinking, plundering Indian property, racing horses, and watching cockfights. A Wheeling Quaker assured Ashe that mores were changing, that the underworld element was about to be driven out. Soon, the godly would gain control of the local government, enforce strict observance of the Sabbath, and outlaw vice. Ashe was sympathetic but doubtful. In Wheeling, only heightened violence and debauchery distinguished Sunday from the rest of the week. The citizens' willingness to close up shop and neglect business on the slightest pretext made it a questionable residence for any respectable group of men, let alone a society of Quakers.

To convey the rough texture of Wheeling life, Ashe described a gouging match. Two men drinking at a public house argued over the merits of their respective horses. Wagers made, they galloped off to the race course. "Two thirds of the population followed:—blacksmiths, shipwrights, all left work: the town appeared a desert. The stores were shut. I asked a proprietor, why the warehouses did not remain open? He told me all good was done for the day: that the people would remain on the ground till night, and many stay till the following morning." Determined to witness an event deemed so important that the entire town went on holiday, Ashe headed for the track. He missed the initial heat but arrived in time to watch the crowd raise the stakes to induce a rematch. Six horses competed, and spectators bet a small fortune, but the results were inconclusive. Umpires' opinions were given and rejected. Heated words, then fists flew. Soon, the melee narrowed to two individuals, a Virginian and a Kentuckian. Because fights were common in such situations, everyone knew the proper procedures, and the combatants quickly decided to "tear and rend" one another—to rough-and-tumble—rather than "fight fair." Ashe elaborated: "You startle at the words tear and rend, and again do not understand me. You have heard these terms, I allow, applied to beasts of prey and to carnivorous animals; and your humanity cannot conceive them applicable to man: It nevertheless is so, and the fact will not permit me the use of any less expressive term."

The battle began—size and power on the Kentuckian's side, science and craft on the Virginian's. They exchanged cautious throws and blows, when suddenly the Virginian lunged at his opponent with a panther's ferocity. The crowd roared its approval as the fight reached its violent denouement:

The shock received by the Kentuckyan, and the want of breath, brought him instantly to the ground. The Virginian never lost his hold; like those bats of the South who never quit the subject on which they fasten till they taste blood, he kept his knees in his enemy's body; fixing his claws in his hair, and his thumbs on his eyes, gave them an instantaneous start from their sockets. The sufferer roared aloud, but uttered no complaint. The citizens again shouted with joy. Doubts were no longer entertained and bets of three to one were offered on the Virginian.

But the fight continued. The Kentuckian grabbed his smaller opponent and held him in a tight bear hug, forcing the Virginian to relinquish his facial grip. Over and over the two rolled, until, getting the Virginian under him, the big man "snapt off his nose so close to his face that no manner of projection remained." The Virginian quickly recovered, seized the Kentuckian's lower lip in his teeth, and ripped it down over his enemy's chin. This was enough: "The Kentuckyan at length *gave out*, on which the people carried off the victor, and he preferring triumph to a doctor, who came to cicatrize his face, suffered himself to be chaired round the ground as the champion of the times, and the first *rougher-and-tumbler*. The poor wretch, whose eyes were started from their spheres, and whose lip refused its office, returned to the town to hide his impotence, and get his countenance repaired." The citizens refreshed themselves with whiskey and biscuits, and then resumed their races.

Ashe's Quaker friend reported that such spontaneous races occurred two or three times a week and that the annual fall and spring meets lasted fourteen uninterrupted days, "aided by the licentious and profligate of all the neighboring states." As for rough-and-tumbles, the Quaker saw no hope of suppressing them. Few nights passed without such fights; few mornings failed to reveal a new citizen with mutilated features. It was a regional taste, unrestrained by law or authority, an inevitable part of life on the left bank of the Ohio.

What can we conclude about the culture and society that nourished rough-and-tumble fighting? The best place to begin is with the material base of life and the nature of daily work. Gamblers, hunters, herders, roustabouts, rivermen, and yeomen farmers were the sorts of persons usually associated with gouging. Such hallmarks of modernity as large-scale production, complex division of labor, and regular work rhythms were alien to their lives. Recent studies have stressed the premodern character of the southern uplands through most of the antebellum period. Even while cotton production boomed and trade expanded, a relatively small number of planters owned the best lands and most slaves, so huge parts of the South remained outside the flow of international markets or staple crop agriculture. Thus, backcountry whites commonly found themselves locked into a semisubsistent pattern of living. Growing crops for home consumption, supplementing food supplies with abundant game, allowing small herds to fatten in the woods, spending scarce money for essential staples, and bartering goods for the services of part-time or itinerant trades people, the upland folk lived in an intensely local, kin-based society. Rural hamlets, impassable roads, and provincial isolation—not growing towns, internal improvements, or international commerce—characterized the backcountry.

Even men whose livelihoods depended on expanding markets often continued their rough, premodern ways. Characteristic of life on a Mississippi barge, for example, were long periods of idleness shattered by intense anxiety, as deadly snags, shoals, and storms approached. Running aground on a sandbar meant back-breaking labor to maneuver a thirty-ton vessel out of trouble. Boredom weighed as heavily as danger, so tale telling, singing, drinking, and gambling filled the empty hours. Once goods were taken on in New Orleans, the men began the thousand-mile return journey against the current. Before steam power replaced muscle, bad food and whiskey fueled the gangs who day after day, exposed to wind and water, poled the river bottoms or strained at the cordelling ropes until their vessel reached the tributaries of the Missouri or the Ohio. Hunters, trappers, herdsmen, subsistence farmers, and other backwoodsmen faced different but equally taxing hardships, and those who endured prided themselves on their strength and daring, their stamina, cunning, and ferocity.

Such men played as lustily as they worked, counterpointing bouts of intense labor with strenuous leisure. What travelers mistook for laziness was a refusal to work and save with compulsive regularity. "I have seen nothing in human form so profligate as they are," James Flint wrote of the boatmen he met around 1820. "Accomplished in depravity, their habits and education seem to comprehend every vice. They make few pretensions to moral character; and their swearing is excessive and perfectly disgusting. Although earning good wages, they are in the most abject poverty; many of them being without anything like clean or comfortable clothing." A generation later, Mark Twain vividly remembered those who manned the great timber and coal rafts gliding past his boyhood home in Hannibal, Missouri: "Rude, uneducated, brave, suffering terrific hardships with sailorlike stoicism; heavy drinkers, course frolickers in moral sties like the Natchez-under-the-hill of that day, heavy fighters, reckless fellows, every one, elephantinely jolly, foul witted, profane; prodigal of their money, bankrupt at the end of the trip, fond of barbaric finery, prodigious braggarts; yet, in the main, honest, trustworthy, faithful to promises and duty, and often picaresquely magnanimous." Details might change, but penury, loose morality, and lack of steady habits endured.

Boatmen, hunters, and herdsmen were often separated from wives and children for long periods. More important, backcountry couples lacked the emotionally intense experience of the bourgeois family. They spent much of their time apart and found companionship with members of their own sex. The frontier town or crossroads tavern brought males together in surrogate brotherhoods, where rough men paid little deference to the civilizing role of women and the moral uplift of the domestic family. On the margins of a booming, modernizing society, they shared an intensely communal yet fiercely competitive way of life. Thus, where work was least rationalized and specialized, domesticity weakest, legal institutions primitive, and the market economy feeble, rough-and-tumble fighting found fertile soil.

Just as the economy of the southern backcountry remained locally oriented, the rough-and-tumblers were local heroes, renowned in their communities. There was no professionalization here. Men fought for informal village and county titles; the red feather in the champion's cap was pay enough because it marked him as first among his peers. Paralleling the primitive division of labor in backwoods society, boundaries between entertainment and daily life, between spectators and participants, were not sharply drawn. "Bully of the Hill" Ab Gaines from the Big Hatchie Country, Neil Brown of Totty's Bend, Vernon's William Holt, and Smithfield's Jim Willis—all of them were renowned Tennessee fighters, local heroes in their day. Legendary champions were real individuals, tested gang leaders who attained their status by being the meanest, toughest, and most ruthless fighters, who faced disfigurement and never backed down. Challenges were ever present; yesterday's spectator was today's champion, today's champion tomorrow's invalid.

Given the lives these men led, a world view that embraced fearlessness made sense. Hunters, trappers, Indian fighters, and herdsmen who knew the smell of warm blood on their hands refused to sentimentalize an environment filled with threatening forces. It was not that backwoodsmen lived in constant danger but that violence was unpredictable. Recreations like cockfighting deadened men to cruelty, and the gratuitous savagery of gouging matches reinforced the daily truth that life was brutal, guided only by the logic of superior nerve, power, and cunning. With families emotionally or physically distant and civil institutions weak, a man's role in the all-male society was defined less by his ability as a breadwinner than by his ferocity. The touchstone of masculinity was unflinching toughness, not chivalry, duty, or piety. Violent sports, heavy drinking, and impulsive pleasure seeking were appropriate for men whose lives were hard, whose futures were unpredictable, and whose opportunities were limited. Gouging champions were group leaders because they embodied the basic values of their peers. The successful rough-and-tumbler proved his manhood by asserting his dominance and rendering his opponent "impotent," as Thomas Ashe put it. And the loser, though literally or symbolically castrated, demonstrated his mettle and maintained his honor.

Here we begin to understand the travelers' refrain about plain folk degradation. Setting out from northern ports, whose inhabitants were increasingly possessed by visions of godly perfection and material progress, they found southern upcountry people slothful and backward. Ashe's Quaker friend in Wheeling, Virginia, made the point. For Quakers and northern evangelicals, labor was a means of moral self-testing, and earthly success was a sign of God's grace, so hard work and steady habits became acts of piety. But not only Yankees endorsed sober restraint. A growing number of southern evangelicals also embraced a life of decorous self-control, rejecting the hedonistic and self-assertive values of old. During the late eighteenth century, as Rhys Isaac has observed, many plain folk disavowed the hegemonic gentry culture of conspicuous display and found individual worth, group pride, and transcendent meaning in religious revivals. By the antebellum era, new evangelical waves washed over class lines as rich and poor alike forswore such sins as drinking, gambling, cursing, fornication, horse racing, and dancing. But conversion was far from universal, and, for many in backcountry settlements like Wheeling, the evangelical idiom remained a foreign tongue. Men worked hard to feed themselves and their kin, to acquire goods and status, but they lacked the calling to prove their godliness through rigid morality. Salvation and self-denial were culturally less compelling values, and the barriers against leisure and self-gratification were lower here than among the converted.

Moreover, primitive markets and the semi-subsistence basis of upcountry life limited men's dependence on goods produced by others and allowed them to maintain the irregular work rhythms of a precapitalist economy. The material base of backwoods life was ill suited to social transformation, and the cultural traditions of the past offered alternatives to rigid new ideals. Closing up shop in midweek for a fight or horse race had always been perfectly acceptable, because men labored so that they might indulge the joys of the flesh. Neither a compulsive need to save time and money nor an obsession with progress haunted people's imaginations. The backcountry folk who lacked a bourgeois or Protestant sense of duty were little disturbed by exhibitions of human passions and were resigned to violence as part of daily life. Thus, the relative dearth of capitalistic values (such as delayed gratification and accumulation), the absence of a strict work ethic, and a cultural tradition that winked at lapses in moral rigor limited society's demands for sober self-control.

Not just unconverted poor whites but also large numbers of the slave-holding gentry still lent their prestige to a regional style that favored conspicuous displays of leisure. As C. Vann Woodward has pointed out, early observers, such as Robert Beverley and William Byrd, as well as modern-day commentators, have described a distinctly "southern ethic" in American history. Whether judged positively as leisure or negatively as laziness, the southern sensibility valued free time and rejected work as the consuming goal of life. Slavery reinforced this tendency, for how could labor be an unmitigated virtue if so much of it was performed by despised black bondsmen? When southerners did esteem commerce and enterprise, it was less because piling up wealth contained religious or moral value than because productivity facilitated the leisure ethos. Southerners could therefore work hard without placing labor at the center of their ethical universe. In important ways, then, the upland folk culture reflected a larger regional style.

Thus, the values, ideas, and institutions that rapidly transformed the North into a modern capitalist society came late to the South. Indeed, conspicuous display, heavy drinking, moral casualness, and love of games and sports had deep roots in much of Western culture. As Woodward has cautioned, we must take care not to interpret the southern ethic as unique or aberrant. The compulsions to subordinate leisure to productivity, to divide work and play into separate compartmentalized realms, and to improve each bright and shining hour were the novel ideas. The southern ethic anticipated

human evil, tolerated ethical lapses, and accepted the finitude of man in contrast to the new style that demanded unprecedented moral rectitude and internalized self-restraint.

The American South also shared with large parts of the Old World a taste for violence and personal vengeance. Long after the settling of the southern colonies, powerful patriarchal clans in Celtic and Mediterranean lands still avenged affronts to family honor with deadly feuds. Norbert Elias has pointed out that postmedieval Europeans routinely spilled blood to settle their private quarrels. Across classes, the story was the same:

> Two associates fall out over business; they quarrel, the conflict grows violent; one day they meet in a public place and one of them strikes the other dead. An innkeeper accuses another of stealing his clients; they become mortal enemies. Someone says a few malicious words about another; a family war develops. . . . Not only among the nobility were there family vengeance, private feuds, vendettas. . . . The little people too—the hatters, the tailors, the shepherds—were all quick to draw their knives.

Emotions were freely expressed: jollity and laughter suddenly gave way to belligerence; guilt and penitence coexisted with hate; cruelty always lurked nearby. The modern middle-class individual, with his subdued, rational, calculating ways, finds it hard to understand the joy sixteenth-century Frenchmen took in ceremonially burning alive one or two dozen cats every Midsummer Day or the pleasure eighteenth-century Englishmen found in watching trained dogs slaughter each other.

Despite enormous cultural differences, inhabitants of the southern uplands exhibited characteristics of their forebears in the Old World. The Scots-Irish brought their reputation for ferocity to the backcountry, but English migrants, too, had a thirst for violence. Central authority was weak, and men reserved the right to settle differences for themselves. Vengeance was part of daily life. Drunken hilarity, good fellowship, and high spirits, especially at crossroads taverns, suddenly turned to violence. Traveler after traveler remarked on how forthright and friendly but quick to anger the backcountry people were. Like their European ancestors, they had not yet internalized the modern world's demand for tight emotional self-control.

Above all, the ancient concept of honor helps explain this shared proclivity for violence. According to the sociologist Peter Berger, modern men have difficulty taking seriously the idea of honor. American jurisprudence, for example, offers legal recourse for slander and libel because they involve material damages. But insult—publicly smearing a man's good name and besmirching his honor—implies no palpable injury and so does not exist in the eyes of the law. Honor is an intensely social concept, resting on reputation, community standing, and the esteem of kin and compatriots. To possess honor requires acknowledgment from others; it cannot exist in solitary conscience. Modern man, Berger has argued, is more responsive to dignity—the belief that personal worth inheres equally in each individual, regardless of his status in society. Dignity frees the evangelical to confront God alone, the capitalist to make contracts without customary encumbrances, and the reformer to uplift the lowly. Naked and alone man has dignity; extolled by peers and covered with ribbons, he has honor.

Anthropologists have also discovered the centrality of honor in several cultures. According to J. G. Peristiany, honor and shame often preoccupy individuals in small-scale settings, where face-to-face relationships predominate over anonymous or bureaucratic ones. Social standing in such communities is never completely secure, because it must be validated by public opinion, whose fickleness compels men constantly to assert and prove their worth. Julian Pitt-Rivers has added that, if society rejects a man's evaluation of himself and treats his claim to honor with ridicule or contempt, his very identity suffers because it is based on the judgment of peers. Shaming refers to that process by which an insult or any public humiliation impugns an individual's honor and thereby threatens his sense of self. By risking injury in a violent encounter, an affronted man—whether victorious or not—restores his sense of status and thus validates anew his claim to honor. Only valorous action, not words, can redeem his place in the ranks of his peer group.

Bertram Wyatt-Brown has argued that this Old World ideal is the key to understanding southern history. Across boundaries of time, geography, and social class, the South was knit together by a primal concept of male valor, part of the ancient heritage of Indo-European folk cultures. Honor demanded clan loyalty, hospitality, protection of women, and defense of patriarchal prerogatives. Honorable men guarded their reputations, bristled at insults, and, where necessary, sought personal vindication through bloodshed. The culture of honor thrived in hierarchical rural communities like the American South and grew out of a fatalistic world view, which assumed that pain and suffering were man's fate. It accounts for the pervasive violence that marked relationships between southerners and explains their insistence on vengeance and their rejection of legal redress in settling quarrels. Honor tied personal identity to public fulfillment of social roles. Neither bourgeois self-control nor internalized conscience determined status; judgment by one's fellows was the wellspring of community standing.

In this light, the seemingly trivial causes for brawls enumerated as early as Fithian's time—name calling, subtle ridicule, breaches of decorum, displays of poor manners—make sense. If a man's good name was his most important possession, then any slight cut him deeply. "Having words" precipitated fights because words brought shame and undermined a man's sense of self. Symbolic acts, such as buying a round of drinks, conferred honor on all, while refusing to share a bottle implied some inequality in social status. Honor inhered not only in individuals but also in kin and peers; when members of two cliques had words, their tested leaders or several men from each side fought to uphold group prestige. Inheritors of primal honor, the southern plain folk were quick to take offense, and any perceived affront forced a man either to devalue himself or strike back violently and avenge the wrong.

The concept of male honor takes us a long way toward understanding the meaning of eye-gouging matches. But backwoods people did not simply acquire some primordial notion without modifying it. Definitions of honorable behavior have always varied enormously across cultures. The southern upcountry fostered a particular style of honor, which grew out of the contradiction between equality and hierarchy. Honorific societies tend to be sharply stratified. Honor is apportioned according to rank, and men fight to maintain personal standing within their social categories. Because black chattel slavery was the basis for the southern hierarchy, slave owners had the most wealth and honor, while other whites scrambled for a bit of each, and bondsmen were permanently impoverished and dishonored. Here was a source of tension for the plain folk. Men of honor shared freedom and equality; those denied honor were implicitly less than equal—perilously close to a slave-like condition. But in the eyes of the gentry, poor whites as well as blacks were outside the circle of honor, so both groups were subordinate. Thus a herdsman's insult failed to shame a planter since the two men were not on the same social level. Without a threat to the gentleman's honor, there was no need for a duel; horsewhipping the insolent fellow sufficed.

Southern plain folk, then, were caught in a social contradiction. Society taught all white men to consider themselves equals, encouraged them to compete for power and status, yet threatened them from below with the specter of servitude and from above with insistence on obedience to rank and authority. Cut off from upper-class tests of honor, backcountry people adopted their own. A rough-and-tumble was more than a poor man's duel, a botched version of genteel combat. Plain folk chose not to ape the dispassionate, antiseptic, gentry style but to invert it. While the gentleman's code of honor insisted on cool restraint, eye gougers gloried in unvarnished brutality. In contrast to duelists' aloof silence, backwoods fighters screamed defiance to the world. As their own unique rites of honor, rough-and-tumble matches allowed backcountry men to shout their equality at each other. And eye-gouging fights also dispelled any stigma of servility. Ritual boasts, soaring oaths, outrageous ferocity, unflinching bloodiness—all proved a man's freedom. Where the slave acted obsequiously, the backwoodsman resisted the slightest affront; where human chattels accepted blows and never raised a hand, plain folk celebrated violence; where blacks could not jeopardize their value as property, poor whites proved their autonomy by risking bodily parts. Symbolically reaffirming their claims to honor, gouging matches helped resolve painful uncertainties arising out of the ambiguous place of plain folk in the southern social structure.

Backwoods fighting reminds us of man's capacity for cruelty and is an excellent corrective to romanticizing premodern life. But a close look also keeps us from drawing facile conclusions about innate human aggressiveness. Eye gouging represented neither the "real" human animal emerging on the frontier, nor nature acting through man in a Darwinian struggle for survival, nor anarchic disorder and communal breakdown. Rather, rough-and-tumble fighting was ritualized behavior—a product of specific cultural assumptions. Men drink together, tongues loosen, a simmering of old rivalry begins to boil; insult is given, offense taken, ritual boasts commence; the fight begins, mettle is tested, blood redeems honor, and equilibrium is restored. Eye gouging was the poor and middling whites' own version of a historical southern tendency to consider personal violence socially useful—indeed, ethically essential.

Rough-and-tumble fighting emerged from the confluence of economic conditions, social relationships, and culture in the southern back-country. Primitive markets and the semisubsistence basis of life threw men back on close ties to kin and community. Violence and poverty were part of daily existence, so endurance, even callousness, became functional values. Loyal to their localities, their occupations, and each other, men came together and found release from life's hardships in strong drink, tall talk, rude practical jokes, and cruel sports. They craved one another's recognition but rejected genteel, pious, or bourgeois values, awarding esteem on the basis of their own traditional standards. The glue that held men together was an intensely competitive status system in which the most prodigious drinker or strongest arm wrestler, the best tale teller, fiddle player, or log roller, the most daring gambler, original liar, skilled hunter, outrageous swearer, or accurate marksman was accorded respect by the others. Reputation was everything, and scars were badges of honor. Rough-and-tumble fighting demonstrated unflinching willingness to inflict pain while risking mutilation—all to defend one's standing among peers—and became a central expression of the all-male subculture.

Eye gouging continued long after the antebellum period. As the market economy absorbed new parts of the backcountry, however, the way of life that supported rough-and-tumbling waned. Certainly by mid-century the number of incidents declined, precisely when expanding international demand brought ever more upcountry acres into staple production. Towns, schools, churches, revivals, and families gradually overtook the backwoods. In a slow and uneven process, keelboats gave way to steamers, then railroads; squatters, to cash crop farmers; hunters and trappers, to preachers. The plain folk code of honor was far from dead, but emergent social institutions engendered a moral ethos that warred against the old

ways. For many individuals, the justifications for personal violence grew stricter, and mayhem became unacceptable.

Ironically, progress also had a darker side. New technologies and modes of production could enhance men's fighting abilities. "Birmingham and Pittsburgh are obliged to complete . . . the equipment of the 'chivalric Kentuckian,'" Charles Agustus Murray observed in the 1840s, as bowie knives ended more and more rough-and-tumbles. Equally important, in 1835 the first modern revolver appeared, and manufacturers marketed cheap, accurate editions in the coming decade. Dueling weapons had been costly, and Kentucky rifles or horse pistols took a full minute to load and prime. The revolver, however, which fitted neatly into a man's pocket, settled more and more personal disputes. Raw and brutal as rough-and-tumbling was, it could not survive the use of arms. Yet precisely because eye gouging was so violent —because combatants cherished maimings, blindings, even castrations—it unleashed death wishes that invited new technologies of destruction.

With improved weaponry, dueling entered its golden age during the antebellum era. Armed combat remained both an expression of gentry sensibility and a mark of social rank. But in a society where status was always shifting and unclear, dueling did not stay confined to the upper class. The habitual carrying of weapons once considered a sign of unmanly fear, now lost some of its stigma. As the backcountry changed, tests of honor continued, but gunplay rather than fighting tooth-and-nail appealed to new men with social aspirations. Thus, progress and technology slowly circumscribed rough-and-tumble fighting, only to substitute a deadlier option. Violence grew neater and more lethal as men checked their savagery to murder each other.

GLOSSARY

Scots-Irish: The people of Scotland who settled in northern Ireland and their descendents, especially those who migrated to America.

Cordelling ropes: Ropes attached to a canal barge allowing the barge to be towed through a canal.

Celtic: Reference to ancient inhabitants of Ireland.

Darwinian: A theory of biological evolution developed by Charles Darwin and others, stating that all species of organisms arise and develop through the natural selection of small, inherited variations that increase the individual's ability to compete, survive, and reproduce.

IMPLICATIONS

Historians have advanced many factors—from frontier expansion to excessive alcohol consumption—to explain the ubiquitous violence that marred antebellum society. From your reading of Gorn's essay, what do you think accounts for the excessive and obsessive violence exhibited on the southern frontier? Do you think this was a particularly southern problem? Or was such violence endemic in all of American society?

Past Traces

The discovery of gold in 1848 brought thousands of men and women to California, each hoping to find fortune and adventure in the Sierra gold fields. One of the largest groups to participate in this national human drama were ordinary, middle-class men who saw in the gold rush a final opportunity to escape, however temporarily, the increasing social regimentation of modern American life. The following letter, written by a middle-class "Argonaut" in 1859, reflects the harsh realities of life among the forty-niners, but also reveals the personal reasons that drew so many men from other parts of the United States to the California gold fields.

William Swain's Letter from the California Gold Fields (1850)

January 6, 1850

Dear George,

It is so long a time since I wrote you and I have passed through so many scenes and changes of condition that I scarcely know what to say among the multitude of things I wish to write. You have probably all had much anxiety about my safe arrival in California, and as you have been unable to hear from me for so long a time, you will be desirous of having a lexicon of our journey.

We arrived at Lawson's Ranch on the 8th day of November, tired and worn down with toil and exposure but hardy, healthy, and in good spirits, buoyant with hope. We were in the Sacramento Valley in the rainy season, destitute of provisions, without shelter, and everything eatable worth from $1 to $1.50 per pound. In fact, all was dear but rain and mud which was everywhere.

We rested three days and put out for the Feather River mines, where we arrived on the 14th of November at Long's Trading Post, the first mines on this stream.

From all that we could hear, we judged the South Fork of the Feather River to be the most likely to yield a pile another summer, for the following reasons: the main part of the Feather River and all the southern rivers have been overrun and consequently the best and richest placers found and worked. The South Fork of the Feather River was reported to be rich, and the gold on it coarse and not much worked. There is good timber for building (not the case on many of the streams of California), which with us is an important consideration as we believed our health next summer depended upon having dry, warm, and comfortable habitation during the rainy season.

In late November we bought provisions at Long's Trading Post and took packs of fifty pounds each. We traveled over the mountains for twenty-five miles through rain, mud and clouds and arrived on the South Fork on the third day.

After prospecting two days, we located a spot favorable for damming and draining the river. We made our claim and then built a house as soon as possible to shelter our heads from the soaking rains. So here we are, snug as school-marms, working at our race and dam. Whenever the rain will permit, a fall of the river will enable us to get into the bed of the river and know what is there. If there is no gold, we shall be off to another place, for there is an abundance of gold here, and if we are blessed with health, we are determined to have a share of it.

You may have some curiosity to know something about our location and dwelling. Our house is a log cabin, sixteen by twenty feet. It is covered with boughs of cedar and is made of nut pine logs from one to two feet in diameter, so that it is quite a blockhouse. It has a good door made of cedar boards hewn our of cedar logs, but no window. It faces the south and is on the north side of the river. In the east end is a family fireplace, in which large backlogs are burning night and day. At the west end is a bedstead framed into the logs of the cabin and running from side to side. The cords of the bedstead are strips of rawhide, crossing at every three inches, thus forming a bottom tight enough to hold large armfuls of dry breaks gathered from the sides of the mountains, which make a substitute for feather beds. On these are our blankets and buffalo skins. Altogether it makes a comfortable bed. Moore has a bunk in one of the other corners. Over the fireplace are our rifles, which are ever ready, cocked and primed, and frequently yield us good

venison. In the other corner may be seen our cupboard with its contents, which consist of a few wooden and tin dishes, bottles, knives and forks and spoons, tin frying pan, boiler, and coffee pot.

Around the sides of the cabin at various points are the few articles of clothing belonging to the different members of the company. Under the bed are five cakes of tallow, under the bunk are three or four large bags of flour. Along the point of the roof is a line of dried beef and sixty or seventy pounds of suet. And out at the corner of the house in a large trough made of pine may be found salt beef in the pickle, in abundance.

At ten in the evening you might see in this cabin, while everything is still, a fire blazing up from the mass of fuel in the large fireplace, myself and Hutchinson on one end of bedstead, Lt. Cannon on the other, and Moore in his bunk. On the roof the incessant rain keeps up its perpetual patter, while the foaming stream howls out a requiem of the rushing torrent as it dashes on its way to the valley. And here, wakeful and listless, are the members of other circles too. But often the mind is far away, filled with other scenes, far distant homes, and relatives.

In front of our cabin a mountain rises from the edge of the river two thousand feet and hides the sun till ten o'clock in the day. Its top is often covered with snow. The live oak and numerous other mountain evergreens, besides the pine and cedar, green as spring, are loaded with snow near the mountain top and dripping with rain on its side and base. And this is only a specimen of the hills and scenery on all sides of us.

We found the most extraordinary state of morals in the mines. Everything in this country is left where the owner wished to leave it, in any place no matter where, as such a thing as stealing is not known.

Miners' rights are well protected. Disputes seldom arise and are settled by referees, as they would be at home.

George, I tell you this mining among the mountains is a dog's life. A man has to make a jackass of himself packing loads over mountains that God never designed man to climb, a barbarian by foregoing all the comforts of civilized life, and a heathen by depriving himself of all communication with men away from his immediate circle.

You can judge my feelings when I inform you that I have not had an opportunity to send to Sacramento City for my letters and papers and have no tidings from home since I received your last letter at Independence, and I have not seen a newspaper since I left the states.

There was some talk between us of your coming to this country. For God's sake think not of it. Stay at home. Tell all whom you know that are thinking of coming that they have to sacrifice everything and face danger in all its forms, for George, thousands have laid and will lay their bones along the routes to and in this country. Tell all that "death is in the pot" if they attempt to cross the plains and hellish mountains. Say to Playter never to think of the journey; and as for you, *stay at home,* for if my health is spared, I can get enough for both of us.

You may think from the tenor of this letter that I am sick of my job, but not so. I have not seen the hour yet when I regretted starting for California, nor have any one of our little party ever regretted that we undertook the enterprise. I have seen hard times, face the dangers of disease and exposure and perils of all kinds, but I count them as nothing if they enable me to place myself and family in comfortable circumstances.

Now you will think that there is a contradiction in the advice that I gave you and others about coming to California and the declaration of my own satisfaction that I have performed the journey. The fact is that gold is plenty here and the accounts received before I left home did not exaggerate the reality. Therefore I am glad that I am here. But the time is past—if it ever existed—when fortunes could be obtained for picking them up. Gold is found in the most rocky and rough places, and the streams and bars that are rich are formed of huge rocks and stones. In such places, you will see, it requires robust labor and hard tugging and lifting to separate the gold from the rock. But this is nothing to the risk of life run in traveling to this country. Therefore, if I was at home and knew all the circumstances, I think I should stay at home; but having passed those dangers in safety, I thank God that I am here in so favorable circumstances.

I hope soon to send for my letters, and God grant that they may bring no sad intelligence from home, for I almost dread to hear from that happy home, fearing that our neighborhood may have been the theater of cholera.

You are better acquainted with the state of things around San Francisco Bay than I am, and therefore I say nothing about them.

I have felt great anxiety about my wife and child, as I left them no means to live upon for so long a time, expecting to send home means before this; and also, their necessities might embarass you. I hope that you will see that they are provided for, and if I can remunerate you for any trouble you may have, I shall feel willing to do so and ever feel grateful for your kindness. Give my love to Mother, if she is yet living, and say to her that I often, very often, think of her.

Tell Sabrina not to be overanxious about me, for I shall be careful of my health, and as soon as I can get the rocks in my pocket I shall hasten as fast as steam can carry me.

Write often, for I may sometime or another get your letters.

17

No Boy's Play: Migration and Settlement in Early Gold Rush California

Malcolm Rohrbough

The discovery of gold near Sutter's Mill outside present-day Sacramento, California, set in motion one of the most dramatic transcontinental migrations in American history. The prospect of wealth, power, advancement, and simple adventure drew tens of thousands of men and several thousand women to seek their fortunes in the California gold fields in the years between 1849 and 1852.

While the California Gold Rush quickly attained mythic status in American culture— a position it has barely lost in the last century and a half—the reality of the Gold Rush has often been more interesting than the myth. In fact, as a number of recent histories have revealed, one of the most intriguing features of the Gold Rush was the ubiquity of its attraction. As Malcolm Rohrbough discusses in this essay, the California gold fields attracted men and women from all ranks of life—rich, poor, and especially those in between. Unlike previous transcontinental migrations of eastern farmers seeking better land in the West, the Gold Rush brought those with more sedentary and urban occupations to abandon their work and families in order to participate in the mid-century "gold craze." In the hands of recent historians, the Gold Rush has become much more than a simple quest for riches: it was equally a quest to prove one's manhood, a way of escaping the drudgery of everyday life, and a means of securing personal and family independence in a rapidly changing world.

In this essay, Rohrbough describes the process of decision making, preparation, travel, and settlement that defined the early stages of the Gold Rush. Though most

Argonauts returned home poorer than when they had begun, all remembered these early years with a fondness reminiscent of a hunting expedition or a stint in military service. Most who wrote about their venture to California described it as the formative experience of their lives.

....

On the morning of April 19, 1775, on the green at Concord, Massachusetts, the militia of the New England towns first faced the power of the British Regular Army. Writing a poem more than half a century later to celebrate this dramatic moment, Ralph Waldo Emerson paid tribute to the "embattled farmers," who "fired the shot heard round the world."

Just as the gunfire on Concord Green echoed around the world, so too did James W. Marshall's discovery of January 24, 1848. Marshall's gold flakes set in motion the events that we know as the California Gold Rush. But what events and over what a vast landscape and seascape! The first Forty-niners came from up and down the West Coast, from Sonora and Oregon, and then from the Hawaiian Islands. By the middle of autumn 1848, the news of the gold in California had reached the eastern states, where it rapidly spread from Maine to Mississippi, from Wisconsin to Florida, and eventually around the world. Marshall's gold discoveries launched a thousand ships and hitched a thousand prairie schooners. The overland schooners embarked from county-seat towns and villages across the breadth of the nation, from subsistence farms in the Ohio Valley to the great plantations of the lower Mississippi River Valley. The Gold Rush's appeal was universal, for those who joined the procession in 1849 and over the next dozen years embraced every class, from the wealthy to those in straited circumstances, from every state and territory, including slaves brought by their owners to the gold fields.

The discovery of gold in California was to trigger the greatest mass migration in the history of the young Republic up to that time, some 80,000 in 1849 alone and probably 300,000 by 1854, an immigration largely male and generally young, but not exclusively either, by land across half a continent and by sea over thousands of miles of ocean to new and heretofore unimagined adventure and wealth. And it would become an international event with immigration from all over the world, including farmers from China and lawyers from Paris, miners from Wales and merchants from Chile. California would become in a few short years the most cosmopolitan place in the world, and San Francisco the most cosmopolitan city.

Initially, the arrival of news about the California gold discoveries in the eastern half of the young continental American nation had been greeted with much skepticism, coming from the distant West Coast after a divisive war of conquest. The evidence for the truth of the stories mounted slowly, and the discoveries achieved universal acceptance only with President James K. Polk's message to Congress of December 5, 1848. Polk confirmed the gold in California and added, "The accounts of the abundance of gold in that territory are of such an extraordinary character as would scarcely command belief were they not corroborated by the authentic reports of officers in the public service." The army officer who brought the letters of confirmation had also carried samples of gold, some 220 ounces. On display in the War Department, the gold became a magnet for visitors, officials, and newspaper reporters. The glittering rocks washed away any lingering doubts, and the public gazed with rapt attention at the sparkling specimens. Their wonder would be repeated by a generation of Forty-niners peering at the nuggets in the bottoms of their pans.

Acceptance was soon followed by wild, uninhibited enthusiasm, and the news spread rapidly to the most remote villages of the American Republic. The impact of the news on one tight-knit community may be summarized by the observations of Prentice Mulford on his village of Sag Harbor on Long Island in the autumn months of 1848: "One June morning, when I was a boy, Captain Eben Latham came to our house, and the first gossip he unloaded was that 'them stories about finding gold in Californy was all true.' The report slumbered during the summer in our village, but in the fall it commenced kindling and by winter it was ablaze. Ours was a whaling village. By November 1848, California was the talk of the village, as it was all that time of the whole country. The Gold Fever raged all winter."

This outbreak of what observers like Prentice Mulford called "gold fever" had an immediate impact. Editors scrambled to set the largest headlines and searched reference books for the best analogies to the past, with references to the "El Dorado of the old Spaniards," "the dreams of Cortez and Pizarro," "the Age of Gold," routinely filling the columns of dailies and weeklies.

A wide range of motives drove future Forty-niners who proposed to go to California. Of course wealth was the first and most public. In addition, the prospect of treasure opened by news of these dazzling discoveries at Sutter's Mill offered young people escape from what they thought of as the limited horizons of the village, the farm, or the shop, and the daily demand of labor associated with these places. It was not the young alone, however, who were propelled into motion. Men of all ages and conditions made plans to go to California, and a surprising number of women wished to join them.

From the welter of newsprint and stories passed from one astonished citizen to another (like Captain Eben Latham) emerged two universal truths. First, the gold in California was real and abundant. Among the most astonishing features of the California Gold Rush was that the most outrageous tales of wealth were true. The Golden State—it would join the Union in 1850—produced a seemingly endless flood of gold. While agricultural laborers in the East earned a dollar a day for twelve hours of work in the fields and artisans and craftsmen perhaps a dollar and a half for the same hours, men who were recently farmers and mechanics made sixteen dollars a day washing gravel in the streambeds of California's foothills. In the six years from 1849 to 1855, the Argonauts harvested some $300 million in gold from California.

The second observation that came to enjoy full acceptance was the notion that gold was available to everyone. The California Gold Rush spoke to American values at midcentury: the democratic belief that wealth would be available to all, that success would reward hard work, and that the largest portion of riches would go to those most moral and worthy by the standards of the day. The discovery of gold in 1848 and its wide, indeed universal, accessibility to Americans everywhere was the reincarnation (or the ultimate continuation) of the American dream, the promise of a better life for themselves and their children through hard work. The search for gold in California became the epitome of American economic democracy: anyone with a pick, pan, and shovel could participate, at least in the early years, regardless of wealth, social standing, education, or family name. Hence this greatest bonanza in the history of the young Republic and newly crowned continental nation was open to all.

The appeal was immediate and universal. Everywhere, citizens of the Republic across the breadth of the land pondered the question of whether to join the rush to the West or whether to stay home. The whole family assembled to canvass the issue. This dilemma raised questions about a host of local and family obligations inherently woven into the miniature world of all Americans at midcentury: marital responsibilities and family obligations, in which the opportunity for wealth was measured against long absences that imposed new duties, often with reduced resources. But the prospective Forty-niners cast the opportunities for wealth in California as something that would benefit the entire family and perhaps in a few short months notably enhance its prospects for generations to come.

The gold fever thus began to disrupt families and communities across the nation, in states and in territories, in regions north and south, slave and free, from urban centers to the most remote farming homesteads. Discussions of whether to go, when to go, who would go, who had gone, and why, occupied many long evenings and evoked emotional outpourings. And for those who decided to go, there was the need to raise the funds for the voyage, whether by sea or overland. Many prospective Forty-niners appealed to their families, with visions of wealth to be shared among all members. Young James Barnes of Washingtonville, New York, summed up the pleas of many Argonauts when he wrote, "Father i need thy assistance; dont send your son emty away. . . . i dont ask you to give me the money, only lend it to me until i am able to repay you."

There were other investors outside the family. Two capitalists each put up $2,500 to finance a company of ten from Monroe, Michigan, in exchange "for a quarter share each in the proceeds of the company" for a two-year period. Another man advised his nephew to invest $500 "by fitting out some young man, on whose integrity he could rely and who had no means of going himself—and agree to divide the profits with him." The sum would support "some poor but hardy man" for two years in California with the prospect of a good return for both parties.

Those who determined to go often did so in a "company" with their friends and neighbors. The company was, in truth, often a replica of the local community from which they came. Within the company, an Argonaut might have one or two special friends. One Forty-niner described such a close friendship with the comment, "me and John stick together like wood ticks to a horse." It was a familiar camaraderie; it was also a support network, confronting an unknown adventure of great distances and strange and alien landscape in which the support of friends would be both welcome and necessary.

The company formed and the officers chosen, a period of intense preparation followed. Men who had been tied to labor on farms and in shops suddenly found themselves officers in companies preparing to depart for California. On them fell such solemn duties as victualling, gathering uniforms and arms, and drafting a constitution. The hum and buzz of activity transformed their communities, and they became the envy of all those who had wished to go but decided to remain.

The outbreak of gold fever and the prospect of a large emigration to the West in search of gold was not greeted with universal enthusiasm. Far from it. Among those sometimes ranged in opposition were ministers, who saw the search for gold as mammon triumphant over the family and community. Such views emerged in a sermon preached by the Reverend James Davis of the First Congregational Church in Woonsocket, Rhode Island. His sermon suggested, among other things, the power and influence of the news of gold. The "gold fever," the Reverend Davis intoned, was a national disease, a true epidemic. It should be treated as such. "The excitement is become truly appalling, and reaching not our cities alone, but our villages and towns and shaking every family. There never has been any excitement equal to it within the remembrance of our oldest cities.— War, Pestilence, Famine, the most astonishing discoveries in the arts and sciences . . . the advancement of civilization and Christianity in the subjugation of heathen lands—all these have never filled our land and the minds of our young men with such intense excitement. . . . The gold pestilence which is more terrific than the cholera, threatens to depopulate our land."

Others argued forcefully that the discovery of gold was a blessing, national resources to be used for the national good. It turned out, according to this justification, that those who went to California in search of wealth did not do so as a selfish gesture, but instead they were patriots spreading American civilization and culture to the distant western parts of the new continental nation. These national heroes (and some heroines) would make California an American land, replace Mexican Catholicism with American Protestantism, supplant the Spanish language with English, and supersede Mexican culture with American values and institutions. This new national purpose gave a powerful patriotic dimension to the rush to California, as many editors and public officials commented in offering their blessing to the departing Argonauts.

Finally, there came the partings. These were public with parades and religious services, or private, with a small gathering at the front gate or stoop. In New York City, "the docks are crowded with fathers and mothers, brothers and sisters and sweethearts, and such embracing and waving of handkerchiefs." One departing Argonaut threw his last five-dollar gold piece toward shore, shouting, "I'm going where there is plenty more." And strangers joined the throngs of family members to celebrate the embarkation for this national adventure. In Philadelphia, companies of Argonauts marching to the ships "were greeted with Cheers from different crowds who stood on the wharves to witness our departure."

For many, these were solemn, even sad, occasions. On the crowded wharves of Boston, ministers conducted final services, with sermons appropriate to the anticipated long absences and somber obligations owed family and country. In Prentice Mulford's village of Sag Harbor, Long Island, the departing men and their families filled the church for a special service where they were admonished to behave virtuously, remember the standards and values of their community, and return rich. As a special reward, these leaving Argonauts were then permitted to stay up late with their girls. In Bloomington, Indiana, two thousand people came together to mark the occasion with religious services (a Bible was presented to each member of the departing company) and to sing missionary hymns to the gold companies as the wagons rolled west toward the unknown. These leave-takings lay with a heavy hand on the families and communities from which had departed their young (and sometimes not so young) men for the Golden West. These adventurers left behind spouses, fiancées, children, siblings, parents, and friends. Their absences would change sometimes forever the configuration of their families and communities.

So America went to California in search of gold. The companies went by sailing ship across the seas and around the Horn in 1849; they went by wagon overland from St. Joseph or Independence, Missouri, to Placerville (or Hangtown, as the Argonauts affectionately referred to it). Many companies bound for California went by sea, especially those within reach of the Atlantic ports. The journey by sea could begin at any season, anywhere along the coast, and could make the long voyage around Cape Horn or could opt for the shorter route across Panama. The cost was substantial, on the order of $1,000 for individual members of the company. But the conditions were ideal for companies or individuals with investment ambitions. The sailing vessel offered the means to transport equipment and other cargoes for use and for sale. Such companies offered opportunities for absentee investors to buy shares and transport goods for resale in California, opening the Gold Rush as a money-making chance to capitalists who would never leave the comfort of their rooms in Boston or New York.

For those who went by sea, there were several kinds of purchases. For the voyage, the Argonauts needed barrels of beef and ship biscuits, butter and pork, rice and salt. And they needed them immediately and at the most favorable price. In addition, they required personal equipment, clothing, tools, and guidebooks. These items were known collectively as the "kit," and companies along the eastern seaboard from Portland, Maine, to New Orleans, Louisiana, advertised heavily as outfitting centers. To these basic articles might be added special equipment, "goldometers" or gold-digging machines of various kinds, and other exotic technology that immediately appeared on the market. Indeed, the first great bonanza of the California Gold Rush was in the port cities along the Atlantic Coast, where outfitters did a heavy business in outfitting prospective Argonauts and their vessels for the gold fields.

The voyage to California, whether by Cape Horn, or the shorter version by way of Panama, was long, routine, and boring. Energetic, ambitious, and sometimes frantic Forty-niners, anxious to confront the wealth that seemed sure to be theirs, were confined on a ship for several months, powerless to do anything to accelerate the pace of their voyage to the golden port of San Francisco. Many Argonauts kept journals, in search of ways to pass the time and also in response to their sense of the significance of the moment. As relief against boredom, seaborne companies organized communal activities, from military drills to amateur theatricals to practical lectures on the geology of California or the customs of peoples in the ports of call. As the gold fields came closer, company officers prepared their members for debarkation and made necessary arrangements for dividing the company into squads of miners (a final gesture to military organization) and doling out supplies.

Members of the companies, idled by the long voyage, read and talked, smoked and fished. Above all, they gambled. It was something of an irony that, having been warned to hold fast to their traditional values in the face of the temptations of California, they would succumb to games of chance on the voyage there. But they did. Like so much else that would come to be associated with California, upright and God-fearing citizens of the Republic would be seduced by bad habits and sinful activities, and in this case, before they ever washed a single pan of dirt in the diggings.

The long sea voyages invariably generated internal tensions and anxieties, sometimes even open conflict. To begin with, there were variations in accommodations and sometimes

in food. Travel by sea to California (whether by Cape Horn or Panama), like sea travel everywhere, had a certain class-conscious element to it. Some could afford better accommodations than others. A few members of the same company brought delicacies for meals, and formed themselves into separate messes to enjoy their special treats. They openly intended to maintain social and economic distinctions between themselves and their fellow company members, as they would have done before the common expedition to California.

Their ocean voyages exposed the seagoing Argonauts to new American places and to foreign cultures. Both often made powerful impressions. Some ships from New England, New York, and Pennsylvania called at Charleston and sometimes New Orleans, and there their passengers had their first encounter with the institution of slavery. By midcentury, slavery had become a dominant influence in American political life. Both Congress and the executive branch were already engaged in the search for an acceptable compromise on the issue of the access of southerners with their slave property to the new territories recently acquired in the war with Mexico. While citizens from the Northeast had heard much about the institution of slavery, few had experienced it firsthand. They now did so. Strolling through the streets of Charleston or New Orleans, they wrote of powerful impressions made by slave auctions.

In the foreign ports of call, whether Panama, Rio de Janeiro, Granada, or Lima, American Protestants had their encounter with a Latin Catholic culture. They were impressed with the landscape and the grandeur of public buildings, especially the cathedrals, and even New Englanders often declared a sense of awe and respect, if not sympathy, for this alien church. The seagoing Argonauts were generally neither impressed by nor sympathetic to the local peoples, however. The Americans deplored local habits that they found lazy or scandalous or both. The universal targets of criticism were music and dancing, especially the enthusiasms of men and women for public entertainments such as the fandango. One Forty-niner expressed shock that men and women bathed together in Granada. Another described Chileans as "a very indolent and idle class of People possessing but little enterprise." And the Americans generally contrasted the beautiful and abundant landscape of Panama with the primitive agriculture and lack of commercial enterprise. Many travelers expressed relief on debarking in San Francisco, not only for the end to the long and boring sea voyage but also for the welcome sight of so many familiar faces and the sound of a familiar language. One Forty-niner wrote of San Francisco streets, "I seemed to feel quite at home among the good honest Saxon countenances . . . everywhere to be seen contrasting favorably with the sallow narrow visaged Spaniards."

Overland travelers faced a formidable journey across half the continent at mid-century. Only a few thousand pioneers had made the trip to Oregon in the previous decade, and these had been farm families headed west in search of land. Never in the history of the Republic had there been a mass migration of tens of thousands overland to the West Coast in a single season. And in the spring and summer of '49, those who made the trek would include city dwellers along with people from small towns and farms, all suddenly caught up the great pioneering challenge of the day. The obstacles included great distances, the monotonous character of much of the landscape, the towering mountain ranges and deserts to be crossed, and fears of attack by Indians.

The migrations of the so-called "overland" Forty-niners shared both similarities and contrasts with those voyaging by sea. Companies were the basic unit of organization here, too, and individuals who went to St. Joseph or Independence, Missouri, without an affiliation always joined a company there. Groups and individuals sought out others with similar origins and values. New Englanders and southerners sought their own kind, of course, but others with special concerns also united. The Sabbath observers joined in companies of those

who would stop for a Sunday of rest; temperance men often banded together. Companies going by sea could depart whenever they wished (within limits of weather), and could match the ship to their size and their cargoes. Overland companies had to conform more to size and schedules dictated by the calendar and the nature of the journey. The trek of twenty-two hundred miles overland was a routine enterprise that, at the same time, imposed certain absolute conditions. The travelers had to leave the Missouri River towns late enough in the spring to find grass for their draft animals on the prairies, but early enough so that they could arrive in California before the first heavy snows closed the passes in the Sierra Nevada. In practice, this meant a departure date somewhere around May 15, and arrival at the base of the Sierra before October 1. The companies were cautioned to travel in groups of no more than sixty, for a larger number would tax the available forage and water, and to limit their loads to a minimum in order to protect the energy and health of the draft animals.

Unlike travel by sea, the overland Forty-niners were constantly aware of crowds along the trails and the growing competition for water and grass, and indirectly, to be the first to arrive in the gold country. This sense of rivalry was the stronger because the Argonauts could literally see their competitors ahead and behind them on the trail. "There are thousands of men going along the road; in fact, it looks like the wagons hauling cotton to Macon just after a rise in the staple," wrote one Forty-niner from Alabama. "I believe there are wagons stretching in sight of one another for 500 miles."

Unlike those suffering the boredom of inaction on the sea voyage, the overlanders performed endless daily chores. One Argonaut's observations summarize the accounts of hundreds: "When traveling, we are up at day break; and by the time the horses are fed, curried and harnessed, the breakfast is ready; as soon as that is dispatched, we hitch up and away. At noon—heretofore we have spent no longer time than is just necessary for the horses and ourselves to eat; but when we get to feeding them on grass, a little longer time will be required. In the evening, after stopping, the horses are to offgear, tie up, curry, and fed and water; the tent is to put up—bed clothes to arrange, supper to prepare and eat—which last is not hard to do—by this time it is bed time, and we 'turn in.' Then again, each member of the company comes upon guard duty once every fourth or fifth night." On the trail, for the first time in a society essentially without women, the Argonauts had their first experiences in sewing, washing, and cooking, and they found these new duties awkward and even burdensome. Little did the overland travelers understand that this domestic work on the overland trail was only the beginning of a new range of chores that would confront them in the gold fields.

Unlike those who went by sea, the overland Forty-niners saw themselves as the vanguard of pioneers, a triumphal march of American people and values across the plains, mountains, and deserts that became the standard for the new Golden State. This journey across half the continent with draft animals was the final large-scale reenactment of America's pioneering past that stretched back for a century, to the migration of frontier families across the Appalachians into Kentucky and the Ohio Country. For the Argonauts of '49, it brought them face to face with the fabled symbols of the American West: the huge herds of buffalo, the dangerous Plains Indians tribes (feared but rarely seen), the towering peaks of the Rockies and the Sierra Nevada, the national monuments of Chimney Rock, Fort Laramie, and the Mormon enclave around the Great Salt Lake.

This great overland migration through the varied landscapes and peoples of the American West ended at Placerville in the late summer or early autumn. There, the companies generally broke up, as smaller groups of six or eight men banded together and headed for the mines. Placerville merchants did a bonanza business in re-outfitting the newcomers and changing them from transcontinental pioneers into miners.

Even those who had brought the proper tools and equipment to California—shovel, pan, pick, tents, blankets, cradle—now had to purchase food and to transport everything to the placers. Supplies for the mines—salt pork, flour, sugar, tea, and coffee—might involve an outlay of one hundred dollars per miner, plus transportation costs of another one hundred.

Arrived in California, the gold seekers found themselves in an alien, new world. It was a world of strangers, not friends and neighbors; it was a world of self-interest, in which individuals had to look out for themselves (hence the great interest in joining together in small groups to mine and to live); it was a world in which prices for staple goods were beyond anything imaginable, and money seemed plentiful and its value diminished. Argonauts from all economic conditions expressed astonishment at the quantities of hard money visible (especially in gambling houses), even passing from hand to hand. "Gold is measured here by bushels and shovel full," wrote one Forty-niner. And another observed, "Money here seems to be of little value, & every person has plenty." This was only one of the many strange qualities of the new land that the voyagers, at last in California, attempted to describe to their disbelieving families and friends at home.

The newly arrived Argonauts—whether by land or by sea—settled in varied places. These destinations included the growing cities of San Francisco, Sacramento, and Stockton; they established themselves in the many small towns and villages dotting the routes to the gold fields or adjacent to the diggings; they went in large numbers into the gold mining country itself. Those who clustered in the cities included professionals such as doctors and lawyers and day laborers who worked on the docks and on the streets. Large numbers also gravitated to the newly energized entertainment industry, which included dance halls, houses of prostitution, and above all, saloons and gambling establishments. These gambling halls were among the most elegant buildings in San Francisco, providing employment for many and making a dramatic impression on the new arrivals in the city. To these groups should be added the laborers in the booming construction industry and the clerks in the numerous merchant houses engaged in importing goods for local consumption and for shipment to the mining camps. Sacramento and Stockton were smaller than San Francisco but no less commercial, for they were the business gateways to the mining camps themselves.

There were hundreds of mining camps in the California gold country. Some were as large as substantial villages; others were simply crossroads with a single street carved out of the forest to accommodate a few stores. These small urban places prospered in proportion to the mines they served. Their commercial establishments included stores for supplies, a boarding-house, a restaurant or two, perhaps a doctor and a lawyer, a small entertainment place with a bowling alley, and one or more saloons. The sale of liquor was a major business, especially on Sundays. Business in the camps was generally defined by the mining cycle of work, and this included a day of rest and recreation on Sundays. So camps would be crowded on Sundays, from first light to sunset. Since mining was seasonal, closing with the beginning of the rainy season in late November or early December, so too, many camps tended to hibernate during the winter months.

By far the largest number of Argonauts in 1849 and subsequent annual migrations headed directly for the gold fields. There, they mined in small companies, or "messes," of from five to eight. These numbers were most efficient for the mining techniques in use in the early years—the pan, but quickly the cradle and a "long tom"—and for domestic arrangements. The small company was more than simply a matter of economic and domestic convenience; it was also a self-selected group committed to one another in the most personal kind of way. The company as a unit of work and living offered support in case of sickness and even in case of death. That the sick should

be cared for was part of the unwritten contract associated with shared living and working. Every gold seeker could tell stories of individuals taken ill and left to fend for themselves. Occasional accounts of Good Samaritan strangers emerged from the hustle and movement of the Gold Rush, but most Argonauts preferred to rely on carefully chosen companions. Here were the companions who would sit up with the miner taken ill, fetch the doctor, and make the soup. Here, also, were the partners who would close the eyes of the dead man, dress the body and bury it, and handle the estate. And, in a final act, they would communicate with the dead man's family and carry out his last wishes.

The mining company had its origins in a work unit. As early as the summer and fall of 1848, observers had commented on the advantages of working in groups of at least three or four. By the mining season of 1849, mining in groups was universal. The work was of the most onerous and repetitive kind. Each day, the members of a mining company trekked to their claim and began a routine of digging, shoveling, carrying, and washing that continued unabated and with little variation throughout the day until dark. In 1849, most companies operated one or more cradles. In a pattern that stretched from one end of the Mother Lode to the other, one man loosened the "dirt," whether by digging or shoveling; a second carried it to the site of the cradle; there, a third washed the materials. The fourth or fifth members of the company would dig or carry. Miners rotated jobs to equalize the work and relieve the monotony. When a company exceeded six or so, it would operate a second cradle.

The basic unit of work in the California Gold Rush—at least for the first half-dozen years—was the human body. The hard, repetitive labor of digging, carrying, and washing was often done in swift, ice-cold, moving water. "You will have to work in water & mud Morning until night it is no boys play," one Forty-niner wrote his parents. Contrasting with the icy water of the snowmelt watercourses was the heat of the summer California sun, beating down on the bars and into the still canyons. The work was exhausting. "Mining is the hardest working imaginable and an occupation which very much endangers health," complained one Argonaut. "A weakly man might about as well to go digging his grave as to dig gold." Under these conditions, the company performed another function: it demanded and received a continuing work commitment on the part of each member. The presence of a member who did not do the expected labor—whether from lack of will or lack of strength made no difference—was a constant source of irritation in a mutually reinforcing group based on equality. So during the long work days that stretched into a long mining season, gold seekers drove themselves forward on a daily basis through a combination of restless energy, hope, self-interest, group loyalty, and sometimes desperation.

The same division appropriate to mining, with its unending physical labor, long hours, and collective work, also helped to define the new living arrangements. For the miners, it was cheaper and more practical to live in groups. From five to eight men would occupy a large tent or cabin as close to the work site as possible, where they would take turns cooking, cleaning, sewing, and making trips to the camps for food and mail. The most important chore was cooking, for it involved all members of the company. The duty of cook rotated on a weekly basis. As all cooks were amateurs, the meals tended to be repetitive. The main evening meal included meat (fresh or preserved), bread or biscuits, and coffee or tea with plenty of sugar. All miners learned how to bake. It was a necessary skill, and most miners later remember their first loaf of bread as vividly as the first sight of buffalo on the plains and gold flakes at the bottom of their cradles.

Through all these frenzied activities, whether in the cities, mining towns and camps, or at the placers themselves, most of the Forty-niners maintained strong ties with their families and communities in the East. Almost all of them, initially at least, fully intended to return home with a full share of California's wealth, to change the future prospects of their family, and to enhance their standing within the family and the community. Their migration overland represented the first steps in a long cycle of adventures in a strange and exotic place and their eventual return home. Their settlement in California completed the first stage of their experiences as the Argonauts of '49.

GLOSSARY

"Shot heard 'round the world":	Reference to the Battle of Lexington and Concord, fought between the British army and American Minutemen on April 19, 1775. It marked the beginning of the Revolutionary War.
Argonaut:	Originally a person who sailed with Jason on the ship *Argo* in the Greek epic, *The Odyssey*. More generally, a person who embarks on a dangerous but rewarding quest, in this case, the California Gold Rush.
Cape Horn:	The passage between the Atlantic and Pacific oceans at the southern tip of South America.
Sierra Nevada:	A mountain range in eastern California that was the site of most gold mining during the California Gold Rush.
Good Samaritan:	A compassionate person who unselfishly helps others.

IMPLICATIONS

In this essay, Rohrbough argues that the California Gold Rush touched on the deepest American values of the mid-nineteenth century. After reading about the experiences of American Argonauts in the California gold fields, what values do you think emerge as the most important to the forty-niners?

American wars have never involved only men. Women were active participants as sutlers, laundresses, and cooks in every major American army from the American Revolution through the frontier campaigns against the Plains Indians in the late nineteenth century. This reading begins with the recollections of Susie King Taylor, a laundress during the Civil War. As she shows, even in wartime, domestic tasks were still widely considered the exclusive realm of women.

Susie King Taylor, *Reminiscences of an Army Laundress (1902)*

I was enrolled as company laundress, but I did very little of it, because I was always busy doing other things through camp, and was employed all the time doing something for the officers and comrades. . . .

The first colored troops did not receive any pay for eighteen months, and the men had to depend wholly on what they received from the commissary, established by Gen. Saxton. A great many of these men had large families, and as they had no money to give them, their wives were obliged to support themselves and children by washing for the officers of the gunboats and the soldiers, and making cakes and pies, which they sold to the boys in camp. Finally, in 1863, the government decided to give them half pay, but the men would not accept this. They wanted "full pay or nothing." They preferred rather to give their services to the state, which they did until 1864, when the government granted them full pay with all the back pay due. . . .

I learned to handle a musket very well while in the regiment and could shoot straight and often hit the target. I assisted in cleaning the guns and used to fire them off, to see if the cartridges were dry, before cleaning and reloading, each day. I thought this was great fun. I was also able to take a gun all apart and put it together again. . . .

We had fresh beef once in a while, and we would have soup, and the vegetables they put in the soup were dried and pressed; they looked like hops. Salt beef was our standby. Sometimes the men would have what we called slapjacks. This was flour made into bread and spread thin on the bottom of the mess-pan to cook; each man had one of them with a pint of tea for his supper, or a pint of tea and five or six hardtack. I often got my own meals and would fix some dishes for the noncommissioned officers also.

About the first of June, 1864, the regiment was ordered to Folly Island, staying there until the latter part of the month, when it was ordered to Morris Island. We landed on Morris Island between June and July, 1864. This island was a narrow strip of sandy soil, nothing growing on it but a few bushes and shrubs. The camp was one mile from the boat landing, called Pawnell Landing, and the landing one mile from Fort Wagner. . . .

About four o'clock, July 2, the charge was made. The firing could be plainly heard in camp. I hastened down to the landing and remained there until eight o'clock that morning. When the wounded arrived, or rather began to arrive, the first one brought in was Samuel Anderson of our company. He was badly wounded. Then others of our boys, some with their legs off, arm gone, foot off, and wounds of all kinds imaginable. They had to wade through creeks and marshes, as they were discovered by the enemy and shelled very badly. A number of the men were lost, some got fastened in the mud and had to cut off the legs of their pants, to free themselves. The 103rd New York suffered the most, as their men were very badly wounded.

My work now began. I gave my assistance to try to alleviate their sufferings. I asked the doctor at the hospital what I could get for them to eat. They wanted soup, but that I could not get; but I had a few cans of condensed milk and some turtle eggs, so I thought I would try to make some custard. I had doubts as to my success, for cooking with turtle eggs was something new to me, but the adage has it, "Nothing ventured, nothing done," so I made a venture and the result was a very delicious custard. This I carried to the men, who enjoyed it very much. My services were given at all times for the comfort of these men. I was on hand to assist whenever needed.

18

Husbands and Wives: Southern Marriages During the Civil War

Drew Gilpin Faust

Like all wars before and since, the American Civil War brought severe domestic disruptions in its train. Husbands, sons, and brothers were taken away from their homes to serve in the Union and Confederate armies, leaving women to maintain families, farms, and businesses. But wartime separation involved more than the added burden of assuming a husband's tasks and responsibilities. As many northern and southern women quickly discovered, wartime separations also deprived them of companionship, friendship, and solace. Not only were women's tasks made more difficult by their husband's absences, but they also often lost their main source of domestic comfort and support.

This loss was felt especially deeply by southern plantation mistresses. Brought up to a life of refined gentility in which their primary duties were to support and adorn their husband's business and personal lives, plantation women folded their lives nearly completely into those of their prominent husbands. In return, plantation wives expected their husbands to pamper and protect them, to make all important family decisions, and to provide comfort and guidance throughout their married lives. Neither experiencing nor desiring much autonomy in normal times, once war broke out and their husbands answered the martial call of the Confederacy, planter's wives were cast adrift in an unfamiliar and unwanted world.

As Drew Gilpin Faust details in this essay, wartime separation weighed heavily on plantation mistresses, turning their privileged lives upside down and challenging almost every expectation they had about adult married life. Deprived of the comfortable and extravagant social life of prewar days and called upon to run plantations, manage slaves, and even cook and clean for themselves, Confederate women met these challenges in numerous ways—some learned to live autonomously, while others simply made do. But most, Faust reveals, wrote angry and impassioned letters to government officials demanding their husbands' swift return and waited impatiently for their former lives of genteel dependency to be restored.

....

Separation Is Always Very Sad

In October 1863 Kate Peddy wrote her absent husband, George, confessing that she dreamed of him "nearly every night." Sometimes she had nightmares filled with distressing anxiety about his safety; other times she was so happy she woke believing he had returned. But his presence was so frequent and so vivid, it was almost as if their disrupted relationship had resumed to thrive in a nighttime world of vision and fantasy.

Emma Crutcher's dreams restored her husband, Will, to his rightful place as her guardian and protector. "Last night," she wrote, "I dreamed of you, and you were watching over me and taking care of me through a long series of adventures and somehow it cheered me, for I knew that you really would care for me." Will continued to appear to her at night, and on one occasion Emma was dismayed and chagrined by the realism of her dreams of reunion. Her "powers of self control," she explained, were "somewhat benumbed" by sleep, and her vision was "something that I never should have allowed had I been fully roused." Her imagination had re-created in all too lifelike and sensual detail the relationship that war had interrupted.

Some Confederate women regarded dreams as predictive of future events and tried to read them as prophecies. Cornelia Noble found particularly ominous a dream that her wedding ring had broken in two. But Emma Crutcher understood the meaning of dreams differently, believing them to reveal "our motives divested of all the self-deceptions and palliations which we all use, even to ourselves." In one dream she regarded as especially revealing, Will came home with a wounded leg. But rather than feeling grief at his suffering, Emma was overjoyed. Lame for life, Will could, Emma reasoned, neither return to battle nor attract another woman; he was forever hers. Emma concluded upon awakening that this dream displayed her "unmitigated selfishness." Her deepest fears were about his fidelity and his survival; her profoundest desires were not for victory or independence or even peace, but for her husband's permanent return.

For Emma Crutcher, as for tens of thousands of other Confederate women, cherished marital ties became for a time, if not for eternity, the stuff of dreams and fantasies. Absent by day, husbands returned in the vividness of their wives' sleeping imagination to fill the emptiness that had replaced the intimacy of domestic life. The warborn transformation of the structures of southern households had altered their hearts and souls as well. Women of the Confederate South confronted a changed emotional landscape in which the most fundamental personal attachments became as elusive as dreams, only as tangible as the letters that served as the residual substance of these ruptured ties.

The emotional lives of Confederate couples separated by war did in fact depend heavily on the mundane inadequacies of the new national postal service. "Writing what I know your eye will rest on," Emma Crutcher explained, "cements me with you more closely than anything else." Communication, professions of love and support, and even the simplest exchanges of information occurred almost exclusively through the mail. For educated members of the South's privileged classes, the challenges of meaningful expression were by no means as great as those confronting the often marginally literate common soldiers who frequently relied on letters dictated to others as the sole means of marital intercourse. But for rich and poor alike, the inefficiencies and expense of the Confederate mail service worked as a significant impediment to maintaining emotional bonds. Confederate statesmen believed that any subsidization of the mail would represent an unwarranted support for the nation's commercial interests. Thus postal rates reflected actual costs, a policy that sent the price of stamps skyrocketing after secession. In the fall of 1861 Gertrude Thomas noted that the price of sending a letter must act as a "serious drawback" to ordinary southerners, and the next year postal rates doubled. When the cost of sending a letter rose to ten cents in May 1862, Emma Holmes expected to feel the impact "considerably as it will restrict my correspondence in these hard times." By the later phases of the war, even members of the upper strata of southern society found themselves unable to write as often as they wished. Caroline Davis of Virginia complained in February 1865 of the scanty news from family members in Richmond. "I wish we could afford to hear from each other every mail."

Despite its high cost, mail delivery was far from reliable, and southerners reported instances where service was interrupted for months at a time. The impact of these failures was wide ranging. Perhaps the most distressing result was the perpetual inadequacy of information about military casualties. Women would sometimes not hear for weeks or even months whether their loved ones had survived particular battles. Waiting became so unbearable that the worst news arrived almost as a relief. Into the void of insupportable uncertainty, Dame Rumor entered to exert her cruel and arbitrary sway. Many women tried to settle near locations—towns and cities, telegraph offices, or junction post offices—that promised regular and reliable information in order to minimize the torture of anxiety. "I feel the impulse each hour stronger to go where I can hear constantly from Hal," wrote Mary Dulany of Virginia. "I cannot bear to wait." Lizzie Ozburn of Georgia had an even better idea. "I wish," she declared to her husband, Jimmie, "you & I had a Telegraph."

But it was not just life and death matters that could not be effectively communicated. The mass of almost trivial details that comprise the emotional intimacy of married life were similarly impeded. As a Louisiana woman wrote after not having received any letters from the front in almost four months, "L'absence est toujours bien triste, même avec la consolation de pouvoir écrire librement, mais lorsque l'on est privé de recevoir des n[ouv]elles de ceux qui sont si chers, c'est horrible à supporter." The Post Office, one study of the Confederacy's mail service has justly observed, played a significant part "in demoralizing the homefront."

Perhaps their cost and scarcity made letters all the more valuable. "I never knew," Emma Crutcher observed, "what precious things letters could be." When Fannie Gordon received an eagerly awaited note from her husband, General John Gordon, she transformed the sheet into a substitute for the man himself. Placing the letter under her veil, hidden from all eyes, "I pressed to my lips over and over the spot that yours had touched and tried to imagine I could feel your own precious lips & that dear moustache that I love so much." For many women, letters were the "highest pleasure" remaining in their lonely and pressured lives. Composing their responses could provide an emotional outlet nowhere else available. Confederate officials and the public press worried about military morale and urged women, "DON'T WRITE GLOOMY LETTERS." But many wives did exactly that, preserving bonds of intimacy by sharing the many troubles war had brought. Mary Bell of North Carolina explained to her husband, Alfred, in 1862, "I know you will think, I wish Mollie would not write such desponding letters but it has always been my notion to confide to my best friend my worst fears it is such a relief, especially if that friend will sympathize with you."

Lizzie Neblett agreed. "I must have someone to tell my troubles too." Her letters to Will served, she told him, as her "safety valves." But they were also, she confessed, "mirrors of my heart." It worried her a bit that she found herself writing "so fully and openly of my feelings," especially since Will remained so self-contained. Emma Crutcher embraced a new openness toward her Will as well. She discovered she "could write more freely to you than I could talk." Separation paradoxically seemed to encourage a new frankness, a new emotional accessibility, and a new intensity of feeling between husbands and wives.

Often men, in particular, struggled with this new language of personal revelation and implicit vulnerability; Will Neblett was not alone in his reserve. George Peddy felt compelled to apologize to Kate for his shortcomings. "I wish I could tell or write to you how well I love you. When I undertake to do so I am at a loss for words & language strong enough to express it. In fact, my letters fall so far short of your[s] that I am ashamed to try to write anything." David McRaven of North Carolina was not ashamed to try but embarrassed at the result. "Amanda I am getting romantic you will laugh at an old fellow 48 years writing Love like a boy." Alfred Bell feared Mary would regard his "loveing letters" as "crazy and foolish," although she promptly assured him "them are just the kind I like to get."

Rose Lewis could not decide if her husband had come to love her more or was simply using letters to say it more frequently. Wartime separations encouraged recognition, acknowledgment, and articulation of emotions that had in peacetime been ignored or taken for granted. Even her new patriotic sentiments, Emma Crutcher proclaimed to Will, paled in comparison to "the intensity of feeling which your absence awakens." But this new love was bittersweet. "I loved you enough before," she wrote, "to make me happy—now it remains to see, whether I don't love you enough to make me miserable." Southerners marveled at the wonders of emotional discovery, at the sudden awareness of what had always been there yet had remained hidden until it was threatened. "Oh Johny," wrote Julia Davidson with both passion and regret, "we little knew how dear we were to each other until we were called on to make this great sacrafice."

This new awareness of marital devotion made at least some Confederate wives confront unprecedented feelings of vulnerability as well. Women's letters are filled with confessions of anxiety about impending loss. Sarah Kennedy of Tennessee wrote her husband about how she was haunted by fears of his death. Her greatest terrors came as she lay down to sleep after the day's round of busy activity. "The idea that you may never return comes often into my mind and I am so distressed that I have to get up, and I spend hours at night in this way." Susan Caldwell of Warrenton, Virginia, explained how her apprehensions compounded the difficulties of being apart from her husband, Lycurgus. "Separation is painful, but with it an anxious heart is almost unbearable."

The survival of their loved ones amidst the appalling carnage of Civil War battles rested uppermost on these women's lists of anxieties. Many wives, though, feared the loss of their husbands' affections almost as intensely as they worried about the loss of their lives. Women's concerns about their husbands' loyalties derived in considerable measure from their sense that southern men passed into a new and uncharted world as they departed for war. In part, wives feared the temptations of lewd women and the promiscuous behavior traditionally associated with army life. But their apprehensions also encompassed a broader sense that their men were traveling into an unknown realm, where past ties and allegiances might become meaningless. In the Confederate army, men often talked of "seeing the elephant," a term used to describe—or perhaps not describe—one's first encounter with combat. Women bore a similar sense of the ineffable mystery inherent in military initiation, and they feared that the experience of this rite of passage might permanently alter and estrange their men. "You ask me," John Davidson wrote in response to the concerns of his wife, Julia, "if my change of life or manor of living, will not wean me from my wife & children. I can answer it at once. never never can there be any change in me my Love for my Wife & children is unceasing." He was, he assured her, "the same man that I was when I went into the service."

Women's frequently voiced feelings of uselessness in the face of men's all-important military contributions reinforced a more profound sense of inadequacy and self-doubt about their continuing attractiveness and significance to these new Confederate heroes. Whenever George Peddy even mentioned a woman in his letters, Kate worried that he was comparing his new acquaintance to "homely sensless me." She often wondered, she wrote, "why do you love me at all." Often her letters dwelt on the differences between them, a contrast that their wartime lives had only intensified. "You are self relient and independant, able and competent to battle with all the whims of fortune, while I am but a weight that retards and keeps you back from the position which nature designed [you] to occupy."

Mary Bell of North Carolina worried explicitly and constantly about Alfred's entanglement with other women. A sudden formality in his letters combined with a spate of rumors about wanton behavior in his company impelled Mary to direct accusation. When Alfred replied with hurt and anger, denying any such transgressions, Mary apologized. But she continued to wonder "if you are satisfied to do without me, and think that some other woman will do you just as well."

These sentiments of insecurity and vulnerability arose from a dependence that was more than simply emotional. Frustrations at the daily tribulations of Confederate life—at managing slaves or providing for families amidst inflation and scarcity—generated profound feelings of inadequacy. Women often felt crippled by what Lizzie Neblett called "my entire inability to help myself." Sarah Kennedy found that by 1864 she was "ready to despair of competency to perform the duties and responsibilities that necessarily devolve upon me." Warborn independence and autonomy were lamented rather than celebrated.

Women mourned the loss of male protection—physical, emotional, and financial. Emma Crutcher wrote revealingly to Will after they had been apart for six months, "I wish I had you to rely on now for somehow . . . I feel wearied of acting for myself and deciding for myself. It is sometimes very pleasant to stand alone, but we women all get tired of it. I have been entirely independent since you went away, for the first time in my life, not even consulting anyone. . . . And your little wife is tired, and wants to give up the reins, and lay her head on your shoulder and *rest*." Throughout their separation Emma repeatedly invited Will to exert his authority over her—to prohibit her hospital work or to direct her how to dress. If, she once warned him, "you . . . tell me to 'do just as I please, that you would not presume to interfere' I shall never forgive you. . . . If you would only *tell me* to do something, I would like it so much—I should feel like I *was* your wife, and that you claimed your property." When Emily Harris's husband returned to the army after a furlough at home in South Carolina, she felt severely depressed and declared, "I shall never get used to being left as the head of affairs at home." Such responsibility was against her nature. "I am constituted," she wrote, "so as to crave a guide and protector. I am not an independent woman nor ever shall be." Soon after R. L.

Dabney's departure for war, his wife, Lavinia, wrote inquiring about his adjustment to military discipline and celebrating the bonds of female subordination. "How do you like having a *Master*?" she asked in language especially resonant within southern society. "I like it if you do not & I can't begin to say how much I miss mine."

Amidst the overwhelming uncertainties and changes brought by Civil War, women clung ever more tenaciously to structures of authority and belonging that had given them both identity and security. As cherished relationships seemed ever more imperiled by the rising death toll, preserving their traditional forms may have appeared all the more important. In a particularly bald affirmation of the continuing power of patriarchy, Susan Caldwell throughout the war addressed her absent husband as "Dear Papa" and signed each of her letters, "Your affectionate daughter."

Although some men, particularly during the initial months of separation, tried to exert control over routine decisions at home, most quickly abdicated their authority. Even letters full of agricultural advice often ended in much the same manner as one written by E. P. Petty to his wife in December 1862. "I approve anything you do. . . . I am not now the head of the family and dont pretend to dictate." Morgan Callaway carefully instructed his wife, Leila, about how to harvest the cotton, ensure a good potato crop, and cultivate turnips. But then he caught himself short. "Dear me," he wondered, "why should I advise an experienced farmer like yourself[?]"

In many cases women seemed more uneasy about their unaccustomed power than did men. John Davidson sought to reassure and encourage his wife to meet the new demands before her. "Julia you must do the best you can. you have to act the Man & Woman both which I fear will go rather hard with you being so timid and reserved but I am happy to see that a great deal of your timidity is waring off. you have traveled alone & had to manage for yourself so long that you have become to be quite a soldier." Female independence, in John Davidson's construction, required the transformation of women into men, of ladies into soldiers. Despite his supportive tone, his very acknowledgment of differing gender capacities might well have alarmed as much as encouraged his reticent wife.

How Queer the Times

The conditions of Civil War exerted significant strains on family relations. Often disappointed in themselves and tormented by feelings of frustration and inadequacy, women began, as the war ground on, to question their men's infallibility as well. In February 1865 Grace Elmore of South Carolina commented, "How queer the times, the women can't count on the men at all to help them; they either laugh at us or when they speak seriously tis to say they know not what to advise, we must do the best of our ability."

For Virginia French of Tennessee this transformation was more than simply queer or curious. In a diary kept throughout the war, French chronicled her rising exasperation with her husband, "the Colonel," who consistently disappointed her expectations about how a man ought to behave. At the beginning of her record, Johns Hopkins French was always "Darling"; but by 1865 the term of endearment had disappeared, and her wedding anniversary, previously noted with great joy, passed unobserved. "I have wished a thousand times," she wrote in September 1864, "that I had never married—that I had no family pressing upon me—no little children over whose present and future welfare to vex and worry."

Lucy Virginia Smith French was a woman of considerable intellectual ambition. Daughter of a college president in Virginia, she had before the war served as associate editor of the *Southern Ladies' Book*, a periodical issued from New Orleans, and she herself had published a play and a collection of poems. Early in the war Union troops overran Tennessee, and French and her family sought safety in their summer house in the mountains near McMinnville. French labored to care for her young children—even worrying about basics such as bread and meat—and at the same time struggled to continue as a productive writer. It was an exhausting regimen. "My work," she wrote "is never done—I toil all the day with my hands and at night abridge my sleep to work with my brain." These unrelenting demands prompted her at last to ask, "Does any other member of my family work as I do? I should think not."

Unlike so many southern wives, French did not have an absent husband. "The Colonel," a wealthy stockman in the prewar years, did not serve in the military. Instead he remained at home, "knock[ing] around," as Virginia described his daily activities. His "principal employment," she reported in disgust in September 1864, seemed to be what he called "'going to town!' I often wonder what men were made for! To keep up the species, I suppose—which is the only thing they are 'always ready' and never slow about doing! For my part I am quite wearied and worn out with their general no-accountability—and wish they were all put into the army where they could kill each other off—the less of them the better! . . . I suppose," she continued after this eloquent outburst, "I am beginning to become embittered by years of hardship, privation and sorrow."

As the war's end drew near and its outcome unmistakable, French grew increasingly upset at her husband's failure to prepare for the future, and she complained of "the passiveness of one on whom I . . . have to depend. It is the inability of that one to make new conditions—who submits to circumstances as Fate, and never lifts a hand to make his circumstances or conquer those which are adverse." Her husband seemed to her too much like Dickens's Micawber—waiting for something to turn up. Virginia wished the Colonel could instead emulate Russell Aubrey, the hero of Alabaman Augusta Jane Evans's 1864 novel *Macaria*, the southern best-seller of the war. "But do such strong men live in reality—no. I expect they only exist in books."

When slaves disappeared to the enemy, it was Virginia who took on their work. When her old house servant Martha died, it was Virginia who read the burial service while another slave sang "When I Can Read My Title Clear." When no other schooling was available, it was Virginia who became her children's teacher. At the same time she was trying to write ten to twenty pages of prose each day. Yet she felt "powerless . . . insignificant . . . incapable," and angry that those for whom she was making her many sacrifices neither recognized nor appreciated them. Virginia French confided to her diary that above all she sought justice for herself; she did not feel she was receiving what she deserved. But, she noted, justice "is the hardest thing for man to give to woman. They will be lenient, affectionate, generous—anything and everything but just." Affection, leniency, and generosity imply patronage, even condescension. The justice French desired presumed equality.

In some ways Virginia French and her experience seem to contrast with the loving proclamations of devotion and loneliness exchanged by many couples separated by war. A closer look, however, shows them to be simply different aspects of a shared phenomenon, different manifestations of a common set of gender definitions displaced and disrupted by war. For French as for many other southern wives, war meant a breakdown in expectations about men's and women's roles within marriage. Wives desperately missed the emotional and material support they had taken for granted as their husbands' obligation, duties previously all but unrecognized because they seemed so natural a part of everyday life. When Julia Davidson wrote John "we little knew," she acknowledged the way in which war's subversions of marital and gender roles prompted unprecedented scrutiny and new awareness of men's and women's mutual devotion as well as responsibilities. One result of this reexamination was the intensification of feeling that arose from recognizing that marital bonds could be destroyed by death or separation and could not simply be taken for granted—absence making the heart grow fonder.

But as women assumed many of the burdens they had regarded as male and sacrificed the privileges of protection they believed their due as female, resentment and dissatisfaction appeared. Both love and anger arose from women's sense of loss—loss of individual men and loss of the world of marital and gender relations in which they had forged their female identities. Not to be able, as Grace Elmore put it, "to count on the men at all to help them" cast into question the whole logic of female subordination. Not to have your husband at your side for the birth of a baby you regarded as his responsibility if not indeed his fault, generated disbelief, then resentment and anger. Some of this rage was directed at the Yankees for causing the war in the first place, some at Confederate statesmen and officers for not winning it sooner or granting the desired furloughs, and some, inevitably, at husbands. Julia Davidson was furious when in obedience to military orders John left her almost ready to deliver in the midst of the siege of Atlanta. "The men of Atlanta," she wrote, including John among them, "have brought everlasting stain upon their name. [I]nstead of remaining to defend their homes they have run & left Atlanta. . . . Well Johny what have you done? . . . [E]very one who has talked to me say you did very wrong, transfer or no transfer, to leave until you saw your family at a safe distance. . . . There is not a man who

would have done as you have." John had, in his wife's view, failed in his fundamental duties as a husband and a man by yielding to his orders as a soldier.

The intensity of feeling so many women articulated when separated from their men was an intricate part of a larger recognition of the tenuousness, the insecurity of the ties of love and obligation southern women had assumed as the foundation of their world. War destabilized these presumptions. The absence of the loved one made him all the more desired and desirable; the absence of protection and of material and emotional support underlined the importance of these male responsibilities and generated resentment at their withdrawal. Thus the same dynamic that enhanced feelings of love and devotion in many instances later yielded sentiments of anger and doubt as women found what they suddenly so much needed was not available to them. As in the case of slavery, the obligations of family life began to outweigh its benefits. Catherine Edmondston, taking up new tasks in the face of the recalcitrance of her disobedient slaves, felt overburdened by "household cares." "What a drag it sometimes is on woman," she remarked in her diary, "to 'lug about' the ladder upon which man plants his foot and ascends . . . in ignorance of the machinery which feeds his daily life." But quickly she stifled her resentment, reiterating the ideology of separate spheres and female subordination. "Yet it is not always so," she consoled herself. "Rightly managed, prayerfully taken, women also may ascend, using each of their petty cares as an advance toward that 'heaven' which is governed by *self conquest*, self abnegation." Woman, she confirmed, should find not anger but fulfillment in martyrdom.

Unlike Edmondston, Virginia French did not stifle her discontent. As the war ended, she still continued to do all that was expected of her as a mother and a wife, but she no longer understood why. "I work for other people's interest—labor for them—make sacrifices for them—deny myself good in order to do them good—yet it is not because I either love them, or wish them to love me. In truth I don't care at all if anybody loves me or not. I do it because somehow I think I ought to." Virginia expressed her anger at her husband and her disillusionment with her domestic role more forcefully and eloquently than most southern wives. She was after all a professional writer. But, perhaps more important, the distribution of wartime sacrifice in her marriage was particularly unbalanced. Her civilian husband went not to war but "to town"; he was not risking his life or, apparently, assuming significant responsibility on the homefront. Yet Virginia French was far from alone in her feeling that southern men were not carrying out their obligations to their wives and children because of a war that seemed as the years wore on less and less a noble and romantic Cause than a bloody and tragic slaughter. "How many lives," Martha Fort wrote bitterly to her husband, George, "are to be laid on the alter of ambition of men. I look on this war as nothing else but to gratify unholy ambition." Men went off to worship at the altar of ambition while women were relegated to the altars of sacrifice. As ambitions failed and sacrifices grew, it was an allocation of roles that became increasingly untenable.

GLOSSARY

Confederate/ Confederacy:	The Confederate States of America, the formal name of the 11 states of the southern nation during the Civil War.
American Freedman's Inquiry Commission:	The investigative arm of the post-Civil War Freedman's Bureau. Created by Congress as part of the War Department in March 1865, the Bureau of Refugees, Freedmen, and Abandoned Lands, commonly known simply as the Freedman's Bureau, was charged with assisting ex-slaves (freedmen and women) following the Civil War and integrating them into American society.
General William T. Sherman (1820–1891):	A union army general famous for his "March to the Sea" in 1864. It was during this military campaign that Sherman sacked the city of Atlanta, Georgia.

IMPLICATIONS

Like the Revolutionary War before it, the Civil War raised the issue of women's roles in wartime. One recent historian has argued that the ultimate inability of planters' wives to maintain southern plantations during the war was an important reason for the Confederate defeat. From what you've read here, do you agree? How would you explain this lack of success on the part of plantation mistresses?